POLITICS AND SOCIETY IN UKRAINE

For LTC Jay Parker —

with warmest Regards and Best wishes to a Genuine Scholar & Gentleman,

Bob Kuztz

Westview Series on the Post-Soviet Republics
Alexander J. Motyl, Series Editor

Politics and Society in Ukraine, Paul D'Anieri,
Robert Kravchuk, and Taras Kuzio

Siberia: Worlds Apart, Victor L. Mote

The Central Asian States: Discovering Independence, Gregory Gleason

Lithuania: The Rebel Nation, V. Stanley Vardys and Judith B. Sedaitis

Belarus: At a Crossroads in History, Jan Zaprudnik

Estonia: Return to Independence, Rein Taagepera

POLITICS AND
■ SOCIETY ■
IN UKRAINE

PAUL D'ANIERI
University of Kansas

ROBERT KRAVCHUK
University of Connecticut

TARAS KUZIO
University of North London

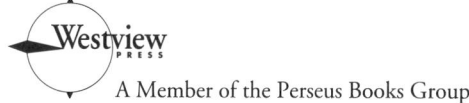
A Member of the Perseus Books Group

Westview Series on the Post-Soviet Republics

All photos courtesy of authors

All rights reserved. Printed in the United States of America. No part of this publication may be reproduced or transmitted in any form or by any means, electronic or mechanical, including photocopy, recording, or any information storage and retrieval system, without permission in writing from the publisher.

Copyright © 1999 by Westview Press, A Member of the Perseus Books Group

Published in 1999 in the United States of America by Westview Press, 5500 Central Avenue, Boulder, Colorado 80301-2877, and in the United Kingdom by Westview Press, 12 Hid's Copse Road, Cumnor Hill, Oxford OX2 9JJ

Find us on the World Wide Web at www.westviewpress.com

Library of Congress Cataloging-in-Publication Data
D'Anieri, Paul J., 1965–
　Politics and society in Ukraine / Paul D'Anieri, Robert Kravchuk, Taras Kuzio.
　　p.　cm. — (Westview series on the post-Soviet republics)
　Includes bibliographical references and index.
　ISBN 0-8133-3537-X (hc). — ISBN 0-8133-3538-8 (pbk.)
　1. Post-communism—Ukraine.　2. Political culture—Ukraine.
3. Ukraine—Politics and government—1991–　.　4. Ukraine—Social conditions—1991–　.　5. Social change—Ukraine.　I. Kravchuk, Robert S., 1955–　.　II. Kuzio, Taras.　III. Title.　IV. Series.
JN6635.D36　1999
306. 2 09477'09049—dc21　　　　　　　　　　　　　　　　　　99-30503
　　　　　　　　　　　　　　　　　　　　　　　　　　　　　　　　CIP

The paper used in this publication meets the requirements of the American National Standard for Permanence of Paper for Printed Library Materials Z39.48-1984.

10　9　8　7　6　5　4　3　2　1

Contents

List of Tables and Illustrations	vii
List of Acronyms	xi
Preface	xiii

	Introduction: The "Quadruple Transition" in Ukrainian Politics and Society	1
1	The Demise of the Soviet Union and the Emergence of Independent Ukraine	10
2	Nation Building and National Identity	45
3	Religion, State, and Society	71
4	Ukraine's Weak State	90
5	Politics and Civil Society	141
6	Economic Crisis and Reform	166
7	Foreign Policy: From Isolation to Engagement	206
8	Ukrainian Defense Policy and the Transformation of the Armed Forces	233
9	Conclusion: Problems and Prospects for Ukraine in the Twenty-First Century	262

Notes	273
Bibliography	321
Index	333

Tables and Illustrations

Tables

2.1	What nationality are you?	62
3.1	Religious communities by region	88
3.2	Number of religious communities in Ukraine, 1996	89
3.3	Eparchies of the Ukrainian-Greek Catholic Church, 1993	89
5.1	Can people freely express their opinions in Ukraine today?	146
5.2	If your rights have been violated, what would you consider to be effective and acceptable?	147
5.3	Membership of civic groups	147
5.4	What should parties do if they do not make it into Parliament?	154
5.5	Development of faction membership in the 1994–1998 Ukrainian Parliament	157
5.6	Factions in the post–March 1998 Rada	158
5.7	Regional variations in the 1998 parliamentary elections	161
6.1	Basic economic indicators of Ukraine, 1991–1998	171
6.2	Ukraine consolidated budget results, 1992–1997	180
6.3	Extent of privatization in Ukraine, 1992–1997	185
6.4	Selected budgetary arrears, 1995–1997	199

Figures

4.1	Tiers of Ukrainian government	103
4.2	Structure of the government of Ukraine, 1997	117
4.3	Ukrainian parliamentary budget process	120

| 4.4 | Structure of the Ukrainian Parliament, 1998 | 122 |
| 4.5 | Vertical structure of power under the 1996 Constitution of Ukraine | 130 |

Graphs

6.1	Change in Ukrainian monetary aggregates, 1991–1996	178
6.2	Ukrainian monetary growth rates, 1992–1996	179
6.3	Real revenues, expenditures, and GDP, January 1992–December 1996	182
6.4	Enterprise and government credits growth in relation to inflation, 1992–1996	183

Photos

1.1	Independence Day celebrations, Kyiv, August 1994	32
2.1	Cossack Days of Glory, Dnipropetrovs'k, September 1990	58
2.2	Old man in uniform of Sich Sharpshooters, demonstration, Kyiv, spring 1994	61
2.3	New monument honoring Mykhailo Hrushevs'kyi, Ukraine's preeminent historian and president, independent Ukraine, 1917–1918	69
3.1	Riot at funeral of patriarch of Ukrainian Orthodox Church–Kyiv Patriarchate, Kyiv, July 1995	84
4.1	Demonstration outside Ukrainian Television headquarters by Christian Democratic Party of Ukraine, protesting against political censorship, Kyiv, June 1995	124
4.2	Ukrainian National Assembly members of Parliament in military fatigues, Parliament, summer 1994	136
5.1	Communist demonstration, Kyiv, summer 1993	149
5.2	Ukrainian National Assembly paramilitaries on parade in central Kyiv, 1993	153
5.3	Leonid Kravchuk, president, 1991–1994	164
7.1	President Bill Clinton and President Leonid Kuchma, Kyiv, May 1995	223

7.2	President Leonid Kuchma and Secretary General Javier Solana of NATO adopt NATO-Ukraine Charter, Madrid, July 1997	223
8.1	National guard parading in Kyiv, Independence Day, August 1994	243
8.2	Presidents Leonid Kuchma and Boris Yeltsin sign agreement on Black Sea Fleet, Sochi, summer 1995	254
8.3	Ukrainian and U.S. troops in a NATO Partnership for Peace exercise, Yavoriv training ground, western Ukraine, 1997	259

Maps

FM.1	Ukraine: Territorial administrative structure	xv
1.1	Referendum on independence	13
2.1	Ethnic Ukrainians	46
2.2	Ukrainian as native language	46
2.3	Proportion of school pupils studying in the Ukrainian language, 1997	47

Acronyms

APA	Ukrainian Academy of Public Administration
CIS	Commonwealth of Independent States
COMECON	Council for Mutual Economic Assistance
ECU	European Currency Unit
EU	European Union
FDI	foreign direct investment
FIGs	Financial-Industrial Groups
G-7	Group of Seven
GDP	gross domestic product
HRV	*hryvnya*, Ukrainian permanent currency
ILO	International Labor Organization
IMF	International Monetary Fund
KBV	*karbovanets*, Ukrainian interim currency
KPU	Communist Party of Ukraine
KUN	Congress of Ukrainian Nationalists
MRBR	Inter-Regional Bloc of Reforms
NATO	North Atlantic Treaty Organization
NBU	National Bank of Ukraine
NDPU	People's Democratic Party
NKVD	Soviet secret police
OECD	Organization for Economic Cooperation and Development
OSCE	Organization for Security and Cooperation in Europe
OUN	Organization of Ukrainian Nationalists
PDVU	Party of Democratic Revival
SPU	Socialist Party of Ukraine
UAPTs	Ukrainian Autocephalous Orthodox Church
UHKTs	Ukrainian-Greek Catholic Church
UICE	Ukrainian Interbank Currency Exchange
UNA	Ukrainian National Assembly
UPA	Ukrainian Insurgent Army
UPTs–KP	UPTs–Kyiv Patriarchate
UPTs–MP	UPTs–Moscow Patriarchate
URP	Ukrainian Republican Party
VAT	value-added tax

Preface

Despite the flowering of scholarship on Ukraine since its independence in 1991, there has not yet been an attempt to provide a coherent overview of Ukrainian political institutions and the political process in Ukraine. For several years, events moved so quickly that to try to cover them in a book-length study was an invitation to immediate obsolescence. Moreover, many of the basic subjects of such a study, such as the structure of the constitution, were unresolved in Ukraine until relatively recently. Since the adoption of the Ukrainian constitution in 1996 and the introduction of a new currency that year, however, the fundamentals of the independent state are now in place in Ukraine. This is not to deny that much is still in flux but rather to assert that an overview of Ukrainian political structures and processes is now both possible and needed. This book aims to fill that need.

The book is deliberately written from an eclectic theoretical approach rather than by advancing a single theory or interpretation of events. This reflects not only the ambiguity of the subject but the varied backgrounds of the authors: D'Anieri was trained in government and international relations, Kravchuk in public administration, and Kuzio in Ukrainian area studies. We hope that this plurality of perspectives enriches the book as much as it has our own discussions. Although all three authors contributed to the various chapters and all take responsibility for the final product, each took responsibility for the drafting of various of the original chapters, and this division of labor should be made clear: D'Anieri drafted Chapters 7 (foreign policy), 8 (defense), and 9 (conclusion). Kravchuk drafted the introduction and Chapters 4 (Ukraine's weak state) and 6 (economic reform). Kuzio drafted Chapters 1 (the Soviet legacy), 2 (nation building), 3 (religion), and 5 (politics and civil society).

The authors would like to acknowledge the support of the institutions and people who made this project possible. We especially thank Rob Williams of Westview Press, whose combination of support and patience was essential to bringing the project to completion. Paul D'Anieri wishes to thank those at the Harvard Ukrainian Research Institute—Director

Roman Szporluk, Executive Director Jim Clem, and Librarian Ksenya Kiebuzynski—who provided a wonderful atmosphere for the original drafting of these chapters when D'Anieri was a visiting professor there in the summer of 1998. Robert Kravchuk wishes to acknowledge support from an NSF-COBASE grant, which was instrumental in his work on this project. Taras Kuzio wishes to acknowledge the support of the Centre for Russian and East European Studies at the University of Birmingham, where, while working on this project between 1995 and 1998, he was on a research fellowship funded by the Leverhulme Trust.

We especially thank our families, who endured patiently as we locked ourselves away to work on this project.

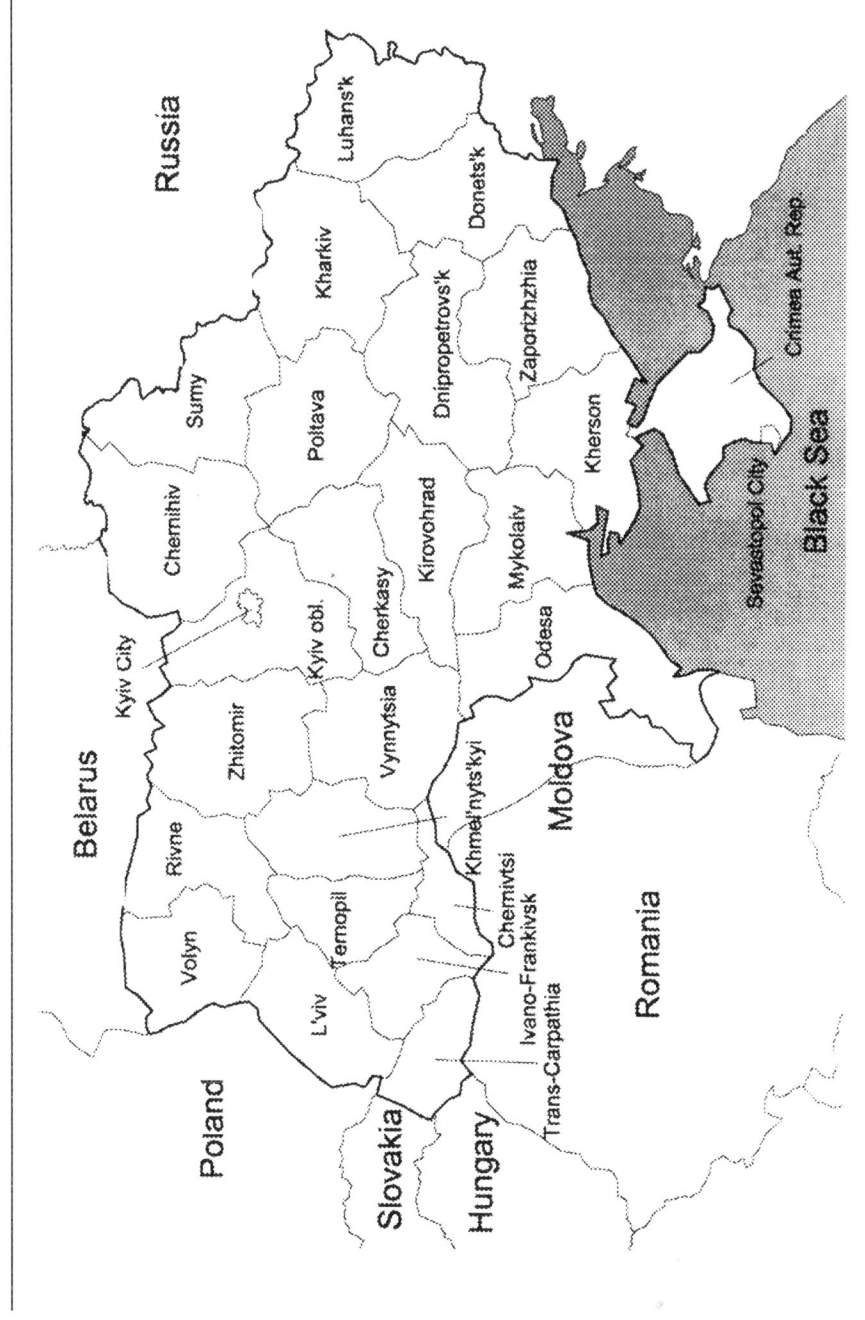

MAP FM.1 Ukraine: Territorial Administrative Structure

Introduction: The "Quadruple Transition" in Ukrainian Politics and Society

Ukraine is important to the West largely because it is seen as the "keystone in the arch" of security in Central Europe. Ukraine is important geopolitically in several ways. First, by putting a powerful state between Germany and Russia, Ukraine ameliorates the security dilemma that led to two wars in the first half of the twentieth century. Second, to the extent that the West continues to feel insecure about a potential threat from Russia, Ukrainian independence creates a strong, independent state through which Russia would have to go before it could renew its threat to the states lying to the west of Ukraine. Third, Ukraine's independence from Russia has positive implications for Russia itself and for Russia's relations with the rest of the world, a notion expressed most clearly by Zbigniew Brzezinski: "It cannot be stressed strongly enough that without Ukraine, Russia ceases to be an empire, but with Ukraine suborned and then subordinated, Russia automatically becomes an empire."[1] Finally, Ukraine is key in a more negative sense: If a state of its size and strategic location should fall into instability, that instability would reverberate throughout the nascent democracies of East-Central Europe.

It is because of Ukraine's key geopolitical role that the United States has made Ukraine the third-largest recipient of American aid (after Israel and Egypt). Ukraine has also become the largest and most frequent participant in the North Atlantic Treaty Organization's (NATO) Partnership for Peace Program. Despite this support, however, the process of reform in Ukraine has been slow, progress has been limited, and there appears a genuine possibility that even the limited economic and political reforms already accomplished will be reversed. The global economic crisis that undercut Russia's economy in 1998 had similar effects on Ukraine, undermining both reform and the reformers and strengthening leftist forces. At the end of 1999, Ukrainian presidential elections will determine who is to guide this process through the next five years. The next few years are therefore a pivotal time for this pivotal country.

However, despite Ukraine's importance, we actually know very little about Ukrainian politics and therefore are ill-equipped either to analyze the problems Ukraine faces or to assess the West's options in dealing with them. Few Western scholars have a deep knowledge of Ukraine, and the vast majority of post-Soviet research on the region has continued to focus on Russia. It is clear that Western economic prescriptions have not worked in Ukraine. But it is unclear whether this is because these prescriptions were flawed or because they were not properly implemented. Moreover, it is unclear whether it is politically possible to implement such policies in Ukraine. Indeed, at a most basic level, we have very little idea what in fact is possible in Ukraine and what is not.

Ukraine's lackluster political and economic performance raises two questions: First, why has reform proceeded so slowly, after the euphoria and optimism that accompanied the Soviet collapse? Second, what possibility is there for reform to be more successful—or to be reversed—in the future? It is to these questions that this book addresses itself. To answer these questions, we bring together detailed empirical research on the Ukrainian case, theoretical observations from political science, and the knowledge gained from the study of other societies in transition. Thus, the book aims to provide both a comprehensive empirical account of *how* Ukrainian politics works and at least a first cut at explaining *why* Ukrainian politics works as it does.

Of these two tasks, the first is perhaps more time-consuming but yields more certain results. Explaining why Ukraine, or any transition society, has followed the path it has, rather than some other, will always be a matter for some debate. But with Ukraine's eight years of independence and its two rounds of national elections now in the past, we can now begin the task with much more confidence than has been possible in recent years. There is now enough stability in Ukrainian politics for the fundamental problems and the basic patterns of the political process to have become clear.

Ukraine's transformation is not occurring in isolation. All around it, states and societies are seeking to move away from the centrally planned economy and authoritarian state that characterized the Communist system. Prior to the collapse of the Communist states of that region, states in Latin America and Southern Europe developed a good deal of experience with the processes of both democratization and economic reform. For policymakers and political scientists alike, these cases provide standards of comparison useful in analysis of the Ukrainian case. We can look at the various successes of Poland, for example, and ask why Ukraine has been unable or unwilling to follow a similar path. Similarly, we can look at Russia and ask why Ukraine has been so much more successful in some areas (e.g., in dealing with regional and ethnic differences) than Russia. More broadly, we can apply to Ukraine the general arguments from political science about the prerequisites and necessary policies for successful reform.

In understanding why transformation occurs differently and with varying degrees of success in different countries, explanations can be broken down into those focusing on prerequisites, or "structural" factors, and those focusing on policies, or "process" factors. This study makes no attempt to advance or defend a single theoretical perspective on transitions but rather borrows where appropriate to help illuminate the case. In Ukraine, two generalizations can be made that serve to structure much of the substance of this book. In terms of process, it is clear that in many cases, most notably in dealing with economic reform, Ukrainian government policies have been demonstrably counterproductive. This raises the question of whether more productive policies were politically infeasible, a question whose answer has important implications for the future. In terms of structure, the situation Ukraine inherited from the Soviet Union was clearly more complex and less favorable for rapid reform than that in its neighbors to the west. Whereas some states (such as those in Latin America) have required democratic transitions and others (in Eastern Europe) have required both democratic and economic transitions, Ukraine must undergo a "quadruple" transition, including not only democratization and marketization but also nation building and state building.

DEALING WITH UKRAINE'S "QUADRUPLE TRANSITION"

The transformation from socialism is often referred to as a "dual transition": a simultaneous change from a party-dominated governmental regime to a more democratic system, coupled with a rearrangement of the economic institutions along market-oriented lines.[2] The major conceptual focus in the "transitions literature" is on the political conditions and factors that will facilitate development of market institutions.[3] There is a particular concern with devising transition schemes that will avoid "transitional incompatibility" between political and economic reforms.[4] What seems clear from international experience, however, is that although economic development can substantially improve a country's chances for democratic consolidation, democratic reform alone is insufficient to bring about economic development.[5] Specifically, consolidation of democracy can be seen as dependent upon the willing participation of self-interested political elites who pursue democratic reform as the means to ensure their own longer-term economic interests.[6] Any beneficial effects of reform for the larger population tend to be secondary concerns for such elites but can be crucial to political sustainability of the reforms. In any case, it seems safe to conclude on both theoretical and empirical grounds that the viability of democracy depends vitally upon economic performance.

Clearly, there are risks and hardships in embarking on and sustaining reforms. It is difficult to identify and nurture a constituency in support of reforms, especially if they are painful.[7] The transition process tends to place pressures on governmental resources at a critical time in the transitioning country's history. Much political capital may be consumed to maintain regime stability as reforms set in. A significant attribute of reforms is that the economic costs of adjustment are immediately felt but the benefits are longer-term in nature and diffused throughout the society. The burdens of reform and adjustment also tend to be unevenly distributed throughout the various social strata. Finally, and partly as a result of these factors, there are profound collective action problems, with reformers bearing a disproportionate amount of the burden of organizing and pressing for reforms and abundant numbers of "free riders" strewn throughout the governmental system.[8] Even a successful reform coalition can be a rather "thin" one, raising the risks of failure. Failed reforms carry with them the risk of loss of legitimacy of governments and diminished credibility of the efficacy of market institutions themselves. Such sentiments are in abundance in Ukraine, and these portend potentially dire consequences for the country's fledgling constitutional system.

What makes the interrelation of political and economic change interesting—and fraught with difficulty—is that both are dependent upon a minimal degree of institutional infrastructure, which takes time to develop.[9] The literature on transitions has largely ignored this aspect of post-Communist transformation (state and institution building), a mistake that Juan J. Linz and Alfred Stepan now acknowledge.[10] Claus Offe therefore defines the "revolution" taking place in post-Communist Europe as fundamentally different from that which took place earlier in Latin America and Southern Europe. In Latin America, democratization was the primary question, as market and state institutions were already in place. In post-Communist Europe, we should add economic reform and state building, which Offe defines as a "triple transition." Within Offe's definition of "state building" are included questions of identity and the social and cultural definition of the political community. In contrast to Offe, we have defined these components as a separate category of "nation building."[11] Hence, in our view, post-Soviet states such as Ukraine are undergoing a "quadruple transition." Offe believes that the simultaneity of these three or four transitions, depending on the definitions used, "generates decision-loads of unprecedented magnitude."[12] The processes tend to complicate and undermine each other in many ways, leading many to wonder whether carrying out such processes simultaneously is even possible.[13]

In the absence of established traditions of democratic self-government, developing the core political institutions will turn on the crucial problem of increasing capacity of the state to govern. This brings the dialogue on the Ukrainian case to the idea of a triple transition: That is the notion that in addition to the usual political and economic dimensions of the transition from socialism, in Ukraine these two processes take place in the presence of a further transition from rule by a foreign, imperial, and colonizing power. The disintegration of the Soviet state left an administrative and institutional void in Ukraine of magnificent proportions that has taken considerable time to "backfill." The political transition thus involves not only development of civic organizations, a free press and media, political parties, and interest groups but also building the capacity of the "quasi-state" inherited from the USSR to enable it to perform even the most minimal functions of modern governance. This represents a considerable constraining factor, insofar as it limits the rate at which Ukraine has been able to absorb change. As Alexander J. Motyl and Taras Kuzio have argued, the lack of administrative and institutional development all but vacated the possibility of rapid and radical transformation for the majority of post-Soviet states, and especially Ukraine.[14]

Finally, linked to the problem of building the new Ukrainian state is that of building the new Ukrainian nation. This brings us to yet a fourth transition currently under way in Ukraine: the need to establish a truly Ukrainian national identity, apart from, and in some respects in opposition to, Russian ethnicity and culture. As argued earlier, questions of "nation building" in the transitions literature are usually either subsumed within "state building" (e.g., Offe) or ignored as irrelevant, because nation building was already complete in the societies in question.

Nation building has many different definitions. We include nation building as a separate category of the "quadruple transition" because we understand all liberal democracies to be composed of *both* civic and ethnic elements. We understand nation building to mean three processes, the first of which is the creation of a new overarching identity that prioritizes the Ukrainian political community (or civic nation) as the homeland of all of its citizens. Thus, Ukraine is building an inclusive "state-nation" or "national state" (not a "nation-state," which assumes a high degree of ethnic homogeneity). Second, nation building also refers to the elements that will constitute the societal, public culture of the new political community. In the Ukrainian case, this is a choice between emphasizing Ukraine's "Western" or "Eastern" heritage. Finally, nation building also refers to national revival for all of the ethnic groups that inhabit Ukraine, whose identities were subjected to denationalization in the Soviet era. The Ukrainian state has supported the granting of polyethnic rights to its national minorities while providing territorial autonomy to one region (the Crimea) where ethnic Ukrainians are a minority.

The implications of this fourth, and ongoing, aspect of the "quadruple transition," the nation-building process, are equally as momentous for Ukraine's future as are the political, economic, and institutional dimensions of transition. Under circumstances where dramatic political, economic, institutional, and nation-building changes are simultaneously under way, the risks are enormous that the four will not be compatible with one another. By far, the most straightforward means of averting such "transitional incompatibilities" is to avoid the simultaneity of reforms altogether—through sequencing.[15] This implies either undertaking political and institutional reforms before economic transition or, possibly, consolidating economic stability and growth prior to nation building and democratization. Many permutations are possible. Ukraine and the other transition societies do not have the luxury of sequencing, however. Determining the proper sequence is extremely difficult on a priori grounds, if not altogether impossible to implement, in the absence of a central political and social force sufficiently powerful to impose its will upon the society.[16] Since the post-Soviet future has largely been defined in direct opposition to the Soviet past, the (re)establishment of such centralizing power in Ukraine appears quite outside the realm of possibility. The interplay of the four transition processes is complex, and highly unpredictable, but consideration of this interplay is necessary if research on transitions is to be either complete or useful.

A "BREAK WITH THE PAST"?

Gaining independence for Ukraine was a bloodless affair, to the relief of all concerned. There was no revolutionary breach with the Soviet past. Thus, the process of transition itself has had an enormous impact on the nature of the problems encountered and the responses to them. Although we think of 1991 as the opening of a new era in Ukrainian history, institutionally and economically, the legacy of the Soviet Union has been powerful. The former Soviet administrative and political elite has retained great power and influence at the center of government and the economy in newly independent Ukraine. The training, instincts, and basic interests of these members of the old Soviet *nomenklatura* are largely incompatible with the needs of a market-oriented democratic state. Further, these groups have perpetuated the corruption of the former system through the persistence of clannish, highly nepotistic networks of relations, based loosely upon regional and industrial groupings.[17] Personalities and groups therefore remain crucial to the flow of events in Ukraine and fill the void that will eventually be filled by viable democratic governing traditions and institutions. But the networks of corruption and influence have proved to be resilient. Consequently, institutional development is likely to be a much longer-term process in Ukraine than the reformers had originally hoped.

Soviet-era social and political attitudes and beliefs also persist. The sense of political helplessness, a culture of victimization, political intolerance, deep distrust of authority, and political passivity have been held over from the former regime.[18] These factors also serve to reinforce perceptions of continuity, but they additionally militate against the institutionalization of liberal democracy. First, a social dialogue concerning the proper size and scope of the state has not taken place in Ukraine, nor is it likely to take place where such attitudes prevail. Second, the weaknesses of the emergent state institutions form a barrier against the organization and development of the institutions of civil society. The diverse interests that exist within this country of 52 million are therefore largely underrepresented in the halls of government at the center. Finally, lack of a common ethnic identity or collective sense of national consciousness prevents the larger society from arriving at any common sense of the "general interest" (or national idea) on which to base public policy. Consequently, politics remains highly particularistic, based largely on patronage, "clans," and often outright nepotism. Anticorruption efforts of the government have been futile.[19]

Paradoxically, there have been many changes in Ukrainian politics and society that would not have been thought possible during the Soviet era, including direct diplomatic and trade ties with the West; an independent foreign policy; membership in international bodies such as the Council of Europe, International Monetary Fund (IMF), and World Bank; a new constitution embodying a separation-of-powers regime and a strong executive; widespread political freedom; nascent political parties; and reasonably free elections. All of these, along with new economic freedoms, are a direct result of the collapse of the USSR. Each represents a discontinuity with the past. And yet as significant as each of these achievements may be, informed observers are as yet unable to conclude that Ukraine has reached the stage of self-sustaining reforms.[20]

AIMS AND OBJECTIVES OF THE BOOK

Among the main purposes for writing this book is our hope of demonstrating that recent events in Ukrainian politics and economics can profitably be interpreted in terms of Western social scientific paradigms. Our purpose is therefore to show that the Ukrainian transition is understandable in the same terms as other recent transitions and that considering the problem in these terms is enlightening, even if Ukraine remains unique. As the chapters that follow seek to make clear, Ukraine's difficulties are not caused by anything unique about the country's geopolitical location, economic endowment, national character, or longer-term relations with its powerful neighbor to the northeast. Rather, these problems may be traced to a series of policy choices that have been conditioned by many of these factors but that are in no sense inevitable or irreversible.

ORGANIZATION OF THE BOOK

The book is organized thematically rather than chronologically to facilitate the analysis of the various issues. This introduction has sketched out Ukraine's strategic importance and the complexities of its "quadruple transition." Subsequent chapters address the themes raised here. Chapter 1 details Ukraine's role in the disintegration of the USSR and explores how the Soviet legacy deeply influences all aspects of post-Soviet Ukraine's politics and society. Chapters 2 and 3, on nation building and religion, respectively, address the fourth prong of the quadruple transition described above: nation building. We treat this issue first because it is in many respects the most fundamental: Problems of state building, politics, and governing that arise in subsequent chapters are traceable in large part to the absence of a coherent unified political community in Ukraine. Chapter 2 focuses on the whole range of nation-building problems. We dedicate a separate chapter (Chapter 3) to the politics of religion, even though the problem overlaps with national identity, because it is analytically distinct from nation building and too complex to simply submerge in that discussion.

Chapters 4 through 6 are in many respects the core of the volume, treating the central questions of economic and political transformation. Chapter 4 focuses on state building, exploring the crucial question of institutional capacity that has been neglected by scholarship but has been fundamental to the failure of reform in Ukraine (as well as in Russia and many other states in the region). We examine at both the micro and macro levels the sources and effects of the Ukrainian state's impotence, including problems of corruption, tax collection, and relations between central and local governments.

Chapter 5 addresses politics more broadly, examining the process of democratization and state-society relations. Largely as a result of the nation-building problems outlined in Chapters 2 and 3, the Ukrainian political spectrum is badly fragmented. This and other factors have translated into a weak and fragmented party system, which in turn has led to a weak Parliament. Thus, Ukraine is in the unenviable position of trying to conduct democratic government with a largely ineffective legislative branch of government.

Chapter 6 turns to the problem of economic reform. In addition to showing why Ukraine's reform policies (if they can be called that) have led to such meager results, we explore the sources of those policies, showing how they emerged from the societal and governmental conditions discussed in the previous chapters. Ukrainian public and elite opinion is divided concerning the desirability of reform, the goals of reform, and the methods for implementing it. Deep divisions within the Verkhovna Rada (the Parliament), and between the Rada and the executive, have made a decisive and coherent reform plan impossible to adopt. The impotence of state institutions has made it difficult to implement even the limited programs that have been adopted.

The final two chapters focus upon the evolution of and the debates surrounding the foreign and defense policies of the independent Ukrainian state. Foreign policy (Chapter 7) has been perhaps the most prominent success for post-Soviet Ukraine. Ukraine managed first to gain acceptance of its independence from a skeptical world and then to transform its relationship with the United States from acrimonious to cooperative. Debates over foreign economic policy and over Ukraine's place between Russia and the West have been strongly influenced by the national identity debates that pervade Ukrainian politics. Ukrainian defense policy (Chapter 8) has been successful in two key areas: downsizing the military and maintaining civilian control. In other areas, though, the state's institutional weakness has led to chaos. Funding for the military is at a fraction of necessary levels, and although the military has been shrunk, it has not been reformed.

Finally, the conclusion (Chapter 9) summarizes the findings of the book and considers Ukraine's future, with its unclear outlook. Ukraine's problems are deep, and to some extent they reinforce each other, and for those reasons, the prospect for rapid improvement in political and economic conditions is unlikely. All the same, there has been sufficient progress in bridging Ukraine's regional divisions, and the shadow economy makes up for enough of the shortcoming in the official economy so that outright collapse seems equally unlikely. Even though Ukraine seems to be in an odd position between its Soviet past and its hoped-for "Western" future, there are powerful forces that, absent a fundamental new shock, will tend to keep Ukraine there for some time to come.

ONE

The Demise of the Soviet Union and the Emergence of Independent Ukraine

The rapid and peaceful disintegration of the USSR came as a surprise to most outside observers of Soviet politics. In retrospect, it appears that the USSR would have disintegrated sooner or later because it was already in long-term imperial decline by the time Mikhail Gorbachev became Soviet leader in 1985. The rapidity of its disintegration came about as a consequence of Gorbachev's mismanagement of the economy and the increasing assertiveness of national minorities that culminated in the failed August 1991 putsch. When Ukraine and Russia decided in late 1991 that the union no longer met their interests, the USSR was doomed.

This chapter is divided into four parts. The first part provides the concise historical background of Ukraine under the late tsarist empire and the USSR. The second surveys the decay of the USSR, the rise of "national communism" in Ukraine, and Ukraine's role in the disintegration of a world superpower. The third part of the chapter analyzes the roles of Russia and Ukraine in ensuring that the USSR undertook a "civilized divorce" in December 1991. This section then discusses the hurried and largely unplanned agreement to replace the USSR with the Commonwealth of Independent States (CIS), which inevitably led to disagreements between Ukraine and Russia during the next six years. It was not until May 1997 that Ukraine and Russia finally hammered the last nail in the coffin of the USSR when they signed an interstate treaty that recognized both countries' territorial integrity. The USSR therefore disintegrated not at once—as in Yugoslavia—but in a "civilized divorce" extending over a six-year period from 1991 to 1997.[1]

The fourth section discusses the Soviet legacy in general and how it specifically affects politics and society in post-Soviet Ukraine. These legacies have had a profound impact upon the four transitions taking place simultaneously in Ukraine (state building, nation building, marketization, and democratization) as well as upon religion and foreign and defense policies. This discussion of the Soviet legacy places the following chapters in perspective because Ukraine, like all newly independent states, was never in a position to start its post-Soviet transformation with a clean slate. These starting points therefore affect and constrain the transformation process.[2]

HISTORICAL BACKGROUND

Prior to the Russian Revolution, Ukrainian territories were divided between tsarist Russia (northwestern, central, eastern, and southern regions), Austria (Bukovina and Galicia), and Hungary (Trans-Carpathia).[3] Ukrainians fared the worst in tsarist Russia and Trans-Carpathia. In tsarist Russia, the autonomous privileges "guaranteed" by the Treaty of Periaslav of 1654 were slowly reduced until eventually the autonomous Hetmanate was dissolved in the 1780s. Ukraine, with no serfdom and a high literacy rate that had been a source of Western cultural influences for Russia in the seventeenth and eighteenth centuries, slowly changed, turning into a provincial backwater by the nineteenth century. Literacy rates plummeted, serfdom was introduced, and Ukrainian language and culture came under state repression after the 1860s. Ukrainians, together with Belarusians, were defined as ethnographic raw material to be homogenized into the Russian nation in the process of nation building.[4]

Russia, unlike France or England, had not become a nation before it became an empire. In this sense it was similar to both Austria and Turkey in the Austro-Hungarian and Ottoman Empires. The late tsarist attempt to build a Russian nation drawing upon the three Eastern Slav groups proved to be impossible due to the short time frame, weakness of the modernization effort (nation building had gone hand in hand with modernization in Western Europe and North America), and incompatibility of empire and nation. A similar fate befell the Russian nation-building project in the USSR, an effort that lasted too briefly between 1990 and 1991 to complete the process. In both the tsarist empire and the USSR, therefore, a premodern Russian identity was submerged within an overall supranational imperial identification with the *state*, not the nation.[5]

In western Ukraine, the Ukrainian ethnos, or ethnic group, fared better. The exception was in Trans-Carpathia, which had come under Hungarian rule in the mid-nineteenth century and where nationality policies discouraged a nation-building project to transform the Rusyny (Ruthenians) into Ukrainians. In contrast, in Galicia and Bukovina, both under Austrian control since the late eighteenth century, the evolution of Rusyny/Ruthenians into Ukrainians had been deliberately encouraged in order to both reduce Russophile sympathies and create a bulwark against the troublesome Poles (see Chapter 2). By the 1880s in Galicia and Bukovina, three orientations were available to nation builders—a separate Eastern Slavic group (Rusyny), Little Russians (a regional branch of the Russian nation), and Ukrainians—and it was the Ukrainians who came out on top. In Trans-Carpathia, the Rusyn option was promoted by the Hungarians (who have still left their mark to this day in northeastern Slovakia), whereas in tsarist Russia, the Little Russian option was backed by the state.[6]

It is therefore little wonder that in 1917 "Ukrainians" were unable to create a united, powerful national movement that was able to successfully create an independent state (in the manner, for example, of the Latvians, Estonians, and Lithuanians). During the civil war of 1917–1921, pro-Ukrainian independence governments were established in Kyiv and L'viv that united Ukraine and western Ukraine in January 1919. The pro-independence Ukrainian authorities fought on many fronts against a variety of forces, including the Bolsheviks, White supporters of the Russian provisional government of 1917, and the anarchist bands of Nestor Makhno.[7] In western Ukraine, conflict was severe against Poles in Galicia and Volhynia, Hungarians in Trans-Carpathia, and Romanians in Bukovina. By the time of the Treaty of Riga in 1921, Soviet Russia had retaken all of the former tsarist territories, apart from Volhynia, and had reconstituted them as the Ukrainian SSR. Volhynia and Galicia became Polish again, Trans-Carpathia went to the Czechoslovak state, and Bukovina to Romania. In all of these three states (Poland, Czechoslovakia, Romania), Ukrainian minorities never received the autonomy they had been promised.

After the 1921 Treaty of Riga and the Union Treaty of 1922, which created the USSR, Ukrainian lands remained divided between four states until they were annexed by the USSR in 1939 as a consequence of the infamous Molotov-Ribbentrop Pact. Of the four states where Ukrainians resided, they fared best in Czechoslovakia. But this state ceased to exist after Germany occupied Bohemia and Moravia in 1938, leaving Trans-Carpathia to hurriedly create its own Ukrainianophile state and declare its independence in March 1939. The ministate proved unable to maintain itself for long, as it soon fell to Hungarian forces who continued to occupy it as allies of the Germans until 1944. In Bukovina, Ukrainian forces fought an unsuccessful war against Romania in 1918–1919, and it too continued to occupy the region as a German ally until the arrival of Soviet troops in 1944.

Poor relations between Poles and Ukrainians dominated Galicia and Volhynia throughout the interwar period. Ukrainian military forces from the Austrian army put up a spirited resistance to the Poles in Galicia but by 1919 were overcome by superior Polish forces dispatched from France. The Poles reneged on their promises of substantial autonomy to Ukrainians and instead sent military colonists to settle the eastern *kresy* (borderlands), while occasionally initiating repressive measures against Ukrainian political and cultural life (for example, the pacification campaign of 1930). Ukrainian nationalists, many of them veterans of the unsuccessful campaign for independence of 1917–1921, organized counterviolence through the Organization of Ukrainian Nationalists (OUN), an integral nationalist movement created in Vienna in 1929. Poland's nationalizing policies in the interwar period toward its German, Ukrainian, and Belarusian minorities mirrored those the Prussian state had applied to Poles prior to 1918.[8] Polish nationality policies replicated those of the Hungarians in Trans-Carpathia prior to 1918 and 1939–1944, in which Ukrainians were defined as regional tribes, such as Lemkos and Hutsuls. In both cases, these Polish efforts produced the opposite of what was intended, as Rogers Brubaker points out:

> Yet, far from furthering the assimilation or even securing the loyalty of borderland Slavs, Poland's inept nationalizing policies and practices in the inter-war period had just the opposite effect, producing by the end of the period what had not existed at the beginning: a consolidated, strongly anti-Polish Belarusian—and to an even greater extent—Ukrainian national consciousness.[9]

MAP 1.1   Referendum on Independence

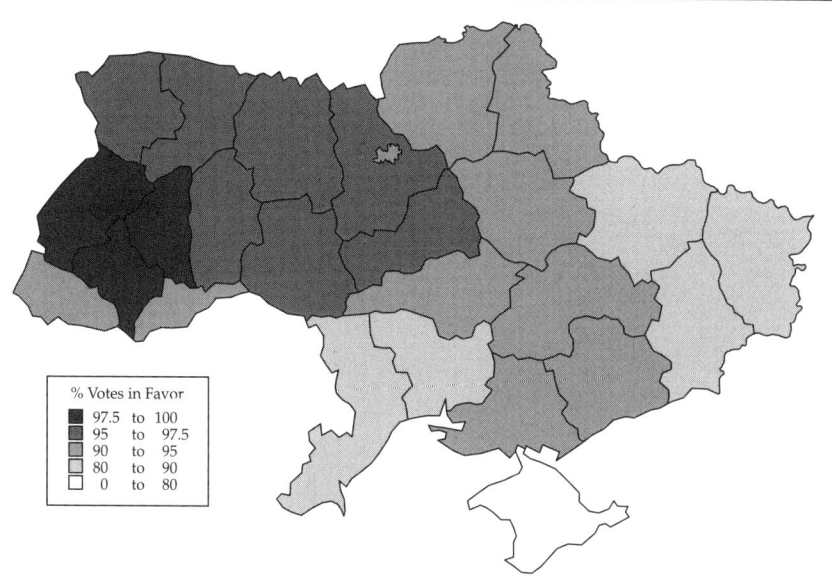

SOURCE: Central Electoral Commission.

It is perhaps little wonder then that by the time of the German-Soviet invasion of September 1939, one-third of the population of interwar Poland, which constituted national minorities, felt little, if any, allegiance to it. Ukrainians saw it as the chance to join in the Nazi anti-Bolshevik crusade and possibly create in the process an independent state (even a puppet one, as in Slovakia). In addition, western Ukrainians were also embittered by nearly two years of Soviet rule (September 1939–June 1941), which had turned them against Soviet power.

A joint crusade against Bolshevism and the creation of a German-aligned state, at least, was the theory. But the Nazis had other plans. The radical younger wing of the OUN led by Stepan Bandera (the OUN split in 1940 into two factions; the conservative wing was led by Andrei Melnyk) declared independence in L'viv on June 30, 1941. The result was widespread Nazi arrests of OUN members and sympathizers, including Bandera himself and Yaroslav Stetsko, who both served the remainder of the war in a Nazi concentration camp. The OUN, under its new temporary leader, Mykola Lebed, organized the Ukrainian Insurgent Army (UPA) and launched a guerrilla war—first against the Nazis and, after 1943–1944, against the Soviets—which lasted until 1953. Postwar Soviet policies of forced collectivization, the forcible union of the Uniate Church with the Russian Orthodox Church (see Chapter 3), and the influx of Russian party and security functionaries all served to further alienate western Ukrainian society from the Soviet regime. The OUN-UPA struggle against the Soviet regime also served to foster an image, as in the three Baltic states, that identified the Soviet regime as "Russian" and therefore as a foreign invasion.[10]

At the same time, nation building in western Ukraine was fostered, perhaps unintentionally, by the Soviet regime. Due to the strength of Ukrainian national consciousness, Soviet nationality policies were not as repressive as those pursued in western Belarusia, where Soviet—not nationalist—partisans had dominated the local scene.[11] Nazi and Soviet policies of genocide and ethnic cleansing removed Jews and Poles from the urban centers of western Ukraine. These urban centers expanded while others were built during the course of the Soviet modernization of western Ukraine after 1945. Urbanization and modernization consequently occurred simultaneously, with the influx of already highly nationality-conscious rural Ukrainians into the urban environment. Unlike in eastern and southern Ukraine, therefore, ethnic Ukrainians came to demographically *and* culturally dominate the urban centers of western Ukraine as was the case with other nation-building projects elsewhere in Europe. This had, of course, been the objective of national Communists in the 1920s in eastern Ukraine, but the policies of indigenization had been halted by the early 1930s (see Chapter 2).[12] Similarly, in Trans-Carpathia after 1945, the very fact that the region became a part of

Ukraine (albeit the Ukrainian SSR) for the first time since the Middle Ages, coupled with certain Soviet policies that encouraged a Ukrainian nation-building project, transformed Rusyny into Ukrainians, over half a century after that was permitted in Galicia and Bukovina.

To recap then, nation building in western Ukraine was fortuitous in being able to forge a modern national identity over six stages, which included:

1. Transfer from Eastern Orthodoxy to a national institution, the Greek Catholic Church, in 1596. Prior to 1918 religion was an important marker of identity (in the tsarist empire all "Orthodox" people were defined as "Russians" [that is, Ruskiy]). The Uniate (or Greek Catholic) Church enabled Ukrainians to define themselves as different from *both* Roman Catholic Poles and Orthodox Russians.
2. Favorable Austrian nationality policies between the 1780s and 1918.[13]
3. Armed conflict with, and prior treatment at the hands of, Poles, Romanians, and Hungarians, which solidified their perception of these as hostile "others."
4. The brutal Soviet annexation of western Ukraine (1939–1941) and Soviet policies after 1945, coupled with a vicious and protracted guerrilla war until 1953, which helped to define the attitude of western Ukrainians toward the Soviet regime as both "foreign" and "Russian," to be dumped when the opportunity arose. This they proceeded to do during the March 1990 parliamentary and local elections, when the Communist Party was removed from the political map of western Ukraine, and the March 1991 referendum, when western Ukraine held a third referendum of its own on independence that won an overwhelming endorsement.
5. Postwar Soviet urbanization and industrialization, which enabled ethnic Ukrainians to dominate the urban centers of western Ukraine *both* culturally and demographically, which they had last done in the Galician-Volhynian Principality of the twelfth to thirteenth centuries.[14]
6. Nation building, transforming Ruthenians (Rusyny) into Ukrainians, which the Austrians had encouraged in Galicia and Bukovina in the second half of the nineteenth century; this was encouraged by Soviet policies after 1945 in Trans-Carpathia, building on the growth of national consciousness in 1938–1939 when the region declared independence from Czechoslovakia.

Ukrainian-Polish relations after the Soviet-Nazi invasion of Poland in September 1939 went from bad to worse. A Polish-Ukrainian civil war raged in Volhynia, where Ukrainian nationalists (of various groups) ethnically cleansed Poles. This was "justified" on the grounds that they were forced settlers from the interwar period and that the Polish partisan groups had cooperated with Soviet partisans against the Nazis and Ukrainian nationalists. Polish nationalist groups, in turn, ethnically cleansed regions such as Chelm and Podlachia, the site of the mass destruction of Ukrainian Orthodox churches in the late interwar period by the Polish authorities.

After the arrival of a puppet Polish Communist regime in 1944, Polish security forces, allied to the notorious Soviet secret police, the NKVD, struggled against the OUN and UPA until 1947. During this period, Poles were this time ethnically cleansed by their "allies," the Soviets, who removed them from western Ukraine to the newly "recovered," as they were dubbed, former German territories in western and northern Poland. Unable to subdue the OUN and UPA by military means alone, the Soviet and Polish authorities launched Akcja Wisla (Action Vistula) in 1947, which ethnically cleansed 250,000 Ukrainians from southeastern Poland to the "recovered" former German territories now in Poland. These were scattered around villages inhabited by Polish newcomers from the eastern *kresy*, with the aim of assimilating them into the newly configured Polish homogeneous nation-state. No provisions were made for their cultural rights until 1956, when government departments were allowed—although these were located within the Ministry of Interior (not the Ministry of Culture) right until the end of the Communist era. Unable to attack the Russians, the Polish Communist regime, through its educational system, the film industry, government propaganda, and the media, produced and published a wide variety of anti-OUN and anti-UPA literature and films. Although ostensibly "antinationalist," as in Soviet Ukraine, they tended to denounce collectively all Ukrainians and the diaspora (in Poland) or the diaspora and western Ukrainians as "nationalists," thereby deliberately fostering a climate of mistrust and enmity.

The thaw in Polish-Ukrainian relations, launched by diaspora groups and publishing houses (such as Kultura and Suchasnist), gathered momentum with the election of a Polish Catholic pope in 1979 and the rise of Solidarity in the 1980s.[15] The contemporary post-Communist Polish-Ukrainian "strategic partnership" has therefore normalized relations between both peoples after decades, if not centuries, of bitterness.

Ukrainians living in the former tsarist territories that became the Ukrainian SSR in 1922 fared far worse. As we have already seen, and as Chapter 2 points out in greater detail, the tsarist regime did everything it could to prevent nation building, hoping that Ukrainians (and Belarusians) would be available as ethnographic "Little" and "White" Russians for the Russian nation-building project (similar to Bretons and Alsatians in

France). The strength of national feeling in Ukraine did not lead to the establishment of an independent state but did allow for the creation of the Ukrainian SSR. Ukraine's large and vocal body of national Communists looked upon the USSR as a confederation of sovereign states that would promote the simultaneous modernization of Ukraine and nation building among those who had been previously labeled as "Little Russians" by the tsarist regime. In the 1920s, such a policy was gradually leading to the demographic and cultural domination of eastern and southern Ukraine's urban centers by ethnic Ukrainians. If these policies had not been abruptly halted in the early 1930s, the post-1992 independent state would be a very different animal than that which actually exists.

For five decades, from the mid-1930s to the mid-1980s, Soviet nationality policies produced ten outcomes that the independent Ukrainian state is now forced to grapple with:[16]

1. The Ukrainian SSR, in the manner of the other thirteen non-Russian republics (but not the Russian Federation), became the territorial and ethnic homeland of Ukrainians, and its territorial integrity came to be supported by all shades of Ukrainian opinion.
2. In the post-Stalin era, ethnic Ukrainians came to dominate the commanding heights of Soviet Ukrainian institutions (including the Communist Party of Ukraine, where they had been weakly represented in 1917–1921).
3. Ethnic Ukrainians came to demographically dominate Ukraine's urban centers, which until then had been dominated by non-Ukrainians (which proved to be a major handicap during the 1917–1921 civil war).
4. The 1932–1933 artificial famine in eastern Ukraine, which claimed upwards of seven million lives, produced two results.[17] First, it destroyed the Ukrainian peasantry as a social and ethnic force, which it had been until then (while simultaneously not allowing their influx into urban centers to culturally dominate Ukraine's cities). Second, it effectively ended any Ukrainian ethnographic claim to the Kuban region and eastern border regions of Ukraine, which had possessed ethnic Ukrainian majorities until then (the Kuban Cossacks, descendants of Zaporozhian Cossacks ethnically cleansed by Tsarina Catherine in the late eighteenth century, had clamored to join independent Ukraine in 1917–1918).
5. Eastern Ukrainians were pitted against "bourgeois nationalist" western Ukrainians who, together with the diaspora in general, were continually vilified as "Nazi collaborators" and "anti-Soviet renegades."

6. The number of Ukrainians with Russian as their first language and Ukrainians who defined themselves as bilingual grew, particularly in the large urban centers of eastern and southern Ukraine. This was undertaken by a conscious state policy of mass Russification. In 1958, 60 percent of book titles published in Ukraine were in Ukrainian, a figure that had declined to only 27 percent in 1978. Meanwhile, the number of pupils enrolled in Ukrainian-language schools dropped from 81 to 47.5 percent between 1950–1951 and 1988–1989.[18]
7. Large numbers of eastern Ukrainians, particularly in regions such as the Donbas, intermarried. They were then encouraged to define themselves as "Russians." Many of these people have reidentified themselves in the post-Soviet era as possessing multiple Ukrainian-Russian identities or "Soviet" ones.
8. Indigenous Ukrainian churches were destroyed in the early 1930s (Autocephalous Orthodox) and 1946 (Greek Catholic), leaving only the collaborationist Russian Orthodox Church to cater to the spiritual needs of Ukrainian Christians. Western Ukraine accounted for upwards of two-thirds of Russian Orthodox parishes by 1985, a reflection of how important Ukraine was to the Russian Orthodox Church. In the post-Soviet era, the Greek Catholic Church has recovered but no longer holds a monopoly in Galicia and Trans-Carpathia, as it did prior to 1939 among Ukrainians in this region. Meanwhile, the largest Orthodox Church in Ukraine remains the Russian, renamed the (Autonomous) Ukrainian Orthodox Church in 1990 (see Chapter 3).
9. Soviet nationality policies and historiography furthered a "Little Russian" complex similar to that promoted by the tsarist regime, in which Ukrainians were defined as raw ethnographic material to be nationalized into the New Soviet Man. Although the three Eastern Slav groups and the Russian language were the source for this Soviet nation-building project, it should *not* be confused as Russian nation building, which the Soviet regime never fostered (the Russian Federation was the only Soviet republic that was *never* promoted as a Russian homeland until Boris Yeltsin became its president in summer 1990). While professing a *territorial* loyalty to the borders of the Ukrainian SSR, some Ukrainians therefore also possess a cultural allegiance to a larger pan–Eastern Slavic unity. As in Belarus, these two identities are incompatible (Soviet territorial sovereignty versus pre-1917 pan–Eastern Slavism) because the former recognizes a separate ethnic group, which was given some formal recognition by the

Soviet regime, while the latter defines them merely as a regional branch of the Russian nation.[19]

10. Tsarist policies of linking Ukrainian language and culture to political demands by articulating oneself as a nationally conscious Ukrainian were revived by the Soviet authorities through their denunciations of "bourgeois nationalism." As the young Ukrainian historian H. V. Kas'ianov points out: "In line with the official ideology the dogmatic understanding of 'Ukrainian bourgeois nationalism' included any kind of show of national consciousness, cultural, ideological or political tendencies which didn't coincide with state ideology on the nationality question and could (or, believed they could) threaten its rule or become the basis for separatist tendencies."[20]

The post-Stalin era lasted for three decades, from the mid-1950s to the mid-1980s.[21] During this period, the Ukrainian SSR developed as a modern, industrial state, although lopsidedly. By the time of the Gorbachev era, upwards of one-third of the gross domestic product (GDP) came from the military-industrial complex, while large industrial giants guzzled subsidized energy inputs from the Russian Federation. Ironically, the Ukrainian SSR had itself been an energy exporter until 1970, but with the decline of the Ukrainian energy sector, thousands of Ukrainian experts were encouraged to migrate to Siberia (300,000 of them still live in Tyumen oblast alone).

The post-Stalin era in Ukraine can be neatly divided into three distinct periods. The first lasted from the 1960s until 1971. Communist Party of Ukraine leader Petro Shelest promoted a national Communist line that increasingly challenged Moscow's nationality and economic policies (Ukrainians were perturbed at having to subsidize economic development in Siberia and Central Asia). The Ukrainian language and culture were promoted, and some of the historical myths promoted by the Soviet state were challenged by the republican leadership. In 1972, though, Shelest was deposed and accused of "nationalism," forced to live in "exile" in Moscow.

The second period is associated with the Volodymyr Shcherbyts'kyi era from 1972 to 1989.[22] During this period, Soviet nationality policies are remembered as having done to Ukrainian language, culture, identity, and historiography what the Stalin era did physically in murdering millions of human beings. The seventeen years of Shcherbyts'kyi rule promoted "Little Russianism"—not Ukrainian nation building, the wishes of national Communists in the 1920s and 1960s. This was undertaken through historiography, the Russian Orthodox Church, Russification, support for bilingualism, and encouraging people to adopt an ethnic Russian identity. At the same time, it was precisely this period of Soviet rule that is remembered as the "era of stagnation," when corruption, nepotism, clannishness, immorality, and nihilism became the hallmarks of Soviet, and Ukrainian, society. The courageous few who became Ukrainian dissidents protested Soviet policies on the nationality question and human rights (hence they were dubbed "national democrats"), leading to Ukraine's becoming the site of the USSR's largest Helsinki movement and contributing proportionately the largest number of political prisoners to the Gulag. When released in 1987, these dissidents became the radical foot soldiers of the Ukrainian Popular Movement from 1988 on. Many of them still play a prominent role in contemporary Ukrainian society in Rukh, in center-right political parties, as parliamentary deputies, and through the creative unions.

The third period of the post-Stalin era began with the arrival of Gorbachev as Soviet leader in 1985 but ultimately did not fully emerge from under Shcherbyts'kyi's influence until his death in September 1989. The drive to independence in the Gorbachev era brought out the paradoxes of Ukrainian society mentioned in this chapter. National consciousness in Ukrainian society proved to be stronger than in 1917–1921, when it was largely a rural phenomenon, but it nevertheless remained insufficiently powerful to encompass the entire country. The drive to independence therefore was inevitably the result of the combined efforts of the national democratic movement in western and central Ukraine, where ethnic nationalism was strong, and the national Communists in eastern and southern Ukraine, where national democrats remain weak in popularity.[23]

Thus, the "national question" inherited by the independent Ukrainian state in January 1992 continues to have a deep influence upon all facets of the post-Communist transition in Ukraine.[24]

IMPERIAL DECAY

A series of events during the late 1980s and into 1990 pushed the Soviet Union ever closer to collapse. In addition to the chaos created by Mikhail Gorbachev's attempts to reform the Soviet economy, nationality issues, largely ignored by rulers in Moscow, increasingly threatened the stability of the USSR. Gorbachev admitted that "unresolved issues have surfaced one after another, errors and deformations that were accumulated over decades have now made themselves felt, and ethnic conflicts have erupted after smoldering for years."[25]

Gorbachev always believed the official Soviet line that nationalists represented only tiny extremist groups with little popular support. He therefore reacted against them in the traditional post-Stalinist Soviet manner through dismissals, rhetoric, military threats, and eventually the use of force. It was not until 1989–1990 that he seriously turned his attention to this question. By then, it was probably already too late, since nationalist agitation was in full swing in the Baltics and was accelerating in Ukraine. By the time Gorbachev recognized the severity of the Soviet nationality crisis, it had overcome him.[26] He was reluctant to adjust nationality policy, and above all, "there was no acknowledgment on its part of the need to offer the non-Russians a new deal."[27] When a new deal was finally reluctantly offered in late 1991 in the form of a confederation, it was too late.

The slow disintegration of Soviet power at the center was embodied in the election of republic-level legislatures in 1990, which gave republic-level governments far greater legitimacy than the nonelected Soviet state in Moscow. Although these elections were far from "free and fair," the success of opposition candidates shredded the aura of dominance of the Communist Party and undermined its claims to legitimate rule. Between March 1990 and August 1991, relations between the center and the republics were dominated by a tug-of-war over whether the USSR should be reconstituted as a "renewed federation" (Moscow's position) or as a confederation of sovereign republics (the view increasingly held in the republics and only adopted by the Soviet center in November 1991).

This tug-of-war also often divided republican Communist Party elites into "imperial" and "national" factions, particularly in republics that included large counterelites, such as Ukraine. Popular legitimacy for the "national" faction was usually vested in the elected parliaments. The legitimacy of the "imperial" faction was subject to constant attack as Gorbachev's glasnost (openness) campaign allowed the central and republican media to publicize the present and past misdeeds of the Soviet government, most notable of which in Ukraine was the famine engineered by Joseph Stalin in 1932–1933. The "imperial" faction was also hampered in its ability to maintain itself as a coherent fighting force because of its conflict with Gorbachev. As the old guard of the Communist Party, these individuals detested Gorbachev's reforms and were likewise viewed by Gorbachev's team as the primary obstacle to progress. The "imperial" or conservative faction therefore had few supporters within the central elites; the ones it did have disgraced their cause in their poorly executed August 1991 putsch.

The growth of "national" factions within the republican Communist Party elites was facilitated by two factors. First, there was a local tradition of national communism that always raised its head during periods of liberalization. In Ukraine, this had occurred in the 1920s and again in the 1960s. Second, the Brezhnev era had encouraged the growth of local elites with ties to their republics. Elites from Moscow and those based in the republics increasingly forged local coalitions at a time when the Soviet center was in a process of slow decay. For a variety of reasons, many republic-level elites had incentives to obtain as much autonomy from Moscow as possible. In some cases these elites were motivated by nationalism, but in many cases there was personal political or economic gain to be had from increased republic autonomy. The growth of national consciousness and the rapid disintegration of the USSR also reflected the failure of Soviet power to create a genuine "Soviet" national identity to replace the ethnic identities of the country's multinational population. Yet democratic movements remained confined to individual republics, and there was little coordination above republican boundaries. Moreover, there remained divisions within republics among those with very different agendas who found a common interest in greater autonomy.

The crisis within the USSR during the late Gorbachev era did not come about either as a consequence of Gorbachev's botched reforms or the growth of the national movements but rather was accelerated by these developments. The USSR on the eve of the Gorbachev era was already in a process of advanced internal decay and slow disintegration, and it is unclear whether any measures could have reversed this decline. In Alexander Motyl's view, the crisis during the Gorbachev era was therefore the logical consequence of long-term imperial decline.

Although the degree of inevitability of the Soviet collapse remains in debate, there is little doubt that Gorbachev's policies accelerated the process. The de-emphasis on repression and encouragement of openness reduced fear of coercion and opened up public space for dissent. At the same time, devolution of economic authority strengthened republic-level governments at the expense of the union government in Moscow. Many have argued that in its basic outlines, the collapse of the Soviet Union was not fundamentally different from the collapse of the tsarist and Austro-Hungarian empires during and after World War I: "Decay sets in not when the relationship has been terminated (that would be imperial collapse), but when the absolute power of the center over the periphery can no longer be effectively maintained and the periphery can, and does, act contrary to the will of the center."[28]

Ukraine's Drive to Independence

That Ukraine was to declare independence, and the USSR to wither away by December 1991, were events that few could have foreseen even a few months beforehand.[29] Dmytro Pavlychko, the well-known writer and member of the Ukrainian Popular Movement who went on to play a leading role in nation-state building and foreign policy in the Kravchuk era, said exactly a year before the declaration of independence that "an immediate secession from the Soviet Union is, first of all, impossible because we (Ukrainians) are not yet mature enough as a people for complete independence."[30]

Until summer 1989, the Ukrainian opposition had remained cautious about clamoring for independence for two reasons. First, as Pavlychko sensed, it was doubtful that independence would be accepted in eastern and southern Ukraine. Russian-speakers dominated left-bank Ukraine and the city of Kyiv, and Volodymyr Shcherbyts'kyi, head of the Communist Party of Ukraine (until his death in September 1989), held tight control over the Ukrainian SSR. A Kharkiv newspaper wrote: "Therefore, a sober assessment will tell us that the declaration of the complete independence of Ukraine in the near future is impossible."[31] Leonid Kravchuk, chairman of the Ukrainian Verkhovna Rada, limited his advocacy to transforming the USSR into a confederation of sovereign republics until the failure of the August 1991 putsch. Only then did he back full Ukrainian independence from the USSR.

In other words, the opposition and the national Communists both championed confederation—not independence—until September 1989 and July 1991, respectively. Up until the August 1991 putsch, it appeared that the Soviet Union would carry on, albeit with a more decentralized system of government. In looking back on this, Kravchuk said that the USSR began to decline beginning in the early 1980s. Gorbachev's new course only brought to the surface all the negative processes that were already in existence within society, Kravchuk argued, which led to public perceptions that the Soviet union had no long-term future. The USSR "started to fall long before, very quickly from 1985. And everyone understood this, that the empire would fall."[32] In Kravchuk's view, the disintegration of the USSR was due to "objective laws of social development; the national movement towards independence and statehood."[33] At the time, however, few acted as though this was obvious, and the suddenness with which the Soviet Union collapsed and Ukraine was vaulted to independence had powerful repercussions for the new country.

The Communist Party of Ukraine

Although in the March 1990 elections to the Verkhovna Rada, less than one-third of the new deputies were elected from the democratic bloc and the democratic platform of the Communist Party of Ukraine (KPU), their influence proved to be disproportionate. Of the 190 deputies who regularly worked in parliamentary committees, half were from the opposition. Only 6 out of 25 members of the Parliamentary Presidium were conservative members of the KPU.[34] Many of the KPU deputies also held other posts (for example, as directors of enterprises) and therefore did not devote their time as energetically to parliamentary affairs as did the opposition. Moreover, they were used to treating the Rada as a rubber-stamp body, whereas the reformers better understood that as a popularly elected assembly, the Rada now had real power.

Kravchuk played a key role in two respects within the KPU during 1989–1991. First, between 1989 and 1990, the positions of KPU and parliamentary chairman were in the same hands (those of Volodymyr Ivashko). After Ivashko's transfer to Moscow, the KPU was divided between two poles of attraction. Whereas the KPU leadership remained in the hands of a conservative leader (Stanislav Hurenko), Parliament was led by a national Communist (Kravchuk). KPU members could choose between two orientations ("imperial" and "national") at a time when public space was opening up for civic activity and fear of state sanction was eroding.

The transfer of power from the Communist Party to parliaments under Gorbachev played into Kravchuk's hands and helped weaken an already divided and demoralized KPU.[35] As parliamentary chairman beginning in mid-1990, Kravchuk was responsible for negotiations on the Union Treaty with Gorbachev and the other union republics. He, together with the poet Borys Oliynyk,[36] drafted the 1989 law "On Languages" and also ensured KPU backing for the June and August 1990 Declaration of Sovereignty and Declaration of Economic Sovereignty, respectively. Kravchuk increasingly played the role of the national Communist, following in the footsteps of his predecessors from the 1920s and 1960s. He was also instrumental in introducing a second republican question in the March 1991 Gorbachev referendum on a "renewed (Soviet) federation." This second question asked whether Ukraine supported the transformation of the USSR into a confederation of sovereign states, and the favorable response added legitimacy to demands for greater autonomy. But Kravchuk and Hurenko were united in one respect: They both detested Gorbachev (as did Boris Yeltsin, as will be discussed later). Hurenko disliked Gorbachev because he was the "ruiner of the (Communist) party." There was little support for Gorbachev, therefore, within *either* wing of the KPU.

THE DECLARATION OF INDEPENDENCE

The democratic opposition never expected to obtain a landslide vote in favor of independence within the Verkhovna Rada on August 24, 1991, five days after the putsch was launched in Moscow. Why then did only two members of the Rada vote against the declaration of independence? Ivan Pliushch, parliamentary chairman between December 1991 and March 1994, recalled that Kravchuk did not have to work hard to persuade the KPU to support the declaration: "They were in such a state of shock . . . so active were the democratic forces . . . In other words, they were under such serious attack in Kyiv, and not only in Kyiv, that they understood they had to save themselves and there was only one salvation: to join their fellow deputies."[37]

None of the members of the Verkhovna Rada wanted to show that they were "conservative" after the collapse of the Moscow putsch. A resolution in favor of adopting a declaration of independence only required 50 percent of deputies to give their approval (that is, 226). The actual number who voted for the declaration proved to be much higher—321 (with only 2 voting against, 6 abstaining, and 31 not voting). In other words, the declaration of independence was backed by a constitutional two-thirds majority, with little parliamentary dissension.

The de facto disintegration of the original "Group of 239" KPU bloc into two factions had left conservative hard-liners with only approximately 100 deputies. The remainder had moved, with Kravchuk and Pliushch, into the national Communist camp. After the August 1991 putsch, they joined forces with the 120 democratic deputies to produce a clear majority in favor of independence. But even the hard-line minority had thrown in the towel after the August 1991 putsch. As Hurenko put it: "Today we will vote for Ukrainian independence, because if we don't we're in the shit."[38]

That the declaration of independence occurred therefore can be attributed to three factors. First, the general trend of the KPU on the defensive in the face of a growing opposition movement since 1989 meant that Ukrainian political life was moving toward this outcome. Second, the extremism of the coup attempt and the incompetence with which it was executed combined to make the orthodox position untenable. Third, the end of Soviet rule in Moscow, as a result of Yeltsin's eclipse of Gorbachev, made a continuation of Soviet rule in Ukraine impossible. Thus, as in 1918, independence was as much dropped upon Ukraine as a deus ex machina as it was a result of a deliberate Ukrainian movement. As a Ukrainian author pointed out: "The declaration of independence occurred in general not as a result of the highly developed national civic political life in Ukrainian lands, but external developments in the capital of the former empire."[39]

The Referendum on Independence

Following the declaration of independence by the Verkhovna Rada, a referendum to confirm the declaration was scheduled for December 1, 1991, and activity in Ukraine in the autumn of 1991 focused on this prospect, as well as on the presidential elections to be held on the same day. No major Ukrainian political party or figure campaigned against independence. Only the small United Social Democratic Party of Ukraine agitated against it. Even the Socialist Party of Ukraine (SPU), established in

October 1991 after the KPU had been banned two months earlier, did not come out against the drive to independence. All of Ukraine's national minorities,[40] apart from Romanians, backed independence, and no local Russian groups agitated against it.[41]

Only Romanian nationalists in Chernivtsi oblast called for a boycott, although this failed to make a dent in the large vote (92.7 percent) in favor of independence in that region.[42] In both Trans-Carpathia and Chernivtsi oblasts, 78 and 89.3 percent, respectively, voted for additional questions in favor of a "special self-governing territory" and providing "special economic status." Hungarians in the Berehove Raion of Trans-Carpathia oblast (where they account for 81.4 percent of the inhabitants) voted heavily in favor of the creation of a "national district." Religious and trade union groups also came out in support of independence.[43] Thus, although there was some desire to push the devolution process even further, especially among national minorities, there was widespread support for detaching Ukraine from the Soviet Union.

Nevertheless, despite signs of nationwide support and high prereferendum support registered in opinion polls, Soviet and Russian leaders remained convinced that Kravchuk's play at obtaining public legitimacy in a nationwide referendum on December 1, 1991, would fail miserably. Kravchuk initially believed that the referendum would obtain only between 60 and 70 percent endorsement (he was concerned that it be at least higher than the two-thirds constitutional majority of 67 percent).[44] National democrats remained afraid that it would not even obtain 50 percent.[45] Gorbachev was even more skeptical, telling Kravchuk: "This will never occur! I know Ukraine well. You are mistaken. No, this will never be! And you will still come to Moscow and sign the Union Treaty."[46] Gorbachev complained to Kravchuk: "What have you dreamt up there, that referendum, it already took place in the Soviet Union, and you are again talking about another referendum."[47] Yeltsin was also surprised after the referendum results came in, asking Kravchuk: "What, and the Donbas (the oblasts of Luhans'k and Donets'k) voted in favor?"[48]

Whether or not to hold a referendum on independence divided the opposition and parliamentary deputies. National democrats at first argued, ironically, against a referendum because parliamentary deputies, who had voted heavily in favor of the declaration of independence, held popular mandates and spoke on behalf of their constituencies. They saw the referendum as a means to undermine, rather than reinforce, the declaration. "It was precisely the democrats who spoke in the Supreme Soviet and on Sophia Square who said that Kravchuk had dreamt up this referendum. We already have independence and we don't need to do anything," Kravchuk recalled.[49] But this was precisely one of Kravchuk's main motives, namely, to annul the results of the March 1991 referendum.[50] In retrospect, the referendum was crucial to Ukraine's independence, because when things became bad in subsequent years, no one could dispute the legitimacy of Ukraine's decision to secede. In contrast, Belarusian president Aleksandr Lukashenka has been able to argue that the March 1991 Soviet referendum holds sway, because no subsequent referendum was held to overturn the earlier one and confirm Belarus's independence declaration on August 25, 1991.

Yet the real reasons that national democrats opposed the holding of a referendum lay with the fear that it would not obtain the two-thirds majority many believed was required. Kravchuk understood that "they [the national democrats] were afraid of a referendum. They did not believe that the Ukrainian people would vote in such numbers for independence. They were even afraid they wouldn't get half."[51] This fear, in turn, was brought home to many of them because of their suspicions and distrust of Kravchuk as well as the strength of influence that the former KPU still wielded in eastern and southern Ukraine. Levko Lukianenko, then leader of the Republican Party of Ukraine and a December 1991 presidential candidate, had therefore opposed the holding of the referendum because if it had failed, the KPU would have been in a position to annul the declaration of independence. "It was not worth the risk to let this happen," he recalled.[52]

By December 1991, the six presidential candidates[53] were divided into two groups—Kravchuk (representing the establishment) and the rest (a mixed bag of opposition leaders who could not agree on advancing one candidate). Viacheslav Chornovil, a leading figure in Rukh and the only serious potential challenger to Kravchuk, pointed out that "[t]here is no great difference in our programs [Chornovil-Kravchuk]; he simply copied mine."[54]

The results of the referendum on independence defied all expectations at 90.3 percent (with 84.1 percent of voters taking part). Kravchuk said, "I did not know there'd be such a high percentage."[55] The highest support for independence was registered in the west Ukrainian Galician oblast of Ternopil', where it obtained 99 percent of the vote, and the lowest was in the Crimea, at 54 percent (in the contested port of Sevastopol, it was higher, at 63.7).[56] Throughout Ukraine, the rate of support varied between 80 and 90 percent (with an average of 84.2 percent).

In four oblasts—Kharkiv, Odesa, Luhans'k, and Donets'k—the vote in favor of independence obtained less than two-thirds (with an average of 65.2 percent). One-fourth of Ukraine's total population lives in these four oblasts. In the Crimea, independence was only supported by 36.5 percent of those eligible to vote, as 63.5 percent of the electorate had not taken part in the referendum. The highest number of "no" votes was made in the Crimean Autonomous Republic (42.2 percent), Luhans'k (13.4), Donets'k

(12.6), Odesa (11.6), Kharkiv (10.4), Mykolayiv (8.2), and Kherson (7.2) oblasts. All of these oblasts lie in Ukraine's eastern and southern regions, that is, in areas that are primarily Russian speaking and low in Ukrainian national consciousness.

Promoting the idea of holding such a referendum on independence and successfully carrying it out was probably Kravchuk's finest hour. Kravchuk, a skilled chess player, compared it to "a grand master's move" because it automatically annulled the March 1991 referendum and ensured Ukraine's diplomatic recognition.[57] In addition, Kravchuk could travel to Belavezha Pushcha seven days later with a strong bargaining hand. Kravchuk used the widespread feelings of fear and revulsion about Yeltsin's victory over Gorbachev in Moscow to stress the importance of distancing Ukraine from the Russian Federation and to achieve a result even the Ukrainian nationalists thought impossible. Kravchuk achieved this in part by utilizing the entire Soviet apparatus in Ukraine to agitate for independence. The period between August and December 1991 turned out to be the zenith of common purpose in Ukrainian politics. "We had a unique event in Ukrainian history after 24 August 1991, when national Communists and others traveled throughout Ukraine and agitated for independence, all on one platform of support for independence."[58]

Why Did People Vote for Independence?

An appeal by the Ukrainian Parliament to the population calling upon people to vote for independence outlined five key arguments:[59]

1. Independence would improve the "economic, political, ecological, and cultural status" of Ukraine on a par with the remainder of the world.
2. Independence would ensure better use of the country's economic potential and "vast resources."
3. Independence would "guarantee prosperity and freedom for people."
4. Independence would halt "the impoverishment of our people."
5. Independence was the only alternative (in other words, the USSR was finished).

The reasons for supporting independence were obviously not uniform throughout Ukraine. As Motyl has argued, "It was not, therefore, the Ukrainian nation that voted for independence in December 1991 but the inhabitants of Ukraine who may, in time, come to constitute a genuine nation." After all, "the inhabitants of Ukraine were (and still are) anything but a nation."[60] The lack of consensus in the reasons for voting for independence in 1991 explains in part why the large majority supporting independence was prone to erosion in subsequent years. For those who based their vote on the belief that independence would bring prosperity, experience would undermine support for independence.

Clearly, in western Ukraine the national idea predominated (the region had overwhelmingly backed independence in its own March 1991 local poll). A banner hung on L'viv's Town Hall said simply: "Remember when you go to vote on December 1 that the eyes of your forefathers who laid down their lives for Ukraine are watching you."[61] Kravchuk looked upon the referendum in a similar manner, pointing to some of the many historical myths that would later be formulated to support Ukraine's independent state:

> The referendum gives you a unique historical chance to renovate the 1,000-year tradition of Ukrainian statehood. Your "yes" to the act of state independence is a guarantee against deliberate famine, state terror, Chernobyl disaster, destruction of national languages, culture and customs and a guarantee that the people will not die for alien interests in adventures like the Afghan war.[62]

Kravchuk also linked the demise of the totalitarian USSR, which he, of course, had at one time faithfully served, and the rise of independent Ukraine to national, political, and economic liberties. This connection has been continuously stressed by Ukrainian leaders since 1991 when they compare life in independent Ukraine to life in the USSR. When Kravchuk was asked if it was good for Ukraine to secede from the USSR, he replied by asking whether you would ask a canary if it would prefer a cage or be allowed to fly away. Kravchuk then added: "Ukraine lived in a cage for 350 years. Today it wants to have its own state, knowing that this is not an easy matter."[63]

In southern and eastern Ukraine, where the national idea remained weak, other factors may have predominated in leading to the large vote for independence. Some of these included dislike for Gorbachev, the Soviet center's perceived exploitation of Ukrainian resources, and the expectation that standards of living would be higher. In a poll conducted one month prior to the referendum, the four largest issues preoccupying voters were the economic crisis, the environment, organized crime, and stabilization. Other factors (for example, cultural revival and democracy) were much further down on their list of priorities.[64] A roundtable discussion held by the National Institute of Strategic Studies and the newspaper *Holos Ukraïiny* on the "Ideology of State Building" also found that "[w]hen people voted for independence, then they were thinking of practical realities, that they would live better."[65]

A second factor that differentiated eastern and southern Ukraine from the remainder of the country was in how independence was perceived, something that the creation of the CIS eight days after the referendum only served to cloud even further. Typical of this confusion, which Kravchuk probably deliberately promoted, were the views of a former Communist Party member and army colonel, Victor Byichkov, who had voted for independence but nevertheless stated, "This is not the end of the Soviet Union."[66] It is probably difficult to estimate what these views actually meant, except to say that the population lacked access to independent media and was highly prone to manipulation by local and republican elites. The confusion also probably rested on how eastern and southern Ukrainians perceived (and, to some extent, still perceive) "independence." Thus, in the 1990 Declaration of Sovereignty, it did not seem to trouble anyone that to be sovereign but remain in the Soviet Union was a logical contradiction. To western Ukrainians, by December 1991, "independence" undoubtedly meant a complete break with the USSR and Russia, hence, their disappointment with the creation of the CIS. To eastern and southern Ukrainians, by contrast, "independence" was probably closer to the view held by the Russian leadership, something lying between confederation and full independence. In other words, eastern and southern Ukrainians greeted the creation of the CIS because it signaled that ties (economic, political, personal, cultural, psychological) with Russia would not be completely severed.

Nevertheless, one cannot either completely discount the influence of national and democratic factors even among eastern and southern Ukrainians as playing a role in their support for independence. In the Donbas, there was a strong anti-Communist and anti-center feeling in late 1991. Hennadiy Turshyns'kyi, a Donets'k-based technician, said, for example: "This is a lost city, a lost region, we have no identity, no Church, no language. I hope that in an independent Ukraine we will be true human beings."[67] Another Russian miner from the same city, Ivan Lukianenko, voted in favor of independence because it was time to "feed ourselves—not Russia. Ukraine's been bled of its wealth and had nothing back in return."[68] Valentyn Symonenko, the former mayor of Odesa, supported Ukrainian independence (like his successor, Eduard Gurfits) because only in an independent Ukraine was it possible to begin work on a local Free Economic Zone.

By December 1991, public opinion throughout Ukraine was fed up with Gorbachev, the dictates of the Soviet center, and his "renewed federation." Eastern and southern Ukrainians may not have wanted the complete break with Russia and the USSR that their western Ukrainian brethren hoped and voted for. But at the same time, they wanted a new relationship between the Soviet republics to replace a USSR that everyone, including Russian democrats, believed had historically come to a dead end. Kravchuk alluded to, and recognized, these views in eastern and southern

Ukraine: "There are forces which understand independence in a particular way, as in the CIS or the former USSR. These forces understand independence partially and not completely, not as sovereign and full independence."[69] His proposal to create the CIS was therefore meant to both pacify the inhabitants of eastern and southern Ukraine and improve relations with Russia. On both of these counts he was successful. But this stunning majority in favor of independence has not again materialized in Ukraine, and having agreed on declaring independence, Ukrainians later found that they agreed on little else, from relations with Russia to the optimal form of the economy.

THE END OF THE USSR

Toward a "Civilized Divorce"

At the parliamentary inauguration ceremony on December 5, 1991, for newly elected President Kravchuk, the Ukrainian Parliament also proceeded to renounce its allegiance to the 1922 Union Treaty. This renunciation of the treaty establishing the USSR was also regarded by some as a de facto renunciation of the 1654 Treaty of Periaslav, which had bound the fate of Ukraine and Russia together for centuries. This was clearly recognized by Kravchuk, who said, "The empire which endured for 337 years no longer exists, and Ukraine is the author of its destruction."[70] At a special session of Parliament held in the National Opera House on November 22, 1991, the one hundred and twenty-fifth anniversary of the birth of Mykhailo Hrushevs'kyi, Ukrainian historian and first (unelected) president, was celebrated. Those creating the new state were said to be following in his footsteps. Two days after his inauguration, Kravchuk flew with his prime minister, Vitold Fokin, to Belarus to discuss further developments.

Having established an independent Ukraine, the status of the Soviet Union became the operative question. Mikhail Gorbachev had campaigned throughout the autumn of 1991 for a new union treaty, and various schemes for economic, military, and political union were advanced by Russian reformers. With Ukraine's overwhelming vote for independence, it became clear to all (except perhaps Gorbachev) that there would be no new union treaty. But because of the highly integrated economies, the single military, and the nuclear arsenal, it was also unthinkable that there would be no central government whatsoever. Moreover, in legal terms, the Soviet Union still existed and Mikhail Gorbachev was still its president.

On December 8, 1991, Kravchuk met with Belarusian parliamentary chairman Stanislav Shushkevich and President Boris Yeltsin to sort out

PHOTO 1.1   Independence Day celebrations, Kyiv, August 1994

this tangled set of relationships. Kravchuk ended up obtaining what he wanted—the legal and political acknowledgment by Russia of Ukraine's independence—and surrendered very little in return. He was able to achieve this because the referendum had put him in an extremely powerful bargaining position, while Boris Yeltsin's position was weakened by his pursuit of two contradictory goals: the preservation of some sort of union and the elimination of Mikhail Gorbachev's power base.

Yeltsin had no desire to end the Soviet Union, and along with others, he imagined that some confederal arrangement would be worked out. But his more pressing problem was Mikhail Gorbachev: Gorbachev and Yeltsin both claimed to be at the top of the same governmental apparatus, Gorbachev as president of the Soviet Union, and Yeltsin as president of a Russian state that had declared its control over much "Soviet" property and institutional apparatus in Moscow. Agreeing with Kravchuk to formally disband the Soviet Union served the goal of eliminating the legal basis of Gorbachev's power and subsequently forced Gorbachev's resignation, as he was president of a country that no longer existed.

Yeltsin sought at the same time to retain common policies in a wide range of areas, in part because it was hard to imagine genuine Ukrainian independence and in part because he understood what sort of problems would emerge from an absence of such collaboration. But there was no way that he could force the dissolution of the Soviet Union (and get rid of Gorbachev) and then somehow get Kravchuk to agree to a meaningful set of common institutions. Kravchuk correctly understood the strength of his position and was happy to cooperate with Yeltsin in the first part of his agenda. Legally dissolving the Soviet Union by renouncing the 1922 Union Treaty cut the final legal tie between Ukraine and the Soviet Union, and that served Kravchuk's interest as much as Yeltsin's. But Kravchuk had no reason to want any serious institutional "center" to remain, perceiving that such a center would serve only as a vehicle for Russian hegemony and as a continuing argument that Ukraine was not completely sovereign and independent. He was able therefore to bargain for a very watered-down agreement on a "Commonwealth of Independent States," which contained a good deal in the way of commitments to cooperate but nothing in the way of the institutional apparatus to implement such cooperation. Much of Russian-Ukrainian relations since 1991 has been the story of Russia's goal to restore the ties that it agreed to sever and Ukraine's resistance to such attempts.

The Gorbachev Factor

The anathema Yeltsin and Kravchuk felt toward Gorbachev was returned in Gorbachev's feeling toward them.[71] Looking back, Gorbachev recalled: "The team that came to power at that time was devoid of conscience and ethics. They are dangerous people. I'll put it this way; it was not a victory for Yeltsin, it was a triumph of boorishness."[72] The conflict in Moscow between Yeltsin and Gorbachev was used by Kravchuk to his advantage when he asked Yeltsin at the Belavezha Pushcha meeting whether Moscow needed "two presidents." As the Belarusian chairman of Parliament, Stanislav Shushkevych, recalled, "It was clear [at Belavezha Pushcha] that it was Gorbachev who more than anything was getting in Boris Nikolayevich's [Yeltsin's] way." Sergei Paskhomenko, a Moscow-based journalist, also believed that "[t]he hatred between Gorbachev and Yeltsin was the engine" that made the latter join forces with Kravchuk to remove him and the country he led.[73]

Russia's Yeltsin and Ukraine's Kravchuk were not alone in detesting Gorbachev; Shushkevych and Nursultan Nazarbayev of Kazakhstan hated him as well. Galina Starovoitova, then an adviser to Yeltsin on nationality questions, found that "[t]he other republican leaders were sick of him . . . Yes, they wanted him out, and the only way they could do this was to abolish his post."[74] Shushkevych's prime minister, Vyacheslau Kebich, added, "We were angry with the way Gorbachev was behaving and we would have signed God knows what just to get rid of him."[75] At the same time, there was little love between Yeltsin and Kravchuk, either.

Kravchuk remembered that "it was easier to talk to him (Gorbachev) than with Yeltsin" because Gorbachev's "level of culture was higher."[76]

Russian Motives

The creation of the CIS, Igor Kliamkin has averred, was the only manner in which democracy could be saved in Russia and the only way for it to obtain its statehood by distancing itself from the USSR.[77] But this was easier said than done. As Gorbachev asked with a sense of irony: "Why did Russia need independence? From whom did they need to be independent? Itself?"[78] Gorbachev was alluding to the fact that the majority of Russians did not perceive "Russia" to be confined to the borders of the Russian SFSR because this republic had never been promoted as a homeland for ethnic Russians by the Soviet regime (unlike the non-Russian republics). Psychologically "Russia," to the majority of Russians, was one and the same as the entire USSR, because tsarist and Soviet nationality policies had not promoted Russian—but rather Soviet—nation building with Russian identity submerged within a supranational tsarist and Soviet identity.

This confusion between the two and over whether "Russia" could actually be divorced from the USSR was made more difficult by subsequent events. The Russian SFSR and the USSR shared the same institutions until 1990, when Russian ones were established. This overlap "made it relatively easy for central Soviet military and bureaucratic elites to reorientate themselves to the RSFSR at pivotal moments."[79] The Soviet center did not therefore disappear; it was simply ambushed and then reannexed by the Russian Federation. Hence, the Russian SFSR was the only Soviet republic that did not declare independence. Russia's "independence day" is therefore celebrated on June 12, the day it declared sovereignty in 1990.

A Confused Beginning to the CIS

Arriving at the Belavezha Pushcha hunting lodge in western Belarus on December 7, 1991, all three East Slavic leaders had no real idea of how their meeting would end. Shushkevych, the meeting's host and the person who claimed to have called the meeting, admitted afterward: "Although we were discussing the fate of our country, I did not have any feeling of the momentous character of the event. Not so long before I was a simple academic."[80] Shushkevych had initially wanted to invite Gorbachev as well, but Yeltsin had threatened not to show up if Gorbachev was also there. Shushkevych therefore chose to invite Yeltsin—not Gorbachev— from Moscow, a reflection of how power had shifted away from the Soviet center to the republics after the August putsch. Shushkevych's main priority was to obtain Yeltsin's consent to Belarusian independence.[81]

Shushkevych was a bystander in an event largely dominated by negotiations between Kravchuk and Yeltsin. Shushkevych, Kravchuk believed, would have signed anything placed in front of him (that is, the Union Treaty or the CIS agreement).[82] Shushkevych's only proposal was to create a "Tripartite Commission," which would then make only recommendations to Gorbachev.[83] This was turned down by Yeltsin and Kravchuk. In the final analysis, Shushkevych's resignation to whatever fate was decided by "you big ones" was seen in his suggestion that "[w]e are a small country, we will accept whatever Russia and Ukraine agree on."[84] Nevertheless, Shushkevych informed Gorbachev of the decision they had reached at the meeting where he had become redundant. Replying to Gorbachev's evident anger, Shushkevych told him: "Well, it seems that the time has ended when everything and all things [are] decided in Moscow."[85]

The Russian delegation certainly possessed no plan when it went to the meeting and did not bring suggestions for a CIS to replace the USSR. Sergei Shakhrai, then a legal adviser to Yeltsin, admitted that they began searching for a formula only during their evening meeting of December 7. The formula they chose was twofold. First, the states that created the USSR in 1922 would annul the Union Treaty and thereby dissolve the USSR.[86] This, in effect, was merely acknowledging reality: "The Soviet Union had already disappeared. We were recognizing formally the reality in which we were all living since the August coup," Gennadii Burbulis, then a Yeltsin adviser, said.[87] Second, a draft proposal from Kravchuk for a CIS "agreement was born on the spot . . . which ensured that the breakup of the Soviet union took place with the minimum of losses and upheavals."[88] Andrei Kozyrev, then Russian foreign minister, began typing the draft at midnight but did not finish and did not want to wake up the typist, so Yegor Gaidar, then Russian prime minister, handwrote the document for signing the next morning.

Ukrainian Motives

Kravchuk had only become convinced to pursue independence after August 1991. Prior to this, he had offered to Gorbachev the confederal solution he had supported as an additional republican question in the March 1991 referendum. "From the very beginning we stood for a confederation," Kravchuk admitted.[89] What had changed to push Kravchuk into the independence camp was the attempted coup: "The putsch quickened the birth of new relations between republics," Kravchuk argued.[90] By the time Gorbachev moved to a confederal position in late 1991, it was already too late. Yeltsin arrived at the Belavezha Pushcha meeting armed with Gorbachev's proposal for a new union treaty based on a confederation. But due to "Ukrainian intransigence," Burbulis recalled, this was rejected and a commonwealth without a center was proposed instead (the original name was the Commonwealth of Democratic States). Kravchuk never told his delegation anything of his plans before the meeting and "did not expect any radical groundbreaking steps from this meeting,"[91] nor did he believe that the meeting would finalize an agreement.[92] He was of the opinion, though, that they should not create a new confederation or union but should only provide for the orderly dissolution of the Soviet Union, which was inevitable.

The manner in which the CIS was created inevitably led to different interpretations of how interstate relations in the former USSR should have evolved at that time. For example, according to Burbulis, Russia did not anticipate Ukraine's nationalization of the Soviet armed forces on its territory. "We believed there would be joint armed forces for a period of five or seven years," Burbulis explained.[93] Yevgennii Shaposhnikov, Soviet minister of defense, agreed at the Belavezha Pushcha meeting to instead become CIS defense chief, clearly signaling Russia's intentions of dominating the CIS even at this early stage. The Russian Federation only launched its own armed forces in spring 1992 after it saw the futility of attempting to preserve CIS armed forces. In addition, it was not immediately decided how political and economic links would be maintained or reformulated after the collapse of the USSR.

Ukrainian-Russian Disagreements Surface

The biggest problem, of course, related to interstate relations within the CIS. Yeltsin saw the removal of Gorbachev and the Soviet center as a means not to establish an equal commonwealth but as a means to ensure that the Russian Federation openly dominated the CIS (as it did the center in the USSR).[94] This was again unsurprising. As we have already noted, the Russian SFSR could not make the clean break from the USSR that the other fourteen non-Russian states attempted, and the Russian SFSR was therefore the only Soviet republic not to declare its independence from the USSR. In addition, former Soviet officials may have worked for the Russian Federation after January 1992, but their psychology still reflected the Russian SFSR mind-set (or even that of the former USSR).[95] Ukraine was therefore set to come into conflict with the Russian Federation over two related issues from the moment the CIS was created. First, Ukraine has continuously insisted upon equality in interstate relations within the CIS and has refused to openly acknowledge any Russian leadership, sphere of influence, or domination. Second, Ukraine has refused mainly

Russian proposals to create suprastate structures for the CIS, for it to be given international legal standing, or for it to possess its own symbols. Consequently, both Yeltsin and Kravchuk had very different ideas as to what the content of the CIS should be and whether it had any real, long-term future, "Obviously, everybody understood in their own way (independence) what this meant," Kravchuk said.[96] Yeltsin believed that all of the former Soviet states could remain sovereign while staying together, a position lying somewhere between a confederation and full independence.[97] Kravchuk, by contrast, saw the CIS purely as a vehicle for a "civilized divorce" that would allow Ukraine to "return to Europe" and be free from Russia's embrace. Yeltsin's understanding of the CIS was therefore closer to that of eastern and southern Ukrainians and not that of the national Communist–national democratic alliance that led Ukraine under Kravchuk.

UKRAINE AND THE SOVIET LEGACY

The Soviet legacy in Ukraine touches every aspect of politics and society, and only a brief overview is possible here.[98] In terms of national identity, the record was mixed, as the Soviet government first promoted the Ukrainian identity and language in the 1920s and then ruthlessly suppressed them but also established the territorial basis for the current Ukrainian state. Politically, the Soviet regime extinguished any citizen-based initiatives that might have provided the beginnings of a civil society and created a set of institutions, largely corrupted by the time of the collapse, that continue, only partially reformed, to drive Ukrainian politics. Economically, the Soviet system led to the depletion of Ukrainian natural resources and to an economic structure that is completely inappropriate for the market. Ecologically, the country is devastated. Thus, while we typically emphasize the fundamental break that occurred in 1991, it is crucial to take into account the important legacies that the Soviet Union has left for independent Ukraine.

The drive to create an independent Ukrainian state between 1917 and 1920 failed, but the strength of national feeling in Ukraine did have the unexpected result of forcing the Soviet Russian state to agree to the creation of the Ukrainian SSR. This weakness of Soviet power in Ukraine, the strength of Ukrainian national communism, and the more liberal environment of the New Economic Policy forced Moscow to allow the Ukrainianization and *korenizatsiia* (indigenization) policies of the 1920s. These policies provided rapid and impressive results in which the development of Soviet power and modernization (urbanization and industrialization) occurred simultaneously with Ukrainian nation building within the Soviet Ukrainian state. In a manner similar to what had taken place in

Western Europe decades earlier, peasants with a local and premodern identity migrated to Ukrainian-speaking urban centers where they exchanged their local identities (*tuteishi*, literally meaning "from here") for a Ukrainian national identity.

But this attempt on the part of Ukrainian intellectuals and elites to create a modern Ukrainian nation was again thwarted (as it had been in the second half of the nineteenth century in tsarist Russia). By the early 1930s, the Soviet authorities had become concerned, just as their tsarist counterparts had earlier, that if *korenizatsiia* were allowed to continue, the Ukrainian ethnos would have evolved into a modern nation, with negative consequences for the centralized state the Soviets were building. George Liber concluded: "Had the Ukrainianization program continued during the height of industrialization, the cities would have become culturally Ukrainianized. They would have followed the pattern of Prague and Warsaw set at the end of the nineteenth century."[99] This modern Ukrainian nation may have then proceeded to raise political demands, such as confederation or even independence (as in 1989–1991).

In 1933, the Soviet state reversed these policies of nation building when it unleashed an artificial famine that claimed upwards of 7 million Ukrainian lives. Russian nationalism returned within the sphere of Soviet nationality policy and historiography. Stalin did not nullify the agreements made between the center and periphery in 1918–1923, and the multinational USSR remained, with its commitment to national homelands. Nationally assertive elites were replaced by more pliant, loyal ones. Nevertheless, republican elites were allowed to grow and identify with their own designated homelands, although they had to be guarded by Moscow's "watchdog" (the ethnic Russian second secretary of the Republican Communist Parties). National consciousness and assertiveness were often allowed to exist within limits and depending upon the strategic significance of the republic.[100]

Ukraine represented a key strategic republic in Moscow's eyes, and any threat from Ukrainian "bourgeois nationalism" was regarded as a greater security threat than that emanating from other non-Russian republics or from Russian human rights activists. From the mid-1930s on, Soviet nationality policies and historiography therefore preferred to maintain the majority of Ukrainians in a frozen prenational ethnos that would gradually assimilate, together with the Belarusians, into Russians as the future East Slavic core of *Homo sovieticus* (that is, the Soviet state promoted Soviet—not Russian—nation building). Ukrainians possessed their own separate republic, but nationality policies and historiography promoted a Little Russian, regional, and geographical identity (not a Ukrainian national identity separate from the Russian). Russian remained the language of "modernity," "progress," and urban life. Ukrainian language and culture, which had been set to dominate the industrial and urban centers of 1920s Ukrainian SSR, became in effect "provincialized."[101] Ukrainians dominated their urban centers demographically but not culturally.

A cursory examination of Soviet nationality policies, especially if one focuses on some of the more brutally repressive aspects of that policy, leads to the conclusion that Soviet policies had a nation-destroying effect. In fact, the Soviet legacy is somewhat more confused. Nation destroying undoubtedly occurred on a great scale physically in the Stalin era and linguistically in the Khrushchev-Brezhnev eras.[102] But as Victor Zaslavsky has noted, "Soviet nationality policy, despite its professed goal of subverting ethnic loyalties and destroying ethnic difficulties, promoted and accelerated the process of nation building."[103] In a postmortem of the USSR, Ronald Suny argued that the USSR had been a "victim not only of its negative effects on the non-Russian peoples but of its own 'progressive' contribution to the process of nation-building."[104] In other words, Soviet repression and its failed socioeconomic policies both turned the republics against the state and provided them with the means to dismantle this state in an orderly fashion into its fifteen component parts. Ultimately, the USSR disintegrated because Soviet nation building failed (Russians, Ukrainians, and others felt more Russian or Ukrainian than Soviet). This, coupled with former Soviet president Mikhail Gorbachev's evident lack of understanding of nationality problems, led the republican elites to turn their backs on the Soviet center in favor of republican nation and state building.[105] Brubaker therefore believes that the USSR pursued a contradictory policy of both repressing nationalism while consolidating "nationhood and nationality."[106] This is probably the case for some former Communist countries more than for others.

Therefore, the Ukrainian state that became independent on January 1, 1992, inherited a contradictory mix of legacies from its Soviet Ukrainian predecessor. In the realm of the state, it inherited a set of institutions that possessed symbols, certain governing bodies, hypertrophied security forces, and a very small elite. Because the transition occurred peacefully, these state institutions were not destroyed. In the short term, this fostered stability; in the longer term, that institutional continuity has led to a powerful inertia obstructing reform, as the following chapters show.

Independent Ukraine is faced with the task of creating a united political nation from this inherited mixture of peoples composed of modern and premodern attributes.[107] Difficulties in state building and in nation building tend to reinforce one another, as deficiencies in one area hamper progress in the other in a vicious cycle that characterizes many of the problems discussed in the following chapters.

A major problem for the Ukrainian leadership in December 1991 was that "[h]aving achieved independence, our Supreme Soviet, one can openly state, did not know what to do with it."[108] Kravchuk admitted: "You have a government that is weak, a president that is just being formed, a Parliament which thinks it is an executive and parliamentary committees which think they should be doing the work of cabinet ministers."[109] A future vision (or even a less ambitious program) was precisely what Ukraine lacked. Lacking at that stage a united shared past, ethnicity, and language, Ukraine needed a forward-looking vision, which President Kravchuk or Parliamentary Chairman Pliushch failed to provide in those crucial early years of independence.[110] Thus, despite the large degree of Ukrainian nationalist activity in society, the government remains fragmented, as Chapter 5 will show in more detail. As Brubaker has noted: "No other state has gone so far in sponsoring, codifying, institutionalizing, even (in some cases) inventing nationhood and nationality on the sub-state level, while at the same time doing nothing to institutionalize them on the level of the state as a whole."[111]

Ukraine, like many other states of the former USSR, therefore inherited *both* a "quasi-state" and a "quasi-nation."[112] The Soviet system partially built—but prevented completion of—both a Ukrainian state and a Ukrainian nation. Post-Soviet Ukraine inherited a people composed of attributes that approached a modern nation much more closely in western Ukraine (where the Austrians had fostered nation building prior to 1918 and postwar modernization had led to the Ukrainianization of urban centers earlier emptied of Jews and Poles by Nazi and Soviet policies) than in eastern Ukraine. Similarly, although Ukraine had many of the institutional attributes of an independent state, that structure was somewhat hollow and incomplete. For example, Ukraine had a foreign ministry prior to 1991, but it functioned only to support the Ukrainian UN mission and was essentially a branch of the Soviet Foreign Ministry. It had no capacity to formulate or direct the foreign policy of an independent state.

The post-Soviet consequences of this legacy upon Russians are also profound. Three-fourths of Russians believed that Ukrainians are not a separate ethnic group and that Ukrainian independence is therefore "artificial" and temporary."[113] Sixty-four percent of Russians supported the union of Ukraine and Russia into one state.[114] The persistence of these views explains why it took Russia until May 1997 to recognize Ukraine's borders in an interstate treaty, a treaty that the Russian media claimed was more difficult to sign than those with the Chechens and NATO during the same month.

Ukraine consequently inherited a number of key launching pads that required further nation- and state-building policies to complete the process in the post-Soviet era of nation creation and state construction (see Chapters 2 and 3).[115] Motyl says of the Ukraine's Soviet inheritance: "[F]or all its vicissitudes, it did endow Ukraine with a linguistically coherent population that resembled a nation, a set of political activists who resembled an elite and an administration that resembled a state."[116]

THE UKRAINIAN SSR: A QUASI-STATE

The Ukrainian SSR was not a complete sham. The myth of the Ukrainian SSR *did* enter the consciousness of the Ukrainian public. Lysiak Rudnytsky, the well-known and respected Canadian-Ukrainian historian, noted nearly two decades prior to the disintegration of the USSR that the Soviet Ukrainian state had helped to partially lift the Ukrainian ethnographic masses of 1917 into a quasi-nation, although in a very distorted and "psychologically mutated" form. He predicted that "[t]he clever manipulators may well find themselves some day in the position of the sorcerer's apprentice, unable to muster the genie who they have conjured."[117] Two decades after Rudnytsky's prophecy, the Ukrainian elites created by the Soviet regime ensured the success of Ukraine's drive for independence.

National consolidation has certainly occurred in Ukraine's capital city in comparison to a century ago. During the elections to the Constituent Assembly and city Duma in 1917–1918, support for Ukrainian political parties in Kyiv hovered between 21 and 26 percent (in Odesa they amounted to only 4 percent in the election to the Constituent Assembly). In the late Soviet and post-Soviet periods, Kyiv has consistently shown itself to be more Ukrainian, as voters back national democrats and rightist parties. In a study of linguistic preferences in Kyiv, Dominique Arel concluded that within a few generations, Kyiv might well become a Ukrainian-speaking city. Without some national consolidation in the Soviet era, this change probably would not have occurred.[118]

A similar picture emerges in western Ukraine, where in some significant ways Ukrainian nation building was aided by the atrocities of Soviet (and Nazi) rule, especially the expulsion of the Polish inhabitants of western Ukraine between 1944 and 1947. With the removal of the two main ethnic urban groups (Poles and Jews), modernization and industrialization in western Ukraine could occur simultaneously with the Ukrainianization of its urban centers (which had been the hope of Ukraine's national Communists in the 1920s in eastern Ukraine). Between 1959 and 1989, Soviet censuses show that the Ukrainian share of L'viv's population increased from 60 to 79.1 percent at the same time as the Russian share declined from 27 to 16.1 percent.[119] Western Ukraine and Kyiv were therefore becoming more Ukrainian under Soviet rule. Overall, it is impossible to say whether Soviet efforts to destroy Ukrainian nationalism outweighed the inadvertent support given to Ukrainian national identity, but it is important to recognize that the record is mixed.

The creation of the Ukrainian SSR with defined boundaries, which after independence in January 1992 became international borders, is an important beneficial legacy of the Soviet era. The secession of Ukraine came about according to constitutional means, as President Kravchuk often noted. Independent Ukraine was not therefore a completely "new" entity because it represented the constitutional continuation of the Ukrainian SSR.[120] The 1977 Ukrainian Constitution, with numerous amendments, held legal force in independent Ukraine until the adoption of Ukraine's post-Soviet Constitution in 1996.[121] The Ukrainian state claimed the right to inherit everything found on its territory in December 1991 (apart from nuclear weapons), as well as the Ukrainian SSR's share of the USSR's assets.

The Soviet internal administrative borders therefore did play a role in changing and molding the identities of the peoples within their respective republics and, more concretely, in creating the juridical basis for Ukrainian secession. As highlighted above, it was the formal act of dissolving the Union Treaty of 1922 that officially liquidated the Soviet Union in terms of international law and removed Gorbachev's last political leg. Had the Soviet state constructed a state that was as unified on paper as it was in reality, this mechanism of secession would have been impossible, and before any Ukrainian independence had been discussed, the question "What is Ukraine?" would had to have been answered. The Soviets, in a move of immense import, answered this question in creating the federal structure.

CONCLUSION

The disintegration of the USSR came about as a consequence of seven interrelated factors. First, the Soviet union was already in long-term imperial decline by the 1980s.

Second, Gorbachev's policies of perestroika and glasnost opened the doors to political opposition. This, as on previous occasions during the 1920s and 1960s, led to the growth of national communism and the division of Republican Communist Parties into "imperial" and "national" factions, particularly in republics, such as Ukraine, where counterelites remained strong.

Third, Gorbachev's policies opened up political space within which counterelites organized mass movements that over time increasingly allied themselves with the national Communists against the Soviet center. This alliance particularly cemented itself during the 1990–1991 period after republican parliaments were elected.

Fourth, Gorbachev's policies were a failure in the economic and nationalities fields. Gorbachev never understood the nationalities question, apparently believing his own regime's propaganda concerning the fraternal friendship among Soviet people and the creation of the New Soviet Man. If he had proposed a confederal solution to the republics prior to August 1991, most national Communists outside the three Baltic states might have been tempted to ditch their more radical nationalist allies and accept these proposals. Instead, Gorbachev insisted upon a revised union treaty until after the August 1991 putsch, by which time it was too late because all of the republics, apart from Russia, had by then declared independence. Gorbachev's increasing reliance upon Russian nationalism after 1990 only served to further antagonize the non-Russian elites in the former USSR.

Fifth, and closely related to the previous point, Gorbachev's mishandling of the Soviet crises only served to turn *both* the "imperial" and the "national" factions within the Republican Communist Parties against him. By late 1991, Gorbachev was therefore left with few domestic allies.

Sixth, in the aftermath of the failed and botched August 1991 putsch, by December of that year the USSR had de facto already disintegrated. It was only left up to the Eastern Slavic core of this state to ensure that the demise of this superpower was given legal formality and as a "civilized divorce." This view of the importance of the CIS as a "civilized divorce" has been endorsed by Kravchuk's successor, President Leonid Kuchma. CIS executive secretary Ivan Korotchenya also conceded that the CIS provided "a historical and, at the same time, a delicate mission of divorcing the former Soviet republics without conflicts and ensuring their independent political development."[122]

In view of the fact that Russia no longer had any interest in propping up the former USSR and because of Yeltsin's personal dislike of Gorbachev, the disintegration of the USSR served Yeltsin's interest as much as that of Ukraine. Finally, the hurried manner and unplanned agreement to create the CIS in December 1991 served to create disagreements and different interpretations of the role and functions of the CIS between its two key members, Ukraine and Russia. The signing of the Russian-Ukrainian interstate treaty and finalization of the Black Sea agreement in May 1997 signaled the second and final stage of the disintegration of the USSR. In the words of Viktor Semenov, mayor of Sevastopol, "at 9.06 [A.M.] the Soviet Union ceased to finally exist," as Soviet flags were lowered on the Black Sea Fleet on June 11, 1997.[123] The symbolic significance of this second, final stage of the disintegration of the USSR could be seen in the Soviet passports still utilized by many Ukrainian citizens, which became invalid on Ukrainian territory only in January 1998.

The Soviet legacy within Ukraine is therefore paradoxical. In terms of national identity, it includes both vicious repression and the institutionalization of the Ukrainian state. Economically, it includes both modernization and profound distortion. Because the collapse of the Soviet Union was accomplished peacefully, there was no chance to completely erase the past and the ancien régime or to start with a clean slate. Ukraine in 1991 depended on the Soviet Union not only for the establishment of its borders but also for its entire government system. The good news is that chaos and violence were avoided. The bad news is that Soviet institutions have in many respects continued to govern post-Soviet Ukraine, and there has been no room to forge new arrangements, as the following chapters show.

▪ TWO ▪

Nation Building and National Identity

The notion of a Ukrainian people or nation distinct from the Russian and Polish peoples was suppressed for many decades but maintained just enough continuity to blossom into widespread Ukrainian national movements when circumstances allowed, as they did briefly under the Soviets in the 1920s and have now again with the establishment of an independent Ukraine. If "nationalism" is defined in part by the idea that a nation should have its own state so that a people not be ruled by "others," then one of the primary goals of Ukrainian nationalism was achieved in 1991. However, the relationship between "states" and "nations" is extremely complex in general, especially so for Ukraine. Despite the widely used term "nation-state," there are very few cases in the world where the two coincide perfectly. The connection between "nation" and "state" is tenuous: In 1972, only twelve of the world's then 122 states were ethnically homogeneous.[1] In that sense, Ukraine's ethnic and linguistic heterogeneity is not especially distinctive in the modern world, and it is not immediately obvious that Ukraine's heterogeneity should be more problematic than that of other states.

The essential nationality problem for Ukraine is the lack of a coherent national identity around which the society and the state can cohere.[2] Democracy is about the rule of "the people," but in Ukraine there remains uncertainty over who "the Ukrainian" people are. The existence of a large Russian minority is only a small part of the problem. More broadly, the suppression of Ukrainian nationalism, combined with the absence of a tradition of a Ukrainian state, leaves the notion of "Ukraine" and "Ukrainians" murky, hence the frequent lament in Ukraine over the absence of a "national idea."

Literature on nationalism typically distinguishes between an "ethnic" notion of nationalism, where states are based on ethnic and national groups, and a "civic" notion of nationalism, which reverses the process and bases the nation on the state. Empirically, the two are not mutually

MAP 2.1 Ethnic Ukrainians

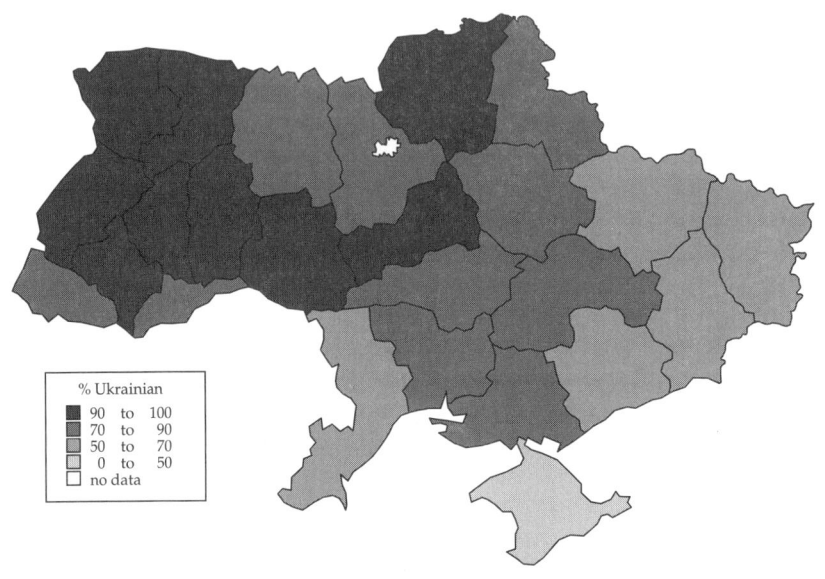

SOURCE: 1989 Soviet Census.

MAP 2.2 Ukrainian as Native Language

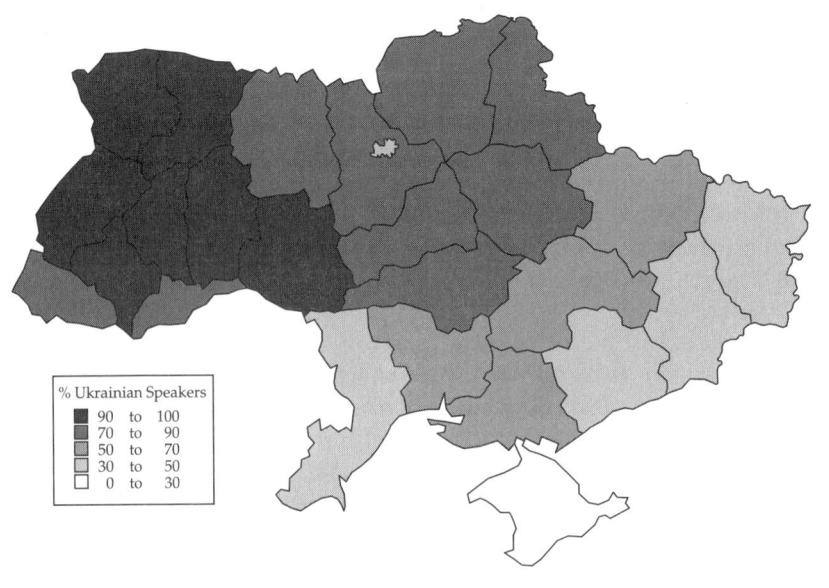

SOURCE: 1989 Soviet Census.

MAP 2.3 Proportion of School Pupils Studying in the Ukrainian Language, 1997

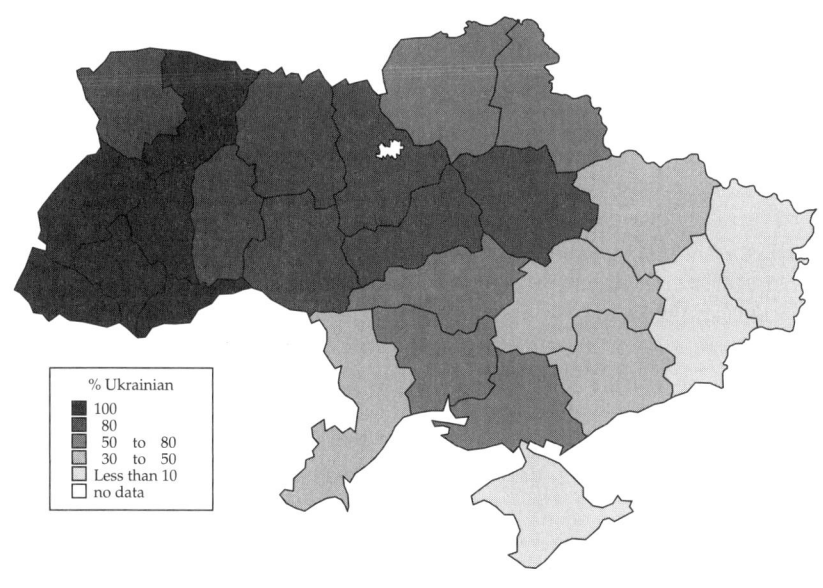

SOURCE: *Z vilnu Ukraiinu*, 8 April 1997.

exclusive, and states tend to combine both notions of nationality in a reflexive relationship between state and nation. The problem for Ukraine is that its history leaves both the state and the nation underdeveloped, so that a vicious cycle appears: The nation cannot be built upon a prominently defined and enduring state, which does not yet exist. But that state cannot be built upon a well-defined and coherent nation, because that too has yet to develop.

For Ukraine today then, the process of nation building is tightly bound up with that of state building. Many argue that a strong democratic state cannot be built without a strong political community and that a strong civil society cannot be built without the notion of commonality that national identity builds. By contrast, many also argue that a strong nation can emerge in the near term only through the nation building that results from a strong and effective state government. Although opinion varies a good deal on just how serious these problems are and how they might be overcome, there is widespread agreement that the "national identity problem" is a profound one in Ukrainian politics today. It shows up in the fragmentation of political parties, in the regional basis of the party structure and of public opinion, and in questions concerning the relationship between central and local governments. The fundamental question is whether the Ukrainian citizenry will come to enough consensus on who they are and what their goals are to make effective democracy a possibility or whether fragmentation will hamper democracy and state building.

WHAT IS A "NATION"?

The conceptual and theoretical issues surrounding the problems of nationality and nationalism are well beyond the scope of this book, but it is worth addressing how Ukraine's situation fits into widely held theories of nationalism. Hugh Seton Watson wrote that "no 'scientific definition' of a nation can be devised.... All that I can find to say is that a nation exists when a significant number of people in a community consider themselves to form a nation, or behave as if they formed one."[3] Using this definition, Ukrainians might already be termed a "nation" by the late 1990s, but it remains unclear how much of the Ukrainian citizenry actually thinks or behaves this way.

The rise of modern "nations" is deemed to have taken place after the French Revolution of 1789, and they are therefore associated with the development of a modern state, parliamentary democracy, and a market economy. The most forthright theorist who linked nations to the modern era was Ernest Gellner.[4] Anthony Smith, however, argued that nations did not just simply arise during the post–French revolutionary era of industrialization, democratization, and marketization. He has said that one should look further back to the premodern era because "nationalists cannot, and do not, create nations *ex nihilo*."[5] Clearly, the development in the premodern era of some of the attributes mentioned later associated with the "nation" is vitally important. Their absence, many argue, has denied success to many former Western colonies in their attempts at nation building. Even if nationalism is a modern phenomenon, national elites always look to the past to legitimize their state's territory and independence. The problem for Ukraine here is obvious: Although Ukraine has more of a national tradition to work with than Belarus, its national tradition was never fully developed and then was seriously undermined in several ways. The division of Ukraine between the Russian and Polish realms led to the absence of a single Ukrainian history, and the suppression of the Ukrainian language and Ukrainian nationalist thought destroyed the materials out of which a strong nation might be built.

This becomes clear when one considers the Ukrainian nation's attributes in the series of qualities that most definitions of nationalism propose as defining a nation. Different nations possess different combinations of these commonly held attributes, among which are:

- Territory
- State

- Language
- Mass culture or ideology
- History[6]
- Economy
- Legal rights and duties[7]

Although it is clear that no one of these qualities is absolutely necessary, Ukraine is strikingly deficient in every one.

NATION BUILDING AND STATE BUILDING

This chapter focuses on the question of nation building; however, as Juan Linz has pointed out, "It might be argued that state building and nation-building can be separated only conceptually but that both processes have gone and are going hand in hand."[8] These two factors should be treated as distinct processes—as they are in this volume—but also as interlinked. A purely civic state cannot by itself provide the "glue" that would unite all of its citizens in loyalty to its constitution. Hence, states are usually underpinned by ethnic elements that provide far stronger bonds of mutual loyalty. These, in turn, exist in an uneasy relationship with the civic elements of the state.[9]

National states or state-nations therefore not only need institutions, constitutions, coercive forces, the rule of law, civil society, and elites (which are covered elsewhere in this volume and are usually regarded as elements of the "state"). They also need a space enclosed by borders,[10] a homeland (*patria* or *heimat*), a national identity, historical myths and symbols, national anthems, and folk culture.

In Ukraine, the processes of state building and nation building are going on hand in hand (together with democratization and marketization), and the need to enact all these transitions simultaneously greatly complicates the matter. In Ukraine, several characteristics of the legacy of Soviet rule complicate the processes of nation and state building.

First, Ukraine inherited what might be called a "quasi-state" from the USSR. This state and the institutions it incorporated were far more developed than those inherited by the nascent Ukrainian state in 1917.[11] At the same time, these new institutions have been insufficient to run a modern state.[12] Nearly a decade after the USSR disintegrated, Ukraine is still a "weak state" and suffers from a severe institutional deficit.

Second, Ukraine, as with other postcolonial states, did not inherit a modern nation. As Robert Jackson pointed out in relation to former Western colonies, "Very few new states are 'nations' either by long history or common ethnicity or successful constitutional integration."[13]

Third, Ukraine today composes an "east" and "west" with vastly different historical experiences. Western Ukraine was never under Russian control until 1939, belonging before that time first to the Austrian Empire and then to independent Poland. A modern Ukrainian nation was allowed to develop in Austrian-controlled Ukraine prior to 1918, a factor that was helped along from 1918 to the 1950s by war and conflict with "others" (Poles, Hungarians, Romanians, and Soviets). In eastern and southern Ukraine, by contrast, modern nation building was forcibly halted on two occasions—in the late tsarist era and then again in the 1930s.[14] Eastern and southern Ukraine, therefore, in general possess less fully developed notions of national identity than do the western regions. Nation building in post-Soviet Ukraine has to therefore undertake two processes before a unified Ukrainian nation will exist.

Fourth, there has been little development of Ukrainian national identity in the east and south, inhibiting the creation of an overarching political community uniting all of the inhabitants of independent Ukraine. To what extent these processes can be accelerated by government policy is hotly debated. Some scholars, such as William Zimmerman, George Liber, Catherine Wanner, and Taras Kuzio believe that such a political community is emerging in Ukraine. Meanwhile, Andrew Wilson and Valeriy Khmelko remain more pessimistic.[15]

NATION BUILDING BY STAGES

Nation building is not a quick process (and is usually far slower than state and institution building). In Western Europe it was "slow and largely unplanned."[16] Although the process is usually credited with beginning in the late eighteenth century, modern nations, as one would understand them today, did not appear in North America or Western Europe until the first half of the twentieth century. This progress of nation building was closely tied to the emerging hegemony of capitalism and bourgeois democracy in long-established states where traditional rulers and archaic, regional customs were gradually replaced by overarching loyalties.[17] The drawn-out process of nation building in Western Europe is being condensed into a much shorter time frame in former Communist countries, such as Ukraine.

Arnold van Gennep divides nation building into three stages that we can apply to Ukraine:

1. Separation: a loosely defined community senses separation. Society is discontented with traditions carried over. Without an overarching national identity, it identifies itself by comparing itself to "others" and noting the differences. Many eastern Ukrainians know that they are different from "Russians" in the Russian Federation but are still unsure as to their own identity.

Western Ukrainians have a stronger sense of "otherness" toward all Ukraine's neighbors.
2. Liminality: a new identity is created. Nevertheless, elements of the old still survive. Society defines itself in terms of its new identity and its traditional beliefs. The majority of Ukrainians have probably reached this stage.
3. Aggregation: a new identity is created incorporating new values and symbols. The old identity is discarded. In Ukraine this is very much linked to generational and socioeconomic factors. The carriers of old values tend to be the older generation, while others who are suffering from the socioeconomic crisis remain nostalgic about these old values and look back at the "good old days" of the Soviet era.

In Ukraine, as elsewhere, nation building has proceeded unevenly, "such that different sectors of the polity at any one time are in different stages of the passage."[18] Nation building in Ukraine is taking place at three levels. At the micro level, Ukrainian national consciousness is growing among individuals, though with great regional variation. At the macro level, a new Ukrainian political community is being created in terms of the symbols and discourses used by the state and mass media. Finally, at the international level, Ukraine has been accepted as an independent state distinct from Russia, implying that Ukraine's inhabitants are distinct from Russians. Only at the international level can the process be said to be complete, and indeed the strong acceptance of Ukraine in the international arena probably contributes to nation building at the macro and micro levels within Ukraine.

The remainder of this chapter is divided into two sections. The first surveys the historical legacy in Ukraine of nationality policies implemented by external powers. The second looks at the record of nation building in Ukraine in the Kravchuk and Kuchma eras by comparing and contrasting their policies and tracing outlines of a growing consensus among Ukraine's elites. This section also goes on to examine border questions, regionalism, Crimean separatism and historiography, myths and legends as elements of the nation-building project, and the socialization of Ukrainian citizens within its polity and society.

NATION BUILDING IN UKRAINE: THE HISTORICAL LEGACY

Ukraine and Russia both trace their roots to the medieval state of Kyivan Rus', centered on what is today Kyiv.[19] After that state decayed, and after the Mongol invasions, a new center of power emerged in Moscow, which from the fifteenth to eighteenth centuries expanded to include much of the territory we presently associate with Russia and Ukraine. Through much of this time, however, considerable portions of Ukraine were included in the Polish-Lithuanian Commonwealth and the subsequent Polish state, and the Crimea was controlled by the Crimean Tatar Khanate, a remnant of the Mongol horde with close ties to the Ottoman Empire. In ongoing wars between Poland and Russia, Ukrainian elites sought to forge independence, most notably in the Cossack uprising of 1648, but in each case, the tsar's armies prevailed, and Ukraine remained divided between Russia and Poland. The last battle for Ukrainian independence was crushed by Peter the Great, and the last vestiges of Ukrainian political autonomy were ended under Catherine the Great at the end of the eighteenth century.

Ukrainian self-awareness initially attempted to find a place for itself within the Polish-Lithuanian Commonwealth, but Polish elites were interested in taking over Ukraine, not in seeing a potential rival emerge there. Failing in its attempts at becoming an equal member of the Polish-Lithuanian Commonwealth, the Ukrainian elites turned to Muscovy in the hope that their separate identity could be maintained there instead. "In both instances, Ukrainians accepted some form of unity while at the same time insisting on maintaining essential differences."[20]

Thus, prior to 1700 there had developed a distinct Ukrainian identity that looked upon both Poles *and* Russians as different "others."[21] Although Russia and Poland controlled much Ukrainian territory at that time, the cultural domination of Russia over much of Ukraine did not occur in earnest until the nineteenth century. Even as late as 1800, Ukraine (or "Little Russia," as it was then called) was a strange, exotic, and foreign land to most Russians.[22] Kyiv was dominated by Polish culture and aristocrats as late as the 1860s.

David Saunders argues that between the seventeenth century and 1914 the "tsars worked hard to prevent a Ukrainian identity from surfacing."[23] The growing assertiveness of Russian nationalism in the second half of the nineteenth century and suppression of all aspects of Ukrainian identity led to a counterreaction and the growth of modern Ukrainian nationalism. This process had its reprise in the latter decades of Soviet rule, when increasing Russification and centralization engendered resistance among the non-Russian nationalities.

Ukraine today is resuming its nation (and state) building after two substantial interruptions (1860s–1870s and 1930s). Miroslav Hroch believes that therefore in Ukraine his three stages of nation building will take place simultaneously. These three stages are the development of a local language and culture as the official language, establishment of an independent state, and the completion of a social structure (for a "nonhistorical" nation whose elites had been assimilated).[24]

The simultaneity of Hroch's three stages applies in particular to those regions of Ukraine where the tsarist authorities prevented the national idea from being transferred from the elites to the masses. As Paul Magosci makes clear: "While Ukrainianism was being suppressed in the Russian Empire, all the fundamentals that make possible a viable national life—history, ideology, language, literature, cultural organization, education, religion and politics—were being formally established in Austrian Galicia."[25] In Austria-Hungary, Ukrainians could remain both patriots of their own ethnic group and loyal subjects to the empire. That is, they could hold multiple loyalties as Scots did in the British Empire after the 1707 union of Scotland and England. In Western empires, multiple loyalties such as these did not necessarily entail assimilation. In the tsarist empire, such an understanding of contractual relationships did not exist, which has led to differing interpretations to this day about the 1654 Periaslav Treaty (the Ukrainian view of a contractual relationship versus the Russian view of Ukraine's unilateral submission).[26]

Industrialization and urbanization did not lead to the domination of urban centers by Ukrainian culture and language. It was precisely to prevent such a Ukrainianization of the cities that Soviet leader Joseph Stalin halted the indigenization campaign of the 1920s, and the brunt of Stalinism befell eastern and southern Ukrainians, through the artificial famine and great terror, but missed western Ukraine, which was not yet under Soviet rule. Thus, eastern Ukraine's cities are largely devoid of Ukrainian culture, and the Russian language is dominant. These areas were less involved in the Ukrainian drive to independence in 1989–1991, which was led by elites from western urban centers which had become Ukrainian in language and culture. In western Ukraine the eradication of Jewish and Polish ethnic groups by the Nazis and Soviets, as well as post-Soviet industrialization and urbanization, had served to make these urban centers thoroughly Ukrainian—which likely would have taken place in eastern Ukraine if indigenization had not been halted in the early 1930s.

In other words, western Ukrainians have a more completely developed sense of Ukrainian national identity because, as Magosci argues, they were able to evolve through the three stages of national revival (that is, nation building). The first stage of "heritage gathering" took place between the 1780s and 1848. During this stage, different orientations competed for the allegiance of western Ukrainians. Magosci's second and third "organizational" and "political" stages took place between 1848 and 1914. Western Ukrainians therefore undertook their nation building during the same period of history as Italians, Germans, other Western Europeans, and Americans. During the second half of the nineteenth century, three orientations competed for the allegiances of western Ukrainians—old Ruthenian (Rusyn, which only referred to western Ukrainians as a separate nation), Ukrainian (which encompassed all Ukrainians), and Russophile (Rus'kiy, including all Eastern Slavs). The Rusyn-Ruthenian outlook remained dominant until the 1860s (this orientation was promoted in Hungarian-controlled regions and still finds adherents in northeastern Slovakia and Trans-Carpathia).

Nevertheless, by the 1890s "Ukrainian" came increasingly to replace the "Russian" nationality and language. Three decades of "organizational" activities by the Prosvita Society, the cooperative movement, and the Shevchenko Scientific Society all led to the victory of the Ukrainianophile movement. In 1893, Ukrainian became recognized as a standard for instruction in education. Seventy-one percent of the 36,000 elementary schools in eastern Galicia taught in Ukrainian, coupled with Ukrainian-language state and private gymnasium and Ukrainian studies departments at L'viv University. The two competing orientations (Rusyn and Russophile) were eliminated de facto from the education system, although both tendencies continued to be supported by the Poles and tsarist authorities.

These successes in nation building inevitably led to the third "political" stage (which, as we have already pointed out, was why the Soviet regime was so afraid of the indigenization of the 1920s). This stage saw the creation of political parties and civic groups demanding universal suffrage, equality in the provision of education to all ethnic groups, local self-administration, independence, the division of Galicia into Polish western and Ukrainian eastern sections, and the unification of all Ukrainians.

Western Ukrainians also benefited from their religious faith (the Uniate, or Ukrainian Catholic, Church combined the Orthodox rite with submission to the Church of Rome), which differentiated them from Catholic Poles *and* Orthodox Russians. The census defined "Poles" therefore as all those who attended Latin-rite churches (in the tsarist empire "Russians" and "Orthodox" were synonymous with all three Eastern Slav nations). Support for the Russophile tendency also declined after the tsar suppressed the Uniate Church in Ukraine and Belarus in the 1830s. John-Paul Himka credits the Uniate Church with contributing the most to nation building in Galicia because it was threatened by both the Roman Catholics and the Orthodox Church. To preserve their religion, they had to therefore stay Ukrainian and not become either Poles (Catholics) or Russians (Orthodox).[27]

In both tsarist Russia and interwar Soviet Ukraine, the Ukrainian ethnos fared far worse. Ukrainians were the *only* ethnic group in the tsarist empire whose language was suppressed. Such a ruling was not applied to the Polish, German, Baltic, Finnish, Hebrew, or Tatar languages despite the threats these ethnic groups posed, the historical animosities that existed, or the anti-Semitism they aroused. Why, then, did the tsarist authorities so fear the Ukrainian language? Saunders argues that the same logic applied in the tsarist era as did in the 1930s, namely, that to allow development of the Ukrainian nation would have led inexorably to the "political" stage of nationalism, including demands for local self-government, confederation, or even independence: "The point of banning books in Ukrainian designed for the common people, and making sure that Ukrainian was not employed as a medium of instruction in primary schools was to prevent Ukrainians at large from developing a sense of their ethnic identity."[28]

These tsarist and post-1933 Soviet policies were accompanied by Russification, particularly in urban centers, by the planned migration of Russians into Ukraine and migration of Ukrainians to Siberia (who by 1917 accounted for 9.39 percent of its population), and by the transformation of Ukraine into an "internal colony" where the commanding heights of the state administration, the government, the economy, and job occupations were dominated by ethnic Russians. The tsarist authorities were particularly disturbed at the aims of the intelligentsia, who wanted to spread, like their colleagues in western Ukraine, the Ukrainian national idea to the masses through the education system. When this was allowed—in western Ukraine prior to 1914 and in the 1920s in eastern Ukraine—national consciousness spread rapidly. In western Ukraine, it had been allowed by the authorities to reach its "political" stage, but in eastern Ukraine, this fear had led to repressive measures in both the 1860s–1870s and in the 1930s. Hrushevs'kyi, the historian and president of the 1917 Central Rada, understood—as did his opponents—that the transfer of the peasantry from villages to towns had to be accompanied by Ukrainianization (i.e., the transfer of the national idea from elites to the masses), which would complete the process of nation building.[29]

From the 1930s to the 1980s, Soviet Ukraine promoted contradictory nationality policies, the legacies of which have been inherited by the independent Ukrainian state. Indigenization (Ukrainianization) was halted in favor of Sovietization. This was accompanied by the physical destruction of Ukrainian elites in the 1930s and 1940s or their forced emigration. Sovietization was increasingly linked to "Little Russianization,"[30] in which nationality policies and historiography promoted the Ukrainian people only as a regional branch of the Russian (here meaning Rus'kiy, or Eastern Slavic) people. The Ukrainian language and culture were portrayed as provincial, rural, and incompatible with the modern era, urbanization, and industrialization. Sovietization and modernization required that Ukrainians (and Belarusians) drop their "local" identities in favor of Russian, the language of Soviet power and modernity. Ukrainians and Belarusians were therefore akin to Breton or Alsatian peasants, whose assimilation into Frenchmen and Frenchwomen was "beneficial" as part of the process of modern nation building.

Russification, intermarriage, and forced migration (out of, and into, Ukraine) in the post-Stalin era led to a growing number of bilingual people and a large Russian minority. In 1958, 60 percent of books were published in the Ukrainian language, a figure that had dropped to 27 percent three decades later. If in the late Stalin era 81 percent of pupils were enrolled in Ukrainian-language schools, by the late Gorbachev era this had dropped to nearly half that (47.5 percent).[31] These factors, Arel and Khmelko found, inevitably diluted the strength of the Ukrainian national idea in favor of a more Russophile, Eastern Slavic orientation.[32] An assertive national identity or even exhibiting Ukrainian national consciousness was equated with radical right "bourgeois nationalism," a tendency only strengthened by the tenacious insurgency by Ukrainian nationalists against the Soviet army during and after World War II.

These policies were contradicted by the monopoly of Ukrainian culture in Ukraine and, at times, even by the Ukrainian language. Each republic was supposed to be the homeland of the titular nation, its language, and its culture. Russian culture therefore was not promoted in Ukraine, which has greatly affected the degree to which Russophones are unable to mobilize in post-Soviet Ukraine. The Writers Union of Ukraine, for example, has always been in alliance with the national democrats and its own lobbying group, the Congress of Ukrainian Intelligentsia, and has a distinctive national democratic orientation.

Soviet development did lead to the establishment of some ruling elites whose ties were closer to their republics than to Moscow or the Soviet Union, including the budding national Communists, ready to jump the Soviet ship when it seemed on the verge of sinking (see Chapter 1). Many of these elites understood the importance of promoting a revival of Ukrainian national identity as a way of maintaining Ukraine's independence (and promoting their own careers). Thus, while the Soviet Union undermined the development of a Ukrainian nation in many respects, it inadvertently supported it through the maintenance of a separate Ukrainian territory and government and the fiction of the sovereignty of the Ukrainian SSR.

By the 1970s, Ukrainians were in a majority in Ukraine's urban centers for the first time. This particularly applied to Kyiv, which became increasingly Ukrainian in culture, language, and ethnicity in the post-Stalin era. In 1917–1920, the low number of ethnic Ukrainians in the urban centers of Ukraine played an important role in the failure of the independence struggle because urban centers gave their votes to parties that opposed independence. In 1917, for example, only 16.4 percent of Kyiv's inhabitants were Ukrainians.[33] By 1991, the proportion of Ukrainians in the capital city had increased dramatically, providing a much more favorable situation for the establishment of a separate state.

NATION BUILDING IN POST-SOVIET UKRAINE

When Ukraine became an independent state in January 1992, it included elements of a modern nation, premodern local identities, a territorial attachment to the boundaries of the Ukrainian SSR (with the exception of the Crimea), a quasi-state with a minimum of institutions, and the ancien régime's ruling elites. It is out of these disparate elements that nation (and state) building was to proceed. The secretary of the National Security and Defense Council, Volodymyr Horbulin, captured popular sentiment, stating that "we have been trying to feel like the real masters of our own life in our own state not for decades, but for centuries."[34] Ukraine's attempts at finding for itself a place within a Polish- or Russian-led commonwealth or union historically failed. It now has to find for itself a place as an independent country between these two neighbors.

Ukraine inherited a population that was essentially loyal to the territorial borders of the Ukrainian SSR. The only exception to this was in the Crimea, which is the only region with a Russian majority. By 1995, the separatist movement in the Crimea had collapsed—without a shot being fired by either party to the dispute. Separatism in eastern Ukraine never got far, and it was based more on dissatisfaction with the economic situation than with the basic fact of independence. Opinion polls indicate little desire of that population to become simply a Russian region, and elites in eastern Ukraine and Crimea seem to have found more to be gained by being major players in Ukraine than minor ones in Russia.

However, support for a pan-Slavic union continues to be high, a result of both continuing feelings of similarity and the socioeconomic crisis, which fed feelings of nostalgia for the economic and social stability of the Soviet era, and debate continues over the questions of nation building, the relative status of the Russian and the Ukrainian language, the definition of a Ukrainian "national idea," the form of relations between Kyiv and the regions, and the status of the Russian population as a minority or as a second titular nationality. Many of these questions were resolved by the June 1996 Constitution. But as with many aspects of this constitution, a weak state, poorly developed institutions, and the socioeconomic crisis mean that many of its provisions cannot be enforced.

Many observers believe that a political community of sorts is gradually emerging in Ukraine. The overwhelming majority of Ukrainians, for example, support an inclusive definition of citizenship and the guarantee of civil rights for national minorities. Nevertheless, although Ukrainians control the large urban centers of eastern Ukraine administratively and demographically, they still do not yet control them culturally.

An independent Ukraine will inevitably change some of these inherited factors. The number of books published in Ukrainian is growing. During

58 ■ NATION BUILDING AND NATIONAL IDENTITY

PHOTO 2.1   Cossack Days of Glory, Dnipropetrovs'k, September 1990

the five-year period from 1992 to 1998, 33,000 book and brochure titles have appeared in Ukraine, of which 15,000 were in Ukrainian. In 1997, 6,308 books and brochures were published in Ukraine, with 49.8 percent of them in Ukrainian (accounting for 24 million out of the total 51.1 million printruns).[35] The Ukrainian language is well established in television (on Channels One and Two, as well as on many independent channels) and on radio (both state and independent). The security forces and education system—two important avenues for nation building—are increasingly becoming Ukrainian in language, culture, and history. Academic historians have increasingly traded in their Soviet-era Russophile biases in favor of the national historiography promoted by Hrushevs'kyi and kept alive in the Ukrainian diaspora. Young Ukrainians, through the media, travel, and the Internet, no longer come into contact with the outside world only through the eyes of Moscow or Russia. The Ukrainian authorities insist on demarcated and delimited borders, not transparent ones. All of these factors, nationalists hope, will gradually differentiate eastern Ukrainian citizens from their Russian neighbors (although not as quickly as President Leonid Kuchma would like).[36]

In many ways, however, Russian language and culture continue to hold sway in Ukraine. Russian-language books from the Russian Federation are deliberately "dumped" in Ukraine.[37] The former Ukrainian Television Channel Three ("Inter"), which broadcasts three-fourths of its airtime in Russian, is still one of Ukraine's two most popular channels. Young Ukrainians are also taking part in globalization largely through Russian and English. Computer programs, the Internet, and instructions for modern technology are often in Russian, not Ukrainian. Three hundred sixty-nine Ukrainian-language publications exist alongside 173 Russian-language ones. But these figures do not tell the full story. The bulk of the publications devoted to business affairs and aimed at the purchasing power of New Ukrainians are in Russian. Finally, the church with the largest number of parishes in Ukraine remains the Ukrainian Orthodox Church (Moscow Patriarchate), whose language and culture continue to adhere to a Russophile, pan–Eastern Slavic orientation.[38]

The Kravchuk Era

Kravchuk was elected president on the same day in December 1991 that a referendum gave a 90 percent endorsement to Ukraine's declaration of independence. The very fact that a former national Communist came to power, beating his nationalist and democratic opponents, suggests that Ukrainians were unwilling to vote for a nationalist president. This made them different from many other Soviet republics (such as Moldova, the Caucasus states, and the Baltics) where nationalist presidents were elected in the early 1990s. This lack of support for a nationalist president repeated itself in the 1994 presidential election held since then and is a reflection of the weakness of Ukrainian national consciousness in eastern and southern Ukraine. Wilson believes that this is a major reason ethnic nationalism has been difficult to mobilize in Ukraine.

Kravchuk's allies within the national Communist wing of the Communist Party sought to compensate for their weak legitimacy as carriers of the national idea by forging a close alliance with the national democrats. Not all national democrats supported overtures made toward them by the former national Communist wing of the Communist Party of Ukraine. The majority within Rukh, led by the arch-oppositionist Viacheslav Chornovil, opposed any alliance. A minority agreed to cooperate with the national Communists, believing that at the time of transition nationalists should rally around the state, and left Rukh to form the Congress of National Democratic Forces.

The *derzhavnyky*, or "statists," were willing to put economic and democratic reform on the back burner in order to pursue their primary goal, building a strong Ukrainian state. This alliance looked for ways to inculcate and instill a new ideology and a more ethnically based national idea through a unified nation. Paul Kubicek finds this view rather destructive to the reform process: "Under the impact of such views, democracy becomes unnecessary and even harmful. Unity is the fundamental requirement of the state-building period."[39] The attempt to impose the values, outlook, and identity of one region (western Ukraine) upon the whole country ultimately failed.

In the Kravchuk era, nationalists focused upon a number of areas important in any nation-building project. They rejected Soviet historiography and promoted the revival of, and elaboration of, Ukrainian historiography, myths, and legends to create cultural allegiance to the new state, believing that the survival of the state is made dependent upon the revival of culture and language. They depicted Russian-speaking Ukrainians as victims of Russification, colonial rule, and genocide rather than as individuals who voluntarily chose or continued to use the Russian language. Thus, Petro Talanchuk, minister of education, compared Soviet policies on language and culture as the equivalent of a second Chernobyl in the degree of their destructiveness.[40] In international affairs (see Chapter 7), the nationalist view portrayed Russia as a foreign "other" and the Russian language and culture as alien and negative. More broadly, this school of thought viewed the Soviet legacy as entirely negative and sought a diametric turn away from the policies of the Soviet era. Finally, nationalists supported the establishment of a state church (see Chapter 3).[41]

At the same time, Kravchuk himself was never a nationalist and sought to use nationalism to build the state rather than the other way around. His support for affirmative action on Ukrainian language in particular was aimed more at state building than at nation building. He always supported centrist policies that recognized Ukraine as a multinational country composed of different regions through policies that aimed to prevent interethnic and interregional strife.[42] Kravchuk's speeches never mentioned the "national struggle," "national goals," or "national mission."[43] Hence, he was criticized by both the national democratic wing,[44] for devoting too little attention to Ukrainian language and culture and not translating words into deeds and finances, and the left and liberals, for being an advocate of a nationalist state.

As a "nationalizing state," Ukraine encountered the same dilemmas that other multiethnic societies face, a problem prominently explored in Rogers Brubaker's theory of "nationalizing states."[45] To begin with, the needs of state building seem to require a certain degree of cultural and linguistic homogenization, but policies to promote homogeneity often spur greater assertion of cultural differences.[46] Both Kravchuk and his successor, Leonid Kuchma, sought to tread this line carefully, adopting centrist nationality policies that rejected the demands of both the radical right and left. Ukraine's post-Soviet nationality policies have therefore evolved and been debated and implemented almost entirely through a democratic process characterized by a good deal of compromise. In the end, almost all ethnic Russians and Russian speakers in Ukraine have

PHOTO 2.2   Old man in uniform of Sich Sharpshooters, demonstration, Kyiv, spring 1994

found the situation sufficiently tolerable that they have neither left the country nor rebelled. Indeed, the greater dissatisfaction is often felt by the nationalists, who lament the almost complete dominance of the Russian language in the eastern and southern regions of the country.

Nevertheless, to Russians and Russian speakers, accustomed to belonging to the ruling class of the Soviet Union, any attempts at affirmative action on behalf of Ukrainian language, culture, and history would inevitably produce opposition. Vasyl'Kremen', former deputy head of the presidential administration under Kuchma and a leading intellectual in the United Social Democrats, remains critical of Kravchuk's nationality policies (perceived or otherwise). Although a supporter of nation and state building in Ukraine, as well as affirmative action, Kremen' nevertheless believes:

> Attempts made during the first years of independence to impose the values acceptable by some of the inhabitants of Ukraine on the whole country and excessive haste in linguistic Ukrainianization resulted in the considerable alienation of the eastern and southern regions from the political capital, and this, along with the worsening of the economic situation, is responsible to a large extent for the abrupt decline in the prestige of the idea of the nation-state.[47]

TABLE 2.1 What Nationality Are You?

Region	Ukrainian	Russian	Other
West	95.5	3.2	1.0
West-Central	86.5	11.7	1.9
East-Central	78.0	17.9	4.1
South	53.4	37.9	8.8
East	59.0	36.6	4.4
Total	74.3	21.6	4.0

SOURCE: "Do vyboriv '98," poll conducted by the Kyiv International Institute of Sociology, vol. 26 (December 1997–11 January 1998).

As Table 2.1 shows, in early 1998 there continued to be profound regional differences in the national identities of Ukrainian citizens.

The Kuchma Era

When Leonid Kuchma was elected president in July 1994, many observers believed that he would reverse many of the nation-building policies instituted in the Kravchuk era, largely because Kuchma had run on an explicitly antinationalist program.[48] As president, however, Kuchma has adopted a more nationalist and statist line, and the changes he has made have been more in tactics than in basic goals. This is probably because, as Wanner argues, "nationalism is a project of the modern state and an integral part of the process of state building."[49] The state has a considerable interest in unifying its citizens behind a single self-conception and in avoiding or eliminating significant cleavages in society.

Kuchma and his advisers do not differ significantly from Kravchuk on the need for nation building to proceed and "complete" the process that previously had not been permitted: "Well, then, the central theme of the twentieth century is the appearance of the Ukrainian nation, its transformation from an ethnographic to a conscious political and cultural community."[50] The secretary of the National Security and Defense Council, Volodymyr Horbulin, concurred when he added that "we have been trying to feel like the real masters of our own life in our own state not for decades, but for centuries."[51] Rhetoric aside, however, Kuchma as well as Kravchuk appears to use nation building to promote state building, rather than using it for its own value, and in that sense is better characterized as a "statist" than a "nationalist."

The Kuchma camp adopted different tactics on nation building in the hope of achieving the same strategic goal as their predecessors. For example, improving Ukrainian-language usage by Russian-speaking Ukrainians remained a strategic goal under Kuchma. Nevertheless, this goal would be pursued more slowly within the constraints of Ukraine's inherited regionalism rather than being forced by central policies regardless of local objections.[52] Kuchma's approach has been based in part on the recognition that the socioeconomic crisis, which Kravchuk's policies exacerbated, made nation and state building more difficult. The state should therefore place greater emphasis upon tackling the economic crisis if it hopes to succeed in building a Ukrainian nation.[53] There was also an increased recognition that changing identities was likely to be a lengthy and traumatic process. Most fundamentally, perhaps, Kuchma's policies have redefined the national idea by de-emphasizing the ethnic component of national identity in favor of a greater emphasis on the civic or state-based component (focusing more on individual over collective rights and more on loyalty to the state of Ukraine, regardless of language or ethnicity, as a marker of "Ukrainianness").[54] Kuchma's nationality policies are defined as "pragmatic" and in favor of the consolidation of all Ukrainians, in contrast to the "romanticism" and western Ukrainian regional bias of the Kravchuk era.[55] Perhaps crucially for winning support in the east and south, Kuchma rejected the view that there was nothing in the Soviet past that was of use in the forging of a new nation.

An added factor that made Kuchma adopt tactics different from those of his predecessor in the realm of nation building was his different political power base. Unlike Kravchuk, who was allied with center-right national democrats, Kuchma came to power allied with social democrats and leftists (although both defined themselves as "centrists"). The two leaders' power bases reflect their different regional origins, Kravchuk being from the west and Kuchma from the east. The gap between the two narrowed considerably after Kuchma came to power, and during his presidency, they had become allies (the United Social Democratic faction, which includes Kravchuk, in the post-1998 Rada is an ally of Kuchma; see Chapter 5).

This left-center of Ukraine's political spectrum has always advocated Ukraine's membership in the CIS, unlike national democrats, but still has restricted this wish to purely economic questions and has preferred bilateral to multilateral ties. At the same time, both Kravchuk and Kuchma have supported Ukraine's "return to Europe." Whereas the national democrats see Ukraine as a "buffer" and therefore Russia as not joining Ukraine in "Europe," many of Kuchma's supporters do not exclude Russia and define Ukraine as a "bridge."[56] Thus, there is still some difference in defining Ukraine's national identity in terms of its distinctiveness or nearness to Russia.

On the question of a unitary versus a federal state, which was prominent in the development of a new constitution, the Kuchma center-left again agreed with the national democrats on the need for a unitary state (allowing only the Crimea as an exception), believing that a unitary state is a stronger state and that federalism would endanger the country's territorial integrity. Kravchuk and Kuchma also agree in their opposition to recognizing officially that Ukraine has two titular nations. Similarly, support for two state languages is mainly confined to the radical left (Kuchma having abandoned the issue shortly after winning the presidency), with most Ukrainian parties supporting only one state language (Ukrainian). No Ukrainian party supports only Russian as a state language.[57]

The nation-building policies pursued by Kuchma have greater support in Ukrainian society because at least half of Ukraine's citizens have a center-left orientation and many see themselves as being of mixed ethnicity and hence do not support rigid ethnic or linguistic categorization. These views have led to a high degree of tolerance toward minorities and toward the Russian language, opposition to a radical break with Russia, and territorial loyalty to Ukraine's frontiers.[58]

Consensus and Outstanding Problems

A growing consensus on nation building among Ukraine's nonradical parties came into existence between 1996 and 1998. Essentially, this consensus contains two components. First, there is agreement that the state of Ukraine should be based on the Ukrainian ethnicity rather than being defined multiethnically or as a dual Ukrainian-Russian entity. Second, the Ukrainian content of the nation and state, however, should be defined inclusively, based on civic rather than ethnic characteristics. In other words, although Ukraine was to be a Ukrainian state, everyone who lived in Ukraine, regardless of ethnicity or language preference, would be regarded as Ukrainian, and minorities would be guaranteed tolerance. Both the June 1996 Ukrainian Constitution and the 1997 National Security Concept supported affirmative action for Ukrainian language, culture, and history and the definition of Ukrainians as the only titular nation with a single state language.[59] This evolution was also witnessed in the choice of political allies made by Kuchma in the October 1999 presidential elections. Both the People's Democratic Party (NDPU) and the United Social Democrats backed Kuchma in the elections, and these parties backed the nationality provisions outlined in the Ukrainian Constitution and the National Security Concept.

To many Ukrainians involved in the debate on nation building as well as to Ukraine's elites, the entire question of nation building in the manner outlined in the Constitution and National Security Concept was imperative because of its ramifications in the foreign policy domain. Ukraine's desire to return to Europe had been proclaimed by both Kravchuk and Kuchma. Nation building would, it was believed, facilitate this return by creating a political nation that was based on the European norm (an ethnic Ukrainian core and a civic, inclusive nation). The perceived alternative to nation building would be to emulate Belarus and return to Russia's embrace.[60]

Success in building a consensus on nation and state building by 1996–1998 rested on a number of factors, including the adoption of the Ukrainian Constitution in June 1996 and the Crimean Constitution in December 1998, both of which signaled that the Soviet era was over; the ratification of the Ukrainian-Russian treaty by the Russian State Duma in December 1998; and the retreat into the past of the Soviet Union. During this period, independence had become a "normal" state of affairs. Kuchma stated that "[t]he voices saying that everything was better in the Soviet period are falling silent. I am convinced that now the people form one nation."[61]

This growing consensus on nation building in the Kuchma era is nonetheless still coming under attack from two wings, just as it did under Kravchuk. The radical left, particularly the two parties that opposed Ukrainian independence outright in the March 1998 parliamentary elections (the Communist Party and the Progressive Socialist Party), attacked Kuchma's policies from the viewpoint of the need for two titular nations and two state languages. Petro Symonenko, the leader of the Communist Party, demanded that the Rada "halt the wave of primitive anti-communism and national and chauvinistic propaganda" in the media.[62] Because of the deep power base of these leftist parties in eastern and southern Ukraine, there remains some possibility that this view will gain ground through the electoral process. However, any leftist elected to high office will find the same incentives that Kuchma did to shift to a state-building agenda.

The national democrats and radical right, meanwhile, continue to distrust Kuchma, believing that he was not firmly committed to supporting nation building based upon the "core" Ukrainian nation.[63] Exponents of these views tend both to demand affirmative action for Ukrainian language and culture and to define Ukrainian identity in very narrow ethnic and linguistic terms.[64] These individuals continue to see themselves as a "national minority"[65] in Ukraine, believing that they are still being exposed to denationalization and Russification.[66] Ukrainian culture is being subjected to "brutal competition," Ihor Kharchenko has argued. "It will either win this competition struggle or lose it. So far it is consistently losing it."[67] In many ways, nationalists feel more threatened by domestic factors (e.g., the large numbers of Russian speakers and the continued dominance of the Russian language in eastern Ukraine) than external ones. This particularly applies in business affairs and the sciences, where the Russian language still dominates.[68]

Regionalism and Separatism

The regional divisions of Ukraine, which have deep historical roots, have led to a fear that the country will fragment along territorial lines. This has not happened, and the threat of separatism, probably exaggerated in the first place, has largely subsided. The problem has centered in Crimea, where there was serious talk of secession, but it has also concerned the Donbas in eastern Ukraine, where there was informal talk of secession but never any formal movement. These movements have been content to stem the tide of western Ukrainian nationalism and to insist on economic ties with Russia. Moreover, during the debate over Ukraine's Constitution, support for transforming Ukraine into a federal state, which was equated with separatist sentiment, also proved to be weak. However, although regionalism has remained bounded and separatism is largely a dead issue, regionalism will continue to play an important role in Ukrainian politics and especially in the process of nation building.

Separatist efforts have been confined to the Crimea, occurring primarily when the Crimea declared independence in May 1992 and then went on to adopt "separatist" draft constitutions. In 1994–1995, a more moderate Crimean leadership was replaced by radical pro-Russian separatists who clamored for Russia's annexation of the region. Five factors worked against their success. First, Russia was in no condition to take advantage of this situation, as it was itself embroiled in a military campaign in defense of its territorial integrity in Chechnya. Separating Crimea from Ukraine was hardly the precedent Russian leaders wanted to set. Second, the Crimean separatists received no support from any mainstream Ukrainian political party in their campaign. The Verkhovna Rada and the executive branch remained united against a Crimean constitution that would permit secession. Third, the executive adopted a tougher line that abolished the institution of Crimean presidency and was also successful in adopting a mix of economic, military, and political pressures against the Crimea. Fourth, the secessionist Russia Bloc in Crimea was divided, incompetent, and opposed by the large Communist political force in the Crimea. Finally, after the adoption of the Ukrainian Constitution, regional parties were forced to reregister as regional branches of all-Ukrainian parties or become themselves all-Ukrainian parties, making maintenance of an institutionalized power base much more difficult.

After the abolition of the Crimean presidency and removal from power of Russian separatists, the levers of power in the Crimea (parliamentary speaker and prime minister) reverted to pro-Kyiv loyalists from the former *nomenklatura*. Initially, these had come from the Party of Economic Revival of the Crimea, but its links to the shadow economy and organized crime led to its gradual disintegration. Its position was taken by the People's Democratic Party, whose regional leader became prime minister in 1998. After the March 1998 elections, the Crimean branch of the Communist Party of Ukraine then took over the reins of the Crimean Supreme Soviet. By 1998, therefore, both main seats of power in the Crimea were in the hands of political forces that strongly supported Ukraine's territorial integrity. During the 1998 Ukrainian parliamentary elections, the Union Party polled less than 2 percent of the all-Ukrainian vote, even though it dropped its separatist program and campaigned instead for Ukraine's membership of the Russian-Belarusian union.

On October 21, 1998, the Crimean Supreme Soviet adopted by a wide margin the fifth Crimean constitution since 1991. Unlike previous drafts, in this one there was no mention of Crimean "statehood" or citizenship rights apart from Ukraine. Moreover, this new draft accepts that Ukrainian is the state language of Ukraine throughout Ukraine, including the Crimea. The most significant "regional" aspect left is the focus on Crimean budgetary autonomy, meaning that revenue collected in the Crimea is to remain there. This is the most pro-Ukrainian constitution of the five and entered into law on December 23, 1998, when it was ratified by the Ukrainian Parliament. Two days later, the Russian State Duma ratified, again with Communist support, the Ukrainian-Russian treaty, signifying Russian recognition that Crimea is part of Ukraine.[69] With that recognition, the issue of secession seems to have been laid to rest, despite ongoing rhetoric to the contrary from some Russian politicians. But though secession is off the agenda, profound regional differences will continue to play a major role in Ukrainian politics, especially in the efforts to build a unified state based on a single coherent "nation."

History, Myths, and Legends

Among the means being used to promote Ukrainian national identity is a rewriting of history to remove the biases of Russian and Soviet historiography and present a historical basis for a Ukrainian state and nation. Petro Tolochko, a leading historian and vice president of the National Academy of Sciences, lamented, "We are faced with a great deal of myth making these days, more than we have ever experienced."[70] Ukraine's new myths and legends portray it as a peaceful "European" country, as a victim of past foreign incursions, and as an entity distinct and different from Russia, with a tradition of democratic institutions and a long history that legitimizes its independent statehood.[71] As with nation-building policies, historiography will represent a "negotiated settlement" among competing political groups. Nevertheless, the importance of history is underscored by Wanner:

> History supplies a vast reservoir of raw materials from which to craft a post-Soviet national culture and underscore the legitimacy of a state. New historical myths and a revised historiography encapsulated in historical reports are

now the cornerstone of the new Ukrainian state's efforts to expand a sense of nation based on common historical experience among an otherwise highly diverse and disenfranchised population.[72]

In Ukraine, where national identity is still debated, history is not only for historians, museums, or academic journals. On the contrary, it has become an important political issue, contested by various actors because the prevailing history is likely to privilege certain actors and policies over others. Thus, the dominant revision of Ukrainian history emphasizes that tragedies such as the artificial famine of 1932–1933 or the Chernobyl accident of 1986 could only have occurred because Ukraine was not then an independent state. Independence therefore has become the norm and is glorified as the only possible outcome to prevent a recurrence of Ukraine's past tragedies. In other words, there "can be no going back." Thus, Deputy Prime Minister Valeriy Smoliy has argued, "[T]he idea of statehood . . . must dominate the media's activities, because Ukraine has achieved its statehood through suffering and will not give it up."[73] History is also useful in defending historical title to Ukrainian territory against foreign claims.[74]

The teaching and popularization of Ukrainian history are part of the process by which the state seeks to promote unity through national identity. The goal is to unite the community of people (Ukrainians) together into one polity while facilitating the revival of links to "world history" and "European civilization." In this view, the teaching of history is the "inculcator of national consciousness, pride and honor in the harmonious unification of national and all-human values."[75] This will increase the interdependency of pupils, "not only to their nation, people and state, but to the European family."[76]

In Ukraine, tsarist and Soviet historiography came under attack in the late 1980s at the same time the national revival and political opposition were gathering momentum. The traditional Russian and Soviet historiographical schemas were rejected first by the cultural intelligentsia and political opposition and then in the early 1990s by the political establishment. The rehabilitation of Mykhailo Hrushevs'kyi, the doyen of Ukrainian history, was of primary concern after five decades of denunciation as a "German agent" and "bourgeois nationalist" (Hrushevs'kyi had been the president of the Ukrainian Central Rada in 1917–1918 but had returned to work as a historian in Soviet Ukraine in the more liberal environment of the 1920s).

Since Ukraine became an independent state, the Hrushevs'kyi schema has to all intents and purposes become the official line followed by historians, literati, and political figures.[77] The extent to which Hrushevs'kyi had become part of the official mainstream could be seen in President

PHOTO 2.3 New monument honoring Mykhailo Hrushevs'kyi, Ukraine's preeminent historian and president, independent Ukraine, 1917–1918

Kuchma's view of him as "the founder of the revived Ukrainian state in the twentieth century, a historian of world renown." Hrushevs'kyi's significance lay in his devotion to "the revival of [Ukraine's] genetic memory, a deep understanding of its own history." Hrushevs'kyi's eleven-volume *History of Ukraine-Rus* "developed a concept of the historical development of the Ukrainian people, [and] proved that our people has its own core origins." Of particular importance, Hrushevs'kyi's work asserts that Ukraine, not Russia, is the successor to the medieval state of Kyivan Rus'. This not only provides Ukraine with a glorious heritage but deprives Russia of its presumed ancestry and hence is rejected by most Russians. Therefore, a work that was largely ignored by Western historians of Russia and denounced by their Soviet counterparts is to Kuchma "the historical Bible of the Ukrainian people, a fundamental work."[78]

The development of a Ukrainian historiography that rejects the pan-Slavic Russian statist school will have a profound influence upon Ukrainian national identity. Ukrainian history is written either from an "ethnic" viewpoint (where the history only pertains to ethnic Ukrainians) or from a "civic" viewpoint (where territory inhabited by the post-Soviet Ukrainian state is the source of the history). Either approach will create difficulties for Russian historiography. Even the "civic" Ukrainian historiography, which is favored by the Kuchma leadership, nevertheless recasts all events and personalities on Ukrainian territory in terms of a Ukrainian history that proceeds from the founding of Kyivan Rus' to Ukrainian independence in 1991.[79] Much of what is positive in Russian historiography is now usually perceived as negative in Ukrainian views.[80] The "tsar liberator" Alexander II banned the Ukrainian and Belarusian languages. Tsarina Catherine may be positive to Russians as a reformer-modernizer and empire builder, but to Ukrainians she is remembered as the destroyer of the autonomous Ukrainian Hetmanate state. Tsarist history, to which Russian historians now return in search of their pre-Soviet Russian identity, is regarded by Ukrainians as a tragedy. This view irks Russians such as Aman Tuleyev, former Russian minister for cooperation with the CIS, who complains that Ukrainian textbooks teach "frankly that Russia is Ukraine's main enemy, which oppresses and suppresses it."[81] It remains to be seen whether this new historiography will ameliorate the differences in national identity in Ukraine, but it is a substantial part of the state's long-term effort to promote the notion of a single, civically defined Ukrainian people.

CONCLUSION

Nation building can mean different things to different people. To many in Western democracies it is synonymous with radical nationalism and ethnic conflict. In some cases, it can be. But in others, it is not. If we accept that all states are composed of *both* civic and ethnic factors, then all states have undergone state and nation building, either in the past or currently. If we also accept that nationalism can play a role in liberal democracy, fascism, or communism, then simply saying that Ukraine is engaged in a nation-building process or that nationalism is strong in parts of Ukraine does not tell us much. This chapter has sought to spell out the way that national identity issues and the nation-building process have influenced the broader political and social situation in Ukraine.

The nation-building (and state-building) program is closely tied to Ukraine's democratic and economic transformation. The process of defining the Ukrainian nation is inseparable from that of ending communism or reforming the political and economic systems. Arguments concerning national identity are not separable from those concerning political and economic reform. Thus, for example, certain market reform proposals are supported (or opposed) in large part because they are perceived as making Ukraine more "Western" in its identity. Similarly, calls for union with Russia are not simply expressions of national identity but are inevitably bound up with nostalgia for the past and a rejection of certain institutions, such as a market economy. Problems of national identity therefore recur in nearly every other issue in Ukrainian politics today.

• THREE •

Religion, State, and Society

Religion is fundamentally linked to politics, to national identity, and to the transformation process in Ukraine. National identity and religion are therefore closely bound together for many Ukrainians, and the highest number of believers are found in regions of Ukraine where national consciousness is high. To Orthodox Ukrainians, for example, the city of Kyiv is 600 years older than Moscow. Why should their church therefore be governed from Moscow? Indeed, the Metropolinate, they believe, was illegally transferred from Kyiv to Moscow by the Russian tsars. In this view, historical justice requires that Kyiv regain its preeminence in the Orthodox world. Thus, the Russian Orthodox Church is regarded as an agent of Russian influence, such that membership in that branch of Orthodoxy, rather than another, has important political implications. Although rooted in religion, these are notions with important political consequences. An understanding of confessional politics in Ukraine is therefore necessary to an understanding of politics more broadly.

As with national identity, examining religion in Ukraine requires looking back into history for the sources of today's divisions and debates. In a manner similar to Poland and Lithuania, the Ukrainian Catholic Church has always remained closely tied to national identity in its heartland of Galicia and Trans-Carpathia. It was therefore not surprising that it was forcibly dissolved in 1946 by the Soviet authorities and its premises handed over to the Russian Orthodox Church. The Orthodox Church in Ukraine has fared worse than the Catholic Church, with only brief revivals in the 1920s and 1940s. The nationalist Ukrainian Autocephalous Orthodox Church (UAPTs) revived in the late Soviet era as part of the growth of the national democratic movement. Although now divided between two churches (UAPTs and Ukrainian Orthodox Church–Kyiv Patriarchate, or UPTs–KP), both branches of this Ukrainian nationalist Orthodoxy have remained close allies of the national democratic camp. The autonomous Orthodox Church–Moscow Patriarchate, in contrast, remains loyal to the Russian Orthodox Church. It espouses a pan-Slavic, "Little Russian" ideology that has given it few allies within the democratic camp. The main defenders of this autonomous branch of Ukrainian Orthodoxy are therefore the left—just as they were in the Soviet era.

During the late Soviet era, and particularly since the disintegration of the USSR, Ukraine has experienced a wide religious revival. The number of religious parishes in Ukraine grew 53.9 percent between 1988 and 1989. Their number increased over 20 percent through 1990 and 1991 before the growth declined to 1.8 percent in 1994.[1] According to a variety of opinion polls, nearly one-half of the Ukrainian population holds religious beliefs, although only one-fourth of the population practices them on a regular basis. The largest number of religious believers are found among the young and the old, with the greatest resistance to religion and attachment to atheism within the middle generation.[2] In a poll conducted in early 1997 that asked "How often do you go to the Church/Synagogue?" 46 percent said "never," and only 31 percent admitted to going once or twice a year. Eleven percent admitted to going once per week, and another 12 percent said they went once a month.[3] As in many developed countries, therefore, the holding of religious beliefs does not always translate into regular church attendance.

Since independence in 1991, confessional politics in Ukraine have been dominated by a battle among competing hierarchies over control of parishes and property. The revival of religious belief in Ukraine and the restoration of property seized by the Communists make the stakes even higher, and the national identity dimension increases the stakes higher still. Finally, the conflict has an international dimension, due to the Russian Orthodox Church's involvement in the issue and its close links to the Russian government. Essentially, the question arises within Orthodoxy over whether Orthodox churches in Ukraine will be led by a separate (autocephalous) Ukrainian Orthodox Church or a Kyiv patriarchate linked to the Russian Orthodox Church or simply remain under the Moscow Patriarchate. All three hierarchies have been active in seeking to win over the allegiance of parishes and in enlisting government support.

The religious fragmentation within Ukraine, particularly within the Orthodox community, is believed by some Ukrainians to be a factor inhibiting national consolidation and the construction of a new Ukrainian national identity. In this view, the three branches of the Orthodox Church in Ukraine should be united (at the very least, two of them share the same ideology). Many feel that this would benefit Ukrainian politics, state building, and civil society by forming a broader basis for consensus in society. Thus, religion in Ukraine is characterized by the divisiveness that characterizes the rest of Ukrainian society and politics.

Nevertheless, the creation of a "state church" on the basis of a united Orthodoxy that was contemplated during the Kravchuk administration was found to be both impossible and undesirable. Ukraine is multiconfessional, with a large and vocal Catholic population. It also has substantial numbers of Jews, Protestants, and Muslims. Creation of a state church was found to be impossible, in that deciding which church would gain that status would have been devastatingly divisive for the new state. It was found to be undesirable because it contradicted the goal of the tolerant civic state that Ukrainian leaders have sought to build. The norm throughout Europe is religious diversity, and Ukraine is no exception to this rule.

This chapter is divided into three sections. The first section discusses the importance of religion to politics, the state, and society in Ukraine. The second section explores the reestablishment of the Ukrainian-Greek Catholic Church (UHKTs), after nearly five decades of illegality and catacomb existence.[4] The final section surveys developments within Ukraine's three main Orthodox churches since the early 1990s. This chapter does not discuss developments within the Protestant,[5] Baptist, Jewish, or Muslim religious communities, which, due to their small size, remain largely marginal to politics in post-Soviet Ukraine.

RELIGION, STATE, AND SOCIETY IN UKRAINE

On the Eve of Independence

The Ukrainian law "On Freedom of Conscience and Religious Organizations" came into force on June 4, 1991, after its adoption by Parliament on April 23 of that same year. The structure of the law was closely modeled on the Soviet law adopted in autumn 1990, although the expansion of certain clauses made it more liberal. The Ukrainian law, however, did not clarify whether churches are recognized in law as national bodies or only as individual parishes and church institutions.[6] One major difference between the Soviet and Ukrainian laws was that the latter provided greater powers to the Council on Religious Affairs. Local councils were to monitor observance of the law, and congregations had the right to subordinate themselves to any religious body in Ukraine, or beyond, and to change their allegiance freely.[7]

One of the most detailed surveys of the strength of religious denominations on the eve of Ukrainian independence divided Ukraine into five regions based upon religious adherence.[8] The first region, with the highest number of parishes, included the four oblasts of Galicia and Trans-Carpathia, which accounted for over 50 percent of the total number of parishes in Ukraine (areas traditionally Ukrainian-Greek Catholic). The second group, in terms of parishes and believers, was composed of the central Ukrainian oblasts of Vinnytsya, Rivne, and Khmel'nyts'kii. The third group consisted of the central Ukrainian and Bukovinian oblasts of

Volyn', Kyiv, and Chernivtsi. The fourth group included the eastern and southern Ukrainian oblasts of Donets'k, Odesa, Sumy, Cherkasy, and Chernihiv. The final group, with the least number of parishes in Ukraine (less than 100 or, in some cases, even less than 50), were the oblasts of Luhans'k, Zaporizhzhya, Kirovohrad, Mykolayiv, Poltava, Kharkiv, and Kherson and the Crimean Autonomous Republic. This survey confirmed that those areas with the most developed national identity and Ukrainian-language proficiency (the first three regions) were also those that possessed the largest number of religious believers.

Although the situation is complex, the simplest explanation for this correlation between religious activity and Ukrainian national identity is that for centuries under the Poles, Russians, and Soviets, the churches were the primary carriers of national identity. Indeed, in past centuries one of the main ways to distinguish Ukrainians from Poles or Russians was by their adherence to the Ukrainian Catholic Church, which by combining the Orthodox rite with subservience to the pope, was neither Roman Catholic nor Orthodox. Especially in western Ukraine (as in Poland), the churches remained one of the primary sources of resistance to Communist rule, though Ukrainian churches were given much less room to operate than were those in Poland.

Much of Ukraine, however, remained Orthodox, and Ukrainian parishes constituted a substantial portion of the Russian Orthodox Church. At the end of the Soviet era, over two-thirds of all Russian Orthodox parishes (3,971) were located in Ukraine.[9] By the mid-1990s, much had changed, including the dramatic growth of Ukraine's two main national churches (Greek Catholic and Autocephalous Orthodox) after decades of repression. Within the Russian Federation, the Russian Orthodox Church possessed the bulk of that country's 10,834 religious communities. But within Ukraine, the Russian Orthodox Church still held on to 6,564 parishes, with approximately 1,500 other parishes in Belarus. Thus, of the total number of the nearly 20,000 Russian Orthodox Church parishes in the three East Slavic states, over 40 percent were still located in Ukraine and Belarus by the mid-1990s. It is easy then to imagine why the Russian Orthodox church, and the Russian nationalists linked to it, could not view Ukrainian secession or the establishment of separate Ukrainian church hierarchies with equanimity.

The religious revival in Ukraine since the late 1980s has meant that Ukraine has maintained its high level of religious adherence in comparison to neighboring countries. By the mid-1990s, Ukraine possessed about as many religious parishes as Poland, though many more than the number found in the Russian Federation or Belarus. As a proportion of religious communities (parishes) to population size, Ukraine had 1:3,159 (with a total of 16,460 parishes), compared with 1:13,786 in Russia and

1:6,038 in Belarus. Ukraine's figure was closer to Poland's (1:3,175),[10] though it is important to recall that Ukraine's average is misleading, in that there is quite a bit of regional deviation from the mean.

Religious Communities in Independent Ukraine

In October 1992, the RFE/RL Research Institute commissioned a survey by the Kyiv International Institute of Sociology, only four months after the unification *sobor* (council) of the pro-autocephalous wing of the Ukrainian Orthodox Church and the Ukrainian Autocephalous Orthodox Church. Atheism was again shown to be strongest among respondents in the eastern Ukrainian cities of Kharkiv and Dnipropetrovs'k, where it was twice as high as in Kyiv and Odesa. Almost half of the respondents identified themselves as Orthodox, with another 3 percent claiming adherence to other denominations. According to this survey, three-fourths of religious believers in Ukraine identified with the Ukrainian Orthodox Church–Kyiv Patriarchate (UPTs–KP), outnumbering those supporting its rival, the UPTs–Moscow Patriarchate (UPTs–MP), by 9:1 (the Ukrainian Orthodox Church has continued to maintain this name, although it is often labeled in the Ukrainian media as the "UPTs–Moscow Patriarchate" to differentiate it from the UPTs–Kyiv Patriarchate).[11] The percentage figures were 72 percent for the UPTs–KP, 20 percent for the Russian Orthodox Church, and 8 percent for the UPTs–MP.

But the strength of support evidenced by this opinion poll in eastern and southern Ukrainian urban areas for the UPTs–KP was not reflected in the total number of religious communities within Ukraine. After the June 1992 unification *sobor* between the UAPTs and the pro-autocephalous wing of the UPTs, the majority of clergy and parishes still remained within the UPTs. The UPTs retains the largest number of registered religious communities in Ukraine (see Appendix). Ukraine's religious believers therefore owe their allegiance primarily to Ukrainian Orthodoxy—not Russian Orthodoxy—whether in an autocephalous or an autonomous variety. This explains why opinion polls that give the respondent a choice of support for either the UPTs–KP *or* the Russian Orthodox Church (that is, the UPTs openly defined as such) invariably show little support for the latter. Purely Russian Orthodox Church support (for the Moscow Patriarch or its émigré competitor) is largely confined to ethnic Russians in the Crimea. Russian-speaking Ukrainians, if they are religious believers, tend to be adherents of Ukrainian Orthodoxy. In sum, although Orthodoxy is widespread, the particular organizational faction of Orthodoxy one supports is an important marker of national identity.

By mid-1993, of those who were religious believers in Ukraine, 52 percent claimed to be Orthodox, 20 percent Greek Catholic, 20 percent

Protestant/Baptist, and the remainder adherents of minority religious sects (Jews, Muslims, Hare Krishna, and so on). Within the total population, though, Orthodox believers, Greek Catholics, and others accounted for 20 percent, 5 percent, and 2 percent, respectively. Forty-two percent of religious believers were not members of any church, and another 32 percent were atheists.[12] In other words, nearly one-half the religious believers in Ukraine were not committed to any particular church.

Although the Protestant and Baptist Churches have a large number of religious communities, these tend to be smaller, with an average of only 100 believers per community. The majority of Roman Catholic communities (71 percent), which tend to be attended by the Polish minority, are to be found in Zhytomir, L'viv, Khmel'nyts'kii, and Ternopil' oblasts, where two-thirds of Ukraine's Polish speakers live. Another 12 percent of Roman Catholic communities are to be found in Trans-Carpathia oblast, where they largely serve the Hungarian minority. Ukrainian-Greek Catholic communities are nearly all based in western Ukraine (91 percent in Galicia and 7.4 percent in Trans-Carpathia oblast). The majority of the newly created parishes in the post-Soviet era were established in Kyiv, Trans-Carpathia, L'viv, and Ternopil' oblasts as well as in the Crimea.

Regional Distribution of Religious Believers

It is important to emphasize the heterogeneity of religious participation in Ukraine, which can be obscured by aggregate statistics. The largest number of religious communities are to be found in Ternopil' oblast, where there is one religious community for every 807 people, compared to only one for 16,900 in Dnipropetrovs'k oblast. The proportion of an oblast's inhabitants to the number of religious parishes is eighteen times higher in Ternopil' than it is in Dnipropetrovs'k.

There are two generally accepted methods by which support for churches can be measured: by counting (1) the number of religious communities or parishes, or (2) the number of faithful who identify with the church, and they can produce radically different results. Regardless of which method is used, however, it is clear that religious activity is much higher in western Ukraine than elsewhere. Fifty percent of the parishes in Ukraine are located in its western oblasts, a region that includes only 20 percent of the country's population. The concentration is especially high in the three Galician oblasts, which contain one-third of all religious parishes in Ukraine.[13] Although only 6 percent of all believers identify with the Greek Catholic Church, it created 20 percent of all religious parishes in Ukraine.[14]

The total number of Orthodox parishes is approximately 8,500, which accounts for approximately one-half of all parishes in Ukraine.[15] A breakdown of parishes by denomination and by region has never been published in the Ukrainian media and is unavailable, the information being regarded as too sensitive for public release by the authorities.[16] By 1996, the UPTs–KP had twenty-two eparchies throughout Ukraine, plus another six in Western Europe, Canada, and Russia. The UAPTs, in contrast, possessed only six eparchies, the bulk of which were in Galicia. The UPTs had thirty-four eparchies in Ukraine.[17]

The UHKTs is based nearly completely in western Ukraine (this church existed originally only in those parts of Ukraine under Polish rather than Russian control). The UPTs–KP has its highest number of parishes located in western and central Ukraine, although it is distributed the most evenly of any of Ukraine's churches. It is noticeable in Tables 3.1, 3.2, and 3.3 in the Appendix that religious believers are far fewer in eastern rather than in western Ukraine. In the Crimean Autonomous Republic, the largest churches are the various competing Russian Orthodox denominations. This reflects Crimea's heavily Russian population. In eastern and southern Ukraine, Russophone Ukrainians and Russians are longtime residents, and the fewer religious believers in those regions tend to give their support to the UPTs or the UPTs–KP (not to Russian Orthodox churches).

Although the majority of the religious believers who identify in polls with the UPTs are located in eastern and southern Ukraine, the majority of their parishes and churches remain nevertheless in Ukrainian-speaking regions, in Vynnytsia, Volyn', Trans-Carpathia, Rivne, and Khmel'nyts'kii oblasts. This confused picture can be explained by the figures given earlier in this chapter. Although nearly one-half of Ukrainians claimed that they were religious believers, only one-fourth of the total population admitted to being practicing believers. Eastern and southern Ukraine are undoubtedly the regions shortest of religious buildings and local religious traditions; therefore, practicing religious beliefs on a regular basis is less possible there.

The UAPTs, meanwhile, has changed its regional support. Whereas during the interwar period it was more prevalent in the Volyn' and Bukovina regions of what was then eastern Poland, today its stronghold is in Galicia.[18] In Kyiv, Orthodox believers are nearly evenly divided between adherents of the UPTs–KP and the UPTs. In Donets'k and Simferopol, though, adherents of the UPTs–KP, the UPTs, and various Russian Orthodox churches are divided 19:55:12 and 5:37:35, respectively.[19]

New Trends

A new development in post-Soviet Ukraine is the growth of Ukrainian Orthodoxy in Galicia, an area that had little, if any, Orthodox tradition prior to 1945, when it became part of the USSR (before this, Galicia had been under Polish and Austrian rule). Two other areas where both of these Orthodox churches are strongly entrenched are Volyn', in northwestern Ukraine, and Kyiv oblast. In Galicia, three Orthodox seminaries function in the cities of L'viv, Ternopil', and Ivano-Frankivs'k. Two others exist in the cities of Kyiv and Luts'k. In addition, one source claimed that the majority of students in the UTPs–KP Kyiv Seminary and Spiritual Academy are from Galicia.[20] This development appears to signal an erosion of a Catholic-Orthodox division that largely overlapped Ukraine's regional division.

THE UKRAINIAN-GREEK CATHOLIC (UNIATE) CHURCH[21]

Uniate Church Reestablishes Itself

By 1992–1993, the Ukrainian-Greek Catholic Church had reestablished itself in Ukraine and had recovered roughly to the number of parishes it had possessed prior to 1939. This was facilitated in part by the strong support it had received from the Ukrainian diaspora, the bulk of which are Uniates (Ukrainian Catholics). In March 1991, Cardinal Myroslav Lubachivs'kyi returned to L'viv from exile in the Vatican, and three months later, the UHKTs was legally registered. This occurred less than a year after national democrats won local and national elections in western Ukraine. Their main target after coming to power was to dismantle Soviet institutions, of which the Russian Orthodox Church was a leading pillar.

In May 1992, the first Synod of Bishops of the UHKTs was held in L'viv since 1946, when the UHKTs was liquidated by the Soviet authorities and its property transferred to the Russian Orthodox Church. In August 1992, the remains of Iosyf Slipyj—the former Metropolitan of the UHKTs who had spent eighteen years in the Soviet Gulag and was then released to the Vatican in the early 1960s—were returned to L'viv, where they were reburied in St. Yury's Cathedral, the central seat of the UHKTs in Ukraine.[22] Over 1 million people paid their respects over the five days that the body lay in state at the cathedral, an event also attended by then President Kravchuk. In September 1993, the first public consecration since World War II of a Greek Catholic bishop on Ukrainian territory took place.

By March 1996, the UHKTs was sufficiently consolidated to hold widescale commemorations of the four hundredth anniversary of the Union of Brest of 1596, which created the UHKTs after the Rusyn-Ruthenian (Ukrainian-Belarusan) Orthodox Church went into union with Rome.[23] At the October 1996 *sobor* of the UHKTs, three resolutions were adopted. First, members called upon the Ukrainian government to officially rehabilitate the UHKTs. Second, they voted to request that President Leonid Kuchma officially invite the pope to visit Ukraine in 1997. Finally, they submitted a proposal to the Synod of Bishops to withdraw condemnation of those Ruthenian Orthodox bishops who had not recognized the 1596 Union of Brest.

Unresolved Issues

Despite the spectacular revival of the UHKTs, three crucial problems remain within this church. First, the issue of territorial jurisdiction has still not been resolved. The territorial question is an important question that could upset relations between the Vatican and the Russian Orthodox Church. The 1596 Union of Brest was first accepted by the Ruthenian Orthodox bishops of central Ukraine and Belarus. The eparchies of Galicia and Peremyshl (in Polish, "Przemysl") accepted church union with the Vatican only a century later. With the liquidation of Ukrainian autonomy within the tsarist Russian empire in the late eighteenth century, the road was cleared for the liquidation of the UHKTs in central Ukraine and Belarus in the 1830s. Greek Catholicism (Uniatism) was therefore de facto eradicated by the state in Ukrainian and Belarusan areas under tsarist Russian control. In Galicia and Trans-Carpathia—under Austrian and Hungarian jurisdiction, respectively, prior to 1918—the UHKTs was allowed to flourish. Until the creation of the eparchy of Kyiv-Vyshorod in the mid-1990s, the Vatican confined the limits of the UHKTs to territories that had traditionally remained outside Russian control (Galicia and Trans-Carpathia). It remains unclear whether the UHKTs and the Vatican will be able to agree on the geographic scope of activity of the church.

Second, the hierarchy and clergy lack complete formal training. Because the church was banned by Soviet authorities, it could not easily operate seminaries, and education was somewhat informal. Many catacomb clergy of the UHKTs were unable to complete or even undertake theological training, something that the L'viv Theological Academy, opened in 1993, hopes to remedy.

Third, the UHKTs has still not been recognized as a church with a right to its own patriarchate, due largely to the Vatican's concern not to irritate the Russian Orthodox Church. The Vatican still holds back from creating this position, a demand long raised in the Ukrainian diaspora and supported unanimously by the bishops' synods of the UHKTs. Before to the disintegration of the USSR, the Vatican had claimed that a patriarchate could not be created in exile but had to wait until the church returned to Ukraine.[24] After the UHKTs reestablished itself in Ukraine, the Vatican changed its tactics, arguing that "the time was not yet right." In other words, the Vatican would prefer not to create a UHKTs patriarchate in order to avoid worsening relations with the Russian Orthodox Church. A UHKTs patriarchate, if and when it were to be created, would encompass the entire territory of Kyiv-Halych (and not only Galicia), thus claiming for the Church of Rome territory previously acknowledged to be under the Russian Orthodox Church. A patriarchal curia has nevertheless already been established by the UHKTs, functioning as a coordinating body over Ukraine's eparchical structures.

This Vatican *ostpolitik* is also reflected in its refusal to sanction the creation of additional eparchies in central Ukraine, which would be seen as an attempt by the UHKTs to move into allegedly "traditional Orthodox territory." The Russian Orthodox Church perceives the entire CIS to be its territory (and not just the Russian Federation), in a manner similar to the way it perceived the entire Russian empire and the USSR. The Russian Orthodox Church does not represent a threat to Uzbeks, Georgians, or Armenians, who are unlikely to join this church. Instead, its believers come from Russians and the largely Slavic Russian-speaking peoples within the CIS. Only one new eparchy (Kyiv-Vyshorod) has been created under Bishop Lubomyr Husar.

It was not only to Galicia, where Orthodoxy is now entrenched, that the Soviet era brought changes. Many western Ukrainians migrated in search of jobs to eastern Ukraine or were sent there after finishing their studies. Others who had been deported to Siberia after World War II were not allowed to return to western Ukraine and had to settle in eastern Ukraine. In central and eastern Ukraine, the UHKTs is therefore also growing, with parishes already established in Sumy, Luhans'k, Poltava, Kharkiv, Donets'k, Zhytomir, Sevastopol, and elsewhere.

The only serious competitor to the UHKTs in Galicia is the UAPTs, whose main base is also located in these three oblasts. In 1989, when the Russian Orthodox Church disintegrated in Galicia, many priests joined the UAPTs rather than defecting to the UHKTs. From its inception, therefore, the UAPTs was in some degree of competition with the UHKTs, often competing for the same church buildings and parishioners.[25]

In addition, regionalism plays a role in dividing the UHKTs. The UHKTs eparchy of Mukachiv-Uzhorod (Trans-Carpathia) has refused to come under the L'viv UHKTs archbishop, instead preferring to be directly subordinated to the Vatican.[26] The UHKTs eparchy of Przemysl (Peremyshl) in Poland was also placed directly under the Vatican. Greek Catholics had been repressed in postwar Communist Poland and their churches and cathedrals in cities such as in Przemysl transferred to Polish control after the expulsion of Ukrainians from southeastern Poland in 1947. The pope had to back down after initially ordering the Carmelites to return the cathedral in Przemysl to the UHKTs. The Carmelites have, in turn, begun changing the architecture of the cathedral to give it a more

Latin-rite look and thereby erase any historical links it had to Ukrainian-Greek Catholicism.[27]

The pope had planned to visit Ukraine for the first time in 1997, after President Kuchma had earlier advised him that 1995–1996 was still too early for such an important visit. An important consideration that had changed was the relative stabilization of interconfessional relations, particularly with regard to disputes over church property. The shortage of properties is being resolved by the dramatic construction of 2,000 churches of all faiths throughout Ukraine.[28] It is unlikely, though, that the pope's visit, which became stalled, would be used to announce the creation of a UHKTs patriarchate, a demand raised by UHKTs lay circles. The Russian Orthodox Church remains adamantly opposed to the visit of the pope, not just to the Russian Federation but to the entire CIS, on behalf of which it claims it has a right to speak.[29]

ORTHODOXY

The Question of Ukrainian Orthodox Autocephaly

Metropolitan Filaret of the UPTs, head of the Russian Orthodox Church in Ukraine, became a surprise convert to autocephaly in early 1992 for three reasons. First, his position within the UPTs was becoming increasingly untenable after he was instructed to resign by the April 1992 Russian Orthodox Church *sobor*. Second, Filaret was being pressured by the national Communist–national democratic alliance under Kravchuk to create a new "state church" from the UPTs. Finally, Filaret and Kravchuk both thought that they could ensure the switch in allegiance of the majority of Ukrainian bishops within the UPTs toward this new "state church." The national Communists were in alliance with national democrats, whose vision of nation and state building assumed that Ukraine required a "state (official) church." In the post-Kravchuk era, national democrats have continued to be the main promoters of a united Orthodox church.

Although Kravchuk officially disclaimed any intention of creating a "state church," this was plainly the objective of the authorities during 1992–1993. The official backing given to this venture was visible and "[a] war was declared on the Muscovite Church."[30] State television and radio were monopolized by pro-autocephaly Orthodox commentators, who regularly denounced the "pro-Russian" UPTs. On June 25–26, 1992, an All-Ukrainian Orthodox *sobor* took place that voted unanimously to unite the Filaret wing of the UPTs with the UAPTs to create a Ukrainian "State Orthodox Church." Émigré-based Patriarch Mstyslav of the UAPTs was elected head of the new Ukrainian Orthodox Church—Kyiv Patriarchate (UPTs–KP). Filaret was made his deputy patriarch, a position that was unusual and only created to accommodate his personal ambitions. After Filaret became patriarch in October 1995, the post was abolished.

After the unification *sobor*, a church council was created that brought together leading national democrats from the pro-Kravchuk Congress of National Democratic Forces and Orthodox leaders. Its first act was to symbolically annul the 1686 act that transferred the Kyivan Metropolinate to Moscow. (Viacheslav Chornovil, as leader of Rukh and hetman of Ukrainian Cossacks, also symbolically annulled the 1654 Russian-Ukrainian Treaty of Periaslav during that same summer.) The historical symbolism of these acts could also be seen in one of the first religious epistles to Orthodox believers in Ukraine drawn up by the UPTs-KP. It claimed that this new church was the rightful heir to the metropolinate of Kyiv Rus' and to the Church of Grand Prince Volodymyr, who had Christianized Kyiv Rus' in A.D. 988.

The Moscow Patriarch dispatched an order to Kyiv Metropolitan Volodymyr to take over the wing of the UPTs that had refused to join Filaret's UPTs-KP. It remained confined to the Kyiv Pecharska Lavra monastery, with Filaret controlling most of the church property of the former UPTs in Ukraine.

The Question of a "State Church"

Despite the backing of the Ukrainian state, the attempt to create a "state church" failed. Only approximately 300 of the then 1,300 UPTs parishes initially defected to the UPTs-KP. Autocephaly from Moscow was not opposed per se by the majority of Ukrainian Orthodox bishops. But they disliked Filaret for a variety of reasons (including his shady past and links to the KGB, and his uncanonical personal life). In addition, the personal motives behind Filaret's and Kravchuk's moves toward independence and Orthodox autocephaly were never entirely patriotic. The UPTs-KP was also faced with the obstacle of recognition of its autocephaly by the Orthodox Patriarch of Constantinople (Orthodox canon does not allow the existence of more than one recognized church on the same territory). Constantinople demanded the unification of all Orthodox churches in Ukraine as the price for recognition of their autocephaly.

By late 1992, Patriarch Mstyslav began denouncing Filaret and the hasty unification *sobor*. After Mstyslav's death on June 11, 1993, those bishops who, like him, had remained critical of the unification *sobor* began a campaign to reregister the former UAPTs. The "state Orthodox church" was beginning to crumble. On September 7, 1993, supporters of the UAPTs held their own *sobor*, which elected a separate Patriarch Dymytriy. Two weeks later, the UPTs-KP held a *sobor* where former dis-

sident Volodymyr Romaniuk was elected as its new "Patriarch of Kyiv and all-Rus'-Ukraine."
Dissension continued within the ranks of the UPts–KP, with defectors going to the UPts and the UAPts. Many of these defectors remained faithful to autocephaly, and their major reason for defection therefore was their continued antipathy toward Filaret.

Kuchma Rejects Concept of "State Church"

Kuchma hailed from the social democratic liberal wing of the Ukrainian political spectrum. He therefore distrusted the UPts–KP and Filaret, whom he saw as allies of Kravchuk and the national democrats. During the 1994 presidential elections, Kravchuk and Kuchma were backed respectively by the UPts–KP and the UPts (the UHKTs, Jewish, and Muslim clergy also backed Kravchuk). Upon being elected, Kuchma showed his gratitude to the UPts by disbanding the Council on Religious Affairs, which had played a leading role in propagating the UPts–KP as the "state church."

Over a year later, however, Kuchma reestablished this body as the State Committee on Religious Affairs to promote dialogue between Ukraine's religious denominations. Kuchma also introduced a new policy of separating the church from the state in reality (not just on paper, as under Kravchuk). The re-creation of a state institution devoted to religious affairs came about as a consequence of Kuchma's realization that the state still had a role to play (particularly with regard to the three Orthodox churches). Kuchma also remained concerned that religion did not play the role he felt it should in "consolidating society."

Lingering Problems

With the death of Patriarch Volodymyr in July 1993, in what some believed to be suspicious circumstances, the way was now clear for Filaret to become patriarch of the UPts–KP, a post he had long coveted. After he was elected patriarch at the October 1995 *sobor* of the UPts–KP, he promptly abolished the post of deputy patriarch. His election to this post again led to defections to the other two Orthodox churches, and by the following year, the UPts–KP and the UAPts had approximately the same number of parishes.

The Ukrainian Orthodox community remains important to the Russian Patriarchate for its finances, numbers of believers, and properties, as well as for its historical and spiritual qualities. Any attempt to remove the autonomous UPts from under the Russian Orthodox Church, in the manner

PHOTO 3.1   Riot at funeral of patriarch of Ukrainian Orthodox Church–Kyiv Patriarchate, Kyiv, July 1995

that occurred within the Estonian Orthodox Church in spring 1996,[31] would lead to another schism in relations between Constantinople and Moscow.

Amid the conflict between the Estonian authorities and the Russian Orthodox Church, Patriarch Filaret of the UPTs–KP called for an end to "Moscow's spiritual empire." Filaret accused Moscow of still maintaining "the essence of an imperialist church. Despite the collapse of the Soviet Union, the Russian church wants to keep a church empire in the form of the Moscow Patriarchate."[32] This is a split waiting to happen. State and nation building in Ukraine will not be complete, in the eyes of some of Ukraine's elites, if the Russian Orthodox Church continues to control over one-third of Ukraine's total number of parishes. The UPTs continues to conduct its services in Church Slavonic and owes its allegiance to a religious leader based in another state. In other words, in this view the UPTs is undermining attempts at state and nation building in Ukraine by propagating a pan–Eastern Slavic cultural and spiritual community.[33] This pan-Slavic notion directly contradicts the main tenet of Ukrainian nation builders that Ukraine is distinct and separate from Russia in all ways. It is therefore little surprise that the Communist Party of Ukraine remains one of the closest allies of the UPTs (despite the obvious irony concerning communism and atheism). The Communist and Socialist media have propagated the views of the UPTs, opposing autocephaly and the creation of one united Orthodox Church.[34]

The adoption of Ukraine's first post-Soviet constitution in June 1996 may usher in a new era for religion in Ukraine. The approach of the new constitution was greeted with an appeal signed by the UPTs, UPTs–KP, UHKTs, Protestant-Baptist churches, Muslims, and Jews, welcoming it as a sign that the church and state would now be separated and that *all* religious bodies in Ukraine would henceforth be equal.[35] Article 35 of the new Ukrainian constitution outlined the separation of the church and state, stressing that "[n]o religion shall be recognized by the State as compulsory."[36] This was a clear rejection of the previous policy of attempting to create a state-backed, national Orthodox church under Kravchuk (the UPTs–KP).

It is noticeable that in the dispute between the Russian Orthodox Church and the Estonian authorities, the pro-autocephaly churches in Ukraine, particularly the UPTs–KP, led by Patriarch Filaret, strongly backed the autocephaly of the Estonian Orthodox Church from Moscow. The pro-autocephaly Ukrainian Orthodox churches also backed the Constantinople Patriarch in the dispute, who sided with the Estonians, arguing that the Moscow Patriarch had pushed the Orthodox Church very close to another schism as alarming as that of 1054.[37] Patriarch Filaret has claimed that the Patriarch of Constantinople is now willing to grant autocephaly after only the unification of the two pro-autocephaly churches in Ukraine (the UPTs–KP and the UAPTs)—and not the unification of all three, which would also include the UPTs.[38] The Estonian path is similar to that taken by the Polish Autocephalous Orthodox Church in 1924 and the Georgian Orthodox Church in 1943 (all three of which were strongly opposed by the Russian Orthodox Church). The paths chosen by these three churches could turn out to be the path chosen by the pro-autocephaly Ukrainian Orthodox churches as well. That is, autocephaly would have to be taken—as it is unlikely to be granted voluntarily by the Moscow Patriarch.

The main problems for the UPTs–KP, according to Filaret, are twofold. First, there is the issue of unification of the UPTs–KP with the UPTs. Second, many parishes remain without spiritual leaders. The UPTs–KP was already an "autocephalous church," in Filaret's eyes. As there could not be two autocephalous churches in Ukraine, Filaret belittled his rival UAPTs as a "temporary phenomenon." This was wishful thinking; within the three years since its revival in 1993, the UAPTs had grown to include approximately as many parishes as the UPTs–KP.[39] Nevertheless, the bulk of this spectacular growth of the UAPTs since 1993 was not due to the active propagation of this church but rather resulted from the defection of a large number of UPts-KP parishes out of personal dislike for Filaret.[40] The UAPts is not therefore a coherently unified church and by the end of 1996 was threatened with internal splits itself. Five hierarchies of the UAPts had long attempted to remove their patriarch, who was finally ousted in October 1996. After removing him, the UAPts bishops quelled rumors that they were dissolving their church.[41] Nevertheless, these two churches are likely to unite sooner or later.

The rift between the UAPts and the UPts-KP increasingly resembled that which divided the democratic camp after 1992. Those who refused to cooperate with national Communists coincided with those who were the strongest supporters of the UAPts and were the most hostile toward Filaret and his church (the UPts-KP). It is also no coincidence that the region of Ukraine (Galicia) that possesses the country's highest national consciousness and the only region that voted against Kravchuk in the December 1991 presidential elections is also the main base of the UAPts. The majority of the six eparchies of the UAPts are to be found in Galicia.

In October 1995, the UAPts and the UPts-KP signed an act of unification with Patriarch Dymytriy as head of the united church, but this was never acted upon (presumably because of Filaret's ambitions to remain patriarch himself).[42] The UAPts had repeatedly stated that it would reunite with the UPts-KP—but only on condition that Filaret went "into retirement."[43] The UAPts had also held talks with the UPts about unity, despite the fact that Patriarch Dymytriy, head of the UAPts, had on a number of occasions ruled out having any dealings with a church under the control of the Russian Orthodox Patriarch and allegedly financed by the "Gorbachev Fund."[44] Therefore, no unification of the UAPts and the UPts would occur as long as the latter remained part of the Russian Orthodox Church. The presence of Filaret and the continued membership of the UPts within the Russian Orthodox Church are the two main factors that are consequently blocking the creation of a unified Orthodox Church in Ukraine.

CONCLUSION

Many, especially among nationalists, see the fragmentation of Ukraine's religious life not only as emblematic of broader societal fragmentation but as the cause of it. As vicar general of the L'viv Archeparchy of the UHKTs, the Reverend Dr. Ivan Dacko, warned, "Today Ukraine continues to suffer from the division of the church. Having endured totalitarianism and persecution, the nation is psychologically, morally, and materially exhausted as well as emotionally drained."[45] It can certainly be debated whether religious pluralism is a sign of weakness or of strength in a society aspiring to liberal democracy, but it is clear that religious fragmentation is part of the regional and national identity diversity that undermines the search for political consensus. As is the case in nation building, there is a strong temptation for the state to take active steps to encourage unity. But just as the Ukrainian government eventually rejected a strong program promoting the use of a single language, so it has also rejected the notion of building Ukrainian national identity through support of an official state church. In both cases, if the state had made such an effort, it would probably have spurred a powerful backlash and would have had the opposite effect of that intended.

The Kravchuk leadership acted hastily, without ensuring there was a sufficient base for its church-building mission. In addition, there were few positive arguments put forward for autocephaly (such as the promotion of historical ties to the spiritual legacy of Kyiv Rus' or the revival of national traditions). The state's policies were instead built around the person of Metropolitan Filaret, a largely discredited figure with close ties to Kravchuk. As an alternative, they could have been built around Mstyslav, who could not have been defrocked by the Russian Orthodox Church (as was Filaret) and had no skeletons in his closet. Finally, the authorities could have repeated the introduction of a law on autocephaly, as was done in January 1919 by the then newly independent Ukrainian state, which imposed legal sanctions against those bishops who refused to break their ties with Moscow.[46] In any of these ways, a policy on a state church could have been pursued more energetically, but it appears that Kravchuk was aware of the hazards of pushing the issue too hard.

President Kuchma's policy of neutrality vis-à-vis religious divisions within Ukraine was initially an extreme response to the interventionist policy of the Kravchuk leadership. Upon coming to power, Kuchma had also wanted to distance himself from the UPTs–KP, from Filaret, and from their national Communist–national democratic allies. Although remaining neutral between rival wings of Ukrainian Orthodoxy, Kuchma increasingly tilted toward backing the UPTs–KP during his 1994–1999 period in office because of its links to reformist political parties and its strong support for domestic state and nation building. In contrast, the leftist-backed UPTs-MP looks increasingly isolated and anachronistic, particularly after the Russian State Duma ratified the Ukrainian-Russian treaty in December 1998.

Nevertheless, the Ukrainian authorities (including both Kravchuk and Kuchma) continue to support the unification of the three Ukrainian Orthodox churches into one church and the granting of autocephaly to it.[47] But there is little support for it to then become a "state church." This process of the coming together of Ukraine's Orthodox churches and their eventual autocephaly is likely to be a drawn-out process, as much a product of domestic state and nation building as it is of the full normalization of relations with Russia. This process could therefore be hastened by the signing and ratification of the Ukrainian-Russian treaty in 1997–1998, which has laid to rest any territorial questions between both countries.

APPENDIX: UKRAINE'S RELIGIOUS COMMUNITIES

TABLE 3.1 Religious Communities by Region

Region/Oblast	1992	1995	% Increase
The Crimea			
Crimea	159	320	101
Sevastopol city	–	30	100
Western Ukraine			
L'viv	2,206	2,386	8
Ternopil'	1,428	1,468	3
Ivano-Frankivs'k	1,078	1,174	9
Rivne	734	862	17
Volyn'	628	788	25
Chernivtsi	599	761	27
Central Ukraine			
Vinnytsya	739	948	28
Khmel'nyts'kii	699	863	23
Kyiv	375	641	71
Kyiv city	89	226	154
Zhytomir	438	603	38
Cherkasy	288	404	40
Dnipropetrovs'k	189	278	47
Poltava	151	235	56
Kirovohrad	153	229	50
Eastern Ukraine			
Donets'k	327	451	38
Chernihiv	279	404	45
Sumy	214	287	34
Kharkiv	174	265	52
Zaporizhzhya	143	253	77
Luhans'k	166	240	45
Southern Ukraine			
Odesa	382	540	41
Mykolayiv	133	219	65
Kherson	139	217	56
Total	13,019	16,460	23

SOURCE: Oleksandr Sahan, "Avtokefaliya: Mizh Politykoiu i Molytvoiu," *Viche* (October 1995), pp. 127–128.

TABLE 3.2 Number of Religious Communities in Ukraine, 1996

Type	No.
Orthodox	
Ukrainian Orthodox Church (Moscow Patriarch)	6,564
Ukrainian Orthodox Church–Kyiv Patriarch	1,332
Ukrainian Autocephalous Orthodox Church	1,209
Other Russian Orthodox churches	101
Catholic	
Ukrainian-Greek Catholic Church	3,079
Roman Catholic	694
Protestant	
Various Baptist/Protestant churches	3,994
National minorities	
Hungarian Reform Church	91
Jews	79
Muslims	176
Krishna	28
German Evangelical-Lutheran Church	17
Buddhist	17
Armenian Apostolic Church	9
Armenian Catholic Church	1
Korean Methodist Church	1
Swedish Evangelical-Lutheran Church	1

SOURCE: *Vechirnyi Kyiv*, 2 October 1996, and *Ukrains'ke Pravoslavne Slovo*, nos. 7–8, 1996.

TABLE 3.3 Eparchies of the Ukrainian-Greek Catholic Church, 1993

Eparchy	Population	Parishes (1989)	Clergy
L'viv	1,826,700	829	289
Ivano-Frankivs'k	736,543	446	204
Mukachevo	1,258,100	136	101
Ternopil'	643,170	316	148
Kolomyia/Chernivtsi	773,691	318	132
Zboriv	414,279	381	96
Sambir/Drohobych	630,900	403	123
Central/Eastern/South	–	30 (approx.)	14
Total	–	2,850	1,107

SOURCE: Press office, UHKTs, "The Ukrainian Greek Catholic Church in Ukraine. Statistics, Analysis, and Development" (September 1993). Copy in the possession of the authors.

• FOUR •

Ukraine's Weak State

The central challenge for Eastern European and former Soviet countries today is to develop the political and economic institutions of a market-oriented democratic system. Especially important in this regard is the changing role of the state in leading and guiding the transition effort.[1] The legacy of the centrally planned and administered economy has prompted many indigenous reformers and their Western advisers to call for a drastic *shrinkage* in the size and scope of the state in transitional economies. As Chester Newland observes, such emphasis is largely due to the current fashion in the West of de-emphasizing the state in favor of market relations.[2] The transition to market does not necessarily imply a smaller, weaker state, however. In fact, successful establishment of a vibrant private sector depends vitally upon the ability of the state to transform itself, not to shrink drastically or disappear altogether. The recent experience of the World Bank with transition economies during 1980–1993 makes it increasingly clear that "reform of the public sector itself is a key ingredient of an enabling environment for the private sector."[3] Remnants of the socialist state are ill-equipped to effectively direct and manage the transition process. What is needed is a *new and different state*, not necessarily a smaller one.

THE "BUREAUCRACY PROBLEM" IN TRANSITIONAL SOCIETIES

An important problem in recent theorizing about economic reform is that institutional and administrative issues have largely been treated as "exogenous" factors.[4] Arturo Israel observes that "the problem is that institutions and managerial capacity are not as visible a resource as capital or labor."[5] Further, governance capacity has never been a priority concern for economists, who generally tend to focus more on the policy aspects of reform. Recently, however, institutional weakness has been recognized as a roadblock to economic reform and development.[6] Other factors undoubtedly intervene, but the "problem area" of structural reform and adjustment is increasingly recognized as one of *implementation*, which ultimately concerns the institutions of government, particularly policy and administrative processes.

The Ukrainian experience illustrates well the connections between institutional-administrative factors—especially the managerial capacity of the state—and economic reform. Its limited governance capacity and administrative capabilities have emerged as the critical constraint on Ukraine's efforts to reform the economy, especially in the areas of fiscal and monetary management and privatization. The most serious problems include: the institutional inertia of Ukraine's inherited Soviet-era bureaucracy; confused and overlapping subject-matter jurisdictions; penetration of the state administration by powerful economic interests; outright corruption; and fluctuating levels of commitment to reform on the part of the political leadership.[7] After seven years of floundering, it has become clear that failure to develop the vital connections between institutional capacity and economic reform, thereby overcoming weaknesses in key functional areas of government, constitutes a gross failure of reform policy. Especially after Ukraine's failure to take advantage of the favorable circumstances for genuine tax and expenditure reform in tandem with the budgetary and monetary successes of 1996, institutional capacity-building can no longer be neglected. In 1997 and after, developing the public administration would have to assume a higher priority.

The institutional basis of market transition in the countries of Eastern Europe and the former Soviet Union is a relatively new area of inquiry. It has received increasing levels of attention by policymakers and scholars concerned with the prospects and possibilities of economic reform. This chapter briefly reviews Ukraine's institutional inheritance, with special emphasis on the administrative roots of the country's lackluster market transition efforts. It focuses throughout on the inadequate institutional-administrative basis of governance in Ukraine. It reviews the major issues in transforming key economic management institutions and explores the critical but misunderstood role of the public administration in the transition effort. The priority of establishing effective governmental administrative institutions in order to more rapidly achieve its reform objectives is highlighted.

Government Institutions and Economic Decline

In late Soviet times, Ukraine contributed over 40 percent of the industrial output and 30 percent of agricultural output of the USSR (measured in terms of "net material product"). The system of central planning was designed to serve the purposes of the central government, particularly Moscow's military machine.[8] Little consideration was given to efficiency concerns. Further, the socialist system was poorly equipped to withstand the economic shock waves that accompanied the collapse of the USSR and the Eastern Bloc trading system.[9] In 1996, the Ukrainian economy was still reeling from the economic shock resulting from the breakup of the Soviet Union in 1991. As can be seen from Table 6.1 in Chapter 6, the postindependence period is unprecedented in terms of the economic decline. From 1991–1997, officially measured real gross domestic product declined nearly 68 percent, industrial output 52 percent, and capital investment 74 percent. Only in periods of war have countries experienced such economic contraction. Ukraine thus inherited from the Soviet system an economic machinery prone to instability and decline in the face of market forces and external trade shocks.[10]

The government's weak response to the crisis clearly aggravated the economic decline. Viewing the fall in output as *the* problem, rather than as the inevitable correction after seventy years of socialism, the government lavished vast amounts of subsidies and credits on state-owned enterprises (see Chapter 6). The intent of Ukraine's macroeconomic policy from 1992 to 1995 was to stem the fall in production in order to maintain robust levels of employment. Until 1996, the result was a stream of inflationary budget deficits. Institutional weaknesses in Ukraine's fiscal management organs resulted in an almost complete monetization of budget deficits. Consequently, there was a fairly continuous flirtation with hyperinflation from 1992 to 1995. The worst year was 1993, when prices increased by over 100 times their 1992 level. The effect is cumulative: From January 1991 to December 1996, prices increased by over 16,610 times.[11] The effect on the population was devastating. Despite regular wage increases, real state-sector wages in September 1996 were but 33 percent of their December 1991 levels.

Wholesale prices climbed even more during this period, on a cumulative basis, placing many state enterprises in a serious cash bind. Further output declines and significant interenterprise payments arrears have been the result. Unable or unwilling to comprehend the situation, the government persisted with its policy of relieving financially strapped enterprises through emission of new credits (most of which were not realistically expected to be repaid). But to no avail. There is compelling statistical evidence that increases in credits and the money supply have had little positive effect on real output.[12] Further, the evidence supports the premise that the government's budget deficits have been driven by increases in fiscal expenditure rather than by changes in revenues, production, or wages, which had no significant influence on Ukraine's deficits in 1992–1996.[13] As we will see in Chapter 6, fiscal discipline has been lax.

Immediately following his election in July 1994, President Kuchma imposed a degree of fiscal discipline, bringing budget deficits in line with requirements of the International Monetary Fund for purposes of stabilization lending. This has been achieved largely by slashing social welfare benefit programs and withholding wages and salaries from state-sector workers, many of whom have experienced many months' delay in payments, now for years. It is not clear for how long such measures can be maintained without structural reform, however, due to persistent lobbying by enterprise directors to continue cheap credits, especially for the agricultural sector. All of this was exacerbated by Parliament's inability to enact budget legislation on time, in some cases causing a delay of many months. By year's end 1996, it was clear that lack of administrative capacity to manage the finer points of fiscal reform would threaten Ukraine's reform efforts, perhaps even jeopardizing its national security. Much valuable time that could have been used to develop the public administration was squandered in Ukraine's crucial first seven years of independence. Capacity-building takes time. The development of modern administrative institutions of government, so critical to successful reform, has been largely neglected by Ukrainian leaders. The Ukrainian experience thus places into sharp relief the vital relationship between policy formulation and administrative implementation.

Theory of Institutions and Public Administration

Modern theories of institutional economics are instructive for understanding the necessity for rapid development of the state in transition economies. The eminent Nobel Prize–winning economic historian and institutionalist Douglass C. North has defined an institution as "a set of rules, compliance procedures, and moral and ethical behavioral norms designed to constrain the behavior of individuals."[14] Stressing the need to distinguish between "institutions" and "organizations," North conceived of institutions as sets of formal and informal rules, distinct from the public organizations that may administer and enforce the rules.[15] Larry Kiser and Elinor Ostrom have provided a definition of institutions that is largely consistent with North's, writing that "institutional arrangements are the rules used by individuals for determining who and what are included in decision situations, how information is structured, what actions can be taken and in what sequence, and how individual actions will be aggregated into collective decisions."[16] In this vein, organizations are sets of processes and procedures that give life to the rules that constitute social institutions. In this theoretical context, development of public organizations is seen as the search for the most efficient set of structures that will enable the effective functioning of the necessary political and economic institutions.

Institutional development can also be conceived as the search for and implementation of more efficient sets of rules.[17] Institutions conceived as *rules* are economically important insofar as they specify the basic structure of incentives in the economy. Proper incentives are necessary for economic development. The causal links thus run from institutions to organizations to economic performance.[18] Each is a necessary link in the chain of economic transition and revitalization. To carry the argument further, institutions are means to reduce basic transactions costs.[19] By their nature, government institutions confer rights and define obligations. Institutions can thus have beneficial effects on the everyday cost of conducting business, by reducing compliance costs and the expense of monitoring contract performance. This is accomplished, for instance, through the enactment and enforcement of civil and commercial law codes. It is useful to view the impact of reducing transactions costs against the backdrop of enforcing property rights. Property rights are essentially exclusionary rights; they concern the power of individuals to control and exclusively enjoy their assets. According to Ronald Coase, transactions costs are inversely related to the efficient functioning of a property rights regime and the institutional arrangements of the state to define, enable, and enforce such rights.[20] Insofar as the value of private property right will be a function of the costs to acquire, secure, and maintain ownership and control over them, the institutional framework of society "influences both how resources are used and the willingness of individuals to acquire and invest in assets."[21]

Institutions that serve to protect clearly defined property rights are therefore crucial to both the allocative and productive efficiency of an economic system. Development of clearly defined and enforceable property rights is the essence of transition to market. There are clearly other institutional factors that influence economic efficiency. The institutional framework of government will facilitate economic reform, to the extent that property rights are defined and enforced by the state; private asset values are affected by the state's taxing and spending policies; and volumes of private commercial activity are influenced by the extent of the state's licensing and registration requirements, laws, and regulations. The institutional basis of the economy, and of economic reform, could not be more clear. The institutional *context* of reform, however, is subtle, as it requires an examination of the specific circumstances and conditions under which governments choose alternative institutional-administrative arrangements.

The Importance of Contextual Factors

The theory of institutions and public organizations highlights the importance of *context*. Context encompasses the connections between institutions and organizations, as well as the factors that condition such connections. The importance of context becomes clear when it is understood that although organizations may not be effectively improved independently of rules modifications, "modification of rules is unlikely to produce results *in an operationally meaningful time frame* unless organizational improvements proceed apace."[22] To paraphrase political theorist David Held: There simply must be a degree of symmetry between the principles of state action (i.e., institutions) and the conditions of their enactment (i.e., administrative organizations).[23] These conditions cannot be specified separately from the historical and contextual circumstances, including ideological, institutional, and organizational dimensions. Institutional choice therefore involves creating an appropriate context in which the operations of government will be conducted. Hence, choosing the right goals alone does not matter; neither does efficiency, alone, matter.

The effects of governmental institutions on the economy are therefore contextual; more precisely, they are *contextually contingent*. They are contingent, precisely, upon the presence or absence of some concrete *capacity* or *capability* for action. In the specific area of economic policy, Dietrich Rueschemeyer and Peter Evans have observed that "an effective bureaucratic machinery is the key to the state's capacity to intervene."[24] Further, to be effective, there must be a certain symmetry or compatibility between the objectives of government and the administrative means to achieve the objectives. Hence: "bureaucratic organizations are geared to do certain things relatively well and, *as organizations,* cannot easily switch to or expand into other fields of action. Organizational structures tend to mesh with specific sets of policy instruments and form a fairly stable amalgam."[25] In a similar vein, Stephan Haggard has observed: "Much of the literature on state 'strength' has failed to specify adequately how we would identify a state as 'autonomous' independently of the policy outcomes to be explained [or sought]."[26] Further, Joan Nelson has argued that "a key component of governmental capacity is the adequacy of management of the bureaucratic and parastatal machinery itself."[27] Arturo Israel has been even more explicit regarding the concrete conditions of institutional effectiveness, writing that "[t]he appropriate unit of analysis for institutional effectiveness is an activity within an organization—that is, a specific function such as . . . planning, budgeting, accounting, . . . personnel management, or training."[28] According to Israel, in order to properly assess the capacity to perform, each administrative function or process must be disaggregated from the organizational whole and examined in detail in light of the objectives sought. To discern the capacity for a particular country to manage the affairs of state, then, it is obvious that attention must be paid to the very details of the public administration. This serves to highlight the critical importance of even the most subtle and opaque aspects of administrative capability.

Primacy of Capacity and the "Paradox of the Reforming State"
Theoretical distinctions between governmental institutions (i.e., rules) and the public administration (i.e., structures) tend to blur considerably when viewed from the perspective of specific *capacities*, or performance capabilities,[29] for although "capable governments utilize a variety of institutions to assure the success of their policy processes, the processes themselves are much more important in determining capacity."[30] In a similar vein, Beth Honadle has said that "capacity building means institutionalizing or embodying strengths in an organization."[31] To the extent that capacity-building is concerned with developing specific administrative and managerial competencies, the process may be characterized as the pursuit of "responsive competence."[32] At base, it concerns the ability of governments to select and fulfill their policy objectives.

What Is "Capacity"? There is a distinct lack of precision in the literature in the use of the term "capacity." Many alternative definitions compete for attention; all are valid, to one extent or another. A basic requirement for analytical purposes is that the notion of capacity must be expansive enough to reflect the specific circumstances (or context) of a particular country, like Ukraine, yet be sufficiently broad to enable generalizations across various states and societies. A most useful conception of capacity for present purposes is that of John Gargan: Simply stated, a government's capacity is its ability to do what it needs and wants to do.[33] The present chapter will largely sidestep issues concerning the appropriate functions, size, and scope of the government sector, therefore avoiding judgments concerning specific policy objectives. Rather, we focus more narrowly on the capability of the state to fulfill its chosen objectives. The concept of "capacity" employed here emphasizes the policy, resource, and program management tasks of the state rather than the legitimacy of particular political institutions and objectives.[34]

Paul Collins has argued that formerly Communist states in transition must develop public service management capabilities in three general areas:[35]

- Core institutions of government (e.g., bureaucratic management, policy development, policy analysis, and so on)
- Public administration per se (including a professional civil service, appropriate center-local relations, levels of decentralization, and the like)
- Enterprise restructuring and management education

It should be clear that issues of state capacity are here conceived largely as action-oriented, in an interventionist sense, as they should be. Thus, after Honadle, we define "capacity" as the government's ability to:

- Identify problems
- Develop policies to deal with these problems
- Devise programs to implement the policies
- Attract and absorb financial, human, informational, and capital resources effectively to operate programs
- Manage these resources well
- Evaluate program outcomes to guide future activities[36]

This definition is consistent with that of World Bank specialist Arturo Israel, who would focus institutional development efforts on building competence in specific functional areas, especially in the effective use of financial and human resources:

> Institutional development (or institutional analysis) is concerned with management systems, including monitoring and evaluation; organizational structure and changes; planning, including planning for an efficient investment process; staffing and personnel policies; staff training; financial performance, including financial management and planning, budgeting, accounting, and auditing; maintenance; and procurement.[37]

The "Paradox of the Reforming State." Building administrative competence poses a certain *paradox* for the transition of the state in a reforming economy. Paraphrasing Leila Frischtak, we term this phenomenon the "paradox of the reforming state."[38] The paradox arises from the observation that economic reform does not necessarily imply a *minimal* state. Quite to the contrary: Reforms aimed at reducing the size and scope of governmental involvement in the economy actually require the enhancement of administrative capabilities.[39] Successful privatization, liberalization of prices, removal of trade restrictions, decentralization of fiscal processes, and redesign of the social safety net all depend upon expanded state capacity. Rather than a weakening of the state, then, just the opposite is prescribed.

This is precisely the paradox of the reforming state: Rather than shrink, the socialist state must expand in new directions in order to support economic reform, even as it abandons its traditional socialist posture of command and control. Unfortunately, international lending institutions traditionally counsel reforming countries that the state ought to be drastically pared back.[40] As we have noted, such sentiments can be traced to the current pro-market, antigovernment fashion in the West. To be fair, public choice economists rightly warn that governments ought to be kept small in size in order to minimize opportunities for powerful interests to penetrate the state for purposes of capturing rents.[41] Further, Frischtak has noted that "the difficulty of clarifying the paradox . . . can partly be attributed to the very elusiveness of the state [itself] as a problem."[42] In order to appreciate the challenge of overcoming the paradox in the case of Ukraine, a more detailed elaboration of the Ukrainian governmental system is in order.

DOMINANT FEATURES OF UKRAINE'S GOVERNMENTAL SYSTEM

Government capacity has become an issue in Ukraine, owing to the apparent gap between its policymaking and administrative capabilities and the magnitude of change demanded by the economic and political transition. Ukraine's governmental system largely consists of vestiges of the former Soviet regime, which have been subject to somewhat piecemeal revision. Consequently, the dominant features of Ukraine's administrative system have militated against effective implementation of reforms. The 1996 Constitution of Ukraine served to clarify somewhat many of the most important issues. However, serious difficulties remain to be resolved, for example:

- A "semipresidential" system that is too weak and fragmented for effective governance
- Complex, confused, and often overlapping jurisdictions among the major political institutions, leading to counterproductive institutional competition
- Centralization in Kyiv of decisionmaking concerning regional and local affairs, owing to the unitary nature of the state
- Excessively executive-oriented, top-down authority structures
- Strictly hierarchical, closed, and exclusionary decisionmaking processes
- "Hollowness" of government ministries
- The existence of "paper ministers," whose roles are almost entirely dominated by the former Communist *nomenklatura*
- Absence of both a rule-of-law tradition and a public service ethic
- Lack of a developed civil service system, with the adequate numbers of appropriately trained and motivated personnel that implies

These problems—which are by no means unique to Ukraine—present certain challenges for the successful pursuit of political and economic reform.[43] Following is a summary of the main features and problems.

A Weak "Semipresidential" System

From 1991 to 1996, Ukraine's constitutional regime may be characterized as a politically stultifying hybrid of the Soviet-era structure, amended (many times) by Parliament since 1991.[44] Both the old Soviet Constitution and the pre-1996 Ukrainian drafts suffered from certain contradictory provisions, which resulted in confused, often overlapping, jurisdictions between the major political institutions.[45] The June 7, 1995, parliamentary vote to establish a "power agreement" with the president was intended to resolve a serious deadlock over the division of powers between them. The so-called Law on State Power and Local Government served, in effect, as a *petite constitution* for one year—until the new constitution was ratified by Parliament, on June 28, 1996. The 1995 deal lent greater clarity to the powers of both president and Parliament and changed the basis for the election of local government officials, all of which had been a major political issue. The situation prior to 1995 had generated a good deal of confusion, inadvertently creating opportunities for bureaucratic entrenchment, which heightened resistance to reforms.[46]

Ukraine's governmental system until June 1996 was a fairly weak "semipresidential" regime.[47] Some have termed this kind of constitutional arrangement a "mixed premier-presidential," or "presidential-parliamentary" regime.[48] It should be noted that all post-Soviet countries have developed mixed presidential regimes, and many of the same factors have been involved in the process of institutional choice.[49] Such *mixed* systems are prone to problems of ambiguity and confusion over the separation of powers among president, Parliament, and prime minister. All three of these actors have constituted the separation of powers system in the early stages of Ukraine's executive branch development.[50] From 1990 to 1995, all three (Parliament through the office of the Speaker) possessed constitutional claims to direct the activities of ministers, who had a double loyalty: The government was subordinated to the president but also accountable and responsible to Parliament. The dual executive structure worked against presidential dominance over the bureaucracy and created tensions that would fester into intensifying conflict until coming to a head with the enactment of the "Power Bill."

Two key conflicts between the president and Parliament emerged from ambiguities in the separation-of-powers regime: a struggle for control over the prime minister and the cabinet; and a struggle for control over subnational governments. Both will be dealt with below. The 1995 Law on Power bolstered, temporarily, the power of the president vis-à-vis Parliament. Under the Power Bill, President Kuchma transformed the presidency into a lawmaking institution. However, as Charles Wise and Trevor Brown have observed, Kuchma's activism highlighted basic contradictions in the division of powers.[51] These contradictions have been addressed considerably, if not resolved completely, by the Constitution of 1996. Ukraine no longer functions as a hybrid "premier-presidential" system, now showing more attributes of a "semistrong presidential" regime. In this system, the prime minister remains weak, insofar as the office is beholden to a popularly elected president, but also depends upon the confidence of Parliament (without being the leader of a dominant party or coalition government). It appears quite likely that, over time, the premiership will become increasingly superfluous.

Nascent National Political Institutions

The key national political institutions are the president, prime minister, Cabinet of Ministers, and Verkhovna Rada (Supreme Council, or Parliament). The president's powers are quite broad. The president appoints the prime minister, who in turn directs the Cabinet of Ministers (Article 106). The president possesses authority to appoint ministers and vice prime ministers nominated by the prime minister. The size of the cabinet leadership cadre has been limited under the new constitution, however, to the prime minister, a first vice prime minister, and three vice prime ministers (Article 114). This necessitated some reshuffling of cabinet portfolios in late 1996, but the organization is now stable. The president's authority under the 1995 Law on Power to establish or eliminate ministries, at his discretion, has been revoked. He may now do so only upon recommendation of the prime minister. Previously, the president was empowered to issue decrees having the force of law and could *annul* (not merely veto) acts of Parliament. Now he must adhere to a formal veto process, which involves the possibility of a parliamentary override (Articles 106, 94). He can still overturn acts taken by the Cabinet of Ministers, but it is not clear that he can revoke actions taken by individual ministries unless they are in direct violation of the Constitution. At the time of this writing (June 1999), such powers have yet to be fully defined. The president appoints the heads of local state administrations, upon recommendation of the Cabinet of Ministers. Through the cabinet, the president only controls indirectly oblast and raion state administrative activities (Article 106), excepting decisions and actions that contravene the Constitution and laws of Ukraine.[52] In that case, the president or any superior executive body may directly revoke their actions (Article 118). However, now only Parliament may dissolve local councils or annul their decisions.

The Constitution designates the Verkhovna Rada as the sole lawmaking body in Ukraine (Article 76). In practice, however, this authority must be shared with the president, Cabinet of Ministers, and National Bank of Ukraine (NBU), all of which possess the right of legislative initiative (Article 93). The Rada possesses broad oversight authority respecting actions of the Cabinet of Ministers (Articles 85, 113). The Rada can dissolve the government via a vote of no confidence (Article 87); however, new elections are not necessarily implied by such a vote. In case of a no-confidence vote, the president will have some sixty days in which to appoint a new cabinet. In his capacity as Speaker, the chair *(holova)* of the Verkhovna Rada previously could suspend actions of the government, Cabinet of Ministers, and other governmental bodies in situations where, in his opinion, they lacked conformity with the Constitution and other national legislation. But no longer. The chairman now presides over and manages the work of Parliament, supervises the parliamentary administration (staff bureaucracy), and represents Parliament in its relations with the president and other governmental bodies (Article 88). The former executive body of Parliament, the Presidium, which possessed the authority to propose legislation and preside over sessions in the Speaker's absence, is eliminated in the new constitution, and with it, a valuable source of patronage controlled by the Speaker.

Due to the dual and highly blended lines of influence and accountability, the Cabinet of Ministers has somewhat divided institutional loyalties between the president and Parliament. In 1991–1995, Parliament employed its institutional leverage, from time to time, to charge the government directly with very specific missions and objectives, often taking little heed of the president's policy agenda. Such a situation permitted entrepreneurial members of the *nomenklatura* to build alliances with parliamentary commissions (now called "committees"), which sometimes directly contravened presidential policy. This has been made much more difficult under the Constitution, as parliamentary committees have been stripped of their ability to directly introduce legislation.[53]

Regarding the judiciary, Parliament elects to the bench all judges (including Supreme Court judges) recommended by a nominating body, the High Council of Justice, except in the case of the Constitutional Court. Constitutional Court justices are appointed jointly by the president and the Congress of Judges of Ukraine. A new court system, comprised of courts of general and specialized jurisdiction, is to be formed within five years of the adoption of the Constitution. In the interim, the existing judicial system remains in place. The courts largely remain vestiges of the Soviet judiciary, with certain new innovations (i.e., the Constitutional Court). According to Article 12 of the Constitution, Ukrainian courts are organized both territorially and functionally. The Supreme Court, Constitutional Court, and Courts of Arbitrage have separate jurisdictions and organizational structures.

The Constitutional Court reviews cases involving interbranch conflict, as well as constitutionality of actions of the president and Parliament. The

Supreme Court is the highest criminal and civil law court in Ukraine. As was the case in the Soviet system, the role of the procurator is dominant in criminal proceedings. The Courts of Arbitrage have jurisdiction over commercial law and disputes involving ministries of government and private business. So far, the courts have not played a major role in the conflicts between president and Parliament, but some recent cases indicate that this may change in the future.

A Unitary State

Like its Soviet predecessor, Ukraine remains a unitary state under the 1996 Constitution (Article 132). Although there are some elementary features of federalism present, oblast and raion governments are essentially subordinated to higher-level governments in virtually every respect (Article 118). The intergovernmental structure remains, formally, a strict hierarchy. There are basically three tiers of government: central government, regional government (oblasts), and local government (which includes cities, city and rural districts, raions, villages, and rural settlements [see Figure 4.1]). To the extent that rural districts are divided into rural settlements and where cities are sufficiently large to be divided into city districts, these effectively constitute yet a *fourth* level of government.[54]

The central government supervises the oblasts, which, in turn, supervise their subordinated units of government (Article 118). The Constitution and laws of Ukraine vest legislative authority in elected oblast and raion councils; the executive authority rests with appointed state administrations. Raion councils and state administrations are strictly subordinated to their oblast counterparts, and, as noted above, the heads of oblast and raion administrations are subordinated to the president. Decisions of lower-level entities may be overturned by superior entities. The unitary state is also reflected in the budget structure of Ukraine, which mirrors the governmental structure. The budgets of lower-level governments are essentially "nested" within the budgets of their corresponding higher-level governments. Intergovernmental fiscal relations are marked by a high degree of revenue dependency, thus retaining the centralization of fiscal management that characterized the Soviet system. From 1991 to 1998, the central government acted largely for its own convenience, with little or no regard for oblast or municipal preferences, needs, or concerns.[55] Indeed, the center often acted to subvert what little fiscal autonomy that was attained, through a steadily increasing stream of unfunded mandates imposed on subnational governments.[56]

The Law on Local Self-Government was enacted in February 1992, and twice amended, in 1995 and 1997.[57] The 1992 law consisted of amendments to the 1991 Law of the Ukrainian SSR, granting rather substantial

FIGURE 4.1 Tiers of Ukrainian Government

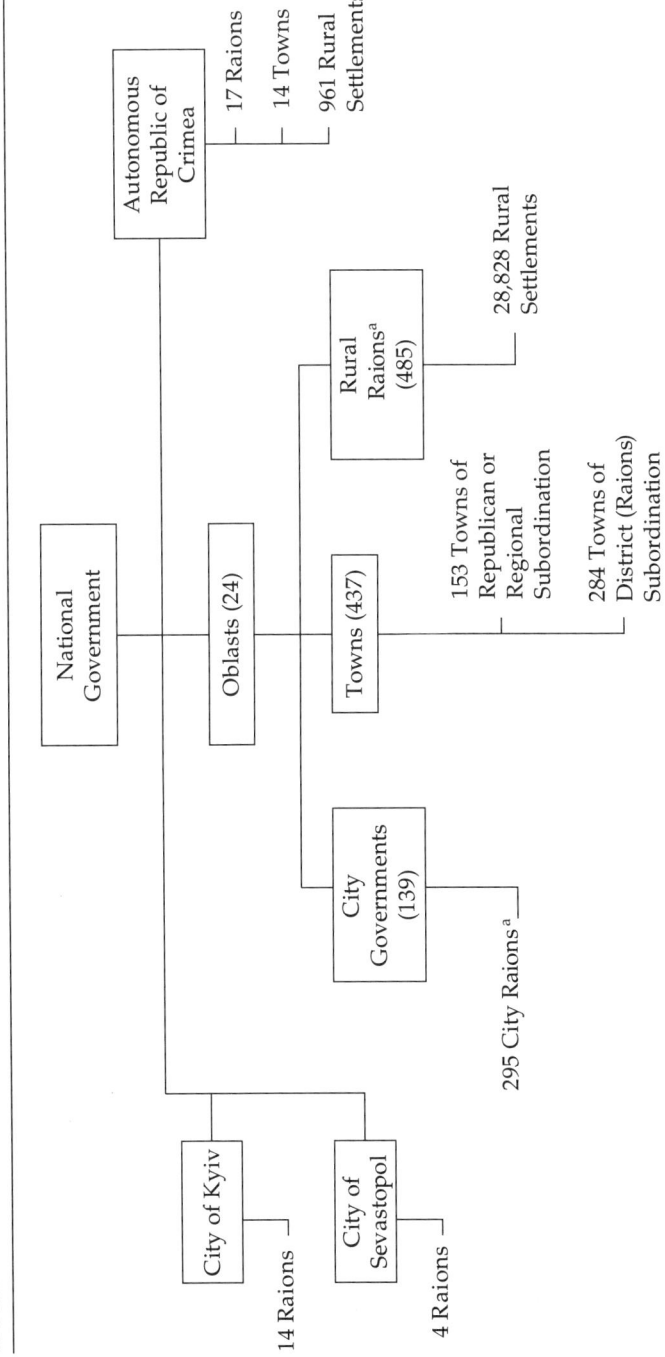

[a] A total of 450 district (rayon) governments are prescribed under the 1996 Constitution of Ukraine. However, Article 140 permits village, settlement and city councils to establish "house, street, block, and other bodies of popular self-organization," thus providing a broad degree of elasticity to the practical number of meaningful governmental districts in Ukraine.

SOURCE: Ministry of Economics of Ukraine.

powers to regional and local governments. In practice, however, owing to contradictions with Ukraine's then existing Law on Budget System, the stunted revenue capacities of municipalities, and the extraordinary role of the Ministry of Finance in local fiscal affairs, the central government has continued to exert a disproportionate influence on local government. In February 1994, Parliament enacted a new Law on Formation of Local Power and Self-Governing Bodies, which established an entirely new structure for local authorities, effectively undermining direct presidential control of regional and local government.[58] Under the 1994 law, subordination of representative bodies became the effective governing principle, whereby oblast and raion Radas were transformed into de facto adjuncts of the national government, rather than operating as truly autonomous bodies of local self-government. The 1996 Constitution is consistent with this schema as far as the legislative power is concerned. The near-total domination of higher-level Radas over subordinates appears certain to result in horizontal conflicts between these Radas and their chairs, insofar as regional and local state administrations are subordinated jointly to the president and Cabinet of Ministers. This type of power structure presents a clear danger of conflict between regional and local Radas and their respective state administrations. The institutional situation at the regional and local level, therefore, will require further elaboration.

Intergovernmental revenues have been shared on a combined retention/subvention basis.[59] Many poor regions are highly dependent on the central government for necessary revenues. Decisions made in Kyiv thus have considerable effect on the regions and localities. In their turn, oblast governments make decisions concerning the intraregional allocation of funds emanating from the center. Local governments, therefore, tend to be "financially captive" to budgetary politics at higher levels. However, under the 1996 Constitution much greater flexibility is granted to local governments to develop own-source revenues; levy and collect taxes; control expenditures; establish, reorganize, and liquidate communal enterprises; and cooperate with other localities in the conduct of joint projects, with provisions for joint financing (Articles 142–143). The lack of buoyant local revenues has made it extremely difficult to establish any meaningful degree of regional or municipal fiscal independence.

Although far from ideal for regional and local governments, the 1996 Constitution is a marked improvement over the previous state of affairs, where the president and Parliament often clashed over the direction and control of local governance. This has been an especially acute issue for both Presidents Kravchuk and Kuchma, but for different reasons. Kravchuk's 1991 electoral support was especially strong in the rural districts. He therefore sought control over the localities as the means to shore up what he perceived was his base of electoral support. Kuchma's concern is that rural areas primarily support leftist parties and parliamentary factions that oppose his reform initiatives. Under Ukrainian privatization law, local councils were also able to block Kuchma's efforts to rapidly privatize small-scale enterprises (i.e., those of communal subordination). In July 1994, the Rada adopted in its first reading the Law on Local Councils, intended by the newly elected Socialist forces in Parliament to reestablish the Soviet system of rule by councils. The president responded in August with a decree that effectively made the heads of all oblast councils, together with the Kyiv and Sevastopol urban councils and their respective committees, accountable to the president.[60] This issue was resolved in the president's favor by the June 7, 1995, constitutional agreement with Parliament and has been largely put to rest in the new constitution.

Hierarchical Organization

The Ukrainian public administration is extremely executive-oriented and top-down in nature. By modern international standards, the internal command structure is excessively centralized. But at the top, vast amounts of "micro management" are exercised, including by cabinet members.[61] The staff expends much time and energy on administrative minutiae, so much so that senior officials are typically unable to properly scrutinize the large number of decisions that are made in their names. The unfortunate consequence has been that key officials devote precious little time to policy planning and development. Further, with their superiors preoccupied with inconsequential detail, lower-level functionaries have been able to exploit opportunities to accumulate influence, exact bribes, and stifle reforms.

In the Ukrainian administrative culture, individual initiative is deemphasized and may be subject to punitive sanctions. This problem, a holdover from the Soviet era, plagues all ministries. Years of subservience to Communist Party authorities have left an indelible mark on administrative routines. Many officials, even today, show little initiative but stand ready to unquestioningly carry out orders. Although the Communist Party apparat is gone, the attitude of unquestioning subservience persists. The political leaders of Ukraine, including reformers (partly owing to their socialization, partly out of distrust of the old-line bureaucrats who remain in the ministries) tend to operate in much the same manner as the former Communist Party bosses. They issue orders, often with little consultation with subordinates, with the expectation that they will be carried out. This has reinforced the already strong expectation that the state primarily serves the interests of its leaders and that the leadership is prone to placing relatively capricious demands upon the bureaucracy.

Closed Decisionmaking

The cultural norm of evading responsibility for incorrect or unpopular decisions has produced an inordinate amount of secrecy in official decisionmaking. Decisions tend to be made in a strictly exclusionary, closed manner. Rather than share authority, thereby diffusing responsibility for decisions and increasing their internal legitimacy, decisions tend to be limited to fairly tight groups of officials within the *nomenklatura* in each ministry. This reinforces an acute awareness of "who's in" and "who's out" among line bureaucrats, which fuels petty jealousies. The large number of operating ministries exacerbates matters, by multiplying centers of decisionmaking and effective "veto points" within the government. Under such conditions, administrative bottlenecks abound. Indeed, in 1997, the World Bank cited Ukraine as among the worst cases of stultifying bureaucracy in the world.[62] Openness concerning issues on the decision agenda is a rarity. New policies and programs tend to be announced with little or no warning, often without official attribution. The rationale behind major policy pronouncements may not be provided. This gives the impression that the state is acting in the service of particular interests. A deep-seated norm of *particularism* thus pervades the bureaucracy, reproducing itself in the decision styles of officials at all levels and engendering public cynicism.

"Hollow" Ministries

The administrative structures that Ukraine inherited from the USSR were wholly inadequate for the governance of a modern, independent state.[63] The basic administrative infrastructure, including but not limited to the fiscal operations of the Ministry of Finance, required institution building "from the ground up," as it were. Basic functions of modern statehood in Ukraine's first seven years therefore underwent a rapid, albeit often haphazard and uneven, development, including: establishing and policing national borders; developing the armed forces; issuing currency and regulating its value; collecting taxes and tariffs; and implementing a national budget. Many mistakes have been made, and the political consensus on basic policy remains unsettled, even after seven years of independent "learning."

A complicating factor is that the basic state functions were developed without adequate numbers of trained administrators to execute them. There is virtually no civil service system to speak of in Ukraine. Like many new states in the region, Ukraine has largely neglected development of the civil service.[64] A serious problem is that there are woefully inadequate numbers of administrators to accomplish the tasks that are entrusted to them.⁶⁵ At the time of independence (August 1991), the central government in Kyiv had only approximately 6,000 civil servants. By late 1995, there were around 13,000 bureaucrats in 112 ministries, departments, and state commissions, supervised by 7 deputy prime ministers in the national government (including 41 ministries).⁶⁶ These were consolidated into 20 ministries and 4 deputy prime ministers in 1996, which now matches the Organization for Economic Cooperation and Development (OECD) average of 20 ministries. Although the number of ministries is large and quite unmanageable, this is far from being the "Soviet-era behemoth" that some contemporary observers have complained of.⁶⁷

Ukraine has not yet come to regard its public servants as a valuable national asset. Little human resource planning occurs, except in the case of individual ministries, which has traditionally produced an intense form of patronage politics.⁶⁸ Like the other Newly Independent States, the government bureaucracy in Ukraine was never truly merit based. Examinations tended to serve as exclusionary devices only. Jobs in the *nomenklatura* were more or less sources of patronage. A constant swirl of reorganizations and imprecisely delineated jurisdictions reinforced the utility of personal loyalties as organizing and expediting devices. Thus, the ideal of an apolitical, professional, neutrally competent civil service never was a part of the Ukrainian administrative landscape. Such a system can take root, in any case, only where some measure of long-term structural stability is achieved.

As late as 1996, skills needs assessments on a government-wide basis were not systematically undertaken. The result is that state officials typically have the wrong skills and education for the needs of the transition economy.⁶⁹ Most were trained as engineers and bookkeepers rather than as economists, policy analysts, or public administrators. They therefore lack the most critical skills and knowledge base. Skills deficiencies are exacerbated by low bureaucratic salaries. This is a most serious problem, as the growing private sector competes with the government for the most skilled workers. Turnover rates are high; in 1995 alone, 14 percent of state employees left for jobs with private sector concerns. Comparable private sector jobs, especially with newly arrived foreign firms, can pay ten or twenty times as much as a government position. Language skills are at a premium. Many civil servants moonlight in order to supplement their salaries. In October 1993, former President Kravchuk took measures to raise administrative salaries some 10–40 percent, depending upon length of service (thereby providing a bonus for longevity).⁷⁰ By late 1998, administrative salaries were some 43 percent higher than the average in the government sector as a whole, though still not competitive with the private sector.⁷¹ Low administrative salaries are therefore a serious problem. Indeed, the most serious and costly obstacles to institutional development and performance on an international basis have been distortions in wages and salaries.[72]

The problem of inadequate numbers of administrators is likely to get worse before it gets better. In fact, both of Ukraine's chief executives took measures to reduce the numbers of state bureaucrats during their terms in office. In 1994, President Kravchuk issued a decree ordering a 30 percent reduction in the numbers of employees in the central state apparatus (and 20 percent at the regional and local levels).[73] President Kuchma in 1995 and 1996 called for reductions in budgeted positions at all levels of government, ostensibly for budgetary savings. It seems clear, however, that Kuchma's main objective was to root out corrupt officials.

The only "pipeline" that is capable of providing a limited number of reasonably well-trained civil servants is the Ukrainian Academy of Public Administration (APA), with branches throughout Ukraine.[74] Established in Kyiv in 1992 as the Institute of Public Administration and Local Government, its Western-style curriculum originally provided around 100 students with a one-year Master's Degree, accredited in Great Britain as a one-year Certificate in Public Administration by the University of North London.[75] In 1995, the institute transferred from the Cabinet of Ministers to the presidential administration, where it came under direct presidential sponsorship. Further, branch campuses were established in L'viv, Odesa, Kharkiv, and Dnipropetrovs'k. Enrollments expanded in 1995 to over 1,000 students per year. The quality and relevance of instruction remain a critical concern, however, as does availability of Ukrainian-language texts in the key subject areas.

A significant problem is that there is no guarantee of employment for APA graduates. Employment remains largely patronage oriented. Recruitment and promotion are highly politicized, in both of which the personal loyalty factor predominates. These features reinforce exclusionary patterns of influence and decisionmaking processes within the bureaucracy. It has only been through the efforts of the APA's energetic Canadian-born associate director, Bohdan Krawchenko, that the issue of building a modern civil service system has remained on the government's agenda. Krawchenko spearheaded the drafting of the new Law on the Civil Service of Ukraine, which was released for public discussion early in 1994 and adopted later that spring.[76] Unfortunately, civil service reform has been displaced by the government's more pressing concerns with economic reform. Exasperated with delays in building the public service, President Kuchma issued a decree in May 1995 instructing the Cabinet of Ministers to draft a program for development of the civil service and establishing the Council on Cadres under the president.[77] The State Commission on Administrative Reform was established in 1997, chaired by former President Leonid Kravchuk. This commission's recommendations are currently under consideration (see below). Despite Kuchma's efforts, however, further progress has proved to be elusive. The consequence of the combined effects of low skills, low wages, and the lack of a systematic approach to government service has been the extremely low level of morale and high turnover rates that pervade the bureaucracy.

The national government is therefore composed largely of "hollow ministries." Many government functions, departments, and divisions within ministries exist primarily in name only. It is not unusual for deputy ministers and department heads to have few staff who may be capable of performing the necessary tasks. The inevitable result is a serious shortfall in administrative performance. Since 1991, the administrative system has been clogged with new laws, decrees, parliamentary resolutions, and orders, many with little realistic hope of implementation.[78] The situation is even more critical at the oblast and local government levels, where resource constraints impinge even more acutely than at the national level.

"Paper Ministers"

It may come as a surprise that ministers themselves have no real job in this system. It has been said that the former Soviet *nomenklatura* runs the government. But it would be more accurate to state that it runs *against* the government or that the government must work against *it* in order to chart an independent course on policy. The problem is that the apparatus of the Cabinet of Ministers, which employs some 700 persons, supervises—and even dominates—the work of cabinet ministers, under the leadership of the minister of the Cabinet of Ministers. In reality, this position has the status of a deputy prime minister and is in fact more influential than any of them, insofar as this is the person who controls the flow of the work of all ministries. Hence, no sense of shared or collective responsibility exists in the system at the top. Cabinet government exists in Ukraine in name only.

Ministers cannot function as "real ministers," in the fullest sense, where they are regarded as mere appendages of the bureaucracy. Under the existing administrative process, they have no independent policymaking responsibility but rather react to the administrative gyrations generated by the *nomenklatura*. Administrative instructions are received by ministers from the civil servants—and *not* the other way around.[79] Bureaucrats clog the system with paperwork, partly as means to occupy ministers, so as to neutralize them. Former Justice Minister Serhiy Holovatiy, for instance, received over 7,000 instructions generated by bureaucrats during his time in office.[80] Thus, despite the presence of reformist ministers like Holovatiy in key posts, little can be accomplished under these circumstances. A radical reform of the Cabinet of Ministers, and perhaps even its abolition, therefore appears necessary. But the draft Law on the Cabinet of Ministers has been held up for some two years, following Kuchma's veto of the initial law. In the meantime, the *nomenklatura* dominates the highest levels of Ukrainian government, where even the president has been unable to overcome its resistance.

Perverse Legal and Ethical Norms

The lack of skilled personnel trained in the most modern methods leads officials to place undue reliance on the entrenched apparatchiks held over from the Soviet period, and with unfortunate results.[81] Since these holdovers are often the only experienced officials, the tendency has been to place them in the most critical and sensitive positions. The persistent influence of the entrenched Communist *nomenklatura* is a problem of long-standing nature, which presents difficulties of inestimable proportions for the post-Communist transition.[82] Raised under the old regime, their "work ethic" and general behavioral instincts are a poor match for the state-building tasks that confront Ukraine. Some exhibit a pronounced contempt for the law, insofar as their positions are still viewed as sources of bribes and other forms of personal aggrandizement. The result has been a steady degeneration toward corruption on a broad basis.[83]

In the absence of norms of ethical conduct and effective accountability and enforcement mechanisms, there has been a trend toward increasing resentment, and in some cases hostility, toward economic reforms on the part of some bureaucrats. Rather than outright opposition, however, some officials prefer to quietly sabotage reforms through lax implementation, red tape, or neglect. The general lack of a civic culture in Ukraine has produced a state where private concerns are routinely substituted for public welfare. This ranges from petty bribery to influence peddling and high-level corruption. A most prominent case has been that of former prime minister Yukhim Zviahils'kyi, who was indicted by the procurator general for embezzlement of some $25 million on illicit oil and gas deals.[84] In 1996, Prime Minister Pavlo Lazarenko was widely rumored to have dispensed privileges to his former business associates in the Dnipropetrovs'k oil and gas company, United Energy Systems.[85] In late 1998, Lazarenko was arrested in Switzerland, accused of violating that country's laws against "money laundering."[86] These and other celebrated cases of official corruption lend an impression that "everyone's doing it," leading to the inevitable "So why shouldn't I?" Despite numerous presidential decrees and the launching of Kuchma's widely publicized Clean Hands anticorruption initiative, no serious effort to combat official corruption has yet been pursued.[87]

Changing Governmental Institutions: Are Western Models Useful?
Throughout 1991–1996, effective policy change in Ukraine's formerly centrally planned economy lagged behind development of the necessary new institutions of government. This provides an important reason that economic transformation in Ukraine has defied "big bang" solutions or "shock therapy."[88] Rapid change is especially critical in the early stages of reform, before political opposition can mobilize to block reform. But the ability of a country to reform rapidly depends on the government's absorptive capacity for change. The extreme difficulty of implementing a wholesale overhaul of the public administration is a critical obstacle to rapid reform. Historical evidence suggests that radical large-scale change can only take place at the margins, that is, in relatively small, incremental chunks.[89] Indeed, in the World Bank's considerable experience, "institutional development is a slow process."[90] Resistance to change is not easily overcome. Not only do institutional norms and customs resist rapid change but all institutional change produces winners and losers. Those who stand to lose will resist the change, with whatever resources are at their disposal. This poses a bit of a dilemma for reformers, who may be compelled by the bureaucracy to keep the pace of reforms within administratively feasible limits. The problem is that a slow adjustment affords reform opponents the time necessary to organize. A slow pace also works to the advantage of influential groups, as against the general interest.

Institutional change is therefore *path dependent*. Existing structures of the administrative status quo constitute the relevant frame of reference for evaluating the future path of institutional change. Going slow in the early stages of reform may preclude accelerating reforms at a later stage. Administrative capacity-building is also *country specific*. Ukraine must work with what it has inherited. Since the stock of institutions changes only at the margins, effective change means overcoming inertia in the physical, technological, and human spheres, as well as changing administrative structures themselves. Technological and human obsolescence can be overcome only in the long run; in the short run, they form the reality of the administrative backdrop of the reforms. The path-dependent (i.e., historically contingent and country specific) nature of institutional change is thus an important factor in explaining why foreign experts have been unable to develop detailed designs for ideally functioning organizations in countries like Ukraine.[91]

Collins has cautioned against a blanket application of "proven Western techniques" of administrative reform to transition states, by noting that although they have many elements in common, the circumstances of change will be different in different countries, due to:

- Differing impetuses for change, both internal and external
- Differing country characteristics, both physical and social
- Differing goals of change[92]

J. J. Hesse has flatly rejected "teaching legislators and administrators in Central and Eastern Europe how to reform their administrative systems," in favor of a gradual, incremental, and contextual reform approach.[93] Newland has decried Western biases, especially the devaluation of government and preoccupation with market economics, as having led to the "export of American practices, with limited knowledge of or attention to varied indigenous experience, institutions and recommendations."[94] Finally, Christopher Hood has questioned the extent to which "Next Generation" administrative practices associated with the "New Public Management" movement in the West can be applied to transitional societies.[95]

The task is monumental. In the absence of a fully developed administrative apparatus to manage reforms, development of specific administrative capabilities must be considered a long-term proposition. Foreign experts can provide a useful diagnosis of the current difficulties, however. Judy Hague, Aidan Rose, and Marko Bojcun have observed that certain Western experiences can be instructive learning devices for development of appropriate administrative systems in the Newly Independent States, including:

- The role of public administrators in the process of policy formulation
- The structures of and processes for evaluating options, making strategic choices, and implementing them
- The role of professional expertise and the relationship between professionals and decisionmakers
- The role of professionals working at the street level and their relationship with service users
- The development of regulatory mechanisms for state- and non-state-owned or -managed agencies
- The development of mechanisms for allowing staff in local agencies to assume responsibility[96]

On the basis of such Western experiences with common problems, the general direction of necessary reforms may be discerned, but not the details or the timing.

The general features of the Ukrainian administrative system make it a cumbersome instrument to lead the country through the trying period of democratic transition and economic reforms. What is increasingly clear is that many of Ukraine's most significant obstacles to economic transition are not economic. Ukraine suffers from an acute *administrative capacity shortage,* the vestige of decades of Soviet underinvestment in the administrative apparatus of the Ukrainian SSR (see Chapter 1).

EARLY DEVELOPMENT OF KEY GOVERNMENTAL INSTITUTIONS

This section discusses recent critical developments in three key areas of government institution building in Ukraine: the Ukrainian presidency, legislative capacity, and the struggle for control of local government (which is largely a reflection of the competition between president and Parliament).

Development of the Executive Branch

In many important respects, development of the Ukrainian presidency must be considered within the context of executive-legislative relations. Under Ukraine's amended Soviet Constitution, at the time of independence in 1991, all power derived from Parliament, as the "Supreme Soviet." But in 1991, the office of president of Ukraine was effectively "grafted" onto the system of government that was inherited from the USSR. The concept of a Ukrainian presidency was originally proposed in early 1991 as the means to facilitate Ukraine's independence. Both rightist elements and the left wing found reasons to support creation of the office. Philip Roeder has argued that Communist deputies in Parliament viewed the office of president as a strong executive power over policymaking and the bureaucracy, that is, an autocratic institution that they could and would control.[97] After all, Leonid Kravchuk, the leading candidate, was *their* man. More probably, leftist forces conceded the presidency to the right in order to hold onto their positions within the apparat and to retain control over state enterprises.

The Dual Executive Structure. The result was that there was no clear "institutional rupture" with the former regime. Many Soviet officeholders retained their positions in the new regime. Especially in the bureaucracy, the continuing influence of these holdovers, coupled with relatively strong leftist forces in Parliament, has slowed the pace of economic reform nearly to a halt. The dual executive structure—having a president and a premier—contributed to the confusion, broadening the independence and latitude of bureaucratic officials to block reforms. The problem was that "the constitutional framework made it difficult for the president to prevail in the normal legislative process, and difficult for the parliament to oversee the administrative process."[98] Competition was heightened, and opportunities for cooperation in precious short supply.

In this constitutional milieu, Ukraine's first president, Leonid Kravchuk (1991–1994), preferred to work within the *nomenklatura*—"behind the scenes," as it were. Rarely confrontational, he displayed a knack for conciliation, coupled with quiet manipulation. Patronage and gamesmanship were his stock-in-trade.[99] He used the prime minister and Cabinet of Ministers more as buffers against Parliament than as a mechanism to make and implement policy.[100] His one truly active attempt to gain control of the cabinet in May–June 1993—in the waning months of Kuchma's premiership—was linked to his dwindling popularity in the face of a worsening economy and thus may be interpreted as a desperate attempt to salvage his presidency. But Parliament resisted placing more power in the presidency.

Kuchma Seeks Expanded Powers. Almost immediately upon his election, Kuchma aggressively sought expansion of presidential powers. Conflict ensued throughout 1994 and into 1995, when Kuchma pressed Parliament to conclude a "constitutional accord," known popularly as the Law on Power, to temporarily fill the role of a permanent constitution while the provisions of the constitution were negotiated. The process of enacting the law was itself the stuff of high political drama. Introduced and adopted in its first reading in December 1994, the draft Law on Power would be continuously revised throughout winter 1995.[101] Over 900 amendments were made to its fifty-six articles. Consequently, the second reading could not take place until April 1995. The process of designing the governmental power structure had become so contentious that representatives of eight parliamentary factions and deputies' groups proposed that an interim "Constitutional Agreement" be executed between president and Parliament, until such time that a new constitution could be adopted and ratified. To work out the details, the Conciliatory Commission was established, with equal membership representing Parliament and the president.[102] By April, the commission was able to agree on all substantive points, save the competence of heads of regional state administrations. Adopted on May 18, 1995, implementation of the Law on Power was to await the appropriate constitutional amendments and other necessary legislative changes.[103]

The mandatory two-thirds parliamentary majority required to amend the Constitution, in order to implement the Law on Power, proved to be an elusive objective, however. The process rapidly bogged down. Kuchma broke the logjam by threatening to hold a national plebiscite on confidence in the president and Parliament.[104] Parliament vetoed Kuchma's call for a referendum, on the basis that it violated the Constitution. Kuchma pressed on, however, issuing a decree in June that the referendum go on. In the face of this threat, and knowing that Kuchma enjoyed broader popular support, Parliament moved quickly to enact the power-sharing agreement in late May, by a vote of 240–81. The president thereby outmaneuvered Parliament into formalizing his actions of the previous year, by making regional councils accountable solely to him.[105] In order to avoid the plebiscite, which it would surely have lost, Parliament had no choice but to accept considerable restrictions on its power or else risk a permanent weakening of its position relative to the president.[106] This was clearly a substantial victory for Kuchma.

The Law on Power defined an entirely new relationship between the president and Parliament. Whereas previously the president, Parliament, and prime minister vied for dominance over policymaking, under the Power Bill, the role of the president became paramount. In effect for one year as an interim "petit constitution," the accord restricted Parliament's formal powers over approval of the budget, ratification of the government's program, and drafting of ordinary legislation. The president, however, received the exclusive right to form a government, issue decrees, appoint elected chairmen of local and regional councils as heads of their respective state administrations, and dismiss the heads of local administrations for violations of the law, the Constitution, or presidential decrees.[107] His appointment powers were sweeping: He could appoint exclusively the prime minister, cabinet, and heads of so-called power ministries (i.e., defense, foreign affairs, internal affairs, security service, and so forth) without parliamentary confirmation. The prime minister was now expressly subordinated to the president. Parliament could express "no confidence" in either the entire government or individual ministers but could not nominate successors, which was the sole prerogative of the president.

The Constitutional Process. As the Power Bill was a temporary agreement, many issues remained to be resolved. For instance, control of local government remained very ambiguous (see below). The president could appoint local and regional executives, but subnational governments remained subject to the laws and decrees of Parliament. In order to resolve this and other issues, as part of the bill's provisions, the Constitutional Committee was established to draft a new constitution within a year's time, by June 1996. The committee was to be chaired jointly by President Kuchma and Speaker of Parliament Oleksandr Moroz, his bitter rival. In many ways, the events preceding ratification of the Constitution of Ukraine, on June 28, 1996, were equally as dramatic as those leading up to the passage of the Law on Power.[108] Kuchma again threatened to hold a binding referendum in order to prod the legislature into action. Again, Parliament relented.

The Constitution establishes the basis for more effective governance in Ukraine by clarifying considerably the role of the president vis-à-vis the cabinet. But it has not completely resolved the relationship between the president and the premier. The president is the head of state (Constitution of Ukraine, Article 102), and the Cabinet of Ministers is the highest executive body, responsible to the president (Article 113). Presidential dominance over the cabinet is therefore ensured, whereas previously they were in direct competition. However, the president must now act in concert with the prime minister in order to exercise various presidential authorities, such as making certain cabinet-level appointments (Article 106). In other areas, they must work collaboratively in order to avoid unnecessary competition and rivalry. In many ways, the prime minister's position is less tenable than before. He is appointed by the president but relies upon the confidence of Parliament. He has no political base in Parliament and few formal powers. As such, he seems destined to occupy the position of "designated fall guy" when things go awry. In order to operationalize the new relationships, further legislative elaboration will be required, as well as development of informal norms and customs. Major overhauls of much existing legislation, enactment of new laws, and revisions to regulations remain necessary in order to fully implement the new constitutional arrangements. A schematic representation of the structure of the executive branch in the wake of the structural reforms of 1997 is presented in Figure 4.2.

Development of the Legislative Function

The legislative function was theoretically preeminent under the Communist system of "rule by People's Soviets." However, although the Ukrainian Verkhovna Rada predated independence, "it was not operationally independent from the institutions of the prior regime."[109] Rather, it functioned as little more than a rubber-stamp assembly for Moscow's pronouncements. Thus, building an independent, functional capacity as a legislative body with genuine policymaking capabilities is a key priority for promoting and establishing democracy in Ukraine. David Olson and Peter Norton have noted the grave dilemma facing the post-Communist legislature: Facing enormous tasks, saddled with crippling underdevelopment, it must literally "rebuild the ship at sea."[110] The key capacity-building tasks relate mainly to internal reforms; as Wise and Brown have observed in the case of Ukraine, "the slowness of establishing the parliament as an independent entity in the evolving institutional landscape is largely due to its internal inefficiencies and incapacities."[111] Legislative capacity-building therefore has several key dimensions:

117

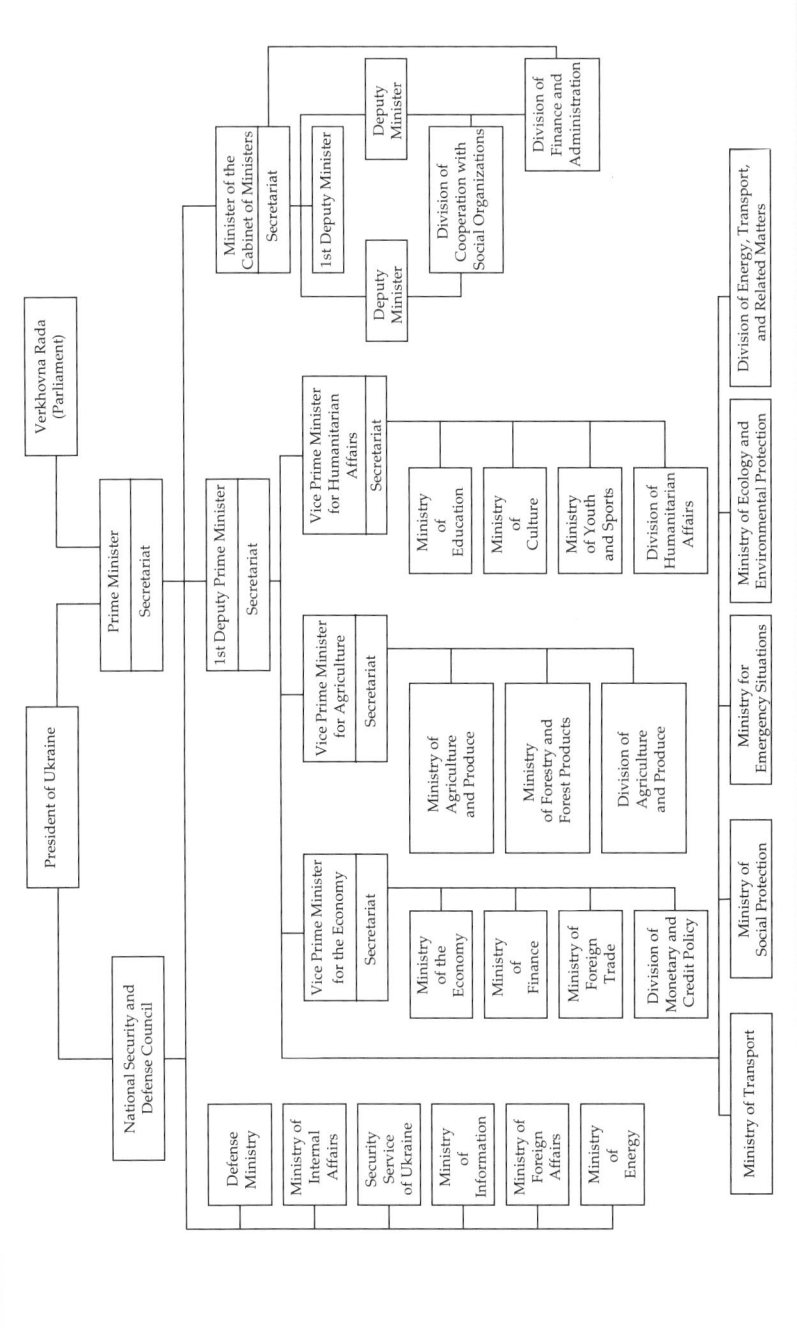

FIGURE 4.2 Structure of the Government of Ukraine, 1997

- Design of the legislative process and adoption of effective rules
- Development of the committee staff and structure
- Conduct of executive branch oversight, especially in the budgetary sphere
- Institutionalization of the role of parties and factions in the legislative process

Much remains to be done in each of these areas before the Ukrainian Parliament will be able to function as an effective lawmaking body.

Legislative Process and Rules. Under the Soviet Constitution, it was not clear which branch or body of government had responsibility for initiating legislation. Consequently, legislative initiation, research, and policy analysis were not emphasized in Parliament. Due to Parliament's largely undeveloped capacity to design and propose new legislation, much of this activity is still conducted by the cabinet ministries, which continue to be dominated by the former Soviet *nomenklatura*. The process has undergone some evolution since independence, however, especially in the role that the parliamentary leadership and committee structure play in enacting new laws.

Before 1996, the legislative process placed a great deal of power in the hands of the Speaker and the (now defunct) Presidium. The Speaker, who serves as the Rada chair, previously possessed power to suspend acts of the government, individual ministries, and other bodies subordinated to the government if they failed to comply with the Constitution and other existing legislation. The Speaker also had power to submit candidates to the Constitutional Court, Arbitrage Court, National Bank governor, and prosecutor general. The Presidium, chaired by the Speaker (and composed of the deputy speakers, chairs of standing commissions), was an important source of patronage. The Presidium determined the weekly agenda of Parliament, issued decrees concerning the structure and functions of Parliament itself, and allocated its internal resources. With the passage of the Law on Power in 1995, the heads of all parliamentary factions and groups were added to this body. Under the 1996 Constitution, the Presidium has been eliminated altogether.

The ordinary legislative process places the right of legislative initiative in the hands of the president, people's deputies, Cabinet of Ministers, and National Bank governor.[112] Committees of Parliament no longer have power to propose legislation. The right of legislative initiative for people's deputies is secured under the law, including compulsory examination of deputies' proposals, and the opportunity for sponsors to address Parliament concerning their initiatives.[113] Referrals of legislative proposals and new bills are made to the appropriate "subject matter" committees of cognizance. In the case of the annual budget bill, this will involve the Budget Committee and other permanent committees. Once a bill reaches the floor, it must be voted on and approved *twice* before it is enacted. These are referred to as votes taken on "first reading" and "second reading." If necessary, bills approved on first reading may be shelved or referred back to committee for revision. The standing committee of Parliament, together with the government, will examine all proposed amendments to the bill and make a final determination as to their acceptability. For the "second reading," all bills will be voted on the basis of an "article-by-article" vote, as well as on the bill as a whole. (If further revisions are appropriate, a "third reading" may be scheduled at this stage.) An outline of the basic legislative process in the case of the annual budget is presented in Figure 4.3.

Upon enactment, the legislation is presented to the president, who has fifteen days within which to either sign the law or veto it. If vetoed, the bill returns to Parliament, together with the president's remarks. Vetoed bills are subject to a two-thirds parliamentary override vote. Ambiguities in the existing process, however, concern whether the president must sign a bill in cases where his veto has been overridden and whether he needs to return bills he does not like at all. The rules of Parliament call for laws coming into effect upon their publication, if the president does not return the law within ten days.[114] Obviously, the president disagrees, insofar as the Constitution indicates that no law may pass into effect without the president's signature.[115] Further, the president does not consider the rules of Parliament to be law but rather an "internal document." President Kuchma clashed with Parliament in this area when he vetoed the 1997 Law on Local Self-Governments three times before relenting, having prompted a signature campaign calling for his impeachment.[116] There is therefore potential for future collisions between the branches over the override process.

Concerning parliamentary rules and procedures, a basic set of rules was enacted on July 27, 1994, replacing a set of provisional rules that were (more or less) informally followed since 1990. The 1994 rules are an amalgam of procedures in use from around the world, and some have argued that they lack consistency. Further, there are no explicit sanctions for rules violations, so that numerous infractions have taken place. The rules have not been amended since the Thirteenth Convocation of Parliament (1994), but amendments to bring them into conformity with the 1996 Constitution await their final disposition.

Committee Structure and Staff. A large amount of legislative activity occurs in plenary session, as opposed to committees. Hearings on individual bills may or may not be held. Committee recommendations are

FIGURE 4.3 Ukrainian Parliamentary Budget Process

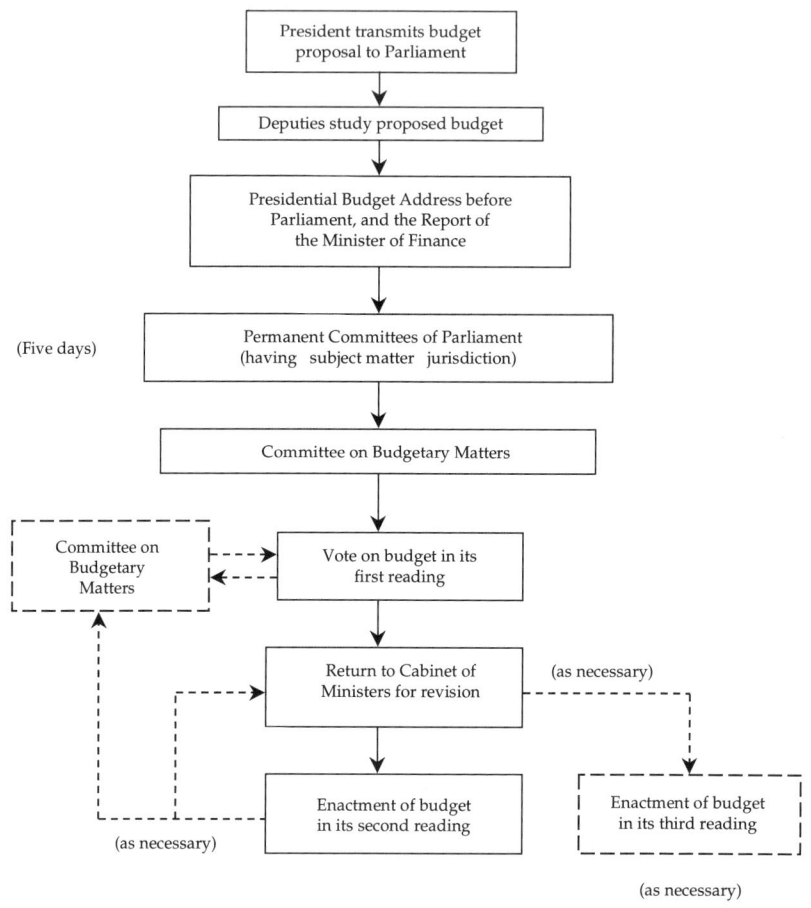

SOURCE: Adapted from Indiana University, Parliamentary Development Project, 1997. Original from "Materials Adopted by the Supreme Council of Ukraine for the Preparation of its Legislative Program, July, 1995."

reported to the full body, along with all proposed amendments, making a sham of committee deliberations. Comprehensive, written committee reports are not ordinarily provided. Consequently, multiple amendments from the floor are common, leading to much rancorous debate during plenary sessions. This creates a serious capacity constraint. Failure to enact laws over time has led to presidential frustration with Parliament, the executives' active use of "coercive decrees," and threats of binding referenda. In order to expand the volume of legislation that Parliament potentially can consider, the role of committees requires further elaboration.

The division of the work of Parliament into subject-matter committees is the common means to deal with the complexity of modern legislation, reduce uncertainty, maintain control, and expand legislative capacity. At the time of Ukraine's independence, there was no working system of parliamentary commissions in place. ("Commissions" is the term that was used to describe committees prior to adoption of the Constitution.) As of the Fourteenth Convocation of Parliament on May 12, 1998, there were twenty-two standing committees (see Figure 4.4). Deputies generally serve on one committee only. According to the rules, representation on committees is supposed to be proportional to the composition of parliamentary factions, with equal membership for all factions. The diverse interests of deputies, coupled with the fairly continuous shifting among factions, has meant that this rule has been difficult to enforce in practice.

Participation in committee work remains low.[117] The typical monthly schedule of parliamentary activity consists of two weeks in committee, one week in plenary session, and another week in the constituency. However, since all proposed amendments are reported by committees and taken up in plenary session, there is little incentive for deputies to participate in committee work. As long as most of the real work of Parliament occurs in plenary session, this will remain so.

Committee work is also hampered by a lack of adequate numbers of competent staff, which places a serious constraint on both the quantity and quality of committee work. The Secretariat of Parliament provides staff, ranging from three to eighteen individuals. Such staff are typically not well versed in the subject-matter areas of the committees to which they are assigned. Consequently, they are not able to provide appropriate levels of research or analytical support to their respective committees. The parliamentary central staff contains data processing support services and a library. However, budgetary support for these services has been low, and staff wages are subject to payments arrears. Parliament's ability to keep itself informed is therefore quite limited. This is an obvious area for future capacity-building efforts.

Budgetary Oversight. Legislative oversight of the executive has been a perennial problem since the fall of the USSR. This was especially true in the critical area of budgetary oversight. Previously, Parliament was not a participant in the formulation or execution of the budget. Budgetary oversight was, in a word, nonexistent. The original post-Soviet Law on the Budget System, and subsequent amendments, firmly established the right of Parliament to scrutinize the budget, enact tax laws, and fix the level of subnational revenues.[118] However, the role of Parliament in

FIGURE 4.4   Structure of the Ukrainian Parliament, 1998 (as of the start of the Fourteenth Convention, May 12)

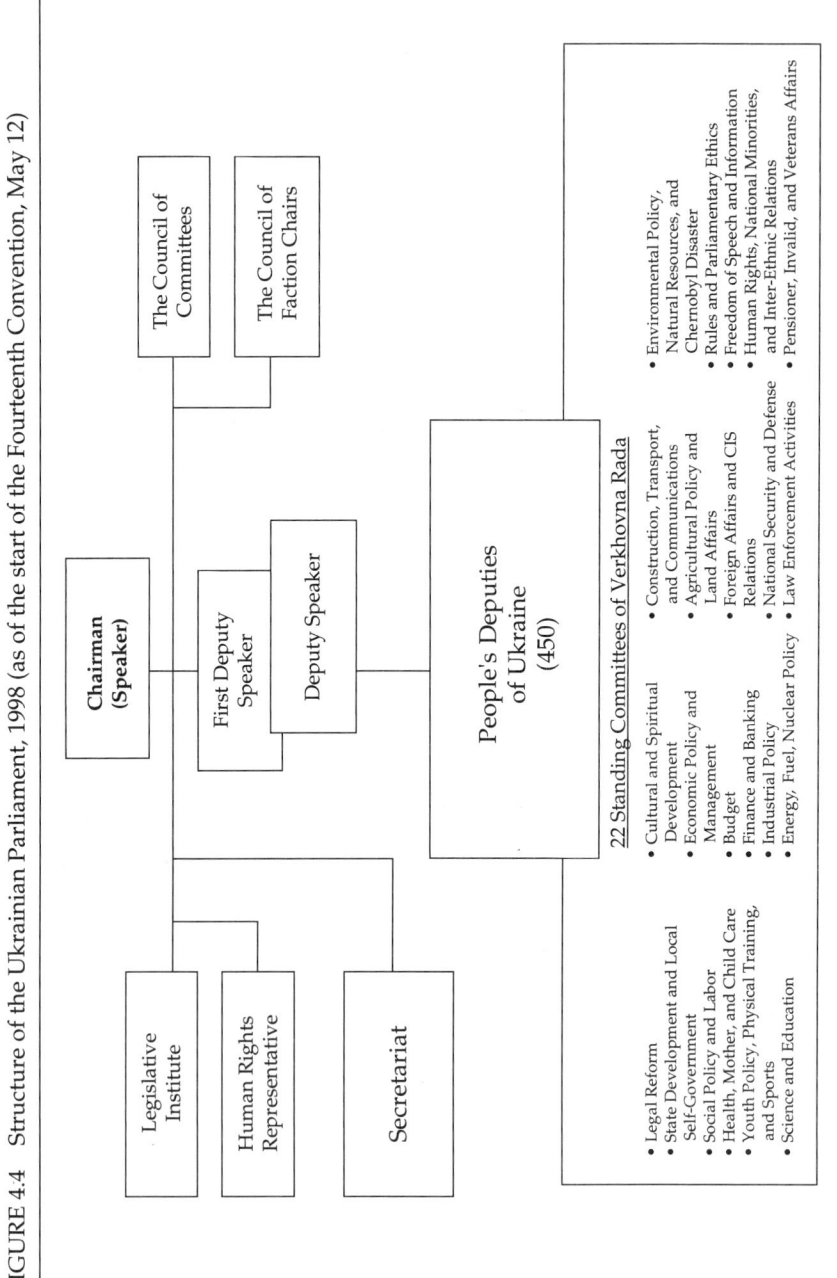

budget execution and that of the Budget Committee are not yet clearly delineated. Creation of the Accounting Chamber in 1997 has provided Parliament with the institutional means to execute budgetary oversight. The chamber has basic authority to provide Parliament with regular and consistent information on the preparation and implementation of the budget. It may perform compliance audits and special investigations of fiscal issues of concern to the parliamentary leadership, much as the U.S. General Accounting Office does for the U.S. Congress.

Parliamentary Parties and Factions. Political parties can serve an important legislative capacity-building role by coordinating legislative initiation and management of legislative business. However, development of political parties has been slow in Ukraine, particularly in the parliamentary arena. Ironically, after the 1990 elections Parliament served as the arena for development of the anti-Communist opposition. In 1990–1994, Parliament did not formally recognize parties or factions within the Verkhovna Rada itself. Deputies were able to register as members of up to two groups, but no privileges attached to their choices and factions had no formal mechanism to represent their members within the larger body. Consequently, the Presidium was predominant in the legislative process, where the factional leadership had some means to express their sentiments to the powerful Speaker, who chaired that body.

Party Discipline. Party discipline was distinctly lacking in Ukraine's first post-Soviet Parliament, except for the Communists in the so-called Group of 239, who tended to vote as a block on important economic issues. Due to their greater activism and participation within the activities of Parliament, democratic forces were able to exert a disproportionate influence in 1990–1994 on the parliamentary agenda, including setting the stage in 1990–1991 for the crucial votes on sovereignty and independence. Their numbers and voting strength, however, were small. For instance, in the March 1990 elections, 128 of the 442 deputies elected were aligned with either Rukh or the newly established democratic group Narodna Rada ("National Council"). The Communist Party of Ukraine (KPU) lost its "leading role" through the repeal of Article 6 of the 1978 Soviet Constitution. A subsequent article was amended to permit multiparty politics in Ukraine. The KPU was banned in 1991 and was to reregister in October 1993 without any of its Soviet-era property. By 1991, the Group of 239 was a divided and spent force, but that did not end leftist dominance of Parliament.

Impact of 1994 and 1998 Elections. Factions became much more crucial to the work of Parliament after the 1994 elections. The election law in effect for those elections resulted in more than 150 deputies in 1994 being

PHOTO 4.1 Demonstration outside Ukrainian Television headquarters by Christian Democratic Party of Ukraine, protesting against political censorship, Kyiv, June 1995

elected as nonparty independents. This prompted many of them to agitate for a resolution to organize Parliament into deputy factions and parliamentary groups. "Factions" were groups that had a corresponding political party outside of Parliament, whereas "groups" did not have political status in society at large but served as an organizing body only within Parliament. In practice, however, all are referred to as "factions" within Parliament. The threshold for faction membership was 25 members. Factions received office space, staff, technical support, and, from 1995 to 1996 on, a seat on the (since disbanded) Presidium. By the end of 1995, 378 out of 417 deputies were members of 11 parliamentary groups or factions. At the end of 1998, 420 deputies belonged to 10 factions (plus 27 in a nonideological faction of "Independents"). The post-1998 election factions are more in the nature of true party factions, owing to the 1997 elections law, which was more encouraging to party development. One-half of the deputies elected in March 1998 were taken from party lists, so that these new members naturally tended to group according to party affiliation. There is therefore an increasingly partisan tide in Parliament, whose development will continue in the coming years. Overall, participation in party factions since 1994 is therefore significant.

Role of Factions in the Legislative Process. Factions have not been very effective in organizing and managing the work of Parliament, however. For one thing, although the ideological poles are well established, there are many factions that fit no easy description. In the vast middle are the bulk of deputies, who, though they are members of factions, reflected no coherent ideological or issue orientation. Known as the *bolota,* or "swamp," in Parliament, their members tended to vote not as a block but according to particular issues. After the 1998 elections, there is still a broad "middle ground" of party factions and a fairly constant shifting of deputies among the factions (with more than three deputies shifting per month, effectively changing parties). Further, although the left won the largest number of seats in the 1998 elections, it does not have the "constitutional majority" necessary to control key votes, nor does it always vote as a cohesive block. Party discipline and cohesiveness, while improving, are not yet sufficiently well developed to organize parliamentary work. Finally, the weak constitutional status and role of the prime minister militate against coalition building and coordination of policymaking. In the absence of a genuine premiership, including the crucial role of party or coalition leadership, and in the face of severe institutional disadvantages vis-à-vis the president, coordination of legislative business will continue to be a haphazard procedure, at best.

The Struggle for Local Government

Regional and municipal government (all referred to as "local government" in Ukraine) has been caught up in the overall struggle between the president and Parliament over development of the executive power. At times, control over local government appeared as a goal in itself. However, at other times the objectives have been much more vague. The legislative basis for local self-government has been subject to dramatic swings, reversals, and shifts in focus, beginning in 1992. The status of local government remained unsettled after adoption of the June 1996 Constitution of Ukraine, which ought to have resolved the basic issues but has not. What follows, then, is a story without a finish, insofar as it is still being written.

Early Legislation for Local Self-Governance. The legislative basis for local government in Ukraine was established soon after the referendum on independence, in February 1992, with enactment of the Law on Local

Self-Government, which amended the 1991 Law of the Ukrainian SSR. The 1992 act granted substantial independence and powers to local governments.[119] Indeed, Article 12 stipulated that "higher-level bodies [of government] may not interfere in the development, approval and execution of local budgets."[120] The act also separated local budgets from those of higher levels, stipulating that "local budgets of single administrative and territorial units may not be included in the budgets of other units and in the state budget of the republic." In practice, however, Ukraine's regions have little fiscal independence.

The 1992 law contradicted directly the centralizing approach embodied in much existing legislation. The 1991 Law on Budget System, for instance, authorized higher-level governments to annually determine the types and levels of responsibilities they would assign to subordinate governments.[121] This provision of the law has been used fairly aggressively by Parliament in a manner that compromised almost completely the fiscal autonomy of Ukraine's regions. The Law on Budget System has been twice amended and now gives clearer definition to local tax and expenditure assignments.[122] However, subnational governments find themselves in a fiscal "vise grip," owing to a significant narrowing of the local tax base by the central government, combined with a substantial devolution of expenditure responsibilities.[123] As a practical matter, local government independence has not proved to be an entirely workable concept in Ukraine.

Kravchuk's Network of President's Representatives. There have been frequent changes to the legislative regime governing local government in Ukraine. For instance, in the very month following enactment of the 1992 law, President Kravchuk issued a decree establishing the system of "president's representatives," who were appointed as the titular heads of the oblast administrations, acting in the name of the president.[124] In April 1992, Kravchuk issued another decree, pursuant to the first, formalizing the role of president's representatives as heads of the oblast state administrations.[125] Kravchuk also terminated activities of the previous state administrations, thereby usurping even those powers previously exercised by the oblast councils but now legally in the hands of president's representatives. Later the same year, another presidential edict subordinated all local state administrations jointly to the president and the Cabinet of Ministers on all matters falling within their respective jurisdictions.[126] Parliament bore some complicity in all of this, enacting in 1992 the Law on the Representatives of the President of Ukraine, which effectively formalized presidential control of local government.[127]

Throughout 1993, discontent over the sorry state of the economy set in, becoming all the more intense during that year. Regionalism was on the rise during this period. Eastern Ukraine and the Crimea were especially adamant that regions should be permitted to reestablish economic links with regions in other former Soviet republics, unimpeded by Kyiv. The president's representatives were widely viewed as an obstacle to the fulfillment of some regions' economic aspirations. Following the June 1993 Donbas coal miners' strike and that summer's agitation for a national referendum of confidence in president and Parliament, Kravchuk issued a decree granting greater autonomy to the administrations of certain eastern oblasts for a two-year period, ending December 31, 1995.[128] Specific privileges granted to these oblasts included the right to manage and dispose of state property. This decree was widely interpreted as the means to counter separatist tendencies in the eastern provinces.

Kravchuk's Impending Exit. With the approach of the 1994 elections, Kravchuk's grip on power was in its waning moments. Popular discontent with the system of president's representatives had become universal.[129] Parliament took advantage of Kravchuk's weakness, passing the Law on Formation of Local Government Bodies, which established an entirely new structure of local government.[130] The act undermined direct presidential control by eliminating the office of president's representatives, effective June 26, 1994, the date on which new elections to local offices were to be held.[131] Far from bolstering regional independence, however, by this act Parliament introduced a new system of subordination of representative bodies, whereby oblast and raion councils were effectively converted into adjuncts of the national Parliament. This set the stage for conflict between higher-level councils and their now-subordinated local councils, as well as between councils and state administrations at all levels. Matters had become worse.

In order to strengthen his support in the regions, Kravchuk undertook two measures in 1994 that were interpreted as preludes to a comprehensive restructuring of the state. In February, he extended by decree property and entrepreneurial powers of the four oblasts of eastern Ukraine, those which had been subject to his November 29, 1993, grant of greater autonomy.[132] In March, Kravchuk ordered the wholesale transfer by July 1, 1994, to oblast capital city governments, the ownership of all state assets in housing and communal services, personal services, trade, public restaurants, urban roads, education, culture, fitness and sports, health care, and other social welfare functions.[133] Oblasts were directed to do the same for their subordinate local governments by September 1, 1994 (although Crimea was excluded from this). Lists of specific objects subject to transfer were developed by the Cabinet of Ministers. This move was intended to improve the economic strength of subnational governments. Presidential adviser Vasyl Rudenko described these actions as "serious steps towards decentralization and power-sharing between ministries and oblast administrations."[134] The regions were ecstatic in their anticipation of receiving real power. But it was not to be.

Kuchma Establishes Presidential Dominance. Kravchuk's efforts to placate the regions were to prove unsuccessful. In July 1994, running on a platform of greater regional autonomy, closer economic ties with Russia, and a looser official language policy, former Prime Minister Kuchma defeated Kravchuk's bid for reelection. Both the new president and Parliament were to make control over local government an issue of ongoing contention, however. In the wake of the presidential election, the recently elected Parliament in July approved in its first reading a new Law on Local Councils. The act—which was never to become law—was an obvious attempt by the Socialist plurality in Parliament to reestablish the Soviet system of "rule by People's Soviets." Kuchma responded in August, subordinating by decree all heads of oblast councils to the president.[135] Acting during a parliamentary recess, the president asserted his direct control over both the Cabinet of Ministers and all independently elected regional authorities. Kuchma was positioned to assume the lead role in formulating state policy.

In order to demonstrate openness on matters of regional concern and to facilitate closer cooperation between his administration and regional leaders, in September 1994, Kuchma established a new Council of Regions, composed of the heads of regional councils.[136] This body was to serve in an advisory capacity to the president on matters of regional concern.[137] But Kuchma soon became frustrated with the ability of the independently elected regional council chairs to stifle his efforts at economic reform, especially privatization. This moved the president in December to introduce a draft Law on Power, containing provisions that would clearly establish what he termed "the vertical structure of legitimate executive power."[138] Kuchma's draft would abolish the hierarchy of legislative authority, putting an end to Soviet power in Ukraine.[139] Kuchma's draft countered a parliamentary draft already in circulation, which would remove executive structures from power altogether, neutering the president in favor of consolidated "people's rule" at all levels, including all enterprises, state-owned and private.[140] The president and Parliament thus appeared headed for collision.

Impact of the "Law on Power." The "collision" resulted in the enactment of the June 8, 1995, Law on Power, whose dramatic passage was discussed above. In order to consolidate his new powers, Kuchma quickly moved to appoint all chairmen of local councils to the position of head of their respective state administrations, effectively unifying regional legislative and executive powers under the president's overall direction. Kuchma issued two decrees in August, subordinating local (municipal, raion, and settlement) councils to the president and asserting the right to dismiss council chairs from their executive position and hold new elections, if necessary.[141] However, Parliament vetoed Kuchma's decrees in November, on the basis that they contradicted existing law. Kuchma responded with a new decree, challenging Parliament's right to veto presidential edicts. In the absence of a constitutional court, the president asserted that he alone was the "guarantor of the Constitution."[142] Matters were again stalemated.[143] In a further effort to strengthen the "vertical structure of power," on January 4, 1996, Kuchma declared that the executive powers of village, settlement, and city council chairs were also subordinated to him.[144] Previously, the executive councils of these bodies, and their chairs, possessed no executive authority. Council chairs at all levels would now be accountable to the president for the administration of executive authority within their jurisdictions.

Local Governance Under the 1996 Constitution. Also in November 1995, Kuchma transmitted to Parliament a draft version of the Constitution of Ukraine. The president's draft envisioned a two-house legislature: One-third of the upper house, or "Senate," was to be represented by the heads of the regional state administrations (which the president could dismiss under his August 21, 1995, decree). All but one parliamentary faction opposed Kuchma's proposal, which was rejected in favor of the unicameral legislature inherited from Soviet times.[145] After much negotiation, the new constitution ultimately rejected the concept of federalism as an internal structure for Ukraine, in favor of a unitary state.[146] Adopted on June 28, 1996, the Constitution contains no provision for regional powers or prerogatives; there is no decentralization approach embodied in the letter of the law; regional councils are granted relatively limited powers.

The vertical structure of power under the 1996 Constitution is summarized in schematic form in Figure 4.5. The executive branch has assumed a more unified vertical authority structure than the legislative side, which is a system of highly independent councils at all levels. Heads of state administrations no longer serve in the dual role of chief of the corresponding council, as was the case under the Law on Power. Actions of lower-level councils are still subject to reversal, if they should contradict the Constitution or existing laws. But they may not now be nullified or overturned by higher-level Radas without cause.

The outcome of constitution making has clearly worked against the interests of the regions. Sarah Birch and Ihor Zinko have observed, "[T]he fact that Ukraine's constitution-making process dragged on as long as it did probably benefited Ukrainian centralists."[147] Of this, there can be no doubt. The problem is that regional governments still have no voice for

130

FIGURE 4.5 Vertical Structure of Power Under the 1996 Constitution of Ukraine[a]

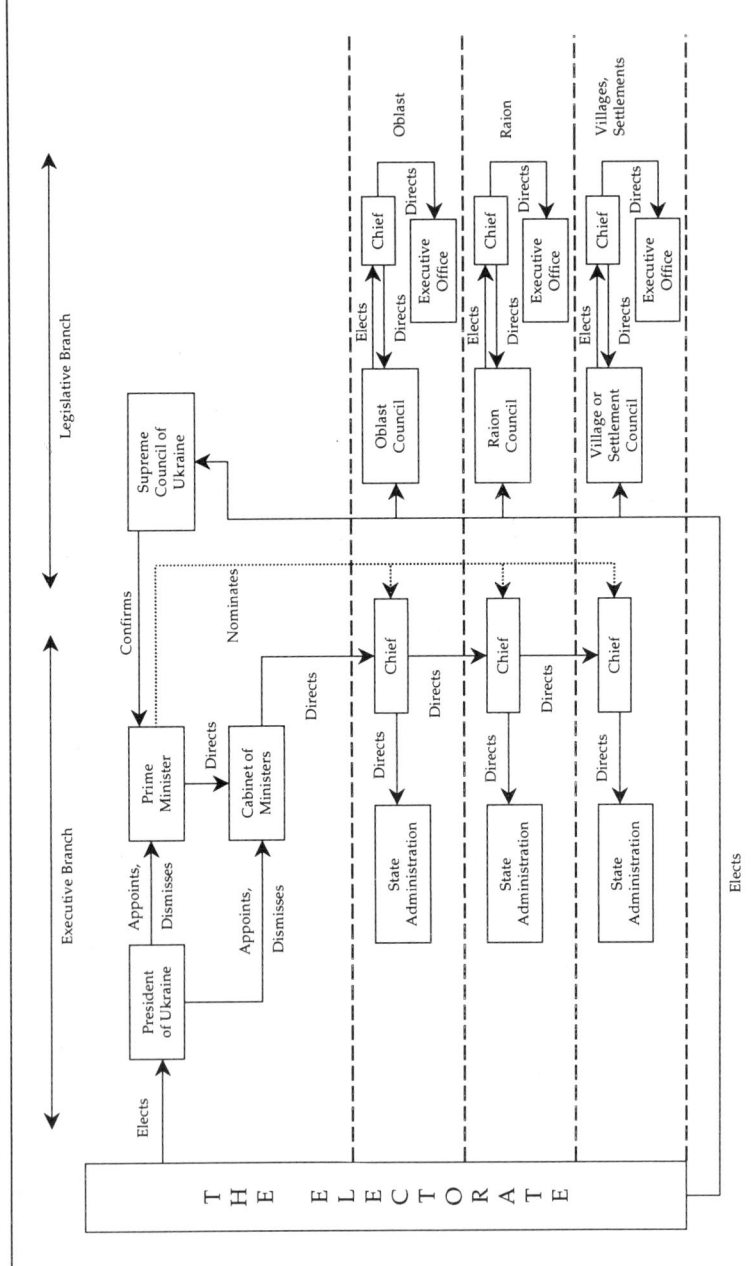

[a] "State" in this chart means "national government."

political expression in the institutional structure as framed in the Constitution. For his part, Kuchma has continued to press for an all-embracing Law on Local Self-Government in order to clarify regional prerogatives and provide well-secured revenue sources to subnational bodies.[148] The law passed in its second reading on May 21, 1997, and despite certain lingering objections to the lack of clarity in the assignment of expenditures and revenues to local government in the law, Kuchma provided his endorsement to far-reaching amendments to the existing law.[149] The new law fixes the legal status and competencies of local and regional governments on a firmer basis than the 1992 law and guarantees the exercise of self-government, in accordance with the 1996 Constitution.

The 1997 law guarantees budgetary independence and spending discretion, permitting a greater degree of fiscal flexibility to local governments, including the right to issue debt (Articles 16, 61, and 70). However, the law also contains an extensive list of "general and specific competencies (functions)" of local governments (Title 2, Articles 25–41). But the principle of subordination of lower-level governments is maintained (Article 4). Central legislative clearance is provided for, insofar as registration of statutory acts of local governments by the Ministry of Justice can be refused on the basis of nonconformance with the Constitution and laws of Ukraine (Article 19). Budgetary authority is shared with the central government, which approves the minimum local budgets sufficient to provide services at the "minimum state social standards level" (Article 61), on the basis of per capita "budgetary norms" (Article 62). In an important feature, the central government guarantees that all subnational governments will be provided with funds necessary to achieve minimum spending levels (Article 62). Unfunded mandates are explicitly prohibited (Article 67), and local governments have unrestricted use of their own off-budget funds (Article 68). Thus, budgetwise, the situation remains very much a "mixed bag."

Revenue assignment remains highly unclear under both the Constitution and 1997 law. Intergovernmental revenues are shared on a combined retention/subvention basis, just as in Soviet times. Many poor regions remain highly dependent upon the central government for necessary revenues.[150] Budgetary decisions made in Kyiv have considerable effects on the regions and localities. In their turn, oblast governments continue to make decisions concerning the intraregional allocation of funds emanating from the center (1997 law, Article 63), as well as the division of functional expenditure responsibilities among their subordinate governments. Consequently, regional and local governments remain largely "captive" to budgetary politics at higher levels. Under current law, however, local governments have much greater flexibility to develop their own-source revenues, levy and collect taxes, and control expenditures. These measures may have been too little, too late for many regions; by

1996, the combined effects of the devolution of functions from above and an eroding revenue base had reached rather dramatic proportions. In the midst of the six-year-long struggle to define the status of Ukraine's regions, many of them had become ever more fiscally dependent upon the center.

THE POLITICS OF INSTITUTION BUILDING IN UKRAINE

The Ukrainian experience with economic reform during its first four years of independent existence has been disastrous. Ukraine has been subjected to a series of unrelenting economic "shocks" (i.e., energy crisis, interruption of trade, new market competition), but without the structural "therapy" required to reallocate resources to more productive uses, which would provide the foundation for its eventual economic recovery. The lack of consistent leadership has been one major reason for Ukraine's poor reform record since 1991. This final section of the chapter illustrates the difficulties that reform leaders have had in developing the institutions necessary for the effective implementation of economic reform.

Presidents, Prime Ministers, and Policies

Since 1990, Ukraine has had three fairly distinct political regimes: a legislatively dominated regime in the period immediately following the August 1990 Declaration of Sovereignty; a mixed premier-presidential regime in the preconstitutional period, roughly from December 1991 to June 1996; and the current semipresidential regime in the post-constitutional period. During the same eight-year stretch, the country has had eight prime ministers (one of them, Vitaliy Masol, twice), twenty-eight deputy prime ministers, four finance ministers, and five ministers of the economy. The average term in office for a prime minister has been thirteen months (through May 1998—the current prime minister, Valeriy Pustovoitenko, may set the record for longevity). The average minister has served no more than twenty-four months in office.[151] The circle of people holding these posts has actually been quite narrow, however. The number of seats in eight governments from 1990 to 1997 is 284, but the number of individual officeholders totals 156. This indicates that there is a good deal of reshuffling taking place. Turnover in office has therefore been a major factor militating against continuity of policy, institutional development, and engendering new norms of political behavior.

No significant reforms were enacted under the first two premiers, Vitaliy Masol and Vitold Fokin. Fokin, in fact, believed that a "third path" between capitalism and communism could be found. Rather than subject state enterprises to the rigors of market competition, Fokin preferred to maintain the elaborate system of state "bailouts" for inefficient state-owned enterprises. Throughout the first year of "reforms," the seeds were sown for Ukraine's mammoth 1993 budget deficits and descent into hyperinflation (see Chapter 6). Masol and Fokin bequeathed to their successor, Kuchma (prime minister from October 13, 1992, through September 21, 1993), a Parliament divided over the need for genuine reforms and in which there was no consensus that expenditures ought to be controlled. Kuchma, the former director of the largest missile factory in the world, initially promised a continuation of Fokin's policies, calling for a process of "evolutionary change" and a search for a uniquely "Ukrainian model" of reform.[152]

Asserting the need for continuing administrative control over the economy, Prime Minister Kuchma proposed reorganizing Ukraine's large state enterprises into joint-stock companies, with the government retaining a controlling interest in these "corporatized" concerns. Kuchma thus initially promised no real structural change. A recurrent theme of Kuchma's policies was the need to reassert state control over the economy and to stabilize production prior to liberalization of prices and trade. On November 18, 1992, the Kuchma government was granted extraordinary powers to rule in the economic sphere for a period of six months. Kuchma's new powers enabled the Cabinet of Ministers to change existing legislation, initiate new measures, and issue decrees in pursuit of economic reforms. The only legislative limitation was that Parliament could act within ten days to reverse any of Kuchma's decrees.

The Kuchma government's "plan of action" was unveiled in January 1993. By any standard, the plan was overly aggressive. The most important objectives of Kuchma's program were to: reduce runaway spending in order to bring the deficit from its estimated level of 35 percent of GDP to within 5–6 percent; reduce inflation to a rate of 2–3 percent a month by December 1993; institute "forced privatization" measures; reform the tax system to become more progressive; break up state monopolies, offer incentives, and spur competition; and free many restrictions on exports.[153] Kuchma pursued the new program with some vigor. Implementation of the government's plan actually began in December 1992, with the passage of some twenty-six special decrees in that month alone. These initial decrees were followed by a spate of fifty-seven others throughout early 1993 (including some that amended, or even repealed, prior decrees). Important decrees passed by the cabinet during this period strengthened privatization law, forbade financing of the budget by printing money, slashed welfare payments, and began the breakup of the state's monopoly on trade.[154]

Although Kuchma's transition program was impressive in its scope and intensity, the prime minister's real powers to enact reforms were significantly limited, in that the National Bank of Ukraine and the State Property Fund remained outside of his control. Hence, the government was from the start deprived of the ability to control monetary and credit policy and move forward aggressively with its privatization agenda. These institutional shortcomings proved fatal to Kuchma's efforts. Further, the Cabinet of Ministers itself was prone to dissension, as the "Red Directors" faction of industrialists (led by Deputy Premier Volodomyr Demianov, minister of the agro-industrial complex) effectively stalled development of administrative means to implement reforms.[155] The state apparatus was, therefore, averse to reforms from the beginning.

The government's ability to execute reforms lagged significantly behind these shifts in policy. Economic performance deteriorated. Public opinion polls registered the citizens' fears that the government was bringing the economy ever closer to the brink of collapse. The government's poor performance in the economic sphere led to Parliament's refusal to extend Kuchma's extraordinary powers, which expired on May 18, 1993. The result was political chaos, without the prime minister or the president or Parliament possessing sufficient unilateral authority to either stop or implement reforms. Consequently, lack of progress on reforms in June prompted a strike by thousands of coal miners in the resource-rich Donbas (Don River Basin) region of eastern Ukraine. With the crippling effects of the 1989 miners' strike still fresh in their minds, Parliament capitulated to the miners, granting generous wage and pension increases.[156] Similar concessions were made to other industrial sectors.

Kuchma was never able to count on the support of his sponsor, President Leonid Kravchuk, who appeared willing to sacrifice the principle of economic reform for the slightest short-term political gain. Consequently, neither the president nor Parliament would wholly embrace Kuchma's economic program. It also became clear that Kravchuk was willing to sacrifice Kuchma to the Donbas mining interests. Institutionally and politically hamstrung, after several attempts, Kuchma resigned in September 1993. He was succeeded by Yukhim Zviahils'kyi, former mayor of the City of Donets'k. He was appointed to the post of acting prime minister as a gesture to the Donbas mining interests. At the same time, President Kravchuk decreed himself to be the head of the Cabinet of Ministers.[157] Now clearly in charge, he called for gradualism in market reforms, as well as a significant continuing presence for the state sector. In November 1993, Kravchuk attempted to reestablish and invigorate in Ukraine certain key features of the central planning system of the former USSR. All firms, whether state-owned, leased, or undergoing privatization, were obliged to fulfill state orders. Other decrees reasserted state intervention in foreign trade, closed the Kyiv Currency Exchange, and severely curtailed privatization activities.

Despite these attempts to "restore order in the economic sphere," inflation soared in 1993 to 45 percent in November and 91 percent in December. Real wages again began falling in the first quarter of 1994. By mid-1994, the system of state orders had broken down, a victim of the market forces that had overtaken the economy.[158] At the same time, the political climate underwent dramatic change, as parliamentary elections were held in March–April and the president was defeated in his bid for reelection in June 1994. Kravchuk's successor was his former prime minister, Leonid Kuchma.

Kuchma and the Politics of Institutional Choice

President Kuchma presented his plan for economic reforms in a speech to Parliament on October 11, 1994. Entitled "Along the Road to Radical Economic Reform," the plan reveals a president more prepared to accelerate market reform than he was as prime minister.[159] In implementing these reforms, the central challenge for Kuchma has been that the lingering ideological biases of the old regime have not permitted a wholesale shift to market-oriented institutions. A significant minority of former Communist Party members, mainly state enterprise directors from the more thoroughly "Russified" regions of eastern Ukraine and directors of state farms and collectives (the so-called lobby of Red Directors), dominated the Rada until the 1994 parliamentary elections. Elected in March 1990, more than a year before Ukraine declared its independence, many of these former Communists remained unrepentant devotees of socialism. A significant proportion of people's deputies were therefore unenthusiastic about reorienting the economy along market lines.

The March 1994 parliamentary elections did not significantly moderate Parliament's opposition to reforms. A significant left bloc of Socialists, Agrarians, and "new Communists" continued to dominate Parliament. The Speaker from 1994 to 1998, Oleksandr Moroz, was head of the Ukrainian Socialist Party and an avowed opponent of Kuchma's reform program, as was the Speaker of the newly elected 1998 Parliament, Oleksandr Tkachenko, of the Peasants Party. Indeed, the March 1998 parliamentary elections brought no significant change in Parliament's ideological "center of gravity." The parliamentary leadership has therefore been aligned against Kuchma's reform efforts since 1994, with a rather fragmented collection of reformist factions unable to bring a shift in the parliamentary focus. A further problem is that the political and personal interests of the governing elites have not favored rapid progress on reforms. Political commitments and major policy concessions made to the left under Kravchuk's regime engendered a form of "populist politics" in Ukraine, which yet seeks to preserve the socialist programs and privileges of the past, especially substantial social safety net commitments and subsidies to loss-making enterprises. Although there are fewer enterprise directors in the post-1998 Rada, they have allied themselves with their respective industry associations and trade unions to oppose reforms, especially large-scale privatization, private ownership of land, and elimination of credit subsidies.

To his credit, President Kuchma has been consistent in his efforts to implement administrative reform. In 1997, Kuchma established by decree the State Commission on Administrative Reform, chaired by former President Leonid Kravchuk. In March 1998, the commission issued a draft "concept paper," which outlines a comprehensive approach to administrative reform, covering the central machinery of government, subnational government, and civil service reform. A draft presidential edict, "On Measures to Accelerate Administrative Reform," has been prepared, envisaging three stages of reform: (1) developing the legislative basis for reform and for experimentation with alternative approaches to reform, (2) transformation of the administrative-territorial system through voluntary combinations of political units at the municipal level, and (3) transformation of the middle (raion) and higher (oblast) levels.[160]

Meanwhile, Kuchma's political objectives include developing an independent basis of support among the emerging commercial interests in

PHOTO 4.2   Ukrainian National Assembly members of Parliament in military fatigues, Parliament, summer 1994

Ukraine—mainly young entrepreneurs—who would benefit the most from his reform policies. These new entrepreneurs could potentially serve as a counterweight to the still powerful "old-guard" Communist apparatchiki and the "new Communists" and Socialists in Parliament. Unfortunately, institutional reform has been caught up in the struggle for control of the state itself, which, due to its poor policy performance, has had the unfortunate effect of reinforcing the struggle. In this environment, the formulation of rational policy for governmental reform has been an elusive goal. Institutional and administrative improvements have been all but completely stymied by the interplay of these factors.

In the Ukrainian situation, the systemic forces operating at the level of administrative-institutional choice have been crucial. The central problem of state capacity development in Ukraine is the capture of various elements of the administrative and policy machinery by powerful interests outside of the state. These groups are far from having a benign interest in the efficient operation of government. Structural changes are evaluated from the standpoint of individual or group interests and opportunities to gain influence over policymaking and execution.[161] It seems clear after eight years that the Ukrainian state has been effectively penetrated by powerful interests that have compromised its ability to represent the broader public interest. The distributional aspects of structural choice have therefore tended to predominate.[162] Institutional choice is contextual, insofar as the preferences of key political actors, the organization of interests supporting these actors, and the context of decisions about institutional choice are major considerations.[163] The formal arrangements have been designed, at least in part, to benefit those who control the process of institutional-administrative choice. In Ukraine, this has been the so-called party of power: influential former Communists who form a fairly tight circle of political allies and who, together with Ukraine's national Communists led by Kravchuk, made an independent Ukraine possible during 1990–1991. In the Kuchma period, these political forces remain in place; he has been unable to unseat them, at times seeming to be one of them. The redistributive effects of state administrative capacity-building would therefore seem to require some insulation from the undue influence of these and other economically powerful groups. This highlights the critical importance of the connection between governance capacity and state autonomy and the special place of the latter in institutional development.

Governance Capacity, State Autonomy, and the Rule of Law

Governance capacity depends vitally upon *state autonomy*, a necessary, but not sufficient, condition for effective public administration. In general, states must be able to pursue goals that are not merely the demands of particular groups, classes, or interests in society. Decisionmakers must be able to pursue the general interest and therefore must possess a minimum degree of insulation from group pressures. This has been recognized by some authorities as a basic prerequisite for effective development policy.[164] It requires, first, that the state itself be differentiated from the society over which it rules. That requires making the intellectual leap from socialism to liberal democracy. Indeed, a central feature of liberal democracy may be the very differentiation of the state from civil society.[165] Increasing differentiation of the state from society poses a particularly difficult undertaking for the remnants of the Soviet political system, which was based on an ideology that admitted of no separate conceptual identities for the people, the party, and the state. The relative autonomy of the state from society will therefore necessitate development of a legal order characterized by a high degree of public and positive law, which are the very foundations of the rule-of-law regime. Natural rights and liberties of citizens are obviously a central concern. But the positive and public aspects of the law also serve to ensure that no single entity—the state included—has sufficient power to capture entirely the public administration, to the exclusion of all other interests.

Ironically, the path by which Ukraine has moved to expand its autonomy has acted so as to constrain its range for autonomous action. President Kravchuk was the key figure in Ukraine's early state-building enterprise. In his efforts to assert state authority over the economy, new mounds of administrative regulations, licensing requirements, and tax laws and selective loopholes were employed. Rather than strengthen the state, these measures positioned the state administration to dispense favors and patronage and to exact valuable rents from commercial interests. Kravchuk thus made the state itself an important arena of economic competition, albeit not the only one. A concomitant effect of the proliferation of administrative controls in 1993–1994 was to encourage "spontaneous" privatization and growth of the informal sector.[166] By early 1996, estimates placed the "underground" economy at 50–60 percent of Ukraine's "real" national product.[167]

CONCLUSION: IS THERE A "GOVERNANCE CRISIS" IN UKRAINE?

Deficiency in administrative capacity is one problem in a complex of factors preventing effective economic and political reform in Ukraine. Building effective governmental institutions should receive greater priority if Ukraine is to successfully make the transition to a market economy. To accomplish this, Ukraine has begun to abandon the tools and instruments by and through which political and economic conflict was managed under the Soviet regime, namely, directed credits, subsidies, patronage, and the selective distribution of rents. But little else has been developed to fill the void left by the receding socialist state. Over time, nonreform of the state has become less of an option. This is precisely because the cost of failure is so high: Sacrifices made and hardships endured for little or no real improvement in the material quality of life will inevitably take a toll on the populace and erode their patience.

There clearly are deep-rooted antimarket biases in Ukraine, vestiges of the former regime. Many view market forces and profit motives, philosophically, as unproductive and even predatory. In the minds of many Ukrainians, the current hardships are associated with capitalism itself rather than with the "aftershocks" of the Soviet collapse. Further, a strong, centralizing statist tradition does much to inhibit acceptance of the state's new, more indirect role in economic management. The paradox for Ukrainian policymakers is that reduced direct government control is called for precisely at the time that their socialistic instincts tell them that *more* controls are necessary in order to moderate, indeed, to "humanize," the market. But at the same time, they know that reassertion of administrative control would only intensify the pain of transition, especially in the short run. In the long run, development of Ukraine's capacity to govern is likely to be an intermittent and punctuated process, not a sustained, smooth, and steady improvement. The intensity of institutional development that is required varies directly with the level of capacity required to achieve particular economic and social objectives. Building institutional capacity takes time and effort and does not follow a smooth, upward-sloping path. Reversals can, and should, be expected. The effective implementation of economic reforms is therefore likely to be similarly punctuated. It will certainly require more time than advocates of the "big bang" approach would prefer.

It is impossible to specify with certainty the precise path of institutional development that Ukraine will follow. The general direction is discernible, however, based on assessment of the most critical needs. It seems clear that over the longer haul, development of governance capacity in Ukraine will depend upon the empowerment of middle-class and commercial interests, which will benefit from the reformed economy. Capacity-building is not only a necessary and important long-run endeavor. It can also make an important contribution to economic reform in the short run, thereby increasing the political sustainability of the entire reform effort. President Kuchma has sought to send a powerful signal to his countrymen by making the commitment necessary to transform the public administration, albeit with much resistance from below and only marginal successes. Many ordinary Ukrainians, and many in the bureaucracy itself, will be unwilling to believe that real change is in the offing, unless and until the government reforms itself from within.

The government's commitment to reform must be clear and unambiguous. Greater clarity is needed concerning the new rules of administrative behavior. At present, ambiguous rules and signals make it difficult for many in the state apparat to accept the inevitability of reforms. The apparatchiki are therefore skeptical about reform generally, and suspicious of the government's motives. Public policy is unfortunately still viewed as a mere "assertion of particular interests" rather than as "promoting the general welfare." Under these conditions, political discourse becomes charged with emotional rhetoric and is vitriolic and lacks credibility. The government's commitment must therefore be genuine and consistently reinforced in order to be credible.

Some indigenous writers have suggested that Ukraine is in a crisis of governance, that the government must first reassert its authority and "restore order" before real reforms are possible.[168] But crises of such intensity generally arise when the state's capacity to maintain law and order is in question. Ukraine clearly has no serious "law and order problem." The crime rate is on the rise and corruption is rampant, but there is nothing in the way of a general breakdown of civic life, let alone on a scale that would threaten the existence of the state. Nonetheless, the government's policies *are* inconsistent and *do* lack coherence; they have been erratically formulated, poorly implemented, and selectively enforced. A high degree of penetration of the state machinery by particularistic interests is much in evidence. These are problems that authoritarianism will not solve and may even exacerbate. But the state remains weak and does not have everything its own way; there are limits to its power, and ordinary Ukrainians are able to sense the limits of state action. On balance, it is safe to say that the Ukrainian state today, while not perfect, suffers no acute crisis of legitimation. There is therefore no "governance crisis," per se. Rather, the state system has reached an unstable political equilibrium at a very low level of institutional development. The status quo is not sustainable over the long run, due to the divergent interests that are placing pressures on the state, particularly increasingly powerful commercial interests. The question remains whether the Ukrainian state will rise to this challenge or fall deeper into the quagmire.

■ FIVE ■

Politics and Civil Society

The Soviet regime sought to eliminate an independent role for society in politics, instead preferring that society participate in politics only in ways prescribed and delimited by the state. For that reason, Ukraine achieved its independence in 1991 with only faint traces of a civil society, that is, a society that sees itself playing an active role in a democratic political system. Among the major tasks for Ukrainian society has been the development of civil society, and one of the major puzzles for social scientists has been understanding how this might occur. Especially in the political party system, we see that Ukraine has a long way to go in this area. The development of Ukrainian civil society and multiparty parliamentary politics has been dominated by four issues.

First, the twin legacies of external rule and totalitarianism impose substantial barriers to the development of civil society. Civil society has deep roots only in western Ukraine, where it has a strong tradition going back to the second half of the nineteenth century. The Soviet totalitarian system destroyed all vestiges of an already weak civil society in eastern and southern Ukraine and undermined that in the western region as well. Centuries of external rule have also created a Ukrainian left that is not fully committed to statehood. Civil society in Ukraine is therefore both being revived *and* invented. President Leonid Kuchma believes that the majority of Ukraine's parties still "express the interests of an insignificant, minuscule part of Ukraine's citizenry. And a number of them are simply oriented towards certain ambitious individuals or exist because of electoral campaign considerations," and further, "the party serves as an umbrella, some as political camouflage, and some as a milking cow."[1]

Second, the fact that the largest political party in Ukraine, the Communist Party, is as much Russian as Ukrainian in its nationalism (as expressed

---

*The authors would like to thank, at the University of Birmingham when this was written, Oliver Vorndran, a Ph.D. student, and Marc Nordberg, an M.A. student, both of whom provided research and writing on earlier drafts that were incorporated into this chapter.

by their support for rejoining Ukraine and Russia) leads to the prioritization by some democratic parties of the "defense of statehood" over political and economic reform. This has played an important role in reducing the political constituency for reform (see Chapter 4). Those who support reform and increasing the distance between Ukraine and its Soviet past are usually also advocates of Ukrainian statehood. This link between support for reform and statehood declines as one moves across Ukraine's political spectrum from the radical right to the radical left.[2]

Third, political reform has developed slowly, with a constitution only adopted in June 1996 (see Chapter 4). This constitution, however, did not resolve the deadlock between the legislature and executive, which has also seriously hampered reform. Finally, it remains questionable whether Ukraine's ruling elites favor a robust civil society, independent media, the rule of law, and strong political parties. They certainly pay lip service to them, particularly in the drive to "return to Europe" (see Chapter 7), but it is not always clear that Ukraine's ruling elites would welcome developments that would circumscribe their ability to pursue their own goals freely. Dmytro Vydryn, a former presidential adviser to Kuchma, believes that a fully developed civil society "is very inconvenient for the authorities," as it would prevent abuse of power, authoritarianism, and large-scale corruption.[3]

This chapter is divided into two parts. The first part places politics, democratization, and civil society in Ukraine within a theoretical framework. The second part is divided into three sections that survey the evolution of Ukraine's civil society since the late Soviet era, the creation of a multiparty system and parliamentary politics in post-Soviet Ukraine.

DEMOCRATIZATION AND CIVIL SOCIETY: THE THEORETICAL FRAMEWORK

In 1992, Ukraine emerged from the Soviet Union after decades of totalitarianism and centuries of external domination. One of the greatest challenges facing states such as Ukraine is the transformation from totalitarian communism and external domination to an independent democratic system. Democratic transition has been studied for many years within the context of Latin America and postcolonial Africa, and the verdict is that all too often these states fail in this democratic transition and revert to authoritarianism. Complicating this picture is the fact, as Valerie Bunce has pointed out, that

> in Eastern Europe, the political tasks of transition are much more complex than in Latin America and Southern Europe, since the question is one of building rather than rebuilding democratic institutions. Unions, parties, in-

terest groups, the institutions of decision making and representation, the rule of law, and other foundations of a liberal political order must be constructed virtually from scratch.[4]

Ukraine's four-pronged transition of democratization, marketization, state building, and nation building during a socioeconomic crisis complicates the process of democratization even further. Only western Ukraine has a tradition of civil society and political parties, both of which are necessary for democratization.[5] Moreover, the overall weakness of national identity in Ukraine calls into question whether there is a single political community in which a civil society can take root.

Political scientists usually define three stages in the transition from totalitarianism/authoritarianism to democracy: liberalization, democratization, and democratic consolidation. Liberalization took place in Ukraine beginning in 1985 and continuing through 1992; essentially, this meant ending authoritarianism and creating space for a variety of political actors to assert themselves. Democratization began in 1991 with the initial setting up of post-Soviet institutions and the first post-Soviet elections. That process continues today. Consolidation remains problematic in the Ukrainian case. Although there is some evidence of consolidation, such as the successful turnover of power, in many basic respects democracy seems to be in its infancy, with consolidation a long way off. The whole question of the "rule of law" and the administration of justice is one example.

Andreas Schedler has explored these stages further by describing two stages between the authoritarian regime and advanced (consolidated) democracy. These are electoral democracy, which is democratic in the most fundamental sense of having free and fair elections, and liberal democracy, which goes beyond elections to include genuine political competition and effective rule of law. The transition from authoritarian rule to advanced democracy is not always a one-way process. Democratic erosion can occur when the regime falls back from a liberal to an electoral democracy. Democracy is deepened when society evolves from electoral through liberal to advanced democracy. However, some societies can revert fully to an authoritarian regime after evolving as far as a liberal democracy. It is rare, though, that societies that have consolidated their democracies revert.[6]

Ukraine is an unstable democracy in which there is extreme pluralism, which creates difficulties for the decisionmaking process and can lead to paralysis of the state.[7] Extreme pluralism is characteristic of countries such as Ukraine that have rapidly become democracies overnight, and as Samuel Huntington argued, when new and weak state institutions are met with increasing demands from a rapidly democratizing society, the state (and democracy) will sometimes collapse under the weight of societal demands.⁸ This, many scholars argue, is the threat to democracy in the post-Communist states.⁹

Ukraine has made some evident progress in democratization. It has passed Samuel Huntington's "two-turnover test," which posits that democracy is established when there have been two handovers of power from the losers of elections to the winners. These turnovers are essential because they indicate that elites have enough confidence in the durability of the democratic process and in the willingness of their opponents to play by the rules to expect that if voted out of office, they will get a reasonable chance to win power back in future elections. In Ukraine, this has happened in parliamentary elections in March 1994 and March 1998 and in presidential elections in July 1994. New presidential elections are scheduled for October 1999, and there are as yet no signs that Leonid Kuchma will not leave office if defeated. Indeed, political power is sufficiently divided in Ukraine that it would likely be impossible for someone who lost an election to simply refuse to go.

A new constitution adopted in June 1996 has won praise from the Organization for Security and Cooperation in Europe (OSCE) and the Council of Europe. Nevertheless, Ukraine still does not possess a consolidated democracy. Paul Kubicek has characterized countries such as Ukraine as "delegative democracies." These possess political systems that meet the formal requirements of democracies "but whose actual practice resembles that of an authoritarian state."[10] In "delegative democracies," elections determine who will run the country, but that person or group then is able to rule largely unchecked. Russia therefore fits in the same category. The Ukrainian media are not completely free. Some newspapers are closed because of their ties to presidential opponents (for example, *Pravda Ukrainy, Vseukrainskiye Vedomosti*). Relations between the executive and legislature are strained. The rule of law is still weak, corruption is widespread, and citizens feel helpless when defending their rights.

Consolidated democratic societies have a high level of information on public affairs, a widespread sense of civic responsibility, capacities to share the values of others, multi-issue rather than single-issue orientations, trust and confidence in the human environment, and freedom from anxiety.[11] Democratic consolidation is also consistent with institution building through the government, parties, parliament, and state bureaucracy.[12] Most of these elements are still missing from Ukraine.

DEMOCRATIZATION AND CIVIL SOCIETY: UKRAINE

Gabriel Almond argued that "every political system is embedded in a particular pattern of orientation to political actions."[13] Politics expresses the collected values and identity of a community that is in the throes of transition from traditional to modern society. If this is so, it follows that a society's culture may in some way make it more or less able to function democratically. A key question for post-Soviet states has been whether they possess the cultural prerequisites for democracy after so many years of authoritarian and totalitarian rule. The need for cultural evolution is a centerpiece of the modernization approach to development. Particularism and diffuse identities will continue to exist in modern societies because old patterns and values are never completely eliminated. These traditions are the basis of the identity in which the new modern community will be grounded.[14]

Political or civic culture provides "guidelines" for acceptable political behavior, while for the community, it provides a "systematic structure of values and rational considerations." These "guidelines" are socialized through the spirit that permeates public institutions; the collective image of citizens; the style and operating codes of leaders, values, beliefs, and symbols; as well as political ideas and norms in the polity. It is not true that newly established states attempt to create political cultures from scratch.[15] Political cultures never replace old ones—they merge with them.[16]

Lucian Pye elaborated this as follows:

> The notion of political culture assumes that the attitudes, sentiments, and cognitions that inform and govern political behavior in any society are not just random categories but represent coherent patterns which fit together and are mutually reinforcing. In spite of the great potential for diversity in political orientations, in any particular community there is a limited and distinct political culture which gives meaning, predictability, and form to the political process. The concept of political culture assumes that each individual must, in his own historical context, learn and incorporate into his own personality the knowledge and feelings about the politics of his own people and community.[17]

Although "political culture" is not in vogue among political scientists, it is clear throughout the post-Communist world that institutional analysis by itself does not explain how polities function. The same set of institutions adopted from some Western democracy into some newly democratizing state can function entirely differently, not only because of the different cultural base on which the institutions are placed but also because through a different process of development, a different set of formal norms and informal practices will develop to determine how the legal language of a constitution is enacted in practice. Thus, the inchoate state of Ukrainian political culture and the absence of a firm tradition of civil society are important to understanding the institutional shortcomings of the Ukrainian state and the slow pace at which democratization appears to be taking place. Only by understanding this relationship can we understand why, for example, an electoral system quite similar to that used in Poland and Germany leads to a very different sort of party system and a parliament that is divided and ineffectual.

The lack of a civil society is a large problem that post-Communist countries, such as Ukraine, have to surmount. Civil society "is a part of society which has a life of its own, which is distinctly different from the state, and which is largely autonomous from it."[18] The right to private property, a middle class with its own business interests separate from those of the state, and plurality of autonomous spheres in religion, economics, culture, and the intelligentsia are still absent. Civil society also requires that the state (or government) be limited in the scope of its activities but that at the same time it also protect civil society and its necessary liberties.

A robust civil society at a time of socioeconomic crisis may not be welcome to the Ukrainian authorities. Such a civil society would protect society from authoritarianism, make the authorities more accountable, and increase the danger of exposure and prosecution of corrupt practices. Civil society, though, remains weak, as can be seen in the following three tables. Table 5.1 shows two things. First, while a majority of people feel that they can speak freely, a substantial minority of them continue to feel they cannot. Second, that number is not decreasing. Table 5.2 shows that Ukrainian citizens feel that there are very few avenues open to pursue their grievances. The feeling that one can get results through the political system is one of the hallmarks of civil society, but it is largely absent in Ukraine, where survey as well as anecdotal data indicate a cynicism toward government that would shock most Americans. Table 5.3, also a staple of research on civic culture in many countries, indicates that few Ukrainians belong to civic organizations of any type. This means that there are few organizations that are not mediated by the state and few organizations in which individuals can combine to make demands on the state. And even on this list, the largest category, labor unions, is still largely under state control. In sum, Ukrainian society remains highly atomized and leaves citizens few ways to make demands on their government.

TABLE 5.1 Can People Freely Express Their Opinions in Ukraine Today (%)?

	1994	1996	1998
Yes	55	60	54
Difficult to answer	30	26	28
No	15	14	18

SOURCE: Poll conducted by Democratic Initiatives, Institute of Sociology, and SOTSIS-Gallup, *Den'*, 23 September 1998.

TABLE 5.2 If Your Rights Have Been Violated, What Would You Consider to Be Effective and Acceptable?

	1994	1995	1996	1997
Election campaigns	15.5	14.8	13.7	10.1
Petition signature collections	17.0	16.7	12.7	11.3
Lawful meetings/demonstrations	16.6	16.2	15.2	14.8
Strikes	7.9	7.9	7.4	6.9
Boycott	7.1	7.0	6.6	5.1
Unlawful meetings/demonstrations	2.2	2.6	2.2	2.7
Unlawful strikes	1.6	1.8	1.9	2.3
Violence	3.0	4.1	2.5	3.9
None	31.9	36.9	33.5	37.3
Difficult to answer	29.8	27.2	33.3	33.4

SOURCE: *Ukrainian Society, 1994–1997* (Kyiv: Democratic Initiatives, 1998).

TABLE 5.3 Membership of Civic Groups

	1994	1995	1996	1997
Club	2.0	1.7	1.6	1.5
Political party	0.7	0.6	0.5	0.4
Movement	0.4	0.3	0.4	0.4
Environmental	1.3	1.7	0.9	0.6
Public org.	0.9	0.4	0.6	0.6
Trade union	6.0	5.2	3.3	2.9
Artist union	1.2	0.8	0.4	0.1
Sports club	3.2	2.5	2.7	3.3
Student	1.7	1.7	1.6	1.4
Religion	3.0	3.7	3.3	2.5
Farmers union	0.7	0.3	0.2	0.2
Other	0.7	1.0	1.1	0.3
None	82.2	84.1	86.7	88.0
No response	0.9	0.1	0.0	0.0

SOURCE: *Ukrainian Society, 1994–1997* (Kyiv: Democratic Initiatives, 1998).

PARLIAMENTARY POLITICS

This section explores the progress made by Ukraine along the path of democratization and the creation of a civil society. In particular, we examine the development of political parties and parliamentary factions in Ukraine in an attempt to judge the stability of the political system and the progress Ukraine has made toward a consolidated democracy. The essential link between society and the state in a democracy is the intermediate associations—political parties and interest groups—that form on behalf of citizens to represent their diverse interests to the state. These intermediate associations, no matter how much we enjoy complaining about them, play an essential role in aggregating and channeling public opinion between the multitude of citizens and the single state.

Ukraine gained independence in December 1991 when the Soviet Union collapsed, due in large measure to the actions of Ukraine and Russia (see Chapter 1). In the years immediately preceding this event, nationalist opposition to Soviet rule had been growing. However, the nationalist opposition alone did not have the institutional strength to gain independence for Ukraine, which was achieved only when a significant portion of the Ukrainian Communist leadership (the so-called national Communists) also chose independence for the state.[19] Essentially a quid pro quo was reached: National Communists supported independence in return for nationalist tolerance of continued rule by the former Communist elite. In a possibly unique situation of imperial disintegration, we then have a country experiencing both replacement in western Ukraine and transformation of the ruling elite.[20] The nationalists had gained legitimacy in much of the country and come to power at the same time as the old Communist elite reinvented itself and thereby retained some popular legitimacy and most of the institutional power. This means that during the process of Ukrainian state building a variety of groups have competing claims on the political and economic resources of the state.

The blessing of the Ukrainian revolution is that it was completely peaceful, but the cost of that peace was the absence of revolution: The ruling elite was not removed from power, and the old institutional system was not decisively rejected. Rather than building new state institutions and political groups from scratch, Ukrainian society has been attempting to transform old Soviet institutions and practices into new, post-Soviet, democratic forms. In the short term, transforming was easier than inventing anew, because there was much to work with and there was no need to start from scratch. But by starting with the Soviet institutions and elites largely intact, the possibilities for transformation have been limited by the materials bequeathed and by the active role played by the Soviet elite in defending its interests in post-Soviet Ukraine.

Parliaments in developed Western democracies are structured along fairly stable party lines. This is not the case in newly democratic states, where political parties as institutions take some time to coalesce into lasting entities. In Ukraine, there is no developed party system due to the legacies of external domination, an atomized post-Communist society, and the legacy of totalitarianism inherited from the Soviet Union. Instead, a multitude of parties have arisen in Ukraine (there are over forty regis-

PHOTO 5.1   Communist demonstration, Kyiv, summer 1993

tered parties). Because of this, few parties in Ukraine possess either the personnel or resources to effectively propagate policy, creating a weak party structure in the country. Most important, the combination of the fragmented party structure and the election laws means that Ukraine has never had a majority party or coalition in Parliament, which is considered a requirement for the legislature to operate in most democracies.

The emergence of a multiparty system in Ukraine is a relatively new phenomenon;[21] the majority of its political parties were only established after the March 1990 republican and local elections during the period from spring 1990 to spring 1991.[22] One author has divided the development of Ukraine's multiparty system into three periods: "preparty" (mid-1988–December 1989), "multiparty" (spring 1990–August 1991), and "post-Communist parties" (August 1991 onward).[23] Pre-1991 parties were often national democratic and propelled Ukraine to independence. From 1992 on, centrist and extreme left-wing parties have grown, with many of them from eastern-southern Ukraine, which largely remained quiescent during Ukraine's drive to independence (with the important exception of Donbas miners).

There is a high degree of overlap among party platforms but relatively little consolidation,[24] because many parties were formed around a particular leader. Parties in general have failed to establish themselves in rural areas or small towns and are still relatively weak and have limited appeal to the public (which is suspicious of the word "party") and to young people. The two largest political parties remain Rukh (the successor to the nationalist movement of the same name) and the Communist Party of Ukraine (KPU). The combined strength of all political parties never exceeds 35–40 percent in opinion polls, and few are still able to establish a solid social base of support because of the lack of development of both civil society and a market economy.

Three factors seem to explain the weakness of political parties in Ukraine. First, due to the Soviet experience, party loyalty tends to be equated with lack of freedom. Therefore, party members who disagree with a given policy are more likely to leave the party than to toe the line. This tendency has plagued Rukh since 1991. Second, party politics in Ukraine is highly personalized, such that many major parties focus not on a key issue but on a leading individual. This makes it much less likely that parties with similar outlooks will combine to increase their power, since one of the individual leaders would have to surrender party leadership (and leaders with close ideological positions are sometimes bitter personal rivals).

Third, the electoral system has only slowly encouraged parties to combine for the sake of survival. Under the new election law, half the members of the Verkhovna Rada are elected under a party list system, in which any party that receives under 4 percent of the vote receives no seats. This creates an incentive for parties to merge, but it may take several election cycles for that result to occur. For example, two similar western Ukrainian reform parties each gained between 3 and 4 percent of the vote, which meant that neither gained seats. With the threshold set low, at 4 percent, there will probably still be a large number of parties in Parliament, as that is not an extremely difficult threshold to meet (in Germany, Poland, and Russia, the threshold is 5 percent, which would have eliminated two parties in Ukraine's 1998 elections).

Apathy is increasing, and the voting public had already become disillusioned with parliamentary politics after only the first general and local election in March 1990. The socioeconomic crisis and failure of independence to bring the fruits of higher standards of living rapidly to the dinner table also played a role. This apathy and growing social discontent are leading to two outcomes. First, support for the left is growing. Second, public apathy is growing, with citizens feeling helpless and thereby believing that they cannot influence their own lives. Apathy is particularly prevalent among young people (a striking 50 percent of Ukrainians do not care about politics).[25] These trends are important because they contradict the intuitively plausible notion that Ukraine's deficit in civil society will naturally erode as it moves further in time away from the Soviet Union and as the most conservative older generations die off. On the contrary, a poorly functioning democracy might undermine civil society. It may not matter if the young are much more reform-oriented than the old if the young opt out of the political process.

The character of Ukraine's multiparty system is such that "the majority of the parties were formed not on the principle around some idea or world view, but grouped round a certain initiative group and after this just a leader."[26] The locality of the parties means that they are often only based in the capital city and oblast centers. Only in Galicia do parties have branches at the local (raion) level.[27] In Autumn 1990, Levko Lukianenko, then leader of the Ukrainian Republican Party (URP), complained that neither Rukh nor the URP had established branches at the raion level: "We, democratic leaders, are still not able to raise five million up from the 52 million people of Ukraine."[28]

Political parties in Ukraine are still weak and largely unpopular among the public at large. When polls have been conducted throughout Ukraine, the popularity of democratic groups is seen to be low in most areas, whereas there always remains a large discrepancy in their popularity between western-central and eastern-southern Ukraine.[29] Opinion polls conducted since the early 1990s have consistently showed that political parties have been unable to break through to achieve widespread popularity. A major factor revealed by opinion polls is that the majority of Ukrainians still do not know the programs of political parties.[30] Rukh and the KPU attract large negative ratings in eastern and western Ukraine, respectively.

Therefore, rural areas and small towns are hardly touched by Ukraine's multiparty system, and the party activists often live in, and work within, their own isolated circles. Although the post-1998 Rada now has several factions, all of which are tied to party membership, there was until recently little recognition in the public's eye of the activity of political parties in parliamentary struggles.[31] Limited access to the mass media and limited foreign links are also additional handicaps for political parties.[32]

In Ukraine *no* political party has yet reached the stage of a mass party. They still remain small in membership, have no social base, and continue attempting to map out an ideological profile. Meanwhile, they have to deal with daily problems (organizing campaigns, printing, finding financial sponsors, and so forth). The results of the various elections and referenda since 1990 have also shown that all non-Communist political parties could command no more than 25–33 percent of the all-Ukrainian vote,[33] and surveys still show that no single political party would be able to obtain more than 10–15 percent.[34]

Many of the political organizations resemble parties less than "political camps" and "movement mentalities."[35] The most significant indicator, perhaps, of the irrelevance of political parties is that neither of Ukraine's presidents has seen the need to belong to one. President Kravchuk's "Party of Power" of "sovereign Communists" was never formalized into a political party or movement. Kuchma first flirted with the Inter-Regional Bloc of Reforms (MRBR) and then threw in his lot with the People's Democratic Party (NDPU) and the Agrarians,[36] his two "Parties of Power." Whereas in most countries, being an independent almost rules out attaining high office, in Ukraine it might well be an advantage, even with the new party list system. If parties convey no advantage to politicians, they will continue to be weak, and political debate will remain chaotic and unstructured.

One of the largest political parties in Ukraine is still, ironically, the Communists. The Communist Party of Ukraine was banned on August 30, 1991, for supporting the putsch against Gorbachev but later got the ban rescinded. The KPU and its allies in the Peasant Party of Ukraine and the Socialist Party have only attracted 150,000 members from the pre-1985 3.5-million KPU, but that still far outnumbers other parties. The democratic platform of the KPU, later renamed the Party of Democratic Revival (PDVU), managed to attract 3,000 members from the KPU when it seceded from it in mid-1990. The pragmatic PDVU and the New Ukraine bloc opposed Kravchuk during his tenure as president. They then united with some smaller parties in 1996 to logically create Kuchma's "Party of Power," the NDPU.

Traditional Western understandings of "left" and "right," although used in this chapter to survey Ukrainian politics and civil society, are not necessarily always applicable to post-Communist countries such as Ukraine. In Ukraine, "right" can refer either to forces supporting economic reform or to nationalist forces that either oppose economic reform or at best give it low priority. Similarly, left can mean either supporting a large state role in the economy or supporting close ties with Russia. But there are those (such as the New Ukraine bloc) that have combined support for close ties with Russia with support for marketization. Policies of economic liberalization policies are just as likely to be advocated by "left" parties as by "right." For example, the chairman of the Social Democrats,

Yuriy Buzduhan, credited Oleksandr Moroz, the leader of the Socialist Party, with having contributed the most to democratization in Ukraine.[37]

Another factor inhibiting consolidation of political parties is the regional nature of Ukrainian politics. Centrist and center-left parties are stronger outside western Ukraine, and the rightist parties have had little success in gaining support outside western Ukraine. In the center of the political spectrum, there are parties in eastern and western Ukraine that have little chance of uniting, despite essentially similar programs.[38] In addition, the ethnic composition of centrist parties is more multicultural and includes a large number of Russians. Opinion polls and election results consistently show that Rukh is strongest in western and central regions and weakest in eastern and southern Ukraine.[39]

The good news in Ukraine's political party system is that support for extremist parties has consistently declined—not increased—during Ukraine's socioeconomic crisis: The ultranationalist Ukrainian National Assembly (UNA) gained a small number of seats in Parliament in 1994 but was shut out in 1998. Centrism has been "at the height of fashion" since 1992: "For some time now almost all the newly created political forces have been placing themselves in the center. They consider a step to the left or a step to the right as an attempt to flee from who knows what. It is very crowded in the center."[40] The lack of popularity of both the extreme left and right, as well as the absence of such figures as Russia's Vladimir Zhirinovsky, leader of

PHOTO 5.2 Ukrainian National Assembly paramilitaries on parade in central Kyiv, 1993

TABLE 5.4 What Should Parties Do If They Do Not Make It into Parliament (%)?

Option	No.
Disband themselves	31
Remain independent	30
Unite with others that did not make it into Parliament	20
Unite with others that made it into Parliament	19

SOURCE: Poll conducted by the Institute of Social and Political Psychology of Ukraine, *Den'*, 15 September 1998.

the so-called Russian Liberal Democratic Party, all testify to a more stable and conservative public than in Russia. Yuriy Shukhevych, leader of the UNA, failed to register the required 100,000 signatures to stand in the December 1991 presidential elections.

The majority of political parties have still not located reliable social bases and constituencies. The exceptions are the Peasant and Agrarian Parties (private farmers and the rural vote), the NDPU, other probusiness parties (the emerging bourgeoisie), and the "toiling masses" (the extreme left). Even in these cases, there is no evidence of any "party loyalty" to speak of (see Table 5.4).

UKRAINIAN PARLIAMENTARISM

In 1994, the first post-Soviet Verkhovna Rada was elected using a pure majoritarian election law (similar in its main provisions to the system used to elect the U.S. House of Representatives: The country is divided up into 450 districts, and the winner in each district goes to Parliament). Because this system put a priority on local popularity, there was little need for candidates to align with a political party to compete, and a large number of those elected were independent or only loosely aligned with a political party. This parliament then created a system of political factions, essentially metaparties that allowed the large number of independents and the large number of relatively small parties to coalesce into a lesser number of factions, bringing greater unity and coherence to Ukraine's Parliament.

The word "faction" means almost the opposite in the Ukrainian context as it does normally. Usually we use the word to describe a portion of a larger grouping (e.g., a faction within a party). In the Ukrainian (and post-Soviet) sense of the term, a faction is defined as an assemblage of parties as a parliamentary group, including members from one or more parties and additional independent deputies. This usage arises because the party system is so fragmented in Ukraine that parties in Parliament have found it necessary to join with others to form larger agglomerations in order to have an impact. Since these parties were unwilling to actually merge but willing only to work together in a limited way, a new designation was needed, and they have been called factions. Official recognition in the Ukrainian Parliament therefore is based not on parties but on these larger factions.

For a faction to be registered and to have official standing in the 1994–1998 Rada, it had to have at least twenty-five members of Parliament from at least two different oblasts. In 1998, the minimum number of members necessary to form a faction was lowered to fifteen, contributing to the proliferation of factions. The two-oblast rule was added after certain factions, such as Unity from the Dnipropetrovs'k region in the 1994–1998 Rada, arose representing a single oblast. There are considerable institutional incentives to forming and joining factions, as opposed to remaining independent. These include the possibility of attaining committee chairmanships, faction staff, increased office space, and automobiles, as well as influence through membership of the parliamentary Presidium (which consists of the heads of each registered faction). Although some factions were very clearly based around a single party (for example, Rukh and the Communists), others represented a combination of parties and may have included deputies unaffiliated with any party. Some parties had no factional representation, particularly those on the radical right, such as the Congress of Ukrainian Nationalists (KUN) or the UNA. There were eleven factions in Ukraine's first post-Soviet Parliament between 1994 and 1998, and the number has varied in the post-1998 Rada.

Ukraine exhibits many of the features of Giovanni Sartori's "polarized pluralism" of five or six major factions (there are many more parties in Ukraine), with some of them forming a pragmatic center.[41] There are major cleavages on the left, where there are large parties, and on the right, which has less voter support. The large center is dominated by members of, or people with links to, the state administration—the so-called Party of Power. In his study of the Ukrainian party system, Victor Chudowsky concluded that regions only play a role at the extreme ends of this political spectrum; region and language do not therefore create the main cleavages between political parties or parliamentary factions.[42] Nevertheless, Maurice Duverger demonstrated that both regional and ethnic divisions are likely to increase the number of parties in a given country, and this seems to be true in Ukraine, where otherwise similar parties from different regions have failed to join forces.[43]

Ukraine's first post-Soviet Rada was elected in single-member district elections in March–April 1994, followed by numerous by-elections in an attempt to fill still-empty seats.[44] These elections brought representatives of nearly all of Ukraine's forty-some parties to Parliament. Duverger's law states that these parties, with time and repeated elections, would be encouraged to coalesce into a smaller number of parties in order to compete against more institutionalized challengers.[45] In Ukraine, however, the single-member district system seemed only to encourage candidates to run as independents and thus to hamper party consolidation. It is not clear that the basic conditions existed for Duverger's law to operate. Therefore, stronger measures were taken to promote party consolidation, and the March 1998 parliamentary elections in Ukraine were held using a different electoral law, in which only half the members were elected in single-member districts, and the other half of the seats (250) were elected by proportional representation, in which votes were cast for parties rather than individuals and seats in Parliament were allotted according to the percentage of votes each party received (with parties receiving under 4 percent being excluded).

The new election law has advantages and disadvantages. It both strengthens individual party unity and also perpetuates Ukraine's vast sprawl of parties. Although the number of candidates elected as independents is inherently limited, thus strengthening party representation overall, other characteristics of the law undermined party consolidation. Most notably, the relatively low 4-percent threshold for entry meant that eight parties made it into Parliament and several others came close enough to possibly succeed in the future. The incentive to consolidate in order to enter Parliament is therefore low in comparison with Germany, Poland, and Russia, which use 5-percent thresholds. However, many parties in Ukraine are based around prominent individuals. When Ukrainians go to the polls, in many cases they will be voting for individuals rather than parties. If so, proportional representation, especially with a low threshold, may not strengthen Ukraine's party system but instead may promote fragmentation.[46] Such disunity would weaken Parliament as an institution, though it may have the benefit of increasing representation of minority interests.[47]

The election law adopted in November 1993 ensured that no deputies would be elected on party lists; nevertheless the Rada structured itself into nine factions even before the election of the Verkhovna Rada leadership in May 1994. Three distinct ideological groups emerged relatively quickly (left, center, and right), ideological divisions that continue to exist in the post-1998 Rada (see Tables 5.5 and 5.6).

The left dominated the 1994–1998 Rada and continues to dominate the Rada elected in 1998. Parliament was led from May 1994 to March 1998 by Oleksandr Moroz (leader of the Socialist Party of Ukraine) and the first deputy Speaker, Oleksandr Tkachenko (deputy leader of the Peasant Party of Ukraine). Moroz and Tkachenko were allied in the Socialist-Peasant elec-

TABLE 5.5 Development of Faction Membership in the 1994–1998 Ukrainian Parliament

	Date						
	6/94[a]	10/94[b]	1/95	6/95[c]	1/96[d]	10/96[e]	9/97[f]
Communists	86	90	90	n.a.	89	87	76
Socialists	n.a.	30	27	n.a.	26	26	36
Peasants	58	52	48	n.a.	27	23	27
Agrarians for Reforms/Agrarians	–	–	–	25	25	24	25
IDG	n.a.	33	31	n.a.	31	24	25
Social-Market Choice	–	–	–	–	31[g]	27[h]	25
Unity	n.a.	34	31	34	33	37	28
Independent	–	–	29	n.a.	27	27	25
Center	n.a.	37	33	37	31	–	–
Constitutional Center	–	–	–	–	–	46	57
Reforms	27	31	36	n.a.	30	29	30
Rukh	27	27	27	n.a.	28	31	26
Statehood	26	28	30	28	29	–	–
Unaffiliated	23	31	19	n.a.	25	n.a.	42
Total number of deputies	335	393	405	405	404	n.a.	422

KEY: – : faction did not exist
n.a.: information not available
[a] Serhiy Hubin, "Up the Down Staircase," *Eastern Economist*, 13 June 1994.
[b] Danylo Yanevsky, "Division of Power, Part IV: Sorting out the Factions," *Eastern Economist*, 23 January 1995.
[c] *Interfax News Agency*, 2 June 1995.
[d] *Ukrainian Weekly*, 21 January 1996.
[e] UNIAR news agency, 1 October 1996.
[f] *Interfax-Ukraine*, 9 September 1997.
[g] *Interfax-Ukraine*, 16 February 1996.
[h] O. Kiliyevch et al., eds., *Khto ye khto v ukraiins'kiy politytsi* (Kyiv: Tov. "K.I.C.," 1996).

tion bloc during the March 1998 elections, and Tkachenko then went on to become Speaker. Oleh Diomin, a member of the People's Democratic Party (the Party of Power) and second deputy Speaker, was replaced by Viktor Musiaka (a reformer) in October 1996. This triumvirate of left-wing Speaker and deputy Speaker with a reformist second deputy Speaker also exists within the post–1998 Rada (where a Communist and Social Democrat are Tkachenko's deputies).

As Speaker (1994–1998), Moroz commanded some popularity beyond the three left-wing factions; a vote on June 5, 1996, to remove him as Speaker failed after it was supported by only 169 deputies, with 168 against (and 12 abstaining).[48] During times of crisis, such as in May 1995

TABLE 5.6   Factions in the Post–March 1998 Rada

Faction	Number of Deputies
Communists	120
Left-Center (Socialists/Peasants)	33
Progressive Socialists	14
Total Left	167
People's Democrats	86
Hromada	45
Independents	26
United Social Democrats	25
Greens	24
Total Center	206
Rukh	47
Unaffiliated	30
Total	450

SOURCE: The Rada, ongoing data.

and June 1996 when President Kuchma threatened to hold referenda, Moroz has always chosen to place his personal career over his ideological convictions, knowing full well that if the Rada had been dissolved, he would have been unlikely to have been reelected parliamentary Speaker. However, Moroz has to tread a finely balanced line between his desire for career advancement (he was one of three top contenders in the October 1999 presidential elections) and his reliance for his position on the Communists (who provided his Socialist Party with the additional twelve deputies, allowing him to create a separate faction in the 1994–1998 Rada).[49]

In the processes leading to the adoption of the Constitutional Agreement of June 1995 and to the Constitution of Ukraine in June 1996,[50] the Communist, Socialist, and Peasant Party factions pursued common strategies and tactics. All three factions tended to oppose the reform program of the executive, favoring a strong Parliament and a weak executive. But this group has never been monolithic. On questions of national security and threats to Ukraine's territorial integrity, the Socialist Party of Ukraine and the Peasant Party of Ukraine adopt *derzhavnyk* (state-supporting) positions, whereas the KPU is divided between two groups, orthodox hard-liners who call for a revived USSR and are generally hostile to Ukrainian independence, and the remainder, who support an independent Ukraine. In addition, the gulf between the Communists and the left (Socialist/Peasant Parties) widened on the eve of the 1998 elections.

The Socialist and Peasant Parties created a unified faction in early 1997 as a prelude to forming their joint election bloc, independent of the Communist Party.

Because of their generally common behavior and aims, both within Parliament and outside, this group of factions is usually called the "left." Many outside commentators usually describe the Rada as dominated by the left. It is more accurate to say that the left is the largest group, controls the speakership, and can effectively scupper any legislation it opposes, but that it has nothing approaching a majority that would allow it to advance and pass its own program of legislation. The three left-wing factions (Communists, Socialists, and the Peasant Party) did not command more than 136 of the 420 elected deputies. This figure is therefore closer to only one-third of the 1994–1998 Rada. In the post-1998 Rada, the left's influence has grown to nearly 167 deputies who sometimes vote together. At other times, the left remains divided because the Progressive Socialists, a Trotskyist splinter group from the Socialists, are often critical of the Communists, Socialists, and Peasants. Nevertheless, the left remains the largest and best-organized bloc in the Rada and it did—and can—effectively mobilize to block reform proposed by the executive.

The various centrist factions in the 1994–1998 Rada (Inter-Regional Deputies Group, Social-Market Choice, Unity, Independents, Center, and Constitutional Center) "can only be distinguished by their amorphousness and an absence of direction in terms of their political and economic orientation. For this reason, this agglomerate of forces can sooner be described as a gray void than as a political center in the European sense of the term."[51] Members of centrist factions had the lowest attendance record of all factions, due to outside interests and lack of ideological commitment to any particular course of action or program. This is also the case in the post-1998 Rada (particularly among the Greens and NDPU).

Rukh chairman Viacheslav Chornovil described these centrist factions as a "parliamentary sludge." "Sometimes they side with the leftists and sometimes with the rightists. They represent what might be called a situational majority, which, unfortunately, does not want to be constructive, and which, in the event of any weakening, disappears," Chornovil complained.[52] In other words, the Ukrainian Rada often followed contradictory policies depending on whether the left or the right had won over the bulk of the center to its side. The centrist factions in the 1994–1998 Rada had the largest number of deputies (160–170) and therefore could often swing a vote in whichever way they moved. Such an example occurred during the vote for the Constitutional Accord in May 1995, with the center and the right voting in favor of its adoption. When there was a vote for the Law on Industrial-Financial Groups, the center joined forces with the left and voted in favor of it.

Within the amorphous center (often termed the *"bolota,"* or "swamp") certain interest groups exist (clan, regional, economic, and so on). These centrists, or "pragmatists," as they prefer to be described, "often act not only independently of, but also contrary to decisions by, the individual factions to which these deputies formally belong. But in general this entire portion of the deputy corps behaves like a typical parliamentary 'bog,' now joining the 'left-wingers,' and now the 'right-wingers,' now looking back at the president and now at the prime minister."[53] This amorphousness weakened party and factional unity in Ukraine and increased the opportunity for splinter groups to form in the 1994–1998 Rada.

The unpredictability of the center affected the Ukrainian Rada in two ways. First, it represented the largest bloc of deputies, who have given stability to the Ukrainian state because parliamentary politics and consensus building evolve around the center, pragmatic ground. Second, it also works to strengthen the executive at the Rada's expense, as the president can often tailor draft legislation presented to the Rada for approval in such a way as to win the support of the center (his natural supporters) in alliance usually with the right or, occasionally, with the left. In a more profound way, however, the amorphousness of the center undermines the entire process of legislation, by making a stable majority in Parliament unattainable. From the perspective of many observers, it is better to have no majority than a leftist majority, but in any case, a parliament without a working majority can hardly legislate, and it is hard to imagine effective democracy without an effective legislature.

The rightist factions in the 1994–1998 Rada (Rukh, Reforms, the former Statehood faction) commanded nearly ninety seats, less than one-fourth of the total. The number represented by these factions fell further to sixty deputies when the Statehood faction was dissolved in October 1996. Although these groups often coordinated their actions against other political forces,[54] they could not create a common agenda. Thus, they have been less coherent than the leftist factions but still more unified than the centrist factions. Their influence on Rada decisions has been restricted because their representation in the Rada commissions has been weak and their small number impedes them from determining decisions in the plenary sessions.

Throughout the history of the 1994–1998 Rada, the number and composition of factions frequently changed because parliamentary structures still had to evolve after the first free elections of March and April 1994. The post-1998 Rada has greater stability because only those eight blocs who made it through the 4-percent threshold were initially allowed to create factions. Nevertheless, two exceptions were made: An "Independents" faction was created from unaffiliated deputies (similar to the

TABLE 5.7   Regional Variations in the 1998 Parliamentary Elections (%)

	West	West-Center	South	East-Center	East
Left wing	6.0	27.5	20.8	20.0	25.7
Right wing	60.8	18.6	7.6	8.4	4.6

SOURCE: "Buileten," *Kievskogo Tsentra Politicheskykh Issledovanyi i Konfliktologii*, no. 15 (July 1998), p. 70.

1994–1998 Rada), and the left-center faction divided into its Socialist and Peasant components (see Table 5.7).

REGIONALISM AND DEMOCRACY

In an emerging democracy, parties are often created along regional lines.[55] Because very few parties began with statewide representation (the Communist Party is the only one with this advantage in Ukraine, although its popularity remains weak in western Ukraine), the majority of parties began on a regional basis. In some cases successful parties will spread across the country, but in some states the regional differences are strong enough to prevent this. Ottorino Cappelli has described the resulting territorial cleavages as "characterized by conflicts over values and cultural identities where this criterion for alignment is commitment to the locality and its dominant culture."[56] In Ukraine, such regional affinity is seen in the nationalists of western Ukraine, the Communists of eastern Ukraine, and the Unity faction (1994–1998) of Dnipropetrovs'k. These cleavages promote an "us versus them" mentality, leading to a rejection of contending values as alien and the suppression of dissent. Therefore, "the territorial cleavage does not constitute the best breeding ground for societal pluralism and democratic party-political competition."[57] Here the questions of national identity and democratization merge, because regionalism, through its effects on the party structure and hence on Parliament, can undermine democratization as well as state and nation building.[58]

In an influential article, Dankwart Rustow argued that national unity is a necessary background condition to democratization.[59] Ukraine has now been independent and democratic for over five years, yet there remains a significant minority in the country and Parliament who are against Ukrainian independence (this group advocates union with Russia or the re-creation of the Soviet Union). Sixty-four deputies (out of 450) in the 1994–1998 Rada refused to take the oath of loyalty to Ukraine.[60] Facts such as this no doubt accounted for Western and Russian predictions of Ukraine's collapse along regional lines because most of these deputies came from one region (eastern Ukraine).

The threat that regionalism poses for the Ukrainian state has been perhaps the most widely studied aspect (in the West) of Ukrainian politics.[61] But the focus on secession or civil war neglects a less dramatic but perhaps ultimately more real problem. Leaving the threat of secession aside (see Chapter 2), factions based on regional loyalties reinforce regionalism, in turn obstructing the process of creating a coherent party system and a functioning legislative branch. In an established state, this is not as much of a problem. Scottish and Welsh regionalism does not necessarily threaten the existence of the United Kingdom, but in a weak state such as Ukraine, such actions could prove destabilizing. Many of the parliamentary factions and political parties are to some degree regionally based. *No political party has an all-Ukrainian following.* That does not necessarily signify a threat of acute regionalism or separatism. Left-wing factions and parties each have a different regional stronghold: the Communists in the east, the Peasants in the east and center, and the Socialists spread across all regions except the west. Membership of the right-wing factions and parties, especially Rukh and other national democratic parties, are regionally based in the west. *Both* the KPU *and* Rukh are regionally based, the former in the east and the Crimea and the latter in the west.

Centrist factions and parties are based mainly between the KPU's and Rukh's two strongholds of the Donbas/Crimea and Galicia/Volhynia respectively. These centrist factions and parties rarely receive high ratings in opinion polls. Nevertheless, they do reflect the views of the majority of Ukrainians who hold conservative (with a lowercase "c"), centrist, pragmatic views. Supporters of Rukh and the KPU are therefore the exception—not the rule—in Ukraine (as reflected in Ukraine's two pragmatic presidents).

In addition to the regional distribution of parties, there is evidence that support for parties is also divided in a manner that Herbert Kitschelt has called "skillwise."[62] Much of the former Communist *nomenklatura* now belongs to the left and other centrist parties, while the troubled agroindustrial sector has split along economic lines between those who have been able to adapt to a market economy and those who have not. Meanwhile, the technical administrative elite and state managers of large corporations—better able to benefit from privatization and a free market—have formed or joined centrist parties supporting both Ukrainian independence and some economic reform.

Although threats of secession have turned out to be less serious than many thought, the problem of regionalism continues. In the bigger picture, the threat is not that regionalism will cause the country to fragment territorially or collapse into civil war but rather that it will make effective democratic rule impossible by creating a political spectrum that is so incoherent, or so bifurcated, that finding any set of policies that commands a majority will be nearly impossible. The result of such a system is gridlock, which has largely characterized the first eight years of Ukrainian parliamentarism. For a well-functioning consolidated democracy, such gridlock may be frustrating, but not fatal. For a brand new democracy in a position that appears economically unsustainable over the medium to long term, the absence of decisive change is much more dangerous.

CONCLUSION

The Ukrainian case is rather unique within the former Soviet Union but perhaps is most similar to Russia, at least in the area of civil society and parliamentary politics. In the three Baltic republics, the level of national identity and civic activism allowed democratic parties to achieve independence without the need for an alliance with national Communists. In Central Asia the national Communists were initially opposed to independence, suppressing democratic groups (which they continue to do). In Ukraine, by contrast, democratic and proindependence groups and parties were never able to establish a mass movement that covered the entire republic or break through the 50-percent popularity mark. They therefore had little choice but to forge an uneasy alliance with the national Communists, led by Kravchuk, in order to achieve their goal.[63] This continues to slow Ukraine's evolution toward democratic consolidation. National identity, civil society, and democratization are closely interrelated.[64]

In this sense, economic reforms have strengthened Ukraine's independence by giving those who can profit from a free market an incentive to support the state (it must be pointed out that this does not prevent those same individuals from participating in corruption). The only region where this analysis breaks down is in the west, where national identity is the driving force behind party affiliation and support for the state. Here the KPU never recovered from its crushing defeat in the March 1990 elections to the Ukrainian SSR Rada.

Three conclusions can be drawn from this chapter. First, though Ukraine's polity is far from consolidated, parliamentary factions and parties are only partially regionalized. This partial regionalization does not represent a threat to Ukrainian statehood and unity, but it does impede effective legislation, and hence democratic consolidation.

Second, the new election laws and the parliamentary faction system have helped begin to consolidate the multiparty system in Ukraine. It is generally believed that "a party not represented in the Supreme Council is not a party at all, but rather a civic organization with an inkling of political pretense."[65] There is evidence that a Ukrainian political community is emerging, but there is also evidence of growing voter apathy and a widening gulf between society and the state.

PHOTO 5.3   Leonid Kravchuk, president, 1991–1994

Finally, although Ukraine's chances of survival as an independent state are therefore no longer in doubt, democratic consolidation, as defined by Juan Linz and Alfred Stepan,[66] is a problem that Ukraine is still in the midst of undertaking. Achieving democratic consolidation would undoubtedly be helped by the establishment of a stronger Weberian state, effective institutions, and a civic national identity in Ukraine, but it remains unclear from what source these assets will emerge.

APPENDIX:
UKRAINE'S POLITICAL SPECTRUM
(MAIN POLITICAL PARTIES)

Extreme Left
  Communist Party
  Socialist Party
  Peasant Party of Ukraine
  Progressive Socialist Party

Centrist (social democratic/liberal)
United Social Democratic Party
Social Democratic Party
Green Party
People's Democratic Party Liberal Party
Labor Party, Democratic Party
Hromada
Agrarian Party
Inter-Regional Bloc of Reforms
Party of Regional Revival

Center-Right (national democrats)
Rukh
Republican Christian Party
Reform and Order
Forward Ukraine!
Republican Party
Peasant Democratic Party
Christian Democratic Party
National Conservative Party

Extreme Right (nationalists)
Federation for Ukrainian State Independence
Ukrainian National Assembly
Social National Party
Congress of Ukrainian Nationalists

▪ SIX ▪

Economic Crisis and Reform

INTRODUCTION

Ukraine's lackluster performance in reforming its economy has been, perhaps, the most perplexing aspect of its post-Soviet experience, mixing some significant successes with an overall record of remarkable failure. In 1996, the World Bank categorized Ukraine as among the "group 4" (slow reform) countries.[1] In 1997, the World Economic Forum ranked Ukraine 52nd of 53 countries in overall competitiveness in its *Global Competitiveness Report*.[2] And in 1998, the Heritage Foundation–*Wall Street Journal*'s *Index of Economic Freedom* ranked Ukraine 125th out of 156 countries, labeling Ukraine as among the "mostly unfree" economies of the world. Economic reform, therefore, remains in 1999 an incomplete project, the government's chief domestic policy challenge. We begin with a review of the basic issues surrounding economic reform in postsocialist Ukraine.

The Essence of "Reform"

Economist János Kornai defines reform in the post-Soviet context as a substantive change, wherein at least one of the three pillars of the centrally planned economy is dramatically altered:

(1) Dominant influence of official ideology;
(2) Dominant position of state and quasi-state ownership; and/or,
(3) Preponderance of bureaucratic coordination.[3]

Dismantling any one of these three building blocks of socialism would effectively bring the other two down as well. It means nothing short of the collapse of the socialist economy. According to this definition, Ukraine is a "reforming economy": The socialist ideology no longer predominates in economic affairs; bureaucratic intrusion, while significant, is much less effective than under the USSR; and state ownership of enterprises has (slowly) given way to privatization, particularly for small and medium-sized firms. Despite progress in these areas, however, there is general consensus that Ukraine has much more to accomplish before the transition to market will be completed and further still before that market functions efficiently.

Moving Forward, Yet Standing Still

Key macroeconomic objectives during the early independence period included establishment of Ukrainian economic sovereignty; rapid privatization and industrial restructuring; liberalization of prices and trade policy; elimination of state subsidies to loss-making enterprises; serious reduction of credit emissions from the banking system; establishment of control over government spending, especially for burgeoning social safety net programs; and stabilizing the currency. During 1993–1998, many of these objectives were substantially achieved, particularly attainment of economic sovereignty, considerable price liberalization, elimination of many consumer and producer subsidies, control of bank emissions, and establishment of a greater degree of fiscal discipline. The main post-Soviet economic achievement came in September 1996, with the end of Ukraine's hyperinflation and the introduction of a new currency.

Despite this progress, Ukraine remains very much an "economic basket case." The tasks not carried out have swamped any positive effects from the tasks completed. The most striking policy failures have been in the areas of large-scale privatization (especially, but not limited to, the agricultural sector), corporate restructuring, enterprise governance, and creation of an "investor friendly" business climate. These are the sine qua non of economic transition, and they have lagged significantly behind progress in other areas. The result is that industrial investment has fallen off sharply, both domestically and from abroad. This portends dire consequences for future growth in productivity, output, and real incomes. Further, Ukraine has tended to "limp along" for several years on massive, periodic infusions of capital from multilateral lending institutions, particularly the International Monetary Fund. Ukraine had emerged from the Soviet period relatively debt-free, but after 1992, it gradually took on such large amounts of new debt that some authorities began to express concerns about its ability to repay these loans. Understanding how Ukraine managed to achieve the gains it has while still avoiding a genuine transition to the market requires consideration of the root causes of the economic crisis, the policy path Ukraine has chosen, and the significant political and institutional impediments to progress on economic reform. Such obstacles have been considerable and, in some instances, decisive. Finally, the government's management of the economy has bred a high level of official corruption. To date, two former prime ministers have had to flee the country to avoid prosecution for offenses committed while in office.

"Shock Therapy": The Road Not Taken

The debate over whether Ukraine should pursue "shock therapy" or "gradualism"—a more evolutionary transition to a market economy—has dominated economic reform debate in Ukraine since it achieved independence. Although there are disagreements over what constitutes a radical reform program, there appear to be several key elements, all of which are to be pursued *simultaneously*:[4] liberalize prices to reach market-clearing levels, freeze wages and salaries to prevent inflation; reduce government expenditures; raise taxes to reduce the budget deficit; tighten bank credit; stabilize the currency; and liberalize external trade.[5] As harsh as these measures appear, studies have shown that countries that have attempted revolutionary change—excepting Russia—have generally raised living standards more rapidly than countries that adopted more gradual approaches.[6]

Ukraine has spent seven years searching for the road to what President Leonid Kuchma calls a "socially oriented market economy." By 1998, there seemed little doubt that the search for a "third way" between the plan and the market would prove fruitless. The only reasonable choices concerned not the direction of change, but its pace. After spinning its wheels for seven years, however, Ukraine's situation raised concerns as to whether it was possible to "become stuck" in a semipermanent state of transition. This could occur, for instance, where a country would achieve a degree of political equilibrium at relatively low levels of institutional development. This condition is commonly found in developing countries, and it is the general view that it hampers economic and political development. With this as a backdrop, Ukraine consciously chose *not* to pursue "shock therapy." Was this a mistake?

The answer to this question turns on the relative importance that the observer ascribes to institutional development. The explicit purpose of shock therapy is to tear down the institutional apparatus of the former regime.[7] This, of course, can be done quickly. But more practical people might agree that the state cannot and should not disappear overnight.[8] In any case, the institutional infrastructure appropriate to a market economy takes time and considerable effort to develop. This calls for a more gradual approach to reform. Proponents of gradualism argue for an iterative process of building a network of market institutions and firms;[9] for proper sequencing of reforms, as opposed to simultaneous implementation;[10] and for building market institutions based on the unique historical traditions of the specific country.[11] The important point is to recognize the time investment required to build effective institutions, the cushioning effect that gradualism can have on the economic dislocations that the crisis imposes on the population, and the political limits to reform.

But gradualism can be painful, too. As two-time Polish finance minister Leszek Balcerowicz has pointed out, "[T]he experience in reform-resistant Ukraine shows that slower change isn't necessarily kinder and gentler."[12] The basic problem is that given sufficient time, coalitions can form around existing nonmarket institutions that will preserve them long past their practical usefulness. This presumes, of course, a "one-size-fits-all" dimension to shock therapy that appears unwarranted.

Perhaps most crucial to the success of shock therapy is the question of political feasibility. In a democratic country, reform can progress only along lines that the public will tolerate. Political support is therefore key, and in Ukraine, it has been mixed at best. A 1993 study of thirteen cases of radical economic change revealed that to be effective, reformers need a strong political base.[13] The slow pace of Ukrainian reforms can be attributed in large part to the difficulty of locating and mobilizing a constituency that supports them. Social support for reform remains thin, with the public possessing divergent opinions on the issue. Further, key governmental and industrial elites still rely heavily on links with the former state planning apparatus to preserve state subsidies, lobby for favors, and maintain existing privileges.[14] Established interest organizations therefore remain very much "bastions of conservatism."[15] Moreover, many business interests have found the transition zone between plan and market extremely lucrative and have no interest in completing the transition. These interests have been much more powerful than those of reformers in the halls of government.

Alexander Motyl has therefore argued that Ukraine's starting point did not lend itself to shock therapy: "The structural legacy of the USSR's collapse, in particular, the kinds of elite Ukraine inherited and its resource endowment, has kept Ukraine on the path of evolutionary change."[16] He concluded that Ukraine seems destined to "muddle along" a more gradualistic path to reform that, due to the absence of significant initial enabling conditions—particularly a dominant revolutionary elite that presses for reform—may simply be the only realistic alternative. It is a matter of debate how to allocate the responsibility for Ukraine's unimpressive performance between the unpropitious circumstances and the policies chosen.

DYNAMICS OF THE ECONOMY

Economic Crisis and Industrial Collapse

Most economic indicators for Ukraine paint a desperate picture. As can be seen from Table 6.1, from 1991 to 1998, Ukraine's real GDP declined by a cumulative 63 percent. This compares to just over a 40-percent decline in

Russia and 50 percent for the CIS average.[17] Industrial output and capital investment fell by similarly large amounts, 52 and 77 percent, respectively. Virtually no sector or industry was spared a deep and broad depression. Heavy industry and raw materials extraction were particularly affected, with even more severe downstream effects on small machine tools enterprises. The data in Table 6.1 also indicate that the industrial collapse has been long and slow to correct. This raises serious questions about the nature of the collapse, its root causes, and secondary effects. As we will see, answers to these questions have significant policy implications.

Why the Output Collapse Was Inevitable

There is some controversy over whether the industrial collapse in former socialist economies was inevitable.[18] In the twenty-five years immediately preceding the fall of the USSR, and certainly by the Gorbachev era, serious misallocations of capital and labor had become obvious. This contributed to a steady decline in productivity, which plagued almost the entire period of Leonid Brezhnev's rule, known euphemistically in the USSR as the *period zastoiy* (period of stagnation). Stagnation gave way to decline even before the collapse of the Soviet Union, so that all postsocialist countries experienced deep recession in the 1990s. By 1994, only Albania, Poland, and the former German Democratic Republic had started on the road to recovery (though not without problems).[19] Conspicuously, both Ukraine and Russia have trailed the pack.

Although official statistics can be notoriously misleading, and may in fact overstate the scale of output decline (particularly by excluding the "shadow sector"—see below), it is widely accepted that a dramatic collapse in real output has occurred. The prolonged recession derives neither from a continuation of the chronic "shortage economy" of the former USSR nor from general excess demand. Rather, the transition from plan to market itself has caused the downturn. In the early postsocialist economy, market forces initially operate in an institutional vacuum left by the withdrawing state, which can have devastating effects. The market has been let loose, but the means to regulate the new economy are lacking. In an important sense, the key task of reform consists of building institutions geared toward the market. The conventional wisdom that reform simply involves getting the government out of the economy is therefore misleading. In the advanced economies, governments perform a host of regulatory and law enforcement functions that are crucial for the successful function of the economy. Economies in transition are trying to form market economies without that key institutional infrastructure.

Demand-side management of the semireformed economy is not possible within the context of the persistent large amounts of state ownership

TABLE 6.1 Basic Economic Indicators of Ukraine, 1991–1998

	1991	1992	1993	1994	1995	1996	1997	Projected 1998
Output and income[a]								
Real GDP	-8.7	-16.8	-14.2	-22.9	-12.2	-10.0	-3.6	-1.0
Gross industrial output	-4.8	-6.8	-8.0	-27.3	-12.0	-5.1	-1.8	-2.1
Employment	-1.7	-4.0	-2.3	-5.4	n.a.	-2.1	-2.5	-3.1
Capital investment	-7.1	-36.9	-10.3	-22.5	-20.5	-22.0	-7.5	n.a.
Prices and wages[a]								
Consumer price index	261	2,830	10,255	501	282	140	10.1	2.3
Wholesale price index	263	3,928	9,767	655	281	117	5.0	n.a.
Average wages	240	2,304	3,948	418	261	22	35.0	-14.0
Government finances[b]								(8 months)
Consolidated budget revenues	36.5	32.8	40.0	49.2	40.2	37.4	28.6	35.4
Consolidated budget expenditures	50.6	45.0	46.5	59.7	48.2	41.9	35.2	37.9
Consolidated budget deficit	-14.1	-12.2	-6.5	-10.5	-8.0	-4.5	-6.6	-2.5
Directed credits	13.6	12.8	8.0	4.2	3.2	1.0	0.0	0.0
Extraordinary funds balance (est.)	0.5	3.5	0.5	0.4	0.4	0.4	0.4	0.4
General government balance	-27.2	-21.5	-14.0	-13.4	-10.8	-5.2	-6.2	-2.1
External sector								(8 months)
Net foreign debt ($US billion)	n.a.	n.a.	1.4	7.2	8.4	9.2	9.8	11.6
Exchange rate (HRV/$, end of period)	n.a.	0.0002	0.126	1.042	1.794	1.889	1.899	2.183
Current account balance (% GDP)	n.a.	n.a.	-2.3	-3.2	-3.1	-2.7	0.5	-0.2
Memorandum: Nominal GDP[c]	299	5,168	142,016	1,080,307	5,083,061	8,051,000	9,484,000	6,109,400

[a] Percent change from previous period.
[b] Percent of GDP.
[c] Billions of KBV.

SOURCES: Ministry of Finance of Ukraine; IMF (1993, 1995); European Expert Service, "Ukraine in Numbers," *Ukrainian Legal and Economic Bulletin* (various issues); European Expert Service, Centre for Macroeconomic Analysis of Ukraine, *Ukrainian Economic Trends* (various issues); source documents; authors' calculations.

of enterprises, nor does it suit the authorities' instinctive preferences for supply-side controls. Property relations must change in order for enterprises to adjust the composition and volume of output to demand, especially for consumer goods. This will be impossible without considerable privatization, corporate governance reform, capital market development, industrial restructuring, and a meaningful bankruptcy law.[20] With privatization will come changes in the composition of entire industries, especially in the size distribution of firms. But, as we will summarize below, meaningful privatization and enterprise reform have come painfully slowly to Ukraine.

Herein lies a dilemma: In the short run, reorganization and restructuring of the real sector will raise unemployment as firms shed excess labor and reduce demand for material and factor inputs. However, in the long run, efficiency and growth are promoted through reallocation of productive resources, reduction of state subsidies, and imposition of a hard budget constraint. It has proved, therefore, to be extraordinarily difficult to avoid contradictory policy measures in the effort to steer a course between a short-run objective to stem the fall in output and employment and a long-run goal to promote efficient growth. This dilemma explains at least some of the more contradictory economic reform measures taken since 1992.

Another equally critical factor has been the severe disruption in state coordination of the economy—a basic withdrawal of the state in many critical sectors—which has left a considerable vacuum, wherein nascent market institutions are slowly developing. The command-administrative system has receded, but the necessary system of market signals to replace it will take time to develop.[21] The backwardness of the financial sector, insolvency of banks, and considerable amounts of favoritism in the allocation of capital also militate against increasing production and investment (see below). Although it is true that financial sector development takes time, the Ukrainian government's sluggishness in cleansing the banking system of bad loans and establishing appropriate regulatory structures is clearly to blame for the lack of progress. Consequently, the transformational recession has proved to be a protracted phenomenon in Ukraine, and it is likely to persist at least a few years longer.

Growth of the "Shadow Economy"

Related to the output collapse and to the institutional deficit has been the emergence of the shadow economy as a significant feature of the transition period. The shadow, or "unofficial," economy in Ukraine is extensive, having grown to an estimated 60 percent of total real GDP by early 1996.[22] Because the shadow economy is not included in official statistics, the decline in output tends to be overstated.[23] The shadow sector is not a new phenomenon. From 1960 to 1989, the unofficial economy in the USSR grew by an estimated factor of 30 times, accounting for more than 20 percent of national income.[24] Shadow activity has continued to grow in post-Soviet Ukraine. As early as 1992, a questionnaire of 223 private firms found that 54 percent of their aggregate profit was derived from shadow activities.[25] In 1994, a poll of 200 companies operating with foreign capital revealed that 55 percent of their business was involved with the shadow economy.[26] Further, approximately 40 percent of all currency in 1996–1997 was circulating outside of the banking system. A significant proportion of the labor force is therefore at least partially employed in shadow activities.[27]

The term "shadow economy" ought not to imply strictly criminal activity. There is an obvious "criminal layer" of illicit activity in the shadow economy, accounting for some 33–50 percent of it. But much, if not most, of it consists of ordinary Ukrainians meeting personal needs, operating more or less openly. The shadow sector thus serves partially as a means to compensate for the collapse of the official economy. It results from individuals and firms protecting themselves from excessive regulation, confiscatory taxation, and rampant corruption. It has softened the blow of economic crisis on the population. Razumkov et al. estimate that at least two-thirds of Ukrainians have benefited from participation in the shadow sector.[28] The benefit to ordinary citizens has been substantial. In a speech before the Verkhovna Rada in January 1996, Deputy Prime Minister Viktor Pynzenyk revealed that the average level of consumption by citizens of Ukraine exceeded their average official monthly incomes by 2.5 times.[29] However, a troublesome aspect of the rise of the unofficial shadow economy is that the larger it becomes, the more state macroeconomic policy becomes superfluous. The government has therefore taken extreme care in its dealing with shadow activity, essentially backing off. In 1998, it remains one of the most significant policy challenges of the postsocialist transition.[30]

The External Trade Sector

To a considerable extent, Ukraine's reform efforts were handicapped in 1992–1995 by an unfavorable economic environment. The collapse of the economic space of the USSR severely disrupted Ukraine's trade patterns. The Western industrialized economies of Europe were weakened by recession, which meant that they were unable to take up the slack left by the demise of the Council for Mutual Economic Assistance, or COMECON. Foreign markets were literally glutted with raw material supplies from former Soviet countries, which brought deterioration in the terms of trade.

Input prices had risen dramatically, especially for energy products, which are Ukraine's economic "Achilles' heel." As we shall see, these developments were accompanied by laggard domestic policy performance, which compounded Ukraine's difficulties.[31]

Trade Patterns Favoring the CIS. Approximately one-half of Ukraine's 1997 foreign trade turnover ($19.2 billion out of $37.6 billion) was with the CIS, and nearly all of that ($15.3 billion) was with Russia. After Russia, Ukraine's major CIS trading partners are Belarus, Turkmenistan, and Uzbekistan.[32] Ukraine runs trade deficits with CIS countries, totaling $2.7 billion in 1997, due mainly to Ukraine's appetite for imported energy. Ukraine usually runs surpluses with non-CIS countries. A damaging trade war with Russia in 1996–1997 dramatically reduced trade with the CIS overall. The dispute arose over imposition of quotas and customs and excise duties on Ukrainian imports, mainly agricultural products. Russia remained Ukraine's most important supplier of oil (100 percent), gas (81 percent), and raw materials (50 percent) in 1997.[33] However, Ukraine's dependence on Russian energy is likely to decline after 1998, as it increases oil imports from Azerbaijan and gas from Turkmenistan. Trade with Russia and CIS countries is frequently conducted on a barter basis, which amounted to some 19.8 percent of exports to the CIS in 1997. However, barter trade fell by three-fourths from 1994 to 1997, due to the Russian-Ukrainian trade dispute.

Ukraine's main export markets are in Russia (26.7 percent of the total in 1997, including 63.7 percent of food, 51.4 percent of machinery and equipment, 37.3 percent of vehicles, and 21.3 percent of chemicals); China (7.7 percent of total); Belarus (5.8 percent); Turkey (4.7 percent); and Germany (3.8 percent). Exports to its neighbors—excluding Russia—accounted for 21.5 percent of the total.[34] Since 1994, Ukraine has also significantly increased its arms exports, from $20 million in 1994, to over $100 million in 1995, to over $1 billion by the end of 1996.[35] In 1996, Ukraine merged three major arms export firms into a single company, Ukrspetsexport, in order to increase competitiveness in what is now its fastest-growing source of foreign exchange.

Ukraine remains interested in bilateral trade and economic cooperation with Russia and the CIS but is careful to avoid any larger political or security linkages. As an associate member of the CIS, Ukraine has rejected all attempts to transform the CIS into a supranational organization.[36] Consequently, Ukraine has refused to join the Russia-Belarus Union, the CIS Customs Union,[37] and the Payments Union. However, consistent with its preference for bilateral relations with CIS countries, in March 1998, Ukraine and Russia concluded the Interstate Economic Treaty. This treaty formalized the two governments' agreement to drop the value-added tax (VAT) and other trade barriers between them that February, an effort that was expected to expand trade between them by some 10–15 percent, in the long run, especially for agricultural products.

Lagging Foreign Investment. Due to insufficient domestic investment capital, Ukraine has turned to foreign capital sources for investment. However, compared to other Eastern European and former Soviet countries, Ukraine has enjoyed relatively little foreign investment. Accumulated per capita foreign direct investment (FDI) in Ukraine totaled only $27 at the start of 1997, compared to $1,376 in Hungary, $696 in the Czech Republic, $250 in Poland, and $48 in Russia.[38] Ukraine had accumulated FDI of just $1.8 billion by November 1, 1997.[39] Surveys of foreign investors provide strong evidence that serious obstacles to investment prevent more ample FDI, including: great legal uncertainty; nonobservance by the state of its commitments; residual effects of central planning; lack of support by state bodies; corruption; unreasonable time delays; and poor economic conditions.[40] Also cited were unsatisfactory transportation and telecommunications infrastructure.[41]

Government policy performance on FDI generally has assumed the following pattern: Repeated statements are made that Ukraine wishes to attract FDI. Laws and regulations are enacted to protect investment inflows, but bureaucratic corruption, ineptitude, or simple indifference leads to selective enforcement. Meanwhile, the government alters dramatically its previous policy in order to serve its momentary convenience, imposing hardships on investors ex post facto. The government thus sends oscillating and mixed signals to investors, heightening their uncertainty, causing many to hold back. The government has appeared content to attract foreign loans in order to finance its budget deficits rather than to engage investors in the necessary work of renewing the capital base.

The Problem of Capital Flight. A related problem concerns the large volume of capital that has actually been leaving Ukraine since 1992. Although capital transactions continue to be strictly controlled, capital has fled the country through ordinary import-export trade, where profits may not be repatriated. There are many opportunities to send capital abroad (especially in the shadow economy). Independent estimates have placed the amount of Ukrainian capital held abroad in the $25–50 billion range.[42] The most common vehicle for capital flight appears to be through barter trade, where volumes of goods are traded at different times and at different price equivalents. It is extremely difficult to verify the relative equivalency—at final market prices—of the goods so exchanged. Capital flight can therefore be hidden in the accounts of enterprises. Studies indicate that the value of exports in barter trade has exceeded the value of imports.[43] There were indications that capital flight was falling from 1994 to 1996, however. The margin of difference between the import and export sides of barter trade fell during this period, implying a drop of over 60 percent. With the currency stabilization in fall 1996, further returns of Ukrainian capital from abroad were expected, as investors would have less to fear from retaining their capital in Ukraine, but the 1998 devaluation of the *hryvnya* (HRV, the Ukrainian permanent currency) has likely delayed progress on this front considerably.

Rising Foreign Debt Levels. At the time of its independence, Ukraine had no foreign debt outstanding, providing its most important initial inherited economic advantage: vast, untapped debt capacity. However, Ukrainian debts rapidly mounted, so that by the start of 1998, there were significant debt accumulations outstanding. From an estimated $1.4 billion in late 1992, Ukraine's indebtedness grew to over $12.5 billion by the end of 1998.[44] Despite this dramatic increase, Ukraine's external debt remains affordable by international standards. The debt-to-GDP ratio stood at between 15 and 20 percent in 1998. Ukraine's principal creditors are Russia, the IMF, the World Bank, and Germany. The overall situation has been exacerbated by additional arrears of over $1 billion owed to Russia's Gazprom for imported gas. In early 1998, the government was seeking to increase its borrowings by over $4 billion, including $1 billion from the World Bank to be used largely to cover the national budget deficit.[45]

Employment and Wages

Under the Soviet planned economy, workers were guaranteed jobs at regulated wages, and universal benefits (including vacations, job training, kindergarten, child care, and often housing) were provided, in part, by the enterprises for which they worked. Some of the paternalism of the former regime has continued in post-Soviet Ukraine, but many of the benefits have been reduced or eliminated, and with the collapse of the socialist economy, unemployment has broken out into the open for the first time. Official unemployment rates still run at around 3 percent, but this does not reflect the actual situation. Many workers have been placed on "administrative leave" or are officially listed as "employed" but are paid part-time wages or not at all. This is the source of the "disguised," or "hidden," unemployment that has become so pervasive in transition economies. In March 1993, inspections of 6,900 enterprises conducted by the State Center of Employment revealed that nearly 572,000 of the 3.9 million workers, or 14.6 percent, were on long-term leave.[46] In certain regions of Ukraine and branches of industry at that time, more than 44 percent were compelled to take leave, which resulted in levels of hidden unemployment reaching 58 percent. Recent estimates place the number of "hidden unemployed" at close to 3.5 million. Many of these workers have turned to "shadow activities" for their sustenance.[47]

Hidden unemployment may be expected to decline, since enterprise-provided benefits are shrinking and the time period for registration for unemployment benefits has been shortened (from three months to seven days).[48] Registered unemployment grew from 162,000 in January 1996 to 351,100 in January 1997, before reaching 1,052,000 by July 1998.[49] The International Labor Organization (ILO), however, estimated actual unemployment levels at closer to 9.8 percent, or three times the official rate. Three-fourths of the unemployed are women, and over one-half possess degrees of higher education. Despite the industrial vacancies that still exist, their higher skills level will make many of them more difficult to place than, for example, dislocated factory workers. Furthermore, in January 1998, there were only 37,600 official vacancies, reflecting low levels of job creation in the highly privatized small and medium-size enterprise sectors (which, in any case, employ only some 5 percent of the labor force).[50] In sum, at the end of 1998, Ukraine continues to suffer from severe unemployment and underemployment problems, two problems that can be solved only through more rapid structural reform, coupled with economic growth.

At the same time, wages have fallen for those fortunate enough to keep their jobs. Real wage levels have been low, highly volatile, and declining. However, government data reflect only wage schedules and not actual wage payments, which have been held up in some cases for several months. At April 1, 1998, some 5,337 million HRV (around $2.5 billion) in wage arrears had accumulated. Further, some 15 percent of wages were being paid "in kind," in the form of finished product. The low wages available in Ukraine have not been sufficient to overcome the substantial disincentives to invest in the country, as mentioned above. This is in part because wages still tend to bear little relationship to productivity levels, which can vary broadly between sectors and even among firms in the same industry. Ukraine therefore has been unable to take full advantage of its relatively low-cost, highly skilled workforce.

Fiscal and Monetary Policy Issues

Perhaps the most pressing issue concerning Ukraine's early economic experience has been the persistent budget deficit and concomitant inflation—especially the slide into hyperinflation by late 1993—and the long drive to monetary stabilization in 1996. Serious expenditure control problems and lavish budget subsidies and directed credits to industry and agriculture combined to produce significant inflationary pressures in 1991–1995.[51] In the absence of adequate domestic debt financing capabilities, inflation broke out into the open as early as 1991. As predicted by economic theory, Ukraine's price inflation was accompanied by rapid increases in the money supply[52] (see Graph 6.1). The period of greatest expansion was 1992–1994, followed by a dramatic reduction, starting in mid-1994, as can be seen in Graph 6.2. Stabilization was largely accomplished by September 1996, when the permanent currency, the *hryvnya*, was introduced.

Fiscal Deficits and Inflation. Ukraine's inflation was largely the result of "soft" budgetary discipline. Quarterly consolidated budget results for 1992–1996 are detailed in Table 6.2. Close examination reveals that real revenues and expenditures were remarkably robust in the face of annual falls in real GDP and the rampant price inflation (see Graph 6.3). This suggests that political as well as economic factors played a significant role in fiscal policy.[53] Especially in relation to credit emission to the government and enterprise sectors, which is highly politically motivated, there has been a direct link to the inflationary impulse (see Graph 6.4). The overall level of public expenditure remains high in Ukraine, relative to most mar-

GRAPH 6.1 Change in Ukrainian Monetary Aggregates, 1991–1996 (by quarter)

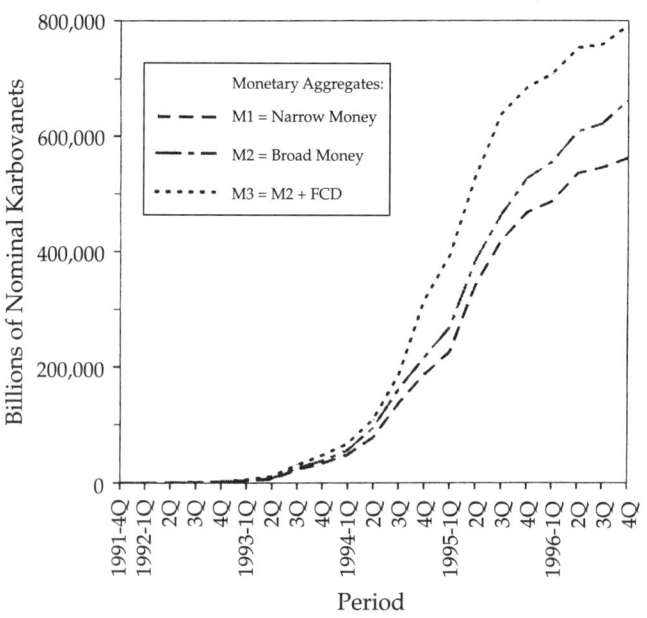

SOURCE: National Bank of Ukraine; authors' computations.

GRAPH 6.2 Ukrainian Monetary Growth Rates, 1992–1996

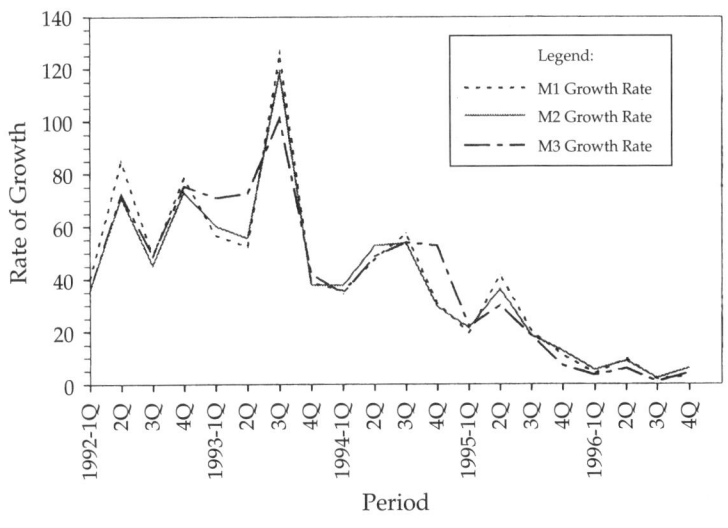

SOURCE: National Bank of Ukraine; authors' computations.

ket economies, running since 1992 at between 40 and 60 percent of GDP, some 20–30 percentage points higher than the average for the European Community. Social expenditures have been fairly constant at 30–35 percent of GDP; however, the country lacks the fiscal resources to afford the overly generous social programs inherited from the USSR. Further, as a relatively aged society, some 25 percent of the population qualify for pension and old-age benefits.[54] The welfare state is thus burdensome by international comparison. Reducing the fiscal expenditure remains an important policy objective.

Lax Expenditure Control.   Although improving, fiscal transparency, control, and accountability are not firmly established in any central governmental body. In the absence of effective expenditure analysis capabilities, the authorities have been unable to "target" programs on the neediest groups and thereby reduce the universal nature of many benefits. Budget and expenditure systems are not geared toward spending control, so ministries and state enterprises have not been subject to "hard budget constraints." Consequently, there has been little incentive to exercise fiscal discipline. Until 1995, the availability of cheap bank credits considerably eroded enterprise accountability. In mid-1999, the lack of a fully functioning treasury continues to hinder expenditure control.

180

TABLE 6.2 Ukraine Consolidated Budget Results, 1992–1997

	Billion KBV (Nominal)						Billion KBV, Constant (1991=100)			Percent of GDP		
Period	Total Revenues	Total Expenditures	Budgetary Balance	Nominal GDP	CPI[a] (1991=100)	Real GDP (1991=100)	Total Revenues	Total Expenditures	Budgetary Balance	Total Revenues	Total Expenditures	Budgetary Balance
1991				299	100	299						
1992	1,695	2,325	−630	5,168	1,159	415	146.2	200.6	−54.4	32.8	45.0	−12.2
1993	5,6826	66,100	−9,275	142,016	59,922	221	94.8	110.3	−15.5	40.0	46.5	−6.5
1994	5,31381	645,348	−113,967	1,080,307	696,972	155	76.2	92.6	−16.4	49.2	59.7	−10.5
1995	2,044,268	2,448,594	−404,326	5,083,061	3,157,181	161	64.7	77.6	−12.8	40.2	48.2	−8.0
1996	3,014,200	3,375,900	−361,700	8,051,000	5,367,333	150	56.2	62.9	−6.7	37.4	41.9	−4.5
1997	2,714,860	3,334,500	−619,400	9,448,400	5,909,434	160	45.9	56.4	−10.5	28.7	35.3	−6.6
1992												
1Q	128	165	−37	513	478	107	26.7	34.5	−7.7	24.9	32.2	−7.3
2Q	284	362	−78	964	787	123	36.1	45.9	−9.9	29.5	37.5	−8.1
3Q	409	536	−127	1,374	1,332	103	30.7	40.2	−9.5	29.7	39.0	−9.3
4Q	867	1,277	−409	2,317	2,830	82	30.6	45.1	−14.5	37.4	55.1	−17.7
1993												
1Q	2,022	2,090	−68	5,984	7,708	78	26.2	27.1	−0.9	33.8	34.9	−1.1
2Q	5,053	6,629	−1,576	11,955	20,872	57	24.2	31.8	−7.6	42.3	55.4	−13.2
3Q	12,679	14,826	−2,147	34,504	63,020	55	20.1	23.5	−3.4	36.7	43.0	−6.2
4Q	37,072	42,555	−5,484	89,573	290,195	31	12.8	14.7	−1.9	41.4	47.5	−6.1

1994										
1Q	55,702	64,113	−9,366	146,949	411,698	36	13.5	15.6	−2.1	37.9	43.6	−6.4
2Q	97,441	113,082	−16,923	189,537	476,548	40	20.4	23.7	−3.3	51.4	59.7	−8.9
3Q	142,813	189,937	−46,663	236,076	535,648	44	26.7	35.5	−8.8	60.5	80.5	−19.8
4Q	234,442	278,216	−41,015	507,746	1,453,691	35	16.1	19.1	−3.0	46.2	54.8	−8.1
1995										
1Q	301,301	368,176	−66,875	843,383	2,317,981	36	12.9	15.9	−3.0	35.7	43.7	−7.9
2Q	465,891	524,507	−58,616	1,114,626	2,688,366	41	17.3	19.5	−2.2	41.8	47.1	−5.3
3Q	572,395	673,919	−101,524	1,460,996	3,378,329	43	16.9	19.9	−3.0	39.2	46.1	−6.9
4Q	704,682	881,993	−177,311	1,664,056	4,094,330	41	17.2	21.5	−4.3	42.3	53.0	−10.7
1996										
1Q	650,465	764,585	−114,120	1,682,737	4,954,978	34	13.1	15.4	−2.3	38.7	46.0	−7.3
2Q	624,183	702,126	−77,943	1,811,393	5,144,524	35	12.1	13.6	−1.5	34.5	38.2	−4.3
3Q	743,661	802,390	−58,729	2,067,800	5,519,687	37	13.5	14.5	−1.0	35.9	38.8	−2.9
4Q	995,900	1,106,800	−110,900	2,489,070	5,720,740	44	17.4	19.3	−1.9	40.0	44.5	−4.5

[a] Average annual CPI for each year; end of quarter CPI for each quarter.

SOURCES: Ministry of Finance of Ukraine; IMF (1993, 1995); European Expert Service, "Ukraine in Numbers," *Ukrainian Legal and Economic Bulletin* (various issues); European Expert Service, Centre for Macroeconomic Analysis of Ukraine, *Ukrainian Economic Trends* (various issues); source documents; authors' calculations.

GRAPH 6.3 Real Revenues, Expenditures, and GDP, January 1992–December 1996 (quarterly exponential growth rates)

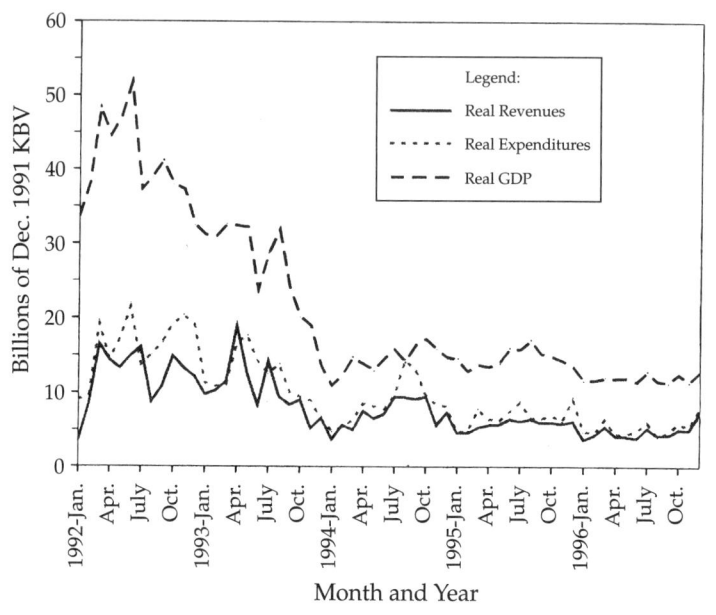

Month and Year

SOURCE: Ministry of Finance of Ukraine; authors' computations.

A Weak Tax System. Since 1992, Ukraine's tax system has exhibited many features of acute crisis, including:

- Falling tax revenue-to-GDP ratios (especially 1994–1996)
- Highly progressive, poorly functioning taxes, with high effective rates but low yields
- Highly differentiated rate structures, narrow tax bases, and extensive exemptions and tax privileges
- Low personal income tax receipts, relative to overall revenues
- Serious compliance problems

A serious problem has been that tax collection rates are particularly low. Frequent and dramatic tax rate and base changes since 1992, combined with high marginal rates, selective enforcement, and the irrational granting of tax privileges, have eroded perceptions of fairness, leading to widespread tax evasion. This has undoubtedly contributed to the rise of the shadow economy, which constitutes an erosion of the official tax base.

GRAPH 6.4 Enterprise and Government Credits Growth in Relation to Inflation, 1992–1996 (by quarter)

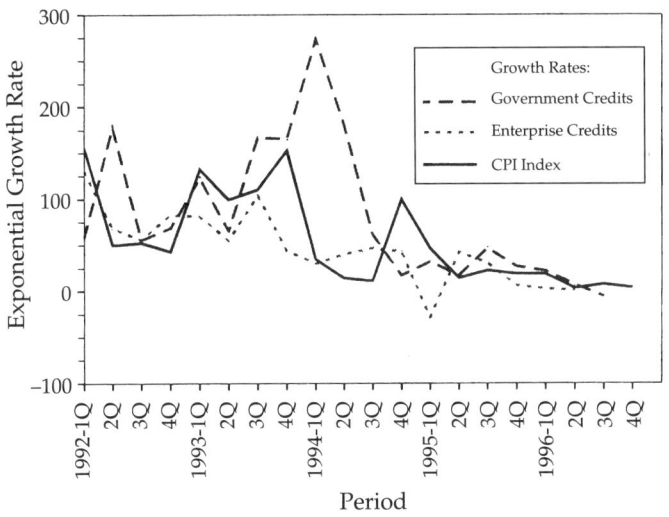

SOURCE: Ministry of Finance of Ukraine; authors' computations.

It is estimated that approximately 32,000 enterprises avoid paying taxes.[55] Further, levels of collection reaching the central government have been lower than expected because controls are inoperative, and much of this potential revenue ends up in regional and tax district offices without being reported to the treasury in Kyiv. The array of taxes, rates, bases, and means of administration in Ukraine are incompatible with the needs of a market economy. The challenge for tax reform is therefore to restore fairness to the system and reduce the serious tax drag on output without increasing the fiscal deficit or resorting to inflationary methods of deficit finance. Effective tax reform has proved elusive, however. The best chance for comprehensive tax reform failed in 1997, when the Rada enacted the president's "Economic Growth '97" tax package on a piecemeal basis, choosing to ignore his more substantive proposals. No further reforms of a comprehensive nature may be expected until after the 1999 presidential elections.

Deficit Financing Capabilities. In the absence of increased tax collections, fiscal deficits will tend to persist. But noninflationary deficit financing (through selling government bonds) has been slow to establish in Ukraine. Until 1996, the National Bank held the dominant role in deficit financing, via credit expansion, which is inherently inflationary. At that time, significant amounts of domestic debt financing became available for the first time. But as of 1998, the financial markets for state bonds were unable to fully cover budget deficits. The slack has been taken up with foreign borrowing, which constituted a substantial 60 percent of the total in 1998. Development of the domestic public debt market thus remains a critical fiscal policy objective. The government's inability to finance its activities has contributed to two much more serious problems: increasing indebtedness to foreign lenders and increasing pressure to finance deficits through monetary expansion, bringing the country back into hyperinflation.

Privatization and Enterprise Governance

Privatization and reform of enterprise governance may be considered the "heart and soul" of transition to the market. Privatization implies a permanent transfer of ownership and control of an enterprise from the state to private investors or managers. It should be emphasized that privatization is not an end in itself but rather a means toward more effective enterprise governance. It is intended to induce a permanent shift in enterprise behavior away from administratively determined modes and toward market-driven considerations. The logic is that privatized enterprises will be more flexible, adaptable, and responsive to markets, increasing their competitiveness and making them engines of growth. Further, rapid privatization—coming at the earliest stages of transition—would bring with it the benefits of shrinking the state sector, including reducing budget subsidies to loss-making concerns; expanding the tax base; curtailing asset-stripping by former directors; and promoting more rapid economic growth.

Mixed Privatization Results. Ukraine's experience with privatization has been quite mixed (see Table 6.3). Although small-scale privatization got off to a slow start, it greatly accelerated in 1995–1996 and was substantially completed by mid-1997. Medium- and large-scale privatization has lagged, however, grinding to a near standstill in 1996. "Scale" is essentially defined under Ukrainian law in terms of the value of an enterprise's asset base, based on book values. Small-scale privatization applies to shops, boutiques, restaurants, and small service establishments. Over 90 percent of the estimated stock of 45,000 small enterprises in Ukraine had been privatized by mid-1997, mainly going to existing managers and employee groups. This appears impressive enough; however, these enterprises collectively account for only around 2 percent of official industrial output. Ukrainian industry thus remains highly concentrated in large conglomerate enterprises, which are resistant to privatization.

TABLE 6.3 Extent of Privatization in Ukraine, 1992–1997

Period	Number Privatized In Period	Number Privatized Cumulative	Used Privatization Accounts (thousands)	Privatized Apartments (thousands)	Number of Private Farms	Land Area of Private Farms (1000s hectares)
1992	30	30	5		14,681	292.3
1993	3,555	3,585	728	902.8	27,739	558.2
1994	7,967	11,552	7,106	1,812.3	31,983	699.7
1995	16,720	28,272	28,000	2,360.8	34,687	788.5
1996	19,453	48,225	43,400	2,927.2	35,353	835.0
1992						
4Q	30	30	5		14,681	292.3
1993						
1Q	400	430	115	61.1	20,665	415.7
2Q	400	830	275	286.1	24,628	482.0
3Q	855	1,685	395	561.3	26,048	510.0
4Q	1,900	3,585	728	902.8	27,739	558.2
1994						
1Q	1,857	5,442	1,503	1,218.3	29,666	620.5
2Q	2,960	8,402	2,873	1,448.0	30,895	657.5
3Q	1,812	10,214	4,883	1,620.1	31,325	675.0
4Q	1,338	11,552	7,106	1,812.3	31,983	699.7
1995						
1Q	1,250	12,802	11,186	1,989.1	33,040	728.9
2Q	2,155	14,957	15,600	2,122.8	33,746	757.0
3Q	4,843	19,800	21,228	2,236.3	34,149	773.0
4Q	8,472	28,272	28,000	2,360.8	34,778	786.4
1996						
1Q	5,928	34,200	31,500	2,499.2	34,783	795.4
2Q	6,500	40,700	38,800	2,616.1	35,266	820.6
3Q	4,300	45,000	42,000	2,746.4	35,353	820.2
4Q	3,225	48,225	43,400	2,927.2	35,353	835.0
1997						
1Q	2,322	50,547	43,800	3,070.0	35,427	848.5
2Q	2,194	52,741	46,317			

SOURCE: European Center for Macroeconomic Analysis of Ukraine, and the Ministry of Economics of Ukraine, *Ukrainian Economic Trends,* July 1997.

Concerning medium- and large-scale privatization, by mid-1997 only 9,649 of the over 18,000 medium- and large-scale firms in Ukraine at the time of independence had entered the corporatization (preprivatization) stage.[56] Of these, 5,087 had transferred more than 70 percent of their shares to private hands.[57] An additional 3,328 enterprises had either entered corporatization or transferred less than 70 percent to the private sector. The sluggish progress on large-scale privatization reflects not only a lingering Soviet preference for bigness but also the parliamentary resistance to substantive cultivation of the private sector. This resistance was manifested most dramatically in the 1994–1995 moratorium on privatization,[58] which was lifted only with the establishment of a standing list of "strategically important" enterprises specifically prohibited from privatization.[59]

Enterprise Governance. Independent observers have concluded that there has been little real change in the behavior of the typical enterprise in Ukraine.[60] Some 85 percent of all shares have gone to incumbent managers and employee groups, through preferred allocations during the initial closed-subscription phase of the process. Among small enterprises, this translates to some 56 percent of all entities being of "collective ownership" as of mid-1997 (plus another 2 percent remaining in state hands). As a result, there has been fairly little behavioral modification in most enterprises. Enterprises purchased by insiders are unlikely to change behavior, pare back costs, or lay off excess labor. In fact, for the postprivatization firm, investment tends to fall, while the wage bill increases.[61] Many continue to seek budgetary and credit subsidies, tax privileges, and state contracts. As Paul Hare et al. have concluded, this is due precisely to the exclusionary nature of most meaningful privatization in Ukraine: "Privatization is often about power and the distribution of property to those already close to power—the *nomenklatura.*"[62] The lack of enterprise behavioral response is obviously of great concern, insofar as there are substantial opportunity costs, not the least of which is slower growth.

Competition Policy. Due to the Soviet penchant for large-scale production, in 1991 Ukraine inherited many monopolies, concerning which privatization alone will not bring market forces to bear. A large proportion of Ukrainian output is produced by industry associations and so-called financial-industrial groups that behave much like conglomerates in the West. Over 98 percent of industrial output is produced by the estimated 18,000 firms classified as medium- and large-scale. The number of monopolies has been expanding, growing 36 percent, increasing in number from 795 to 1,078 in 1993 alone. The Ministry of Industrial Policy reported in February 1998 that the 200 largest enterprises in Ukraine accounted for 90 percent of industrial output.[63] Many of these entities successfully lobby for exemptions from existing antimonopoly laws, which poses a serious policy problem for promoting competition.

Ukraine's law "On Containing Monopolization and Preventing Unfair Competition" was enacted on February 18, 1992. The Anti-Monopoly Committee was established under Ukrainian law on November 26, 1993, to act in concert with the Ministries of Economics and Statistics to list and monitor enterprises that are to be regulated under the law. The threshold was set very high, however, at 35 percent of the market for certain goods and services, at either the national or regional level.[64] Unfortunately, the threshold level means that of the more than 700 markets that are affected by monopolies, only around 30 percent require regulation under the law.

General Business Climate. The business climate in Ukraine is complicated, to say the least. Quite apart from the Byzantine tax system, complex and burdensome business registration requirements and regulations burden commerce with delays, great uncertainty, and opportunities for bureaucratic corruption. A count by the State Committee on Problems of Development of Business Enterprise in late 1997 indicated that some 1,050 types of commercial activity had been subject to licensing by law, edict, or regulation.[65] Further, it was reported that 25 organs of the state possess the right to audit businesses, and that the average number of such annual checks had risen from 34 to 296. In surveys of small businesses, it has been reported that the two most painful legal problems are registration and government audits.[66] The sheer "deadweight loss" to the economy is very great, with Ukrainian enterprises spending the equivalent of an estimated 3 percent of GDP on regulatory compliance each year.

Ironically, all this regulation has not had the effect of providing a firm legal and regulatory base for businesses. On the contrary, because the regulations frequently change, often contradict one another, and are enforced selectively, the regulatory environment has stifled legitimate business and contributed to the growth of the shadow economy.[67] Other problems consistently cited by business leaders include high tax rates and inadequacy of the banking system. In addition, the commercial code is underdeveloped; property rights are unclear and difficult to enforce, as are owners' rights under the law. Protection of intellectual property is especially lacking.

Deregulation of commercial activity has been a major emphasis of the Kuchma administration since early 1998, when the president issued a decree ordering significant deregulation.[68] The decree set a deadline of April 1, 1998, to simplify business registration, reduce the number of activities that require registration, shorten the review time necessary for licensing, limit the number of audits and inspections of businesses, and establish a fixed tax for small businesses. The purpose was to coax some 1.5 million "shadow sector" entrepreneurs into the official economy, thereby increasing the number of registered businesses in Ukraine from around 90,000 (compared to Poland's 2 million small businesses). Little real progress was made on deregulation throughout 1998, however, as election year politics took precedence, and the administration encountered considerable bureaucratic resistance to the decree (many bureaucrats

188 ■ ECONOMIC CRISIS AND REFORM

earn their living by taking bribes from businesses that cannot possibly meet the tangle of regulatory requirements). All of this places private firms at a disadvantage to entities owned and operated by the state. It seems that Ukraine will slowly evolve in the direction of a market economy but will encounter on the way serious competition between private enterprises and state-run and state-protected firms for access to and control over markets.

THE EVOLUTION OF REFORMS

As noted in the introduction to this chapter, transition from socialism is a path-dependent process. It depends as much on initial conditions, policies pursued, and personalities as it does on the assertion of market forces. The evolution of reform policy in Ukraine demonstrates how the interplay of economic and political factors shapes reform policy and how reform can become captive to institutional competition at the highest levels of government. It is to this problem that we now turn.

Kravchuk's Confused Policies, 1991–1994

It is important at this point to recall the compromise between nationalists and Communists at the time of Ukrainian independence: In return for national Communists supporting independence, nationalists did not attempt a revolutionary removal of the ruling elite. The same people who had run the Soviet Ukrainian economy were therefore charged with creating a market economy, about which they had little knowledge and perhaps even less enthusiasm. The rule of Leonid Kravchuk demonstrated these problems.

The twin sagas of President Kravchuk's management of the economy were massive emissions of cheap credit and budget subsidies to industry, paired with the imposition of administrative controls over prices and exchange rates, in the vain attempt to reduce the consequent inflationary pressures or to suppress inflation altogether. Throughout the Kravchuk period (December 1991–July 1994), state-owned enterprises and powerful sectoral lobbies petitioned Kyiv aggressively for large amounts of "soft credits" in order to "stem the fall in output." Ukrainian authorities in this period remained under the spell of what has been described as the "cult of production."[69] Kravchuk himself seemed to believe that Ukraine's rapid price inflation was the result of a tragic imbalance between goods and money, a problem that could be solved by giving cheap credit to industry to increase production. Instead, ample cheap credits led to massive inflation and frustrated monetary stabilization and structural reform.[70]

Kravchuk's confused and often contradictory policies must be seen against the political backdrop of the period of his presidency. As president, he managed to maintain peace and domestic order and to establish Kyiv's economic sovereignty over Ukraine with a minimum of violence and almost no ethnic strife. Given the historical strength of Ukrainian nationalism, this was no small accomplishment. But the relative peace has been bought at the expense of forward progress on economic reforms. Kravchuk's preference for ruling through the old Communist network and his appointment to key governmental posts of former members of the *nomenklatura* promoted stability at the expense of reform. As Volodymyr Zviglyanich has put it, "[U]nder pretext of moving toward liberal democracy, rule of law and ... a market economy, a revamped collectivist elite entrenched itself in power, with Mr. Kravchuk as its leader and symbol."[71] A trade-off, therefore, existed between domestic order and economic reform. However, Ukraine's would-be reformers were growing nervous throughout this period over just how long Ukraine would be able to have the one without the other.

Establishing Economic Sovereignty. Kyiv's chief economic objective in the aftermath of attaining political independence was to establish economic sovereignty over the territory of Ukraine. This objective was pursued even prior to Ukraine's independence.[72] After the Declaration of State Sovereignty on July 16, 1990, Ukraine's first reform program was designed mainly to permit Ukraine to exert greater control over its own economy rather than to facilitate genuine market reforms. Indeed, the cornerstone of the program was to prevent consumer goods from being diverted to Russia, where higher prices could be obtained, by issuing rationing coupons with the payment of salaries. The Rada established the National Bank of Ukraine (NBU) on the basis of the Kyiv branch of Gosbank, extended Kyiv's control over all Soviet enterprises in Ukraine, and established the legal basis for Kyiv to levy its own taxes.

In the year following the August coup and Ukraine's declaration of independence in August 1991, little real reform activity took place. Instead, there was a proliferation of reform programs and plans, from sources both inside and outside of government. Prime Minister Vitold Fokin himself presented at least two detailed reform programs for the Rada's consideration.[73] The first failed to be adopted in fall 1991. But the second was adopted "in principle," in March 1992.[74] The plan was aimed much more at separating Ukraine's economy from that of Russia than at any real reform. That same month, on March 3, 1992, based on an alternative plan containing many provisions contradictory to Fokin's, the International Monetary Fund (IMF) admitted Ukraine to membership.[75] Ukraine also attained membership in the World Bank that year. These were immensely positive developments, especially as both lenders would come to provide critically needed capital as Ukraine's transition unfolded during 1993–1998. But first, Ukraine had to achieve economic sovereignty over its territory.

Establishing full sovereignty over the Ukrainian economy would involve disentangling trade and monetary policies from Russia and other former Soviet countries.[76] Since the old Soviet ruble continued to circulate in Ukraine throughout 1991–1992, the immediate problem was coordinating monetary policy with Moscow. This was an increasingly critical matter. Acute goods shortages resulted from price differentials between the two countries, caused by the apparent inability of the Central Bank of Russia to supply sufficient quantities of banknotes to ruble-zone countries. Substantial amounts of goods were therefore diverted to Russia, to be purchased with its more ample supply of rubles.

In response to shortages of critical consumer items, Ukraine had previously issued multi-use rationing scrip to citizens, in June 1991, which circulated as a parallel currency to the ruble. However, the shortage of currency led in January 1992 to introduction of a noncash counterpart to the ruble, the *karbovanets* (KBV), or "kupon," which was good for use in state stores. That same month, the Russian government liberalized prices broadly, forcing Ukraine to follow suit in order to maintain supplies of critical consumer goods. Hence, prices in general were raised an average of 435 percent during January 1992. Although this imposed a severe hardship on most of the public, the government had little choice: Without higher prices in Ukraine, goods would have fled the country toward higher prices in Russia, since there were as yet no customs controls between the two states. There were more price increases to come. On July 1, 1992, the government freed prices on major food items, causing waves of criticism from the Rada and the public.[77] The people were seeking a political solution, but the real problem was Ukraine's continued vulnerability to Russian monetary policy. In a final effort to "normalize trade with Russia" and on the advice of the IMF, Ukraine formally exited the ruble zone on November 12, 1992, making the *karbovanets* legal tender for all transactions. Ukraine's departure from the ruble area was generally smooth and orderly. However, full monetary independence removed the last remaining restriction on the unlimited issuance of bank credits to Ukrainian industry, paving the way for the tragic descent into hyperinflation in 1993.

"Kuchma I": Kravchuk's Reformist Prime Minister. Due to discontent over the July 1992 price increases and with little positive accomplishment in the economic sphere in his two years as premier, Fokin was compelled to resign in September 1992.[78] Kravchuk chose to replace Fokin with another former apparatchik, Leonid D. Kuchma, an industrialist and former di-

rector of the Pivden'mash missile factory in Dnipropetrovs'k.[79] Confirmed on October 13, Kuchma was given ten days in which to formulate an economic recovery program. At first, Kuchma promised little more than a continuation of Fokin's foot-dragging on the economy.[80] Despite his conviction that "Ukraine is on the verge of collapse," Kuchma initially mixed vague references to the market with calls to develop a uniquely "Ukrainian model" of reform, based on "evolutionary change." However, the new prime minister surprised the Rada by requesting six months' emergency powers "to rule the economy by decree," which the Rada speedily approved.[81] Further, he developed and submitted an economic reform package that enjoyed broad support from the IMF, the World Bank, and other international lenders.[82]

Kuchma brought into his cabinet several young reformers to help him formulate his program.[83] The new team immediately enacted measures aimed at reducing the budget deficit, improving tax collections, liberalizing trade, and promoting rapid privatization. In December 1992 and January 1993, dozens of new decrees were enacted.[84] The Law on Privatization was strengthened, welfare payments were slashed, and retail trade was opened to private competition. Further, the prime minister pledged to disband collective farms, raise energy prices, and fight corruption. These concrete steps were in line with the basic elements of Kuchma's program, which embraced an end to price speculation, imposed regulation of monopoly pricing, placed strict limits on monetary emissions, freed restrictions on investment by foreigners, and sought to conserve energy.[85] The economic climate would improve dramatically if these early reforms were implemented.

Kuchma's bold moves clearly had taken President Kravchuk by surprise. Outmaneuvered by his prime minister, Kravchuk's reluctance to embrace economic reform was becoming ever more apparent. The president had no choice but to endorse the government's program, thereby sharing responsibility with Kuchma.[86] But Kuchma's aggressive stance on the economy earned him Kravchuk's enmity. The president grew increasingly critical of his prime minister's failure to stem the fall in output, which remained an important governmental focus.[87] Upon the expiration of his six months' special powers in May, Kuchma asked for a six-month extension, expressing his desire to introduce a "state of emergency" in order to overcome opposition to his reforms.[88] Further, he asked for direct control over the National Bank and State Property Fund, both of which were subordinated to the Rada, but without which it would be impossible to stabilize the currency or accelerate privatization. Kravchuk interpreted Kuchma's proposals as a direct challenge to his status as chief executive.

The president responded to Kuchma's boldness by seeking direct control over the Cabinet of Ministers and over economic policy. Failing to obtain the parliamentary support for direct presidential government, Kravchuk issued a decree that would establish an "extraordinary committee" of the cabinet to deal with economic matters and asserted the president's control over the government.[89] Thus, by May 1993, economic reform had become fully entwined in the struggle between president and prime minister for control of the executive branch. A significant complicating factor was that these events coincided with a crippling ten-day strike by coal miners in the Donbas region of eastern Ukraine. The strike threatened the economy with chaos. The miners' demands for increased wages were coupled with a demand for a national referendum of confidence in the president and the Rada. The Rada initially met the demand for a referendum to be held in September but rescinded its decision a few days later, calling instead for early parliamentary and presidential elections.[90] The immediate effect of the strike was to prompt Kuchma to issue a more detailed economic reform program.[91] Kravchuk rescinded his June 16 decree extending presidential control over the government when the Rada restored his power to issue decrees and gave him interim control over the cabinet. In order to appease the strikers, he appointed as first deputy prime minister a former mine director and mayor of Donets'k, Yukhim Zviahils'kyi, who was also leader of the Donbas Strike Committee. Frustrated, Kuchma offered his resignation.

The Rada had rejected Kravchuk's bid for direct presidential rule, but it also rejected Kuchma's resignation, playing one off against the other and strengthening its hand at their expense. Kuchma offered his resignation twice more until, in September, the Rada finally accepted it, passing a vote of no confidence in the entire Cabinet of Ministers.[92] This was the final chapter in a long struggle for control of the executive branch. Conservative elements within the presidential administration, in order to weaken his position relative to Kravchuk's, had quietly sabotaged Kuchma by refusing to implement his reform measures.[93] For its part, the Rada had undermined Kuchma's program by ordering fresh credit emissions and by hampering efforts of the State Property Fund to accelerate privatization. Despite ostensible support for reforms *in principle,* a majority of deputies were critical of Kuchma's policies, claiming that they were "ill-conceived and hasty."[94] The opposition Kuchma's plans earned from both the president and the Rada demonstrated how weak the political base for reform was in Ukraine.

The Late 1993 "Anti-Hyperinflation Program." On September 22, 1993, Kravchuk named as acting premier the recently appointed first deputy prime minister, Yukhim Zviahils'kyi.[95] Considered a member of the "Red Directors" group in the Rada, Zviahils'kyi was one of a number of former Communist lawmakers who were opposed to radical economic reforms.

Kravchuk clearly viewed his new premier as the key to consolidating his political support in eastern Ukraine prior to the 1994 elections. During late 1993 and into 1994, his policies tended to favor his electoral constituency, including rural districts where he had always been popular. In the fall of 1993, he ordered Zviahils'kyi to lavish huge amounts of credits on the agricultural sector, in order to finance the harvest, and on state enterprises, which were now perpetually strapped for cash due to a continuing crisis of payments arrears.[96] Wedded to the notion that such credits were necessary to reduce inflation by increasing industrial production, Zviahils'kyi would refer to the October 1, 1993, release of 16 trillion KBV (approximately $500 million) as a "nonmonetary emission."[97] The *karbovanets* went into a virtual "free fall."

Unable or unwilling to see the linkage between bank credits, budget deficits, and inflation, President Kravchuk responded in November 1993 with intensified efforts to impose administrative control. He decreed the temporary suspension of trading operations at the Ukrainian Interbank Currency Exchange (UICE), imposed measures to halt the flight of hard currency from Ukraine, and instructed the NBU to establish control over the official exchange rate.[98] The "street rate" revealed the true extent of the currency devaluation, however, reaching more than 25,000 KBV per U.S. dollar by mid-November, down from the official rate of 5,970 KBV.[99] This new round of inflation was also fought administratively, with efforts to extend governmental control over hard currency transactions.[100]

To make matters worse, the government adopted a resolution to establish a system of some four different exchange rates as of January 1, 1994.[101] This cumbersome system reserved to the government maximal discretion over currency trades. But this did nothing to dampen inflationary pressures, as it did not stem the flows of credits to agriculture and industry. It did, however, provide the opportunity for huge illicit profits for those who could use the multirate system to buy dollars at a low exchange rate and sell them back at a higher rate. The combination of high inflation and cheap government credits was also extremely profitable for a privileged few enterprise directors who could get low-interest government loans, convert them into dollars, wait for the currency to fall, and then convert a fraction of the dollars back into *karbovantsy* to pay off the loan, pocketing the excess dollars.

The consequence was that prices rose by an enormous 93 percent in December, which was also the sixth straight month of price rises in excess of 50 percent. It was now abundantly clear that hyperinflation had broken out in Ukraine.[102] This prompted Kravchuk to respond with further measures to address inflation in a more explicit way. In early December, the government instituted a series of emergency measures called the "Anti-Hyperinflation Program."[103] The first stage of the plan was to "establish strict control over all forms of ownership." Specific measures included a general increase in prices by two times (thereafter, prices were to be frozen); issuance of ration cards for butter; ending the workday at 4:00 P.M. in order to conserve energy; elimination of all daytime television broadcasts; closing universities until the end of February; rationing heat in some cities; and selective "brownouts" of residential districts in Kyiv and certain other cities.

The Cabinet of Ministers further directed the National Bank to issue restrictions that effectively prohibited all commercial banks from making new loans or extending credit to enterprises until the end of the year.[104] The government thereby revoked all credits previously authorized and demanded immediate repayment.[105] Rather than a step toward fiscal sanity, this measure was apparently in order to prepare the way for the NBU to issue some 23 trillion KBV of new credits in December and January.[106] The bulk of the fresh emission was slated for agriculture (9 trillion) and industry (8 trillion), with the remainder for pension indexing (5 trillion). This was sure to bring further inflationary pressures. Led by the antireformist "Red Directors" group, the Rada rejected the more rational features of Kravchuk's program, however, demanding that the NBU immediately lift its December 2 ban on credits to enterprises, preferring not to delay even for a few weeks' time.[107]

By the end of 1993, the government's policies had become incoherent and self-contradictory, with increasing controls coupled with an announced plan to dramatically liberalize prices, removing controls from all but 20 percent of prices by the end of 1994. This would have the effect of both increasing allocative efficiency and reducing the budget deficit. In another contradictory measure, in conjunction with the planned price liberalization, the government proposed to adjust wages so as to cushion the effects of the price rises on consumers. Further, the Ministry of Economics pressed for a gradual ratcheting of prices and incomes, until prices for basic goods—especially raw materials and energy products—rose to world market levels. Although intended to protect consumers, this policy could not help but fuel inflation.[108] Such policies thus are ultimately self-defeating.

Kravchuk's Attempt to Renew the Command Economy. Parallel with the effort to control prices and inflation, Kravchuk also attempted to reestablish the system of "state orders and state contract" for certain critical goods and consumer products.[109] The intent of the policy was to stabilize production; however, the practical result was to continue support for inefficient enterprises and to encourage increased capital flight.[110] Enterprises that fulfilled state orders were guaranteed supplies of fuel, raw materials, and other privileges under the decree. In addition, the government established a list of resources whose production and consumption were to be tightly controlled.[111]

This attempt failed miserably, however. By mid-1994, it was clear that the system of state orders had broken down altogether, for a number of reasons.[112] The effort to reestablish the system of state orders collapsed because government direction of the economy had long since been displaced by market forces, a phenomenon that the authorities apparently failed to understand. State enterprises began searching for domestic and foreign markets. Such enterprise independence became possible only when the state abandoned the crucial control mechanism of allocating material inputs. Bowing to the inevitable, the system of state orders was officially abolished as of January 1, 1995. An important exception was in the agricultural sector, where the state still continues to claim a large proportion of the marketable output (see below).

"Kuchma II": The Course of Radical Reforms, 1994–1998
Economic reform received renewed impetus with the election of Leonid D. Kuchma as Ukraine's second president in July 1994. Candidate Kuchma had run on a platform of renewed economic ties to Russia, greater autonomy for Ukraine's regions, and an "evolutionary approach" to reforms. As president, Kuchma surprised observers by immediately setting about developing plans for accelerating Ukraine's transition to the market. The result was the October 11, 1994, release of an ambitious program of reforms, entitled "Along the Road of Radical Economic Reform."[113] Overwhelmingly approved by the Rada on October 19, the package received immediate support from numerous Western institutions, including the IMF and Group of Seven (G-7) industrialized nations.[114]

The Basic Reform Package. Kuchma's program was comprehensive, embracing the objectives of reducing the budget deficit from 20 percent of GDP to 8 percent in 1995 (and to no more than 4 percent in 1997); stabilizing the currency and introducing the *hryvnya*; accelerating medium- and large-scale privatization; liberalizing prices; reducing heavy tax burdens; cutting business regulation; and easing foreign currency restrictions. The World Bank predicted that if Kuchma's reforms were aggressively implemented, Ukraine could expect real economic growth of 6 to 7 percent by 1996.[115]

The sheer ambition of Kuchma's reforms generated widespread opposition in the Rada, which almost immediately engaged him in battle over the authority to implement the reforms. The game appeared to be one of giving Kuchma just enough rope to hang himself. Thus, despite ostensible parliamentary approval for his program, the legislature continuously handicapped his efforts, ensuring their failure. For instance, the very day after approving his program, the Rada endorsed broad-based wage increases of between 4 and 6 times, a doubling of monthly pensions, and a tripling of social security payments. This move was certain to lead to further deterioration of the *karbovanets*.[116] Kuchma responded by aggressively pursuing his plans for freeing exchange rates and liberalizing prices, which the Rada, reluctantly, also approved on November 9. A unified exchange rate to be set by the UICE went into effect on October 28. But these efforts would be fruitless unless privatization was accelerated and enterprise governance reformed. The Rada remained obstinate, however, blocking entirely any effort to restructure Ukrainian industry. On July 29, 1994, the Rada placed a moratorium on most significant privatization activities.[117] The ban lasted four months, and was lifted only after the cabinet adopted a list of some 6,147 enterprises to be excluded from privatization, owing to their "national significance and value to the state."[118] In this way, the Rada effectively removed from consideration the "cream" of Ukrainian industry, the most desirable enterprises.

In its efforts to handicap Kuchma, the Rada had a willing ally in Prime Minister Vitaliy Masol. Appointed by Kravchuk just nine days before the June presidential election, Masol marked a return to the Soviet period (he had previously served as Ukraine's Soviet-era premier) and was ideologically opposed to much of Kuchma's program. Frustrated with the cabinet, the president forced Masol out of government "for reasons of his advanced age," appointing former KGB general and First Deputy Prime Minister Yevhen Marchuk as acting premier.[119] Initially loyal to Kuchma, Marchuk had not yet exhibited the personal ambitions that would later cause him to run afoul of the president and his policies.

Kuchma on "Correcting Reforms," 1995. Early in 1995, Kuchma's commitment to reforms apparently "softened." He began to speak publicly of the need for a "correction" of reforms, indicating on April 4 in his economic report to the Rada his desire to shift emphasis from achieving stabilization through monetary means to spurring growth in industrial output.[120] The president criticized "blind monetarism," calling instead for creation of a "socially oriented market economy."[121] Kuchma's concept of "correction" implied strengthening the state in order to enhance control over the economic process, to be accomplished through the establishment of "Financial-Industrial Groups" (FIGs). These would essentially be "seamless" networks of banking and industrial enterprises, involving a degree of economic integration not seen since Soviet times.

In late January 1995, Kuchma had decreed that the Cabinet of Ministers draft a law to organize entrepreneurial activity into FIGs, patterned after the Russian model decreed there two years earlier.[122] These entities were viewed as means to reestablish desirable economic links with Russian enterprises, in recognition of the high degree of interdependence that still existed between some firms in the two countries.[123] FIGs are established under Ukrainian law as conglomerates of banks and manufacturers, operating under a single organizational shell. As in Russia, a FIG is a group of companies that band together to share technology and capital in order to improve competitiveness. Initially lukewarm on the idea, the Rada approved establishment of FIGs on November 21, 1995, after stripping away certain special privileges (including tax concessions and access to credits) from Kuchma's draft bill.[124] Certain of the parliamentary factions—especially those on the right—feared that FIGs would constitute a vehicle for Russian domination of key Ukrainian industries. However, the law was enacted after amendments that permitted establishment of FIGs only in "priority industries," to be designated by the Rada itself. Throughout 1995–1998, Ukrainian and Russian enterprises employed this law extensively to create interstate FIGs in the heavy machinery, defense, metallurgical, and chemical industries, among others.[125]

FIGs can combine both vertical and horizontal integration to such an extent that new monopolies may be formed. Although these are obviously subject to the antimonopoly legislation of both countries, the FIG structure militates against domestic competition. Further, the FIG organization "closely corresponds to the ministries to which these manufacturers [previously] belonged" under the USSR.[126] As such, FIGs appear substantially to re-create in the private sector the same kind of patronage-based economic system that Mikhail Gorbachev expended so much effort to bring down. Creating FIGs reconstructs much of the "ministry system," albeit on a decentralized basis, including more coordinated resource allocation, lax incentives, and sluggish response to markets. Cross-national FIGs partially re-create pieces of the former supply system of the Soviet economy. Opponents object that they will favor entrenched powerful economic interests possessing privileged access to government authorities in both countries. Thus, the basic question remains whether FIGs are a vehicle for "crony capitalism" or a "Trojan horse" for Russian penetration of Ukrainian industry, or both.

These developments were complicated in mid-1995, by the ongoing struggle between the president and the Rada over adoption of a post-Soviet constitution for Ukraine. In the absence of general agreement on the basic provisions of a new fundamental law, the struggle over economic reform and exercise of executive powers remained problematic. On May 18, 1995, however, conclusion of the Constitutional Accord between the president and the Rada provided the framework for orderly governance in the face of the daunting task of negotiating a new constitution.[127] But its implementation was delayed owing to the required constitutional amendments that were needed in order to bring it fully into force. The accord would operate as a *"petite constitution."* It was signed on June 8, after Kuchma threatened to call a nationwide referendum of confidence in himself and the Rada on June 28.[128] The accord gave the president exclusive rights to form the government, issue decrees, and overrule local councils that attempted to block his reforms.[129] The new agreement did not end contention between the executive and legislature, however. The Rada continuously debated legislation on issues that were now formally within the president's competence, refusing even to consider over 100 laws submitted by the president.[130] Economic reform was thus still captive to the as yet unresolved institutional competition.

Marchuk's Economic Program. Prime Minister Yevhen Marchuk entered the economic reform arena in October 1995, with the presentation to the Rada of his reform proposals.[131] The ninth such program to be submitted since August 1991, Marchuk's wide-ranging program embraced Kuchma's concept of "correcting reforms," calling for a more evolutionary approach to economic transition.[132] Although the new program echoed much of Kuchma's October 1994 program, Marchuk's would slow reforms "in recognition of the prolonged and deep crisis afflicting Ukraine." However, the plan was full of measures that would militate against development of free markets.[133] The main tenets of the program were: state-regulated transition to a socially oriented market economy; social protection of the population from the worst excesses of transition; protection from foreign competition for domestic producers; corporatization of enterprises (with the state maintaining a controlling interest); state control of prices; and preservation of monopoly status of key enterprises.[134]

The Rada almost immediately voted for measures that were inconsistent with the Marchuk program, however. For instance, a key feature of the program was the elimination of possible wage-push inflation by strictly limiting the rate of growth in wages and salaries to 80 percent of the growth of industrial output. But the very next day after enacting the program, the Rada endorsed an increase in the minimum wage, which would result in fresh emissions of some 600 trillion KBV, thereby aggravating inflation. At the time, Labor Minister Mykhailo Kaskevych stated that "this decision by the Rada has actually canceled the government program of action adopted yesterday."[135] The Rada once again publicly supported the reform program, but it placed itself at odds with the government over its implementation.

Monetary Reform and Fiscal Discipline, 1996. Prime Minister Marchuk vowed to reduce budget expenditures and credit subsidies in 1996.[136] In fact, throughout the year the government made serious efforts to reduce subsidies and credits, with the result that a dangerous crisis was generated in unpaid wages, pensions, and interenterprise debts. Fears arose that a chain of bankruptcies would be set in motion.[137] Efforts were made throughout the year to clear the arrears, but with little success. Wages and salaries lagged significantly behind schedule, often for months. It seems clear that the government used the arrears to meet inflation targets negotiated with foreign lenders, notably the IMF. Further, the arrears crisis failed to dissipate, even after introduction (finally) of Ukraine's permanent national currency, the *hryvnya*. Passage of an austere budget almost three months late, on March 22, barely satisfied conditions for resumption of installments under a previously suspended IMF standby loan agreement, providing around $300 million in immediate fiscal relief.[138] However, as Table 6.4 shows, the payments crisis intensified throughout the year, reaching 82 trillion HRV by December 31, 1996.[139] The arrears would persist into 1997–1998, considerably aggravating social and political tensions.

A serious rift developed between Kuchma and Marchuk over various aspects of reform, costing Marchuk the premiership on May 27, 1996. In dismissing him, Kuchma cited inefficiency in the management of the cabinet.[140] In reality, Kuchma feared that Marchuk had become a serious

TABLE 6.4 Selected Budgetary Arrears, 1995–1997 (millions of end-of-period HRV)

Period	Wages	Social Insurance[a]	Student Stipends	Pensions[b]	Total Arrears[c]	Percent of YTD Deficit
1995						
4Q	384	155	0	102	641	24%
1996						
1Q	591	275	0	421	1,288	–
2Q	919	364	0	1,173	2,456	167%
3Q	1,305	387	85	928	2,705	–
4Q	1,231	399	96	1,255	2,981	116%
1997						
1Q	1,764	383	92	1,380	3,619	–
2Q	1,733	341	89	1,559	3,721	199%

[a] Includes Chernobyl Fund arrears and those of other social funds; excludes Pension Fund.
[b] Includes Pension Fund arrears, Chernobyl Fund, and budgetary pension arrears to the military and security services.
[c] Consolidated budget wage arrears (including the military), pension arrears, and consolidated budget social benefit arrears.
SOURCE: IMF (1997), table 31, page 86; authors' calculations.

political rival, publicly opposing the president over a national referendum on the June 1996 Constitution and engaging in an apparent rapprochement with the left on easing the course of economic reforms.[141] Marchuk, the fifth prime minister since 1992, was replaced by First Deputy Prime Minister Pavlo Lazarenko, a forty-three-year-old oil tycoon from Kuchma's native city of Dnipropetrovs'k.

In firing Marchuk, Kuchma reaffirmed his commitment to economic reforms, stating that "Ukraine has passed the point of historic return, and there will be no going back."[142] For his part, Lazarenko affirmed his support for Kuchma's reforms.[143] To simplify implementation of reforms, Kuchma extensively reorganized the government by decree in July, streamlining the cabinet and ordering the layoffs of 20 percent of government employees (some 10,000) as a cost-cutting measure. In fact, this was a direct move against the midlevel bureaucracy, the so-called *nomenklatura*, widely viewed as blocking reforms. These measures, however, obscured from the public's view preparation for a far more important event, the introduction of Ukraine's permanent currency, the *hryvnya*, in September.

The currency reform of September 2 was announced with great fanfare on August 24, the fifth anniversary of Ukrainian independence. With few restrictions on currency conversion, the reform was entirely nonconfiscatory, which enhanced acceptability of the *hryvnya*. The process went so smoothly that an anti-inflationary retail price freeze was lifted after just two weeks, and the period of conversion was extended until mid-October. To the credit of NBU governor Victor Yushchenko, the *hryvnya*-to-dollar exchange rate remained stable from its inception until autumn 1998, when effects of the Asian economic crisis began to be felt on Ukraine's domestic government debt market. As of early 1999, the currency reform of 1996 stands as the greatest achievement to date of Ukraine's economic reform efforts.

Tax Reform Fails, 1997. Lazarenko's government made its most important reform efforts in the budgetary sphere, proposing a radical reform of the entire tax system. With high marginal tax rates, narrow bases, and hundreds of exemptions, exclusions, and privileges, Ukraine's tax system was in crisis. It is blamed for driving over one-half of the entire economy into the shadow sector. By 1997, it was abundantly clear that the situation had long since become untenable. Dubbed "Economic Growth '97," the program would have greatly simplified taxes through a series of seven draft laws that, collectively, would promote growth by cutting overall taxes by 7.3 percent. The program's centerpiece was to be a cut in the average enterprise tax burden from 7.6 to 4.1 percent of GDP. A key objective was to bring "shadow-sector" businesses into the official economy.

The budget package also included deep cuts in social spending, eliminating all subsidies for rents and utilities.

The fight over tax reform delayed enactment of the budget for almost six months, to June 27, placing acute pressure on the government, with the IMF threatening to temporarily suspend or considerably reduce promised 1997 funding of more than $1.2 billion.[144] This would severely constrain Ukraine's ability to repay energy debts to Russia and Turkmenistan. In the end, the tax package was only partially enacted, including minor changes to the VAT, a major amendment to the enterprise profits tax (levying the tax on "net profits"), and withdrawal of tax incentives for foreign investors (of which the IMF did *not* approve). To the great disappointment of reformers, the remaining five bills were shelved indefinitely. Tax reform had failed abysmally.

Failure to secure enactment of the tax package meant that Lazarenko also would be removed, less than one year after taking office.[145] Dismissed by Kuchma on June 19, 1997, for "health reasons," pressure for Lazarenko's removal had been building for several months, over both his inability to gain passage of Kuchma's tax reforms and his inaction on a major anticorruption package.[146] The prime minister himself had been accused of corruption and money laundering.[147] Owing to these factors, Lazarenko was replaced on July 16, 1997, by a Kuchma crony, Minister of the Cabinet Valeriy Pustovoitenko.[148] Known for his fierce loyalty to the president, Pustovoitenko first came to Kyiv with Kuchma in 1992, when the latter was named premier. A member of the pro-Kuchma National Democratic Party, unlike his predecessors, he was expected to support his patron unquestioningly.[149]

Kuchma Veers Further off Course, 1998. The presence of Kuchma loyalist Pustovoitenko at the helm meant that rivalry between president and premier was at an end, so that responsibility for the government's economic policy now rested squarely with Kuchma. The parliamentary elections of March 29, 1998, failed to break the political logjam between the president and the Rada, with leftists capturing 180 of the 450 seats contested. Election of Oleksandr Tkachenko of the leftist Agrarian Party as the parliamentary Speaker also boded ill for reforms. Predictably, the new Rada has been as obstructionist as its predecessor, attempting in October 1998 to remove Pustovoitenko in a no-confidence vote, due to the government's compliance with stringent IMF conditions. Kuchma himself is now slipping in popularity polls. He ranked third as a 1999 presidential contender, behind the likely Socialist and Communist candidates, in a November 1998 survey conducted by his own administration. In the midst of what may prove to be a divisive presidential campaign, the president is veering to the left. That he sees this direction as the way to move to capture votes underscores the fundamental lack of a popular political base for economic reform in Ukraine.

In May 1998, Kuchma outlined a new program that he believed would appeal to the new, left-leaning Rada. The program, "Concept of and Strategy for Economic Growth, 1999–2005," takes account of the successes previously achieved under the October 1994 program of IMF-approved "radical reforms," updated to the needs of the current situation.[150] Kuchma's 1998 program was designed to increase the regulatory role of the state, reduce foreign and domestic borrowing, increase financial support for industry, and reduce the budget deficit permanently. The objective was to halt the decline in output and actually to increase real growth to 5 percent annually by 2002. Kuchma's plan was to "turn stabilization [gradually] into positive growth." By focusing on the output collapse, however, he was appealing to populist sentiments in the Rada and society, which had always seen the decline in production as *the problem* to be solved.

It is easy to understand Kuchma's frustration with the situation. Originally expected to experience positive growth of 1.0 percent in 1997, Ukrainian GDP actually fell 3.2 percent that year, then grew by a modest 0.2 percent in the first nine months of 1998. In autumn, the Asian crisis, by way of the Russian crisis, sent certain key industries into a tailspin (e.g., steel, which declined 22 percent from its September 1997 level). To compound matters, the worldwide crisis also negatively affected government treasury bill sales, raising the likelihood that Ukraine would have to resort to printing money to cover the ongoing budget deficit of 3.7 percent of GDP. Although the exchange rate had remained relatively stable for two years, in September the NBU was forced to abandon its defense of its "trading band" against the U.S. dollar, which resulted in a devaluation of nearly 60 percent after August 17, when Russia announced its devaluation and debt moratorium.

Kuchma acted in late summer to reduce the deficit by decree, ordering draconian spending cuts to pare the annual deficit to 2.5 percent of GDP, from 3.7 percent, by year's end.[151] Nominal cuts of an average 19.4 percent were ordered.[152] Despite his efforts, Kuchma was unable to prevent the downgrading in September of Ukrainian currency bonds by Moody's, from a B2 to a B3 rating, with a negative forecast.[153] A decline in gold and hard currency reserves to critically low levels also raised the risk of default on external debt, prompting Standard and Poor's to rate Ukraine's fiscal position as "unreliable."[154] As a result of these downgradings, Kuchma took the more drastic step of (more or less) forcibly rescheduling Ukraine's debt, effectively postponing the crisis until 2000.[155] In order to meet the government's immediate cash needs and prop up industrial production, in a major speech on November 19, Kuchma explicitly rejected the advice of the

IMF and Western governments, choosing instead to follow Russia's lead by combating the financial crisis with Soviet-era tools.[156] In so doing, he called for printing more money, as well as new legislation stripping the NBU of its independence.[157]

Vacillating on reforms, and unable to use his prime minister as scapegoat, Kuchma now harshly criticized the monetary policies of the NBU for "artificially restricting the *hryvnya* rate," thereby depriving the economy of money necessary for growth.[158] To increase liquidity in the enterprise sector, Kuchma explicitly reneged on previous agreements with the IMF, reestablishing government control over the NBU and nationalizing the former agroinvestment bank, Bank Ukraiina, which had been led into bankruptcy by the government's policy of directing credits to unworthy growers in the agricultural sector. By prior agreement, Ukraine was also to cancel all tax privileges in order to boost revenue flow, but Kuchma now called for agricultural producers to be exempt from all taxes for three years, except pension fund contributions. Finally, stating that he was against cash emissions, he nevertheless called for reviving the previous practice of direct NBU crediting of the budget, which would amount to the same thing: renewed inflation.

The reaction of the World Bank and the IMF was swift and certain. They announced jointly on December 7 that Ukraine would receive no installments on existing loans or any new loans until February 1999, at the earliest.[159] The European Union (EU) also froze a 150 million ECU credit line (European Currency Unit, roughly equal in value to the U.S. dollar), pending a final decision by the IMF. Hence, a further bailout of Ukraine by Western lenders is highly unlikely. The amounts at stake are not trivial. Ukraine received two IMF tranches worth $335 million, and $340 million in loans from the World Bank, in autumn 1998; but the third IMF tranche was suspended. The NBU badly needs the IMF funds to replenish its hard currency reserves, which stood at just $1 billion after repeated intervention to defend the *hryvnya* after the Russian crisis. However, without IMF funding, Ukraine will not be able to redeem $860 million in treasury bills and another $1.5 billion in external debt that must be paid in 1999. Further devaluation of the *hryvnya* appears likely in 1999, especially in light of the growing current account deficit and minimal foreign currency reserves. At the time of this writing (June 1999), the crisis is as yet unresolved.

Summary: The Politics of Reform

Certain lessons emerge from this examination of the evolution of Ukraine's reforms. What comes through most clearly is the lack of strong, consistent leadership. Presidential vacillation on the direction of reforms, combined with the frequent turnover of prime ministers (and, in fact, other key ministerial posts), militates against implementation of a consistent, longer-term program. These trends call into doubt Kuchma's understanding and genuine commitment to reform and indicate that the division of powers within Ukraine's executive branch remains unclear. Further, the competition between president and the Rada over the course of reforms indicates an unhealthy degree of institutional competition that was not resolved by the Constitution of Ukraine, enacted in 1996. As if this were not enough, at the middle level of the state bureaucracy, the government is plagued by holdovers, former Soviet apparatchiks, who lack imagination, drive, or patriotic fervor.

Most fundamentally, however, there is little underlying political support for reform in Ukraine. The absence of a reform coalition in the Rada is especially disruptive. The parliamentary reformers also tend to be the most fervent nationalists.[160] They are kept continuously off balance by a much stronger left wing, which calls into question Ukraine's legitimate existence as an independent state. The reformers' attention thus tends to be more focused on maintaining and building Ukraine's statehood, quite apart from the question of market reforms. The situation in the Rada reflects a general lack of consensus among the public, which in opinion polls expresses either great confusion or outright hostility toward reform. The public sees the economy worsening, at the same time observing that managers and other elites have preferential access to government and enrich themselves at the state's expense. The president, unable or unwilling to confront and overcome the corrupt forces within the government, only appears to condone the situation. Indeed, when his energetic justice minister, Serhii Holovatyi, attempted to enforce anticorruption laws in 1997, Kuchma summarily discharged him. The Ukrainian public has never strongly supported reform or reformist politicians, and the complete corruption that has characterized reform to this point has undermined the credibility of the idea even further.

The parliamentary leftists, it appears, may have been first to recognize that Ukrainian independence depends vitally upon substantive progress on reforms. Their strategy of paying lip service to reforms, formally supporting the government's programs, and then hamstringing reform in the implementation stage has proved to be very effective. The result is that high-profile reform plans have been adopted on many occasions but have been undermined and forced to fail, thus undermining the whole notion of reform. Many reform measures have been quite piecemeal in nature, lacking a comprehensive scope. The partial reforms themselves have been the cause of subsequent problems, which have been addressed, in their turn, by further piecemeal measures, thereby compounding matters. In the meantime, Ukraine has managed to survive largely on the basis of foreign loans, which have propped it up in the face of its economic policy failures. This has also made the country more susceptible to external economic shocks, as evidenced by the effects of the Asian economic crisis on the economy in late 1998.

CONCLUSION: WHITHER REFORM?

The Ukrainian transition experience is an interesting one for students of economic reform, precisely because it is characterized by such outrageous extremes. The economic record is abysmal. Some four years after Kuchma's "original" 1994 Program of Radical Reforms, there has been little real structural change, save that of small-scale privatization, which is reversible in any case. Large-scale privatization has lagged, with a flow of subsidies and preferential loans to unprofitable enterprises. A labyrinthine tax system, excessively regulated foreign and domestic trade, and low-paid, unfriendly bureaucrats prone to selective enforcement of the laws prevent meaningful development of the business sector. Unclear and mutually contradictory legal and regulatory provisions reserve a great deal of discretion to the bureaucracy. This is especially true of tax administration, where corruption is rampant. In some industries, enterprises have more to gain from securing favorable tax treatment than from making product. The failure of privatization policy has seriously constrained growth of the tax base, which has contributed to keeping the budget in its state of perpetual deficit. External debts to cover budget deficits and finance industrial renewal have been used to pay for energy imports and government salaries and not for their intended purpose. Finally, as Dominique Arel has noted, "[D]espite sustained pressure from the IMF, the World Bank, and the United States, this destructive cycle has not been broken."[161] In late 1998, these creditors' patience was exhausted, and they suspended their loans. Thus, despite certain successes, notably the currency reform of 1996, Ukraine seems further from enacting genuine market reforms than it once was. After seven years of "nonreform," it appears that Ukraine will continue to "muddle through," perhaps, until hyperinflation reemerges or until a severe debt crisis breaks the current political logjam. Whether a crisis, when it comes, finally forces serious reform or whether it leads to the state's collapse remains to be seen.

■ SEVEN ■

Foreign Policy: From Isolation to Engagement

Ukraine's foreign policy represents the most substantial political success story for the young state. Whereas other areas of Ukrainian politics have been characterized by stagnation and crisis, foreign policy has been remarkable for its rapid transition from isolation and uncertainty in the early post-Soviet years to confidence in Ukraine's security and its political importance in recent years. How has this immense change come about? In this chapter, we describe the evolution of Ukraine's policy from 1991 to 1999 as well as the changes other nations have made in their policies toward Ukraine. The most notable successes in Ukraine's foreign policy have been establishing a close relationship with the United States, on the one hand, and settling differences with Russia, on the other. Both these changes, however, have their basic causes in the 1994 shift in the triangular relationship among Russia, the United States, and Ukraine.

This chapter will describe how both Ukraine's inclinations and its options have evolved since 1991, beginning with a discussion of the immense tasks Ukraine faced in the international arena at the time of independence. It does not, however, seek to be a complete history, instead focusing on key events and trends at the expense of a chronological account of all that went on. For the first few years, asserting Ukrainian sovereignty was the primary goal of foreign policy, and other more concrete issues took a backseat. Ties with Russia were severed in many areas, and efforts to build ties with the West were undermined by the West's single-minded focus on Ukraine's nuclear status. By 1994, the policy of asserting sovereignty had reached its limits: It had achieved much, but it was impeding further improvement in Ukraine's international position. After the election of Leonid Kuchma, priorities changed in a subtle but crucial way. The mission of establishing Ukraine's separateness was slowly replaced with an effort to rebuild connections with Russia and to improve them with the West, though the underlying goal of sovereignty was not surrendered. From 1994 to 1997, ties were increased, and tensions were reduced, both with Russia and the West, so that in both directions, Ukraine moved from isolation to engagement. As Ukraine has increased ties with both East and West, a new and very different debate has arisen as the state's leaders contemplate the future: How should Ukraine balance these two axes of its foreign policy, and how far should it move from its previously declared policy of neutrality?

PREHISTORY: UKRAINIAN FOREIGN POLICY BEFORE AUGUST 1991

Prior to August 1991, Ukraine had not conducted an independent foreign policy, and the lack of experience showed after independence. For a short time from 1918 to 1920, various incarnations of an independent Ukrainian republic existed and carried on foreign relations, most notably with Germany. But this period was brief, characterized primarily by civil war, and left no institutional remnants. Under the Union Treaty of 1922, Ukraine was technically a sovereign state with its own foreign policy, but in fact all substantial decisions, both foreign and domestic, were centralized in Moscow. The fiction of a sovereign Ukraine was revived by Stalin after World War II, to justify three, rather than one, Soviet seats at the United Nations. Thus, throughout the postwar period, both Ukraine and Belarus, as well as the USSR, had seats at the UN. There was therefore a small Ukrainian foreign policy apparatus and an international institute in Kyiv, but by all accounts, these played no independent role and functioned merely as additional arms of Soviet foreign policy. Ukraine, for example, had a mission to the UN, but not to any other country. The most talented people in foreign policy, as in all other governmental affairs, moved on to Moscow.

As Ukrainian nationalists began asserting independence from Moscow in the late 1980s, the question of a foreign policy slowly reappeared on the agenda in a number of ways. Clearly, many nationalists dreamed not only of breaking away from the Soviet Union but of aligning Ukraine with the West. As was discussed in Chapter 2, a strong part of Ukrainian national identity continued to look west, via historical links with Warsaw and Vienna, rather than east to Moscow. And underlying the entire notion of independence was an attitude toward Ukraine's historical relations with Russia that had immense implications for subsequent relations. Initially, however, more pragmatic issues were addressed. Most immediate was the desire to bring back to Ukraine the Ukrainian servicemen serving elsewhere in the USSR. Most significant in the long term was policy on nuclear weapons. The Chernobyl disaster had linked nuclear issues with the goal of political independence, and Ukrainian nationalists sought to stress their moderation. For both reasons, the 1990 declaration of sovereignty explicitly stated Ukraine's desire to become a neutral and nonnuclear state. This intention played an important role in the subsequent misunderstandings that plagued the first years of Ukraine's foreign policy.

FROM THE COUP TO THE COMMONWEALTH: 1991

We have discussed above in some detail the pivotal role of Ukraine in the dissolution of the Soviet Union (see Chapter 1), but it is useful to summarize this in the context of foreign policy because the principles behind Ukrainian policy on the Soviet Union continued to define Ukrainian policy long after 1991, both in policy toward Russia and toward the CIS.

Following the August 1991 coup and Ukraine's declaration of independence on August 24, the course toward complete Ukrainian independence was set. Exactly what that meant, however, was unclear, and the process of bargaining between Russian and Ukrainian leaders in this period set the stage for the tension that has persisted ever since. In this brief chaotic period, the biggest questions of defining the two states' relationship—questions that still have enormous political salience in both countries—were hammered out. Although opinion in neither country was uniform, we speak here of "Russian" and "Ukrainian" policies because the gaps between the two states' policies were far more significant than debates within them. Essentially, Russian leaders sought to minimize the fragmentation of the Soviet Union, while Ukrainian leaders sought to maximize it. In the end, Ukraine was successful, which led to considerable resentment on the part of Russian leaders.

Throughout the autumn of 1991, Russian leaders put forth plans for new union-level institutions—first for a redrawn union treaty to replace the one that had prompted the coup, then for an economic treaty modeled on the European Community, then for a unified military based on the NATO model. All of these efforts were aimed at preventing the collapse of central institutions and had practical goals as well as the more obvious goal of maintaining Russia's dominance. Economically, the republics of the Soviet Union were more interdependent than those of the EU, and severing ties abruptly promised untold economic damage. Militarily, the thought of splitting a single army into fifteen seemed institutionally impossible, as well as highly destabilizing. The fear of conflict among the new armies was surpassed by the fear of nuclear weapons, which to many constituted the greatest reason to retain certain central institutions.

For Ukrainian leaders, and especially for Ukrainian nationalists, all such talk from Moscow was dismissed as an effort by Russia to continue its hegemony in any way possible. Independence meant complete independence, and it also meant that Ukraine and Russia should have relations no different from any other two sovereign states. This bottom line for Ukraine was anathema to Russia, but after the overwhelming support for this policy in the December 1, 1991, referendum, there was little reason for Ukrainian leaders to compromise.

Boris Yeltsin, however, had much reason to compromise, and understanding Ukrainian-Russian relations in this period requires a brief digression into Russia's domestic politics. In early December 1991, as Yeltsin traveled to Belavezha Pushcha in Belarus to negotiate a new relationship with Ukraine and Belarus, he was still locked in a struggle with Mikhail Gorbachev for control of Russia. Yeltsin was the president of Russia and had gained both popular and institutional power from this position. But Gorbachev remained president of the USSR, technically above Yeltsin, and continued to argue that much of what Yeltsin did was illegal. The only way for Yeltsin to get rid of Gorbachev in legal terms was to agree to the dissolution of the USSR in legal terms, by agreeing with Ukraine and Belarus, the other signatories of the 1922 Union Treaty, to dissolve that treaty. In negotiating over the terms of a new arrangement, therefore, Kravchuk had all the cards and Yeltsin had none. Ukrainian independence was becoming a de facto reality, was widely endorsed in Ukraine, and had been recognized internationally. And Kravchuk's need to dissolve the Soviet Union in legal terms was not so significant. Legally, it would assert something that was already being established in fact, but Kravchuk had no domestic rival that he needed to dispatch with such a measure. The resulting CIS treaty, then, was written largely to meet Ukraine's needs. Although it declared a whole range of measures on which the states would continue to cooperate, it made such cooperation voluntary and set up no institutional mechanism to carry out such plans. Only in the area of strategic nuclear forces, and there only for a short time, did the agreement amount to much.

Ukraine thus succeeded in establishing its preferred view of the CIS as a "civilized divorce." And Yeltsin got what he needed and forced Gorbachev to resign a few weeks later. But having gotten rid of Gorbachev, Yeltsin and Russia proceeded for the next several years to try to regain what had been surrendered in terms of central control. In December 1991, the issue had been settled largely on Ukraine's terms, and Russia's efforts to alter that outcome became the major source of tension as the two countries moved forward into the post-Soviet era.

THE EARLY AGENDA: RECOGNITION AND SEPARATION

Initially, Ukrainian foreign policy was focused on establishing the state's independence. It is a truism in the study of international politics that the overarching goal of foreign policy is preserving the independence of the state. For most states, independence represents the status quo, but for Ukraine in late 1991, it was a desired goal, not a given fact. Thus, all of Ukraine's foreign policy efforts were aimed at establishing what other states take for granted. This goal was pursued by two means: gaining recognition of Ukraine's independence and completing the process of separating the state from Russia. The former was relatively straightforward and can be dealt with briefly, whereas the latter was much more complex.

Recognition is largely a symbolic notion in international politics, but it has immense practical importance. Ukraine had two separate recognition problems, one focused on Russia and the other focused on the major states of the West. Only with Poland, Canada, and Hungary was recognition noncontroversial; these three states recognized Ukraine immediately after the December 1 independence referendum. The majority of other Western states, however, delayed recognition, beginning an era of mistrust and misunderstanding that lasted until 1994.

The United States and most other NATO and EU states delayed recognition for two reasons. First, they were afraid of seeing the Soviet Union collapse. The West had built a very stable relationship with the Soviet Union, and with Mikhail Gorbachev in particular, and was hesitant to see it go. Most Westerners looked at the collapse of the Soviet Union and saw not liberation but instability. This sentiment was famously expressed by George Bush even prior to the coup, when he visited Kyiv in July 1991 and warned Ukrainians against "suicidal nationalism." Thus, the United States continued to back Gorbachev over Yeltsin up until Gorbachev's resignation. Beyond the hope of seeing the Soviet Union preserved, Western leaders recognized that among the Soviet successor states, Russia was clearly the most important in economic, diplomatic, and military terms. Therefore, even after acknowledging the demise of the Soviet Union, Western leaders played down relations with the non-Russian states (except for the Baltics) in order to avoid antagonizing Moscow. This policy, too, was to continue for some time.

The second reason to delay recognizing Ukraine's independence was to use diplomatic recognition as a "lever" to prod Ukraine on the key issue of concern to the West: nuclear weapons. If Western leaders tended to see instability when they looked at the Soviet collapse, they tended in particular to see the dangers of nuclear weapons. The fear was that three new nuclear states were being born, that fragmenting the old centralized command system would undermine control over the nuclear weapons, and that instability in the region might actually lead to nuclear weapons being used. Fear over nuclear weapons was a main reason the West supported maintaining the Soviet Union, and the reason the West supported the maintenance of a single military control even after the collapse. U.S. Secretary of State James Baker captured the prevailing attitude: "We really do run the risk of seeing a situation created there not unlike what we've seen in Yugoslavia, with nukes—with nuclear weapons thrown in."[1] The United States and most of its allies therefore delayed recognition until after Gorbachev had resigned and after Ukraine had reasserted its intention of becoming a nonnuclear state.

As we will see below, Ukrainian promises and Western recognition did not end the problem. Moreover, this episode caused a good deal of confusion and resentment in Ukraine, feelings that were both to grow. Ukrainian leaders and citizens alike had believed that as the adversary of the Soviet Union, the West would rush to the aid and support of the country most responsible for destroying "the evil empire." Instead, they found that Ukraine was facing demands to return weapons to Russia and that the West seemed to be giving priority to Russia, the former enemy, rather than to Ukraine, which supported the goals of the West. Misunderstandings concerning each other's perspectives continued to plague Ukraine's relations with the West.

Ukraine sought recognition of its independence from Russia as well as from the West, but here the problems were quite different. Yeltsin was more than happy to recognize Ukrainian sovereignty in formal terms, because it was the direct parallel of his assertion of Russia's sovereignty vis-à-vis the Soviet Union. However, having granted recognition in principle, Russia seemed unwilling to grant in fact the degree of autonomy Ukrainian leaders expected. That tussle still creates tension in the relationship. This disagreement over genuine Ukrainian independence defined the relations between the two states on almost every issue. For Russia, the goal was to preserve the role of Russia as the "center" of the region and as the "first among equals." For Ukraine, both of these ideas implied a second-class status that was intolerable.

This question of recognition influenced every issue, major and minor, that Ukraine and Russia had to work out as they dismantled Soviet institutions and developed new ones. A few examples serve to illustrate. Perhaps the major area of dispute early on was the question of the CIS. For Russia, this institution was key both practically, to avert chaos, and symbolically, to indicate that the post-Soviet states, and especially the three Slavic states (Russia, Ukraine, Belarus), were still in some way joined together and to assert that the historical connection was not completely severed. Politically, the CIS was seen by many in both Russia and Ukraine as embodying the dominant role that Russia continued to seek in the region. For Ukraine, the CIS was opposed for exactly the same reasons. Ukrainian nationalists (by which we mean not only those who were members of the nationalist parties but also the Kravchuk government and many "national Communists") approached questions of sovereignty with an exacting standard, fearing that any blurring of sovereignty put Ukraine on a slippery slope to again becoming subjugated by Russia. Thus, the idea that the CIS had any decisionmaking power was steadfastly rejected. Instead, Ukraine insisted that all joint decisions be made bilaterally or, if multilaterally, that every state have a veto. This process, which prevailed, made the CIS a completely ineffectual institution, much to the consternation of Russia.[2]

The lengthy struggle over the Black Sea Fleet had similar roots. Ukraine declared ownership over the fleet for a simple reason: The fleet was based on Ukrainian territory, and according to the practice applied to splitting up Soviet property, each republic was entitled to whatever was on its territory. To make an exception to this rule would be to acknowledge in some way Russia's superior rights over Ukraine. To do so on a military question was especially disturbing to the Ukrainian state. Nonetheless, Russia viewed the action as highly provocative. For most Russians, the Black Sea Fleet was not a Ukrainian asset but a Russian asset, or at least one that should be split.

This dispute was linked to different views of the city of Sevastopol, where the fleet was based, and, more broadly, the entire territory of Crimea. Most Russians viewed Crimea as Russian territory, for several reasons: Historically, the territory had been seized from the Crimean Tatars by the Russian forces of Catherine the Great. It had been part of Russia through the remainder of the tsarist era and into the Soviet era (though with autonomous status under the Soviets). The territory became Ukrainian only in 1954, when the Soviet government decided to transfer the territory to Ukrainian jurisdiction. Hence, Russians tend to argue that the territory is historically Russian and should continue to be Russian. In addition to the historical justification, Russians point to the ethnolinguistic composition of Crimea: It is the only region in Ukraine where ethnic Russians constitute a majority (according to the last Soviet census), and the Ukrainian language is nearly absent there. Due to the heavy military presence in Sevastopol and to the region's status as a favorite vacation and retirement spot for Soviet functionaries, many native-born Russians live in Crimea. Thus, in terms of the doctrine of national self-determination, Russians also argue that Crimea, Sevastopol, and the Black Sea Fleet should be theirs.

Ukraine concentrated above all on the legal status quo. If the agreed rule was that no borders were to be changed with the collapse of the Soviet Union, then no borders were to be changed. Ukrainians could just as easily point to regions in southwestern Russia that were traditionally Ukrainian. Moreover, the 1954 transfer of Crimea to Ukrainian jurisdiction was completely legal in terms of international law and thus had to be recognized. Because Crimea was in question, the question of the Black Sea Fleet became even more important. For Ukraine, any compromise on sovereignty concerning the fleet would open the door to further Russian claims. Russian leaders probably had the same hope: Use the Black Sea Fleet issue to keep the territorial status of Crimea open. This issue continued to plague relations and was only finally resolved in 1997, but it was significant in this early period as one of the main arenas in which Ukraine's push for total sovereign equality clashed with Russia's presumption of superior status.[3]

In addition to achieving recognition from the West and from Russia of Ukraine's independence, Ukrainian policy in the early period of independence was based on making that independence a reality in practical terms. Essentially, this meant a policy of *separation*—of disconnecting Ukraine from Russia as much as possible in every area. If the pursuit of recognition was important primarily in symbolic and legal terms, the policy of separation had profound practical consequences.

The embodiment of the policy of separation was the "Fundamentals of National Economic Policy" advanced by Kravchuk's government and adopted by the Verkhovna Rada in March 1992. The policy provided for little domestic reform and focused instead on establishing economic independence from Russia, including a plan for a separate currency and a rapid departure from the ruble zone, barriers on imports from Russia, and a refocus of exports toward Western markets.[4]

The plan for economic isolation was supported by three distinct groups in Ukraine: the *nomenklatura*, the nationalists, and the national Communists.[5] They had in common not only a focus on nationalism and fear of Russia but a lack of enthusiasm for reform. Although the nationalists' views on reform varied, reform in any case was a secondary issue to strengthening independence. The *nomenklatura* opposed anything that would endanger their privileged positions, and the national Communists shared the nationalists' fear of Russia and the *nomenklatura*'s opposition to reform.

From the nationalist perspective, Ukrainian independence (and even reform) could be achieved only in isolation from Russia, for three reasons. First, Russia would use any connections to reassert its domination of Ukraine, as it had in the past and as it seemed to be doing with reform programs and with energy. Second, instability in Russian society and economy would be more likely to overflow into Ukraine if the two economies were connected. For those who supported reform, there was a third reason: Many Ukrainians, especially in the western region, believed at this point that western Ukraine's historical experience with liberalism would lead to speedy reform and that connection with Russia would only slow down the process.[6] In May 1992, Rukh advocated withdrawal from the CIS on the grounds that the CIS hindered economic development.[7] For those who believed the first two arguments, the efficiency costs of isolation were an acceptable price to pay for independence. For those who believed the third, there was no cost of isolation. One nationalist advocated a "great wall of China" between Ukraine and Russia.[8]

The economic plan focused on independence rather than reform and was based on the contention (in Kravchuk's words) that:

> at a time when Ukraine has become an independent state and the Union center has ceased to exist, our economy continues to be managed from afar. ... In practice Ukraine has not taken, indeed has not been able to take, any serious independent decisions on the economy. ... Ukraine's complete dependence on the existing integration in the two states' economies, Russia's usurpation of functions bequeathed by Union financial, banking, and other systems, and its monopoly on ruble printing facilities across the whole ruble area—all of these things place our economy in a very difficult position, which is growing steadily worse.[9]

The program contained four main policies:[10] First, it called for the establishment of a Ukrainian currency and a rapid exit from the ruble zone. This policy was based both on the recent and ongoing experience with currency shortages and on the nationalist desire to have a Ukrainian currency for its symbolic value. Second, it called for a restriction on imports from Russia, in order to reduce Ukraine's vulnerability. Third, it called for a reorientation of exports to other, less imposing states of the former Soviet Union and the West. Fourth, it envisioned using Ukraine's economic power to negotiate favorable deals where possible by taking advantage of its monopoly position on certain goods and the large amount of transit through Ukraine: "The structural reform policy should include: ... the exploitation of Ukraine's monopoly in producing certain types of products when forming relations ... with states in the ruble zone; [and] the introduction of a system of payment for freight transported through Ukraine's territory."[11]

The policy of isolation turned out not to have the desired consequences. The policy also exacerbated political relations with Russia, which bristled at the high degree of separation, at Ukraine's rejection of collaboration with Russia, and at the unwillingness to participate in endeavors such as the single currency (the ruble) and later the CIS Economic Union. Back in the fall of 1991, both Gorbachev and Yeltsin had recognized that a continued union was impossible without Ukraine, and this was true in economic as well as political terms. Ukraine's insistence on cutting off its economy from Russia and on shunning the CIS effectively scuttled Russian plans for a unified regional economic bloc.

It was more significant, however, that the policy failed on Ukraine's own terms. Reform in Ukraine actually proceeded more slowly than in Russia. Separation of the two economies caused upheaval in industries that had tight cross-border links, causing problems for Ukrainian firms that depended on supplies from Russia as well as for firms that relied on Russian markets. By 1994 (see below) the policy of isolation was blamed for the collapse of Ukraine's economy. Isolated politically and collapsing economically, Ukraine's foreign policy was somewhat disastrous in this period. Irritating Russia was not a problem for most Ukrainian leaders, but irritating Russia and the West at the same time put Ukraine's independence at risk. It is to this combination we now turn.

THE UKRAINIAN-RUSSIAN-U.S. TRIANGLE, VARIANT ONE

It did not take Ukraine's leaders long to become disabused of the notion that Ukraine's juridical sovereignty would mean that other states would treat the new country with respect. From 1991 to 1994, Ukrainian foreign policymakers shed their more naive and idealistic hopes and (with some bitterness) came to understand the rough-and-tumble world of international politics. Most important, Ukrainian leaders learned that Ukraine mattered to the West primarily in terms of the West's relationship with Russia and that as a small power situated next to a great one, its options were limited. Ukraine would achieve its goals not if those goals were justified, but if Ukraine could successfully bargain for them with other states.

In the initial period of independence, Ukraine failed to bargain successfully for three reasons. First, Ukrainian leaders were still figuring out the rules of the game. Second, the congenial state of U.S.-Russian relations meant that Ukraine had little to offer the United States. Third, the U.S. government focused its policy on only one facet of U.S.-Ukrainian relations—nuclear weapons—to the exclusion of all else. The result was a period of acrimony and misunderstanding that left Ukraine politically isolated. The key point of this section and the next is that Ukraine's relations with the West and with Russia are largely constrained by the nature of the West's relations with Russia, which of course are completely beyond Ukraine's control. In the first phase of Ukrainian independence, the strong side of the triangle was the one linking the United States and Russia, and Ukraine was the odd man out. By mid-1994, changes in U.S.-Russian relations, combined with Ukraine's own choice to surrender its nuclear weapons, opened up new options for Ukraine's relations with both states.

The period prior to late 1993 or early 1994 was one of very close relations between the United States and Russia. U.S.-Soviet relations had been improving rapidly since Gorbachev's rise in 1985, and the process continued between the United States and Russia after the Soviet collapse.

Even before that collapse, the Bush administration had supported the interests of Russia over those of the non-Baltic republics, preferring to maintain order and keep Russia happy rather than embracing the uncertainties of national liberation. Following the Soviet collapse, U.S.-Russian relations continued to improve along three axes. First, the United States approved and supported Russia's shift to a democratic form of government. While the United States was pleased to see the development of democracy, Yeltsin received the support of the West in his battles with domestic conservatives. Second, Russia embraced the West's preferred economic course of "shock therapy," while the West promised to deliver substantial sums of aid in order to fuel economic reform and reduce the hardship it would cause. Third, the two states completed the task of dismantling their global rivalry, both in style and in substance. Most important in this process, which moved from rapprochement to close collaboration, was a series of agreements to reduce the threat of nuclear war, including both the detargeting of nuclear weapons as well as two substantial agreements to reduce their numbers (START I and START II).

In this last area, that of nuclear weapons, the mutual interest of Russia and the United States in reducing the nuclear threat put both at odds with Ukraine. And here the passive disregard for Ukraine in the United States turned to active opposition and led to collaboration between Russia and the United States to pressure Ukraine. If U.S.-Russian rapprochement was the enabling condition for Ukraine's political isolation, Ukraine's nuclear policy was the motivating factor. By January 1994, Ukraine finally gave in to demands to rid itself of all nuclear weapons, but until then, the issue resulted in an immense amount of mistrust between Ukraine on one side and the United States and Russia together on the other. It was a battle Ukraine could hardly win.

Once again, Ukraine relied for its policies on the legal position of sovereignty, as well as on a genuine fear for its security.[12] In asserting its desire to be a nonnuclear state, Ukraine had not, in its view, made a unilateral commitment or a commitment binding on it with the force of a treaty. Rather, it was a statement of an intention, the details of which would be worked out later. As Ukraine later sought compensation and security guarantees, such requests were seen in Russia and the West as backtracking on a prior obligation, a view that only caused frustration in Ukraine.

Between 1991 and the Trilateral Agreement of January 1994, which finally resolved the issue, Ukraine's fixation on asserting its sovereignty drove the negotiations.[13] First, Ukraine consistently battled the notion that Russia was the sole legal successor to the Soviet Union. It therefore claimed a share of all Soviet assets, including embassies abroad and military forces and equipment on Ukrainian territory. Nuclear forces, in Ukraine's view, fell into this category, and though it intended to surrender the weapons, it insisted on its rights until that point. Initially, that meant insisting that Ukraine become a party to the START I Treaty if that treaty were to bind Ukraine and insisting that Ukraine participate in future negotiations concerning the weapons on its territory. Jack Snyder has stated that Ukraine's assertive policy on ownership of the weapons "stems not from confident swagger, but rather from its own self-doubts about the solidity of newly won sovereignty."[14]

Ukraine's ongoing preoccupation with sovereignty meant asserting Ukraine's ownership of the weapons. In a policy statement issued on September 10, 1991, opposition leader and presidential candidate Viacheslav Chornovil reasserted his support for a nonnuclear Ukraine but questioned transferring the weapons to Russia because Ukraine was "a rightful heir to all the material and technical resources, including weapons, of the former Soviet Union."[15] From the perspective of the United States and Russia, Russia was the nuclear successor to the Soviet Union, hence all nuclear weapons should be moved to Russia. The problem with simply transferring Ukrainian weapons to Russia was that it implied that Russia had a special status in the region, including sole rights to certain assets of the former Soviet Union. In February 1992, Kravchuk protested Yeltsin's announcement that nuclear weapons would be cut further as part of START II: "The strategic weapons belong to the Commonwealth of Independent States. So how can the Russian president cut weapons he does not have? . . . Our strategic potential may not be very great, but it is not up to him to decide its fate."[16] Because Ukraine was so focused on the principles of sovereign equality, the idea of denying ownership rights of any assets was difficult to accept, even if it made sense on political and strategic grounds.

The ownership of the weapons was significant in particular in relation to the START I Treaty. Ukraine insisted that further negotiations concerning nuclear weapons could not be conducted simply by Russia and the United States, because that would imply that Russia was the sole successor of the Soviet Union and the owner of nuclear weapons in Ukraine.[17] U.S. and Russian negotiators feared this position because it meant trying to reconcile the position of five states (Belarus and Kazakhstan would also be included) rather than just two in the ensuing negotiations. The ownership question was linked to a more practical one in the short term: control of the weapons for the time they remained in Ukraine. The Ukrainian Parliament asserted its sovereign (if temporary) rights to "control over the non-use of nuclear weapons on its territory."[18] By focusing on its ownership rights, Ukraine unintentionally convinced many in Russia and the West that it intended to retain the weapons and scuttle the START I Treaty. The dispute was resolved only with the signing in May 1992 of the Lisbon Protocol, which finessed the problem by making

Ukraine, Belarus, and Kazakhstan parties to START I, while simultaneously committing them to surrendering their weapons, thus making their participation in future negotiations moot. Ukraine gave in on the substance in return for vindication of its sovereignty, appending to the protocol a letter stating that Ukraine had "voluntarily renounced the right to possess nuclear weapons, to which it was entitled as one of the equal legal successor states of the former USSR."[19]

In addition to demanding a role in the treaty process, Ukraine, in its focus on sovereignty, insisted that because it owned the weapons, it should be compensated for getting rid of them. This, too, increased tensions. Ukraine felt that it was simply getting its share of money out of the weapons, many of which were partially constructed in Ukraine. In light of Ukraine's voluntary decision to surrender the weapons, Ukrainian leaders saw compensation not only as just, but as a small price for the other states to pay given their fears. In the West and Russia, the demand for compensation was seen at best as a cynical ploy to get some additional aid and at worst as another attempt to retract the earlier commitments to disarm. The West and Russia never viewed Ukrainian disarmament as a voluntary step but rather as a compulsory one, and they were therefore less inclined to compensate Ukraine for it.

In its effects as well as in its causes, Ukrainian disarmament was more a question of identity than of military security, in which the material issue, nuclear weapons, took a backseat to the symbolic one, sovereignty. Ukraine became convinced that Russia did not respect its sovereignty, and Ukraine's hesitation to give up the weapons convinced many Russian and American leaders that Ukraine was a threat to global security.

Ukraine's political isolation exacerbated a much more immediate problem for the country: a collapsing economy. As shown in Chapter 6, by 1992 Ukraine's economy was in shambles. Although the political effects of economic collapse were felt domestically, some of the sources of the problem were international. First, as discussed above, Ukraine's deliberate policy of severing trade ties with Russia contributed to the economic problems. Because of its policies on nuclear weapons, Ukraine received almost no economic assistance from the West in this period and was threatened with more severe sanctions. The absence of outside support became more important when Russia began using the supply of energy to pressure Ukraine on a range of issues.

No single issue has demonstrated the danger to Ukraine created by its vulnerability to Russia more vividly than its reliance on Russia for much of its energy supply.[20] By early 1993, Russia predicated the continuation of fuel deliveries to Ukraine on Ukrainian concessions on the repayment of Soviet debt.[21] In March 1993, Ukraine's inability to pay for what energy it did receive became acute, and Russia's state-run gas firm, Gazprom, threatened a complete cutoff if debts were not paid. Prime Minister Kuchma accused Russia of inducing "a full paralysis" in the Ukrainian economy.[22] Soon it became clear that Gazprom's actions were part of a concerted Russian effort to use Ukraine's energy dependence to coerce it on a range of issues.

The energy war intensified at the Massandra Summit in early September 1993. The summit was aimed at resolving two issues: the Black Sea Fleet and Ukraine's nuclear disarmament. A week before the summit, Gazprom cut its supply of gas to Ukraine by 25 percent, citing Ukrainian nonpayment as the reason. At Massandra, Russian negotiators proposed a cancellation of Ukrainian gas debt in return for full control of the Black Sea Fleet and the surrender of Ukraine's nuclear warheads. If Ukraine did not agree, the Russians said, gas supplies would be halted.

It was somewhat unthinkable what chaos would ensue if the gas were turned off. Industry would halt, as would generation of electricity that relied on gas. People would be unable to cook their food or heat their apartments. Civil disorder and the collapse of the state might ensue. Given this prospect, Kravchuk did what the Russian negotiators expected, accepting "economic realities," including the reliance of Ukraine's economy on Russian energy, the massive debt, and the inability of Ukraine to come up with the cash necessary to pay the debt. "We had to act on the basis of realism. Suppose we had slammed the door and left. The gas would have been turned off and there would have been nothing else left to do."[23] After furious domestic protest, Ukraine backed away from the commitments made at the summit, but the episode demonstrated how much was at stake in the energy relationship. Russia's control over Ukraine's energy supplies gave it a powerful lever, and the Russian government would use it to coerce Ukraine. This represented a more assertive Russian policy and highlighted to Ukrainian diplomats (who accused Russia of "economic diktat") the vulnerability to economic pressure not only of Ukraine's economy, but of the whole range of Ukraine's political and security interests.[24]

For Ukrainian leaders, the "energy war" emphasized the seriousness of their predicament. If Russia actually decided to cut off energy supplies, where could Ukraine turn? The West was still unwilling to talk before Ukraine had agreed to nonnuclear status. In broader economic terms, Ukraine's separation from Russia was predicated upon the assumption of quickly establishing ties with the West. Again, the West was not eager to expedite the process until Ukraine's nuclear status was resolved. Moreover, as all of the post-Soviet states had found, European consumers were not nearly as eager to purchase post-Soviet goods as had been hoped. Regardless of political pressure, there was little hope that ties with Europe could replace those with Russia anytime soon.

In sum, the first phase of the Ukrainian-Russian-U.S. triangle had two points, Russia and the United States, very close together, with the third, Ukraine, rather distant. The United States and Russia essentially allied with each other to pressure Ukraine on the nuclear issue. Russia applied the economic pressure and the United States and its allies refused to do anything to help. Ukrainian leaders reacted bitterly to the realization that the United States and Russia were joining forces, but there was little they could do without cutting a deal with either one or the other. By January 1994, Ukraine faced the possibility of becoming an international outcast, and its economic problems raised the specter of social disorder.

THE UKRAINIAN-RUSSIAN-U.S. TRIANGLE, VARIANT TWO

By the end of 1994, the situation had changed dramatically. The United States and Ukraine were developing an informal alliance to protect the interests of both at the expense of Russia. What had changed? As implied above, the main change that occurred was external to Ukraine, taking the form of a souring of U.S.-Russian relations. Coupled with Ukraine's willingness to meet U.S. demands on nuclear weapons, Ukraine became an acceptable partner to the United States just when the United States was looking for a counterweight to Russia in the region.

The chilling of U.S.-Russian relations occurred gradually between autumn 1993 and spring 1994. The process was complex, but it can be briefly summarized. The overall trend was that both states began to question the underlying assumption of the previous few years that they had only common and not conflicting interests. Both sides recognized that in several key areas, they were still struggling against one another. At the same time, domestic events in Russia weakened Yeltsin's pro-Western policy while simultaneously making Americans wonder whether democracy and Yeltsin would last in Russia. A few events highlight this process of reevaluation.

First, in September 1993, Boris Yeltsin dissolved the Russian Parliament (in violation of the Constitution) and had to order the army to shell the Parliament building to evict recalcitrant members. Western leaders supported Yeltsin, but they also began to think about the possibility that Russia would revert to authoritarianism. This concern increased in December 1995, when in elections for a new parliament, nationalist and Communist parties routed proreform movements. For Yeltsin, this challenge to his rule made it more difficult for him to ignore domestic opinion on foreign policy, and Russia began a more assertive foreign policy, both within the region and regarding the West.

Regionally, this meant more assertion of Russian influence in the "near abroad," which heightened Western fears of renewed Russian expansionism. In relations with the West, the major challenge concerned Yugoslavia, where Yeltsin and his American supporters found themselves on opposite sides (as they still do). In February 1994, as NATO finally resolved to use military force against Serbian forces besieging Sarajevo, Russia intervened, saying it had brokered a peace deal that made bombing unnecessary. Not only were Western leaders upset that their plans had been scuttled and that Russia had bailed out Serbia, but there ensued an old-fashioned power politics battle over who was to be the dominant international player in Serbia: the United States and NATO, or Russia. In Russia as well, the notion that Russia should always work with the West became discredited. When a CIA agent was arrested for spying for Russia in March 1994, itself a relatively insignificant event, the tone of discussions in Washington, as well as those between Washington and Moscow, returned to the cold war notion of Russia and the United States as adversaries. The U.S.-Russia link was broken, and American strategists had to think about ways to contain what they perceived as increasing Russian assertiveness. Ukraine was ready, and since early 1994, the United States and Ukraine have remained close partners, allowing Ukraine in particular more latitude in dealing with Russia.

Ukraine became an eligible geopolitical partner in January 1994, when it signed (along with Russia and the United States) the Trilateral Agreement on Nuclear Weapons.[25] The agreement essentially resolved the lengthy conflict over Ukraine's nuclear weapons, committing Ukraine to surrender all its nuclear weapons and to "accede to the Nuclear Non-Proliferation Treaty in the shortest possible time," while acknowledging the equality of the three states and their "respect for the independence, sovereignty, and territorial integrity of each nation." Whereas Russia had other disputes with Ukraine that continued to fester, for the United States, the only major obstacle to a close relationship with Ukraine had been removed. Essentially the Ukrainian-Russian-U.S. triangle was reconfigured, such that the United States and Ukraine were closely linked at the expense of Russia, which had always been in tension with Ukraine and was now in tension with the United States as well. Replacing Russia as the focus of U.S. partnership in the region has been the major triumph of Ukrainian foreign policy since 1991.

For the United States, apart from ensuring that Ukraine fulfilled its commitments under the Trilateral Agreement, the primary motive in improving the relationship was geopolitical. Simply by looking at the map, it was clear to many that as long as Ukraine remained independent, any Russia expansion to the west would be largely contained. More broadly, as long as Ukraine remained independent, the other smaller states of the region had an alternative to succumbing to Russian pressure. If Ukraine were to succumb to Russian influence and pressure, the smaller states (notably in the Caucasus region) might give up any hope of remaining independent. Symbolically as well, American leaders tended to agree with the earlier assessment by Russian leaders that there could be no renewed Soviet Union without Ukraine, which was key geographically, economically, and culturally. The argument was made most influentially by Zbigniew Brzezinski: "It cannot be stressed strongly enough that without Ukraine, Russia ceases to be an empire, but with Ukraine suborned and then subordinated, Russia automatically becomes an empire."[26] The United States has taken a number of steps to help Ukraine resist Russian blandishments, to ensure that NATO expansion does not leave Ukraine with no other choice than alliance with Russia, to strengthen Ukraine's connections with NATO and the EU (short of membership,) and to reform the Ukrainian economy to increase the society's self-sufficiency.

For Ukraine, alliance with the United States against Russia was long intended and was warmly embraced when finally offered. From being squeezed diplomatically between the West and Russia until 1994, Ukraine now found that not only was Western pressure removed but that in its place came the opportunity to better resist Russian hegemony. Economic aid from the West meant an ability to pay Ukraine's debts to Russia, which decreased the potential for economic coercion. Western pressure on Russia led to more moderate Russian positions on debt repayment. Most significant perhaps has been extensive Ukrainian participation in NATO's Partnership for Peace program, which sponsored cooperation between NATO and the post-Communist states. Although relatively small-scale, this cooperation has been symbolically essential for Ukraine's efforts to recast itself as a Western state and for Ukraine's feeling that it was not isolated in its dealings with Russia. Precisely because of these far-reaching symbolic effects, Ukraine's relations with NATO have generated some controversy within Ukrainian society, especially after NATO's intervention in Kosovo, though the Kuchma administration remained committed to the partnership.

To summarize, beginning in 1994, the United States became increasingly concerned that Ukraine would be unable to remain independent of Russia and intervened initially to help ease Ukraine's energy crisis. First, it has prodded the International Monetary Fund to help Ukraine restructure its energy debts, despite the fact that Ukraine seems unable to meet IMF fiscal and monetary targets. Second, it has pressured Russia and Turkmenistan, Ukraine's two largest energy suppliers, to reschedule Ukraine's energy debt, first at the end of 1994, and then again after new debts were accrued in early 1995.[27] Together, these arrangements helped Ukraine eliminate its energy debts by the end of 1995. By early 1996, U.S.

PHOTO 7.1   President Bill Clinton and President Leonid Kuchma, Kyiv, May 1995

PHOTO 7.2   President Leonid Kuchma and Secretary General Javier Solana of NATO adopt NATO-Ukraine Charter, Madrid, July 1997

State Department spokesman Nicholas Burns was able to state: "There is no government closer to us right now than Ukraine."[28]

More broadly, through its influence at the IMF and the World Bank, the United States has helped Ukraine gain massive international assistance to reform its economy. The United States has also granted a large amount of bilateral aid to Ukraine, so much that Ukraine has become the third-largest recipient of bilateral U.S. aid (surpassing Russia, and remaining behind only Israel and Egypt). How much difference this has made in Ukraine is debatable, and Ukraine's persistent inability or unwillingness to initiate an effective reform program has been one of the factors discouraging the United States from granting even more aid.

RELATIONS WITH RUSSIA SINCE 1994

As the Ukrainian leadership hoped, the changed structure of the Ukrainian-Russian-U.S. triangle has helped Ukraine improve its relationship with Russia. Improvement in the relationship with Russia is not attributable solely to this geopolitical shift, however. A change in Ukrainian strategy and tactics helped as well. In combination, the two changes meant that Ukraine adopted a policy that was less belligerent to Russia at the same time as its ability to resist Russian pressure increased. For Russia, it became both less desirable and less possible to resolve its disputes with Ukraine through coercion. By the end of 1997, the crucial issues in the relationship had been resolved largely on Ukraine's terms.

When Leonid Kuchma defeated Leonid Kravchuk to become Ukraine's president in mid-1994, many Ukrainian nationalists feared that Kuchma would adopt a very pro-Russian line to replace Kravchuk's anti-Russian policy. Restoring ties with Russia had been one of Kuchma's primary campaign themes and presumably helped him win a large majority of the vote in eastern Ukraine. However, the policy Kuchma adopted was slightly more restrained than that which he had advocated and made a firm distinction between increasing trade flows and reintegrating the two countries or their economies.

On the question of trade ties, Kuchma worked to reestablish the level of profitable trade that had existed between the two states. In his view, it was simply economically infeasible and unwise to surrender all that profitable trade when few other alternatives were available. By 1994, many Ukrainians had come to see economic collapse as a greater threat than Russian expansionism. Not only did economic collapse undermine support for the state and raise the specter of civil unrest, but it made Russia's economic pressure more effective and strengthened arguments that Ukrainians would be better off if their country were closely linked to Russia.[29] One commentator put the situation bluntly: "The existence of Ukraine as a sovereign European state is directly connected with the solution of the problem of energy in all the basic sectors of the economy."[30] Kuchma's trade policy followed that line of thought. There were few concrete options Kuchma could pursue to increase trade, but he was able to erase the notion that any trade with Russia is inherently dangerous to Ukraine's independence. The policy change was rhetorical as well as practical, as embodied by the notion of "strategic partnership" that was used to describe the Ukrainian-Russian relationship. In 1996, one of Kuchma's bureaucrats declared: "Russia is our strategic partner number one, including in economic relations."[31]

At the same time, however, Kuchma surprised many people by holding the line on an issue that was dear to Ukrainian nationalists and to the Russian agenda: economic and political integration. He continued to reject, as Kravchuk had, any formation of joint policymaking bodies, any measure that might surrender some of Ukraine's sovereignty, or any strengthening of the CIS. His attitude was succinctly captured in a November 1994 speech: "Anyone who does not regret the disintegration of the USSR has no heart, anyone who hopes to revive it has no head."[32] This mix of a desire to increase trade and a refusal to form any multilateral bodies to regulate those ties has led to a policy of bilateralism.[33] Bilateralism now has an organizational basis in the Ministry of International Economic Relations and Trade, which has two pertinent sections, the Administration for Bilateral Relations with Russia and the Administration of Bilateral Relations with CIS Countries. Rather than having any particular virtue, bilateralism works for Ukraine because it represents a political as well as an economic compromise. Economically, bilateralism represents a compromise between the most efficient policy of integration and the least efficient position of isolation. Politically, it represents a compromise between the nationalists' isolationist position and the integrationist view held by more pro-Russian segments of society.

Despite Kuchma's more conciliatory approach to relations with Moscow, two issues continued to plague the relationship, explaining in part why Kuchma was not even more friendly. These two issues—the signing of a state treaty between the two states and the resolution of the Black Sea Fleet dispute—continued to breed mistrust in Ukraine. From Ukraine's perspective, the issues were very different in substance but identical in their importance: Both raised the question of whether Russia could or ever would accept Ukraine's independence and equality. The question of a state treaty is largely a formal one, in which neighboring states acknowledge the status of their border and promise to recognize each other's territorial integrity. Ukraine had reached such agreements quickly with all other neighbors except Romania, despite the fact that all had potential territorial claims against Ukraine as a result of World War II boundary settlements (an agreement with Romania was reached shortly before that with Russia). In each case, the signatories found it more advantageous to put such issues in the past and avoid acrimony. Russia, however, had steadfastly refused to sign a treaty with Ukraine and had sought to insert provisions that Ukraine found unacceptable. Initially, Russia insisted that Ukraine allow its citizens to have dual citizenship, which Ukrainians viewed as a ploy to allow Russia a pretext for involvement in Ukrainian domestic politics. Later, Russia insisted on a resolution of the Black Sea Fleet issue before moving forward. Throughout, Russia displayed an unwillingness to say the one thing Ukraine wanted, that Russia recognized the borders of Ukraine. Russia did not want to give this assurance until it had extracted concessions from Ukraine, but Ukrainians saw this refusal as demonstrating Russia's continued hopes of retaking Ukraine. Serhii Holovatiy, Ukraine's justice minister, asserted shortly before the final agreement: "I think that Russia still has as its strategic goal returning Ukraine to its sphere of influence. That is why Russia does not de jure recognize Ukraine as an independent state."[34] By May 1997, with NATO expanding eastward and Ukraine seeking ever-closer alliance, Russian leaders felt more pressure to reach a settlement with Ukraine to avoid pushing it even further westward. The pace of negotiations increased on both issues.

The Black Sea Fleet represented a similar problem: The practical issues were solved much more easily than the symbolic ones. Over time, the two sides had slowly agreed on how to split up the actual assets of the fleet—which were rapidly deteriorating anyway. But the status of Russian bases remained disputed, with Russia insisting that it retain ownership of part of Sevastopol, and Ukraine finding such ownership a violation of its territorial integrity. Eventually, it was agreed that Russia would lease port facilities from Ukraine, but even then the two sides disagreed on the length of the lease, with Russia seeking semipermanent status in a lease of several decades and Ukraine supporting only a transitional (five to seven years) lease until Russia could set up its own facilities. Finally, agreement was reached that Ukraine would retain complete sovereignty and Russia would lease the facilities for twenty years, with rent paid in the form of a reduction of Ukraine's energy debts. Although some Ukrainians were displeased with the length of the lease, in legal terms Ukraine achieved its goal: Russian recognition of Ukraine's sovereignty. At the end of May 1997, Boris Yeltsin finally traveled to Kyiv and signed the agreement on the Black Sea Fleet and the Friendship Treaty, saying, "This is the first time that Ukraine and Russia have signed a treaty as democratic and equal states. There are no more problems in Ukrainian-Russian relations."[35]

Yeltsin perhaps exaggerated, but there is no doubt that the Friendship Treaty and Black Sea Fleet issues represent two of the longest-running disputes in Ukrainian-Russian relations, the two that most caused Ukrainian leaders to mistrust and resent Russian intentions. With Russia officially recognizing Ukraine's sovereignty and its borders, the remaining issues on the agenda are of much less significance. Only if someone comes to power in Russia who seeks to abrogate these agreements would this situation be reversed. Since 1991, the Yeltsin government has consistently taken a more moderate stance toward Ukraine than has Russia's political elite more broadly. There are still many in Russia, most notably Moscow mayor Yuri Luzhkov, who continue to assert a more substantial role for Russia in Sevastopol. Even if Luzhkov or someone like him becomes president, however, it will be quite difficult for that leader to reverse Yeltsin's commitments without causing a major foreign policy crisis.

WHO MAKES UKRAINIAN FOREIGN POLICY?

Throughout this discussion, we have spoken of "Ukraine," or of "Ukrainian leaders," or of "Kuchma" as making the key decisions concerning foreign policy. Although these terms are a useful shorthand, we need to ask exactly what they are shorthand for. In other words, who makes Ukraine's foreign policy? By what process is that policy made? Unfortunately, there has been relatively little scholarly analysis of the Ukrainian foreign policy apparatus and the process by which foreign policy is made. This discussion therefore is necessarily brief.

By all accounts, major foreign policy decisions are made by a very small circle of officials surrounding the president. During the Kravchuk administration (1991–1994), this was to some extent necessary because more permanent institutions had not yet been set up. But the situation has persisted into the Kuchma era as well and looks to be well institutionalized. However, although key decisions continue to be closely held within the presidential apparatus, there has been a significant development of governmental and academic research institutes providing research and analysis to policymakers.

Important decisions tend to be made at the top of the government, but they are not necessarily made at the top of the Foreign Ministry, as one might expect. Instead, a more ad-hoc group, the National Security and Defense Council, has been formed to coordinate policymaking. As far as we can tell, this is the key locus of discussion and decisionmaking. This structure does not vary considerably from the sort we find, for example, in the United States, where two large bureaucracies, the Departments of State and Defense, perform a great number of tasks but are generally superseded by the National Security Council, with less than one hundred staffers. Unfortunately, we do not know the extent to which Ukraine's National Security and Defense Council confers with the relevant ministries or how tasks tend to be divided up among them.

A completely separate institution that has sought a role in foreign policy has been the Verkhovna Rada. Because of its fragmented nature, however, Parliament has had little ability to formulate and put forward concrete foreign policy plans. Instead, it has become active mainly in opposition, when the government has sought to enact a policy that a majority of Parliament opposes. This parliamentary opposition has played a significant role on at least two occasions. In September 1993, when Yeltsin and Kravchuk met at Massandra in Crimea to attempt to resolve the Black Sea Fleet dispute, the agreement they reached was so quickly and so resolutely opposed in the Ukrainian Parliament that Kravchuk quickly had to back away from it. The Rada, and the public opinion it represented, were crucial in forcing the agreement to be scuttled. A second issue on which parliamentary opposition played some role was nuclear disarmament, where Parliament tended to be much more belligerent than the Kravchuk government about giving up Ukraine's nuclear weapons. Initially, Kravchuk was able to ignore the Rada's opposition, but in the end, he (and then Kuchma) was able to win parliamentary acquiescence for disarmament. Nonetheless, the Rada's intervention seriously complicated the process by making Kravchuk's American and Russian negotiating partners doubt his ability to deliver on his commitments. In foreign policy, struggles between the executive and Parliament have generally been won by the president.

It is very difficult to evaluate the roles of some of the other entities that are often viewed as important actors in the foreign policy processes of democracies. Concerning public opinion, for example, there is a good deal of polling data indicating public opinion on a wide variety of foreign policy concerns, but it is impossible to know whether it has any effect on what leaders decide to do. Similarly, one can surmise that the media might have a role, but this, too, is difficult to assess. Given the large influence the Ukrainian government has over much of the media, it seems unlikely that these institutions play an independent role. More difficult still to assess is the role of what might be called "interest groups" or "lobbies." Here we are talking mostly about firms or business groups that might advocate particular foreign policy measures (especially involving trade) that would increase the profitability of the firms. Given what we know of corruption in Ukraine, it seems highly unlikely that there has been no attempt by economic interest groups to alter the government's foreign policy, but there is little concrete evidence. Either way, such efforts are more likely to affect less essential foreign policy issues, such as tariffs, quotas, and subsidies, rather than the big questions of the day, such as nuclear disarmament or relations with Russia. As this discussion shows, however, we still know relatively little about the internal workings of Ukrainian foreign policy.

TOWARD THE FUTURE: UKRAINE BETWEEN EAST AND WEST

For several years, Ukraine's options were quite narrowly defined as a result of others' policies and Ukraine's own weakness. As Ukraine's position has improved, it now has more room to maneuver, which raises difficult questions concerning the best route to take. Most profound for Ukraine domestically and internationally is how the Ukrainian state and society will conceive of Ukraine's place between East and West. The question is by no means a new one—as early as 1991, there was debate over a pro-Western or pro-Russian policy. But since the forging of the NATO-Ukraine agreement and the resolution of key outstanding issues with Russia in 1997, Ukraine can actually choose its own course to some extent. Should Ukraine seek to join the West and turn its back on Russia, as most of the former Warsaw Pact states have and as the Baltic states have? Or should it recognize the primary importance of its cultural and economic ties with Russia and emphasize an eastward orientation? Or can Ukraine find some intermediate position that capitalizes on its key geographic location between Russia and the West?

For Ukraine, the problem poses intense dilemmas at both the domestic and international levels. At the domestic level, choosing a foreign policy orientation becomes entangled with division over conceptions of Ukrainian national identity that we have discussed in previous chapters. For those who define Ukrainian national identity largely in terms of the Ukrainian ethnic group and focus on Ukraine's democratic traditions and historical links with Austria and Central Europe, it seems only natural to link Ukraine to the West. Since many in this category are Ukrainian nationalists who view Ukraine's historical interaction with Russia primarily in negative terms, links with Russia seem unnatural or even dangerous. They point out that Ukraine should rejoin the West, emphasizing that Ukraine was linked to the West before being forcibly separated from it. This view naturally is more widely held in western Ukraine than in other regions.

Others, however, view the issue in very different terms. For those who emphasize the Slavic character of Ukraine, who speak predominantly Russian or consider themselves ethnically Russian, and who have no historical resentment toward Russia, cutting Ukraine off from Russia would equal cutting Ukraine off from its history and from its closest relatives. If the pro-Western view dominated during Kravchuk's presidency (but could not be acted on), this Russophile view has gained ground since. Those who identify Ukraine with Russia and Eurasia also tend to be more skeptical of American plans and intentions, of the virtues of Western Europe, and of the desirability of Western-inspired reforms. Overall,

Ukrainians' images of themselves play a substantial role in their evaluations of the state's geopolitical orientation, with holders of different conceptions of Ukrainian identities seeking verification and extension of their view in foreign policy. As is true in much of Ukrainian politics, identity issues play an important role in all other issues, derailing debate from more pragmatic consideration.

At the international level, the pragmatic considerations are formidable and have not been ignored by strategists or policymakers. So far, Ukraine has sought a hybrid of the three potential positions outlined above. First, Ukraine has strengthened its relations with the West, though with some restraint. Second, in doing so, Ukrainian leaders have taken care not to alienate Russia. Third, although policymakers have retreated from Ukraine's formal policy of neutrality, there remains strong support from a broad band of the political spectrum for continuing Ukraine's "nonbloc" policy. Put together, they indicate that Ukraine will seek increased ties with the West, but not at the expense of relations with Russia.

Ukraine has continued to place a high priority on increasing ties with the West. So far, the most prominent avenue has been through NATO's Partnership for Peace, in which Ukraine has been a very active participant. The relationship is valued enough for NATO to have negotiated a special bilateral agreement with Ukraine so that Russia, which was also to receive such an agreement, would not have a status superior to that of Ukraine. Nonetheless, there are powerful limits on how far this relationship can advance, most basically because neither side is willing to take the next step: full Ukrainian membership. NATO rejects such an idea for the foreseeable future for several reasons: Ukraine is not ready economically or politically; Russia would view such step as threatening; and most important, Western states do not want to guarantee the security of Ukraine. Among Ukrainians, there is more talk of full membership, but it is limited even among those who are enthusiastic about expanding ties, because such a step would be highly provocative to Russia. Many other Ukrainians strongly oppose the notion.

The more practically significant group for Ukraine to join would be the European Union, but this, too, is highly unlikely for some time to come. The EU is more significant because Ukraine's problems are much more economic than military. Hence, EU membership would have a much more positive impact on the country. Moreover, it would not be nearly as threatening to Russia as it would be if Ukraine were to join NATO, a military alliance.

Whereas NATO membership is largely driven by political considerations, EU membership rests upon a very large number of specific technical economic, political, and legal requirements, and Ukraine is a very long way off from meeting these. The issue is complicated by the fact that

Ukraine's principal exports are of goods that are overproduced in the EU, most notably agricultural products and steel.

This tension over the Eastern or Western emphasis in Ukrainian foreign policy was initially avoided by declarations at the time of independence that Ukraine was to be neutral. Although that policy has not officially been rejected, Ukraine has found that the technical requirements for neutrality in the international legal sense are too stringent for Ukraine. In particular, Ukraine's desire to have a close relationship with NATO and to be a member of various international organizations was hampered by that doctrine. More recently, Ukrainian leaders have used a different formulation—"nonbloc status"—to indicate their preferred policy. This less formal doctrine permits wide-ranging cooperation between Ukraine and other countries but still implies that it will join no formal political or economic blocs. Any move to join the EU or NATO (or the CIS) would require another doctrinal revision, but since none of those things are at all likely, this looser formula is likely to endure. Both the doctrine of neutrality and that of nonbloc status have especially robust domestic support because they serve the interests of two groups that are in general in complete disagreement with one another. Ukrainian nationalists, who see Russia as a potential threat, have backed neutrality as a barrier against some future government deciding to join the CIS. Their opponents—supporters of close ties with Russia—support neutrality as a barrier against Ukraine's joining NATO and turning its back on Russia.

Ukraine's intermediate position between East and West is therefore reinforced by both domestic and international conditions. Domestically, it embodies a compromise between pro-Western and pro-Russian forces. Internationally, it embodies the reality that Ukraine will not be admitted into the EU or NATO in the foreseeable future. If this "in between" status is likely to persist, the key question is this: What will the nature of Ukraine's intermediate status be?

The fear in Ukraine is that Ukraine will find itself cut off from the West and therefore with no option but to come to terms with Russia. Economically, Ukrainian leaders fear that extending the European Union's trade barriers to Poland and Hungary will isolate Ukraine from those markets and make Ukraine even more dependent on Russia.[36] Politically, Ukrainians fear that NATO will focus its diplomatic efforts on its new members rather than on countries such as Ukraine that continue to lie outside the alliance. This notion of Ukraine as a "buffer" between NATO/EU and a potentially dangerous Russia works well for Western geopolitics but would put Ukraine in a difficult economic and political position.

Both EU and NATO officials have stressed that the enlargement of their organizations will not cut Ukraine off, and indeed the bilateral NATO-Ukraine agreement was reached in large part to reassure Ukraine and to build the base for a close relationship between Ukraine and the enlarged NATO. In the eyes of President Kuchma and much of the Ukrainian leadership, this was a major foreign policy accomplishment, and it supports their preferred notion of Ukraine as a "bridge" rather than a buffer between East and West. In economic terms, Ukraine already plays an important role as a transport corridor between Russia and the West, and its leaders hope to establish a similar political role. Ukraine has not yet provided any sort of diplomatic mediation between East and West but rather has been careful on key issues to establish positions that are compatible with both sides' views. Thus, on NATO enlargement, Ukraine defended NATO's right to expand but argued that Russia's sensitivities should be taken into account. Ukraine hopes to position itself at the center of a new single "Europe" rather than being at the backwaters of both Russia and Western Europe, as it has traditionally been. So far, the situation is emerging largely as Ukrainian leaders have hoped, but change in the region is still rapid.

SUMMARY

Ukraine's foreign policy agenda is determined in large part beyond Ukraine's borders, as are its potential options. Although Ukraine is a large and populous state, it is relatively weak in international economic and diplomatic terms and therefore has little ability to change its own agenda. Within the tight constraints Ukraine has faced, its foreign policy position has improved dramatically since 1991, for two reasons. First, Ukraine eliminated the major barrier to good relations with the West by agreeing to surrender its nuclear weapons. Second, the souring of the West's relationship with Russia has made the West eager to align with Ukraine and hence has made Russia more conciliatory. By 1998, most of Ukraine's major foreign policy goals had been achieved, including the creation of close relations with the United States, recognition of Ukraine's borders by Moscow, and a resolution to the Black Sea Fleet problem on terms favorable to Ukraine. Current debates over the optimal emphasis on relations with the West and Russia are relatively mild issues to deal with, considering that only five years ago, the survival of Ukrainian independence was still in question. This bright picture has only one cloud in it, but it is a significant one: Ukraine's dismal domestic economy may undermine Ukrainian successes by causing the West to rethink its commitment and by increasing Ukraine's dependence on Russia. Increasingly in years to come, Ukraine's foreign and security policy will overlap with domestic reform.

• EIGHT •

Ukrainian Defense Policy and the Transformation of the Armed Forces

One of the potentially most dangerous missions for independent Ukraine has been the transformation of its armed forces and the development of defense and security policy. In several areas, these projects have been carried out with great success, measured in positive terms: The armed forces have been downsized, denuclearization has been completed, and a revised security doctrine has begun to take shape. In other areas, success has been measured in negative terms—in terms of potential dangers that have been averted. The avoidance of a strong military role in politics and the establishment of civilian control over the military have been significant. Finally, there have been some notable failures, most prominent among which has been the inability to maintain funding for the military at a level adequate enough to ensure the viability of the forces.

OVERVIEW

The establishment of a separate Ukrainian military and defense apparatus was initially a means to dissolve the Soviet Union, only later becoming important in its own right. The collapse of the Soviet Union and the establishment of independent Ukraine created what we might describe as problems of both supply and demand, as well as of a disjuncture between them. On the supply side, Ukraine inherited an enormous military, numbering approximately 750,000, which was far beyond its needs or its ability to maintain. Simply reducing the size of the military has been a basic mission, successfully carried out so far. In addition to the *size* of the military, Ukraine inherited a military that was *structured* to help fight a war between the Warsaw Pact and NATO and was thus inappropriate to new circumstances. In addition, Ukraine inherited a mammoth military-industrial complex far out of proportion to its needs.

234 ■ THE TRANSFORMATION OF THE ARMED FORCES

On the demand side, Ukraine needed an independent military to safeguard its independence from potential encroachment (or simply the threat of it), most likely from Russia. In numbers, this potential already existed, but in structure, deployment, and planning, it did not. Even more troubling, since the primary threat was from Russia, Ukraine needed an officer corps whose primary loyalty was to Ukraine rather than to Russia or to the former Soviet Union. This initially did not exist. Ukraine also needed a security doctrine to guide the development of its military forces. And fundamentally, like any other country, Ukraine needed the economic capability to pursue these needs. That economic foundation has been entirely lacking so far.

Ukraine inherited much from the Soviet Union, but much of what it inherited was not what it needed. In that sense the situation in military and defense issues parallels that in much of the rest of society. The key task was transformation: transformation of an enormous army prepared for global and total war into a smaller army prepared for local and limited war; transformation of a heavily Russified army with Soviet indoctrination into a Ukrainian army with loyalty to Ukraine; transformation of a massive military-industrial complex completely integrated with the defense industry throughout the former Soviet Union into a smaller Ukrainian military-industrial complex capable of independently producing military equipment. Finally, independent Ukraine required a transformation from a political system in which the military was one of the most prominent actors into a system where the military was accountable to and controlled by civilian authority.

This chapter seeks to explore all of these issues to show how defense and military issues have evolved in post-Soviet Ukraine. Because defense and security issues naturally concern relations with other states, some of the issues relevant here have been treated in the preceding chapter on foreign policy, and we have striven to avoid repetition. Following a brief discussion of theoretical issues, the chapter proceeds as follows: First, we discuss the role of military issues in the breakup of the Soviet Union and the links between establishing an independent Ukraine and establishing a Ukrainian military. The specific problems involved in separating the Ukrainian military from the Soviet/Russian military are then discussed. Second, we discuss the problem that followed separation—reforming the military and its doctrine for the entirely new job it faced—and we consider the debates over reform and the progress made so far. Third, we examine the problems that have emerged in sustaining the military, which has not been immune from Ukraine's economic woes. Fourth, we discuss the related issue of transforming the military industrial complex, which was one of Soviet Ukraine's great strengths and is one of independent Ukraine's great liabilities. Fifth, we focus on the military side of a theme from the previous chapter, examining the effort to determine the major threats to Ukrainian security and the best means of meeting them. Sixth, we explore the increasing interaction between Ukraine's military forces and those of other countries, which has occurred both through NATO's Partnership for Peace and through Ukraine's participation in UN peacekeeping missions. Last, we examine potentially the most important issue of all for Ukrainian politics: the role of the military in politics.

THEORETICAL ISSUES IN THE STUDY OF UKRAINIAN DEFENSE ISSUES

Because this chapter considers such a wide range of issues, there is not a single theoretical issue or even a single body of literature on which the discussion can center. The two most basic issues, which we focus on here, concern the role of the military in politics and society. The first question is that of state building: What role can the military play in building the Ukrainian state, and what role has it played? The second issue is that of state-society relations: How autonomous is the military from civilian control, and how prominent a role does the military play in the broader political arena?

Charles Tilly has shown that the military was tightly bound up with the process of state building in Western Europe, so the following question naturally arises here: What is the role of the military in state building in Ukraine, a state with a massive military and imposing obstacles to state building?[1] However, Tilly's perspective does not take us far in the Ukrainian case, because the role that the military played in the European states is not the one primarily required in Ukraine. In Western Europe, the military contributed to state building by securing that most fundamental state attribute, a monopoly on violence, which needed to be secured from both internal and external challengers. The military made it both necessary and possible to extract increased taxes from subjects and to create an efficient central bureaucracy.

In Ukraine, the monopoly on violence has not been the state's primary concern, either internally or externally, because "stateness" was not arising from scratch but rather was being devolved from Moscow to Kyiv. As we describe in more detail below, however, the military did play an important role in state building. That role was symbolic and institutional rather than material and coercive and was centered on using the establishment of an independent Ukrainian military as one of the essential and undeniable markers of the establishment of a Ukrainian state, separate from Russia. Along with the successful referendum in December 1991 and the subsequent recognition from world powers, the establishment of a separate military was key in making Ukraine's independence an accepted fact rather than a contentious issue.

A second, and less prominent, role for the military in state building has been the role of the military in forging national identity and loyalty to the state. This role has been secondary because the role of the armed forces as a nation-building tool has been controversial within the military itself and because the military has itself been an object of "nationalizing." Because the "Ukrainianness" of the military has itself been suspect, the armed forces have been able to play a unifying role in society only symbolically. Nevertheless, in discussions over moving from a conscripted to a contract force, the potential role of the military as a unifying institution continues to be relevant.

Traditional theories of civil-military relations can more readily be applied to this case, though again the circumstances in which Ukraine and its military find themselves make the case atypical. The most relevant literature to apply here is the well-developed literature on civil-military relations in the Soviet Union, which allows us to examine both continuity and change from the preceding system. As Dale Herspring has shown, the questions asked about Soviet civil-military relations did not differ substantially from those concerning other societies, and indeed Roman Kolkowicz's influential study of Soviet civil-military relations was heavily influenced by Samuel Huntington's study of the United States.[2] In all these cases, the two key questions were: To what extent is the military autonomous from political forces or penetrated by them? And to what extent is the military able to exert itself in the country's politics? The first question concerns the military's power in controlling "its own" domain; the second concerns the military's ability to control political issues outside its own domain. In practice, these two issues are often folded together into the catchall phrase "civilian control of the military." Is the military a tool of the state, or the other way around? As we will see below, these questions have become essential for contemporary Ukraine, with its massive military, weak state, and desperate need for transformation. In particular, the question of whether the military can resist encroachment on "its" prerogatives from politicians has been hotly contested in Ukraine. At the same time, the military has not sought a broader role in the state's politics and has largely remained under civilian control.[3]

SEPARATING MILITARIES AND SEPARATING STATES

Ukraine's declaration of independence in August 1991 established Ukraine's separation from the Soviet Union and from Russia in theory, but not in fact. The Soviet Union still existed, and throughout the fall of 1991, officials in Moscow—both those siding with Boris Yeltsin and those siding with Mikhail Gorbachev—put forth a series of plans for continued "federation" or "confederation" or "union" of some type. It was still somewhat incomprehensible that separation would be complete. Foremost on the agenda, even ahead of the goal of maintaining a common economic space, was the goal of maintaining a single military. As early as September 12, only three weeks after the coup attempt, Russian Federation Defense Committee deputy chairman Vladimir Lopatin advocated a new defense organization similar to NATO, and Soviet defense minister Yevgennii Shaposhnikov said that republic leaders agreed that military forces should remain unified. The idea of separate militaries was threatening, or even unthinkable, in Moscow for several reasons. First, the Soviet army, following its sacrifices and successes in World War II, held a hallowed place in society, not just in official propaganda. Second, the military was structured such that it was not easily dividable: Soldiers were permanently stationed outside their native republics and facilities such as air defense consisted of a single network that could not function in separated pieces. Third, and most troubling, the breakup of the Soviet army meant the creation of three new nuclear states, in Ukraine, Belarus, and Kazakhstan, where nonmobile strategic systems were stationed permanently.

Those who supported complete Ukrainian independence recognized, as did leaders in Moscow, that complete political independence and sovereignty were possible only through creation of all the vestiges of a sovereign state, including a military.[4] Symbolically, the establishment of a Ukrainian army was seen as the sine qua non of the establishment of a Ukrainian state, and the dividing up of the Soviet army decisively signaled the end of any union arrangement. Practically, the need for a separate Ukrainian military was equally apparent in the days and weeks following the coup. On August 19, one of the plotters, General Varrenikov, flew to Kyiv and issued an ultimatum: If Ukrainian leaders did not follow the orders of the plotters, the Soviet army would invade. A special forces unit was flown in from Brest and stationed outside Kyiv, and helicopters hovered over the capital. Kravchuk stated in a press conference shortly afterward: "I realized that I had no one to defend me, [and] sensed that armed people could walk in at any time and take me away."[5] Having declared independence, Ukraine and its leaders became concerned for their security and began thinking about repelling intervention by Russian or Soviet forces. The lessons of 1918, when the demise of the fledgling Ukrainian state was blamed on an inadequate military, were also prominent in the motivation to focus on the military aspects of independence.[6] In sum, for Ukrainian leaders, seizing jurisdiction of troops on its territory and declaring ownership of their assets became—both symbolically and practically—a means important to making Ukraine's independence a reality.

Accordingly, Ukraine's declaration of independence on August 24, 1991, was accompanied by a parliamentary decree asserting Ukrainian ownership and control over all military units on Ukrainian territory and the intention of creating a separate military.[7] On September 3, General Konstantin Morozov was named defense minister, and he made Ukraine's priorities clear: "We reject the idea of a unified military command. Our approach will be step-by-step towards an independent Ukrainian army."[8] In October, the Council of Defense was created to oversee defense matters, and in November, the Verkhovna Rada passed a measure requiring troops in Ukraine to take an oath of loyalty to Ukraine. In April 1992, Kravchuk decreed that except for nuclear forces, all military forces on Ukrainian territory were to be put under the jurisdiction of the Ukrainian minister of defense.[9]

As with declaring independence, however, it was easier to declare the establishment of a Ukrainian military than to accomplish it in fact. The period from the fall of 1991 through early 1993 was consumed with sorting out Ukrainian military assets from Soviet military assets and with the process of getting soldiers to either take a loyalty oath or leave the armed forces. All of this had to be accomplished in the conditions of turmoil that characterized both Ukrainian domestic politics and Ukrainian-Russian relations.

The question of the disposition of "strategic forces," meaning primarily nuclear weapons and their delivery systems, topped the agenda, and a discussion of this issue helps explain why Ukraine flirted with "going nuclear" by declaring ownership of the nuclear weapons on its soil. Prior to independence, Ukraine had declared its desire to be a nonnuclear state, but the process of splitting up the Soviet military made that policy untenable. Initially, when the Soviet Union was dissolved and the CIS formed in December 1991, it was agreed that although individual republics would form their own militaries, strategic forces would remain under the control of a centralized CIS command. When Russian president Boris Yeltsin announced in September 1991 his intention to transfer all nuclear weapons in the Soviet Union to Russia, Rukh leader Viacheslav Chornovil adamantly opposed the notion.[10] Although Ukraine was leery of the CIS, the arrangement was useful in that it allowed Ukraine to establish a separate military without adopting nuclear status. In every other way, however, Ukraine worked to undercut the CIS military command, arguing that the CIS had jurisdiction over nothing but nuclear weapons and even then that those weapons could not be used without Ukrainian permission.

Russia during this period continued to support a strong CIS apparatus as the only way of preserving some vestige of the Soviet Union and particularly as the only way to maintain the military unity that many saw as crucial to the region's stability. Thus, Russia did not form its own army until May 1992. The Russian defense apparatus developed in large part by taking over many of the former USSR structures that in the interim had been delegated to the CIS. Over time, it became clearer that the notion that nuclear weapons in Ukraine were jointly controlled (through the CIS) was a fiction and that in fact those weapons were controlled by Russia, which had essentially absorbed the Soviet/CIS defense structures.[11] Although Ukraine grudgingly accepted CIS control, it would not countenance Russian control and took a series of steps to declare "ownership" of the weapons (though by all accounts Ukraine never had the ability to launch the weapons).

Thus the process of building a Ukrainian military was closely bound up with the process of building a Ukrainian state. Not only did an independent military give Ukraine the physical power to back up its claim to independence, but the establishment of a military led that process symbolically. Moreover, for Kravchuk, whose nationalist credentials were weak and whose support among nationalist sections of the population was nearly nonexistent, supporting an activist policy toward establishment of Ukraine's military was politically beneficial. As has been true with many states throughout history, the centralizing ability of military power and the patriotism instilled by the military were used by a new and insecure state to build loyalty and legitimacy internally as well as to prevent external interference.[12]

The process was not without its difficulties, which arose primarily in the controversy concerning the military oath of allegiance to Ukraine. Due to Soviet policy, many of the conscripts serving in Ukraine were not Ukrainian, and they had no desire to take a loyalty oath to the new state. Although there was a vocal core of pro-Ukrainian officers, who organized themselves as the Union of Ukrainian Officers, over 70 percent of the officer corps were from outside Ukraine, most from Russia.[13] Many had no desire to see the Ukrainian army split off from the Soviet army and were put in a very difficult bind by the proposition: They could either pledge an oath of loyalty to a country to which they felt no attachment, or they could abandon their careers and their housing. Theoretically, one might expect that Russian soldiers in Ukraine would go back to Russia and join the Russian military, but in fact there were no positions for most of them in Russia and no housing for them. For them, the solution was not to return to Russia but rather for Ukraine's army to continue to be linked to a CIS force and for them to pledge their loyalty to that entity rather than Ukraine. In the end, the vast majority of those who were not released from the military due to downsizing (see below) accepted their fate and grudgingly pledged loyalty to Ukraine. Ukraine thus succeeded in forcing its soldiers to pledge loyalty, but the result was a military with many in it who objected to the very existence of a Ukrainian army and whose loyalties were rather suspect.

REFORMING AND RECONSTRUCTING THE ARMED FORCES

Following the establishment of a separate Ukrainian military, it was necessary to make the military Ukrainian in policy terms as well as in fact. In other words, Ukraine inherited a military that was set up to do tasks that had little or no relevance to Ukraine's national security. The military inherited from the Soviet Union was clearly inappropriate for Ukraine in at least two ways. First, it was far too big for Ukraine's needs and for its economic means. Second, it was designed as part of a larger army intended to wage war either in a massive armored campaign in Central Europe or in a strategic nuclear campaign. Neither those types of campaigns nor their prospective targets are currently relevant. The initial problem was to change the identity of the military from a Soviet force to a Ukrainian force. A more substantive problem was to develop an agreed plan of reform, which in turn required some notion of national security challenges. The more fundamental problem was that whatever mandate for reform was given to the military, there was no money forthcoming to carry it out. Finally, an issue for the present and future is whether the basis of military service should be shifted from conscription to a professional army. This section deals with the issue of a plan of reform, and the following section deals with the funding crisis.

Ukrainianization

The events of late 1991 and early 1992 created a military that was Ukrainian in the sense that it was the acknowledged possession of the Ukrainian state. As discussed above, however, this military was not Ukrainian in content or in the self-identification of the troops. Many of those serving in the units appropriated by Ukraine were not born in Ukraine or were not ethnically Ukrainian but chose to stay in Ukraine's armed forces because they had no other real choice. That many, especially in the officer corps, were Russian presented an enormous problem for Ukraine's defense planners. It appeared very questionable whether such an army would loyally protect the state, especially if the challenge came from Russia. There was an urgent need to transform the military from a force composed of a mass of Russian-speaking forces, most of whom never thought of Ukraine as a separate country prior to 1991, and a core of Ukrainian nationalists to a force that was genuinely Ukrainian in its patriotism.

Essentially, the process involved three tasks. Each of them was risky in that by pushing the agenda of Ukrainianization, it might spur rebellion on the part of non-Ukrainians rather than forestall it. First, the oath of loyalty was administered very quickly after the declaration of independence.

The oath prompted protest from many, but the government did not retreat, and those who refused to take the oath were released from service. Nonetheless, some units insisted on flying the Russian flag. Second, there was a desire to shift the primary language from Russian to Ukrainian. As the "language of interethnic communication" in the Soviet Union, Russian dominated the armed forces even in Ukraine, not only in its spoken form but also in manuals and all the written material associated with the army. Even among those actually from Ukraine, Russian was the dominant language. Nationalists sought to reverse this practice because they felt a Ukrainian military should use the Ukrainian language, especially since the military was to play an important role in building the Ukrainian national identity. Third, there was a need to indoctrinate Ukraine's servicemen into what it meant to be Ukrainian. Beyond language, there was a desire to familiarize the military with Ukrainian history and Ukrainian culture and, above all, to infuse them with loyalty to Ukraine rather than to Russia or the Soviet Union. The means adopted to this task were somewhat heavy-handed, however, and sparked protest, as the Main Directorate for Education and Social-Psychological Work, which had formerly indoctrinated soldiers in Marxism-Leninism, was redirected to indoctrinate them in Ukrainian national identity. Over time, as the existence of the Ukrainian state, and hence the Ukrainian armed forces, has become an established fact, the officer corps seems to have accepted the situation. The army remains, however, heavily Russian speaking, in that sense mirroring Ukrainian society well.

Downsizing

Ukraine inherited 726,000 military personnel from the Soviet army, and the goal is to cut this force roughly in half—to 350,000 by 2005. Originally, the goal of 350,000 was to be reached by the end of 1996 (forces had been reduced to 420,000 by 1995). The timing of the final reductions was reconsidered due to the shortage of funding needed to transfer people to civilian life and due to arguments that in fact the proposed reductions were too drastic. This was one of many cases in which reforming the military, even if it would save money in the long run, required a short-term injection of funds that were unavailable.[14] The process of downsizing has been both motivated and constrained by the severe economic problems in the country. On the one hand, budgetary pressures on the government made cutting military spending a priority, and cutting force levels was a primary means to that goal. On the other hand, the transitional costs associated with downsizing—most especially finding housing for newly released soldiers—have slowed the process. Nonetheless, the reduction since 1991 has been drastic, and that has substantially decreased the burden on Ukraine's overstretched budget. As force levels came down, however, disagreement over the ultimately desirable level has been an increasingly important factor in slowing the process. Hence, the issues of restructuring and reorienting are closely linked to that of downsizing.

Restructuring and Reorienting

After the formation of the Ukrainian military, there was initially much more emphasis on consolidation, that is, on completing the process of separating the military from the Soviet army, than on reform. In that period, returning Ukrainian citizens from units in other countries, enacting the loyalty oath, and rechanneling basic chains of command from Moscow to Kyiv occupied the Ukrainian defense establishment. Completing these basic tasks was all that could be achieved in a time of chaos. Genuine military reform therefore did not begin until Leonid Kuchma took over as president in mid-1994 and appointed a new defense minister, Valeriy Shmarov.[15]

Shmarov, the first civilian defense minister in the CIS, came to office with a mandate from President Kuchma for reform. As is true in most countries, efforts to reform the military encountered stiff resistance from within the military establishment (and from some societal groups) and had to be substantially scaled back. What was originally intended as a radical reform of Ukraine's military to meet the new challenges and new constraints of the post-Soviet era has been watered down into an evolutionary reform that will maintain much of the current force structure and orientation.

The reform plan was based on a revised notion of Ukraine's security threats as well as on the need to save money. The Soviet army, from which the Ukrainian army emerged, had been structured to fight a large-scale and protracted conventional war. It was equipped for that task with emphasis on armor and artillery. In the early years of Ukraine's independence, the most likely foe changed from NATO to Russia, but the guiding assumption remained that the threat was from an attack by an aggressive state that would require a total war effort. In that sense, the composition inherited from the Soviet Union was more or less appropriate, though a complete geographical reorientation was required. Kuchma came to office believing, as many Ukrainians did, that an all-out war with Russia was highly unlikely and that it made no sense to base the military on that scenario. In military terms, it seemed that Russia would never think that it could easily defeat Ukraine (this became even clearer after Russia's fiasco in Chechnya). In political terms, none of Russia's aspirations toward Ukraine would be met by an all-out invasion. Moreover, in diplomatic terms, Kuchma and others saw little difficulty in working out Ukraine's

THE TRANSFORMATION OF THE ARMED FORCES ▪ 243

PHOTO 8.1   National guard parading in Kyiv, Independence Day, August 1994

differences with Russia. A different view of Ukraine's security threats emerged at this time. After the economic collapse and hints of unrest in 1993–1994, it appeared that the primary threats to Ukraine were domestic, not international. Moreover, to the extent that international threats remained, the danger seemed to come from the small-scale (and not so small) ethnic civil wars that were popping up all over the former Soviet Union, in Chechnya, Nagorno-Karabakh, Georgia, and Moldova. From this perspective, it appeared that Ukraine did not need a big force as much as it needed an agile one, capable of being rapidly deployed to put out fires that might arise due to conflicts either outside Ukraine on its borders or, in a worst case, within Ukraine itself. If Russia were to try to subject Ukraine, in this view, it would do so either through economic pressure or by stirring up Ukraine's ethnic Russians. Either way, the army as structured in 1994 seemed almost irrelevant. For these reasons, Ukraine's domestic security forces have grown rapidly even as the regular military has been drastically scaled back.

The reform plan, designed by Defense Minister Shmarov and Deputy Defense Minister Ivan Bizhan, contained the following major components:[16]

- Reducing troop levels to 220,000 by the year 2000
- Focusing expenditure on equipment rather than size
- Focusing on mobility rather than size
- Changing the geographical basis of deployment from three Soviet-era military districts to seven operational groups

- Eventually moving to a professional or "contract" military rather than relying on universal conscription

The reform plan was opposed not only by a large portion of the general staff of the military but also by Ukrainian nationalists. Both groups opposed the underlying reevaluation of threats on which the plan was based and feared the changes would endanger Ukraine's security. In the military, resistance stemmed also from a fear of lost prerogatives that seems to characterize almost all military reforms, especially those that envision a smaller military and less funding. Ukrainian nationalists opposed the plan primarily on the grounds that it was based on an underestimation of the threats to Ukraine and hence left the country vulnerable. The nationalists, almost all of whom had opposed Kuchma's candidacy, were much less sanguine than Kuchma about Russia's unwillingness to attack. For them, the invasion of Chechnya demonstrated not Russia's weakness as much as its continued willingness to apply massive military force in the pursuit of its goals. Ukrainian nationalists were also much more attentive to the rhetoric of Russian hard-liners, notably Vladimir Zhirinovsky, who continued to talk of conquest. More abstractly, perhaps, their notion of a strong state included in it a large and powerful military. A second point of opposition was the proposed shift to seven operational groups. Nationalists feared that the regional deployment of the army would contribute to different regions of Ukraine having their "own" armies, whose loyalty to the region might surpass that to the state. Instead, they advocated maintaining the inherited Kyiv, Odesa, and Trans-Carpathian military districts from the Soviet Union and adding a fourth district centered on Dnipropetrovs'k to cover Ukraine's border with Russia. Finally, nationalists sought to maintain the system of conscription (despite their opposition to that practice under the Soviet Union) because universal military service was viewed as an important builder of national unity and of Ukrainian national identity, as it has been in France and Germany.

In the military, the leader of the opposition to the Shmarov plan was Colonel General Anatoliy Lopata, chief of staff of the army until February 1996. Friction between the first civilian defense minister and the senior military officer was perhaps inevitable, but conflict over the reform program was intense, such that Shmarov constructed a completely separate working group under Bizhan, which some characterized as an "underground general staff," to complete the plan beyond the reach of Lopata and the general staff. Lopata was popular within the officer corps, and the dispute spurred resentment that officers faced political pressure from the Ministry of Defense to side against their leader. On the other side, Bizhan published an open letter signed by himself and 700 officers supporting the reform plan. The reform, it seemed, threatened to split the armed forces as well as to split the general staff from the political leadership. Rather than force a showdown to decisively enforce civilian control, Kuchma backed down from his support for Shmarov's plan, but not before firing Lopata in February 1996 (Shmarov himself was fired in June of that year).

Faced with two different concepts for Ukrainian military reform, Kuchma supported neither decisively, fired the two main opponents, Shmarov and Lopata, and proceeded to compromise: The military district system has been maintained but redrawn, with districts based on Kyiv, L'viv, Odesa, and Chernihiv (to cover the border with Russia); troop levels will be brought to a compromise figure of 350,000, but only slowly; the army will be rearmed as resources permit to provide for greater mobility and faster deployment; and conscription will be maintained in the short term (though it is not well enforced), while the move to a professional army will remain on the agenda. The most major structural change has been the merging of the air force and the air defense forces, which was carried out without major opposition before the more sweeping reform plans were introduced.[17]

Professionalization

Many have advocated professionalizing the Ukrainian military, that is, relying on voluntary enlistments rather than on conscription, but it appears that for the time being the army will continue to staff itself through conscription. The benefits of a professional army for Ukraine are perceived to be similar to those in states such as the United States and Britain. Using a smaller number of more highly paid soldiers who serve for longer periods can lead to a more effective force. Such a shift was a significant part of the Shmarov reform plan, which would have required more technically proficient and more highly trained soldiers. In a massive infantry-based army, a lower overall skill level is needed. A second reason for moving to a professional army is that conscription strikes many as a rather coercive measure, inappropriate for a democratic state except in wartime. Much of the movement for a separate Ukrainian army prior to August 1991 arose in opposition to the practices of conscription in the Soviet Union and to the fate of conscripted recruits. Some of the same problems persist in independent Ukraine, though not the problem of Ukrainian soldiers being forced to serve in distant parts of the Soviet Union. Finally, professionalization is viewed as more "Western," despite the fact that Germany and France are only now moving in that direction.

Nonetheless, there are several objections to such a move. First, unless professionalization is accompanied by substantial cuts in troop numbers, it will be costly. A primary virtue of conscription is that conscripts can be paid very little above subsistence. Second, the notion of the military as an incubator of national unity implies that conscription has benefits apart from military effectiveness or cost. Discussing professionalization in 1998, Defense Minister Oleksandr Kuzmuk said, "[D]espite the attractiveness of the tenet of a fully professional army, I am convinced that we will preserve the call-up system of staffing our army because it is a traditional and tested path ensuring the closeness between our Armed Forces and society."[18]

SUSTAINING THE ARMED FORCES

In the Soviet system, the military and its associated industries received priority in all funding decisions. In all of the post-Soviet states, Ukraine included, this priority has eroded for two reasons. First, with the adoption of democratic institutions, the military has lost its previous impregnable position in the budgeting process. Second, economic collapse has made it impossible to fund the military at previous levels even where such funding was considered desirable. By increasing the incentives for speedy downsizing, this condition has in one way facilitated military transformation. But the dearth of funding has made it nearly impossible to undertake any positive program of reform. Rather than a reform of the military, Ukraine has essentially had a shrinking of the military. The funding problems have eroded readiness and morale and have spurred widespread crime and corruption in the military and defense organs.

The statistics concerning the underfunding of Ukraine's military are staggering, and the hardship faced by normal soldiers appalling. A brief review of some of these statistics is illustrative:[19]

- In 1995, the Ukrainian defense budget met only 16.9 percent of financial needs, down from 28 percent in 1993–1994 and 34 percent in 1992.
- In 1995, only 5–12 percent of needed funds were provided for training and new technology.
- In late 1994, 73,000 officers and 34,000 reserve officers had no housing.
- Twenty percent of officers surveyed "moonlighted" in commercial firms to make ends meet.
- Half of Ukraine's suicides involve soldiers or officers.
- Of 305,000 tons of fuel needed in 1994, the military received only 40,500.
- By 1995, 40 percent of Ukraine's fighter jets were out of action due to fuel shortages and a lack of spare parts.

THE TRANSFORMATION OF THE ARMED FORCES ■ 247

- Naval headquarters in Sevastopol lost its phone service in early 1996 because it could not pay its bill.

Simply put, Ukraine inherited a military that it cannot sustain. Even after halving the number of active servicemen, the military is drastically underfunded and undersupplied. The situation shows no signs of improving: Ukraine's 1999 budget foresees actually cutting the defense budget by approximately 20 percent, even though Defense Minister Kuzmuk complained that only 46 percent of needs are met within the current budget and that "tragic consequences" could result from further cuts.[20] The economic causes of these budgetary shortfalls are obvious, and perhaps unavoidable, but the consequences are far-reaching, having effects on morale, corruption, and preparedness.

As noted above, the rate of suicide is extremely high in the armed forces, only one of several indicators of a social crisis in the military that is completely undermining morale. The physical conditions in which troops exist—with inadequate housing, food, and training—have led to a situation where almost anyone who can get out of the military does. The broader social crisis in Ukrainian society itself is making it more difficult to find adequate conscripts: In 1993, 120,000 conscripts were found to be unfit for military service for health reasons. Problems continue within the military. Most notable, but probably not unique, was a scandal in 1994 in which eighty conscripts in the Carpathian military district were found to be suffering from severe malnutrition, having lost between ten and twenty-five kilograms while serving. The cause of their malnutrition, it was discovered, was that the conscripts were receiving only one-third of their already meager rations because the rest was being pilfered by officers and sold on the civilian market. The widespread nature of this problem was recognized when a special inspectorate was formed at the Ministry of Defense to investigate "the dishonest and illegitimate doings of officers, their inability to discharge their duties, and abuses of official positions."[21] Another blow to morale has been the continuation of the practice of hazing of new conscripts, or *dedovshchina*. The topic of major complaints about the treatment of Ukrainian recruits in the Soviet army, hazing has continued apace in the Ukrainian military, making service even less desirable. In addition to all that, payment of salaries is often delayed.

The housing crisis has continued, despite downsizing of the army, for several reasons. First, officers do not generally give up their housing when they leave the military, so downsizing does not lead to many vacancies in housing. Second, downsizing has largely bypassed the officer corps, leaving Ukraine with an officer corps proportionally much larger than it needs. Third, the influx of Ukrainian officers, first from the withdrawal of

Soviet forces from the Warsaw Pact and then from the other post-Soviet states, has offset any internal decline in the number of officers needing housing. Originally, Ukraine planned to solve the problem by paying for the construction of new housing with money earned selling surplus military equipment. But although Shmarov pledged to add 20,000 units of housing per year, Ukraine's economic turmoil has prevented this. Sale of military equipment has been much less profitable than anticipated, and it is not clear whether any such profits were actually earmarked for housing construction. Instead, local city governments have been encouraged to provide apartments for the military. Although several city governments have provided between 50 and 100 apartments each, the effort amounts to only a small fraction of the overall needs of the armed forces.

Surveys of military personnel indicate how much all of this has lowered morale. Nearly 60 percent of officers expressed a negative view of their situation in July 1994. This percentage declined slightly under Shmarov, who did a better job of paying salaries on time, but dissatisfaction among sergeants and conscripts remained near 60 percent. Forty percent of conscripts do not want to join the army. Surveys show also that about one-half of all young officers would like to quit the armed forces.[22] They stay in the military largely because of their family situation or the fear of unemployment rather than out of any genuine desire to be officers.[23]

It is difficult to know precisely how much the material and emotional declines in the armed forces have reduced the forces' preparedness for action, for until they are called upon to perform, we will not know how well they will do. There can be little doubt, however, that reduced training time, declining operability of equipment, and shattered morale have severely degraded the ability of the army to do its job. The one good test case we have, of Ukrainian units serving under the UN in Bosnia, shows that they generally performed up to par but ran into serious allegations of corruption. Their performance should not lead to much confidence, because these are the very best units in Ukraine and have been allowed most of the material benefits that the rest of the army has been denied.

The corruption that showed up even in Bosnia has perhaps been the most widespread response in the military to its underfunding. If sufficient funds are not obtained from the government, much more of a soldier's livelihood depends on his own resources, and in the military, there are many opportunities to make money on the side. Although the state has hoped to raise funds through the sale of surplus equipment, lower-level officials have taken to selling off equipment on their own and embezzling the proceeds, whether the equipment is surplus or not. The Interim Investigating Commission of the Verkhovna Rada concluded that there was no control at all over arms sales and that embezzlement of proceeds was rife.[24] The corruption that occurs involves sales of weapons not only on the international market but also on a smaller scale and at a more local level, as well as sales of any military assets that have a civilian purpose, diversion of foodstuffs to local markets, or simply embezzlement of money allocated for salaries.

The only potential silver lining in this massive cloud is that the armed forces will probably not be called upon for any serious mission anytime soon. But clearly, the crisis of the military will limit the political leadership's foreign policy options. One must assume that in a crisis, decision-makers will have to be much more doubtful than they otherwise might be about the army's ability to carry out any key mission entrusted to it.

RESTRUCTURING THE MILITARY-INDUSTRIAL COMPLEX

With the collapse of the Soviet Union, it was immediately recognized that decreased military budgets would put a massive strain on many industries producing for the military. In the Soviet Union, as much as 20 percent of GNP was spent on defense, and approximately 1.3 million Ukrainians were employed in the defense sector in 1985.[25] Because military industries contained some of Ukraine's best technical minds and some of its most advanced equipment, they could not be simply shut down. Rather, the hope was that their technical expertise could be rechanneled into high-quality production for the civilian market. Restructuring was an oft-repeated goal in the early 1990s, but it has proven much more difficult than anticipated. Instead, defense factories have gone into decline with the rest of the Ukrainian economy. There have been a few bright spots, but most successes for Ukrainian military industries have come not by restructuring but by continuing to build military hardware and selling it on the world market. Indeed, the sale of military equipment is one of Ukraine's best sources of hard currency earnings.

The Soviet Union was the world's second leading arms exporter, and Ukraine, which constituted about 20 percent of the Soviet defense industry, played an important role as a supplier for the international market. After 1991, both Russian and Ukrainian arms sales collapsed, due to chaos in the industries, problems of dividing interdependent industries across borders, and the perceived need to convert defense industry to civilian purposes. Thus, Ukraine sold only $28 million worth of military goods in 1993 and $42 million in 1994.[26] Conversion, though a good idea, has not worked in practice throughout the former Soviet Union. Such conversion required substantial investment, which was often unavailable, and assumed the ability to enter markets already fully supplied by leading Western and Asian firms. Thus, attempts such as converting an aviation electronics factory into a manufacturer of cellular phones never got off the ground, despite some investment incentives provided by the U.S. government.

Following the collapse of military exports through 1994, President Kuchma, himself a veteran of the world's largest ballistic missile factory, placed a much higher priority on the issue. The new priority was based on the simple free-market realization that Ukraine's firms had competitive advantage in weapons, not cellular phones or vacuum cleaners. Firms such as Pivden'mash in missiles and Antonov in aircraft were among the best and most experienced in the world at their areas of the arms bazaar. Rather than move away from this strength, Kuchma sought to exploit it, appointing Volodymyr Mukhin as head of Ukraine's Commission for Defense and State Security. Mukhin approached his job with zeal, saying that "our bombs will become smart" to compete with those from Western manufacturers and predicting that the profits from selling the enormous inventory of Soviet ammunition and supplies "will feed the country for the next ten to twenty years."[27] Rather than dissolving or converting these factories, then, the Ukrainian government has elected to keep approximately 150 of the most important enterprises under state control and to privatize another 550. In 1996, the government combined arms export efforts under a single administration, rather than maintaining the three separate firms that had existed earlier.[28]

Initially, exports focused on relatively unsophisticated small-dollar commodities, such as ammunition, grenades, torpedoes, and rockets that were left over in huge supply from the Soviet Union. Because these surplus materials were essentially free to Ukraine, exporters could gain market share and still make a profit selling at prices 20 percent below those of others (leading to charges by Western competitors of "dumping"). By 1995, sales had reached $100 million, and Ukraine's determination to reestablish itself in the international arms market was announced boldly at the world's major arms fair, IDEX-95, held in the United Arab Emirates in March 1995. Ukraine exhibited over 200 products from over fifty enterprises, as much as any country except the United Kingdom. Particular emphasis was given to the T-80UD and T-84 tanks.[29] In July 1996, when Pakistan agreed to purchase 320 T-80UD tanks for $550 million, Ukraine achieved the breakthrough it had been looking for. Ukraine beat out competitors from Russia and China to win the deal, apparently because only the Malyshev plant, in Kharkiv, can produce the tank with diesel engines, which are optimal for the hot desert conditions in Pakistan. Given the Ukrainian tank's advantage in desert conditions, Ukraine hopes to continue its success in the rapidly expanding Middle East arms market.

Ukraine has proven capable of competing on world markets in two other areas of defense-related production. In aviation, Kyiv's Antonov works has pressed forward with designing new aircraft to sell on the world market. It has been particularly successful in the area of large transport aircraft, where its AN-22 behemoth was leased by France on several occasions to airlift support to Africa to aid friendly governments there. The United Kingdom even considered restocking its transport fleet with AN-22s before settling on the American C-130J.[30] More recently, Antonov has developed a new heavy transport aircraft that has raised considerable attention. The German Ministry of Defense commissioned a study into the possibility of developing a "Westernized" variant of the AN-70 as a less costly alternative to the Future Large Aircraft under development by a Western European consortium. Although the success of that project is questionable, Ukraine and Russia have already agreed to begin production of the aircraft, with 150 to go to the Russian air force and more to be sold on the world market for both civilian and military purposes.[31]

In the area of missiles, Kuchma's old factory, Pivden'mash, has positioned itself to compete in the market for satellite launches. The Zenit rocket booster, produced jointly with Russia and launched from the Baikonur Cosmodrome in Kazakhstan, has been used to launch a series of satellites for the American Globalstar consortium. It is also the basis for a rocket being developed by Boeing to launch satellites from sea. The large lifting capacity and low cost were major advantages of the Ukrainian rocket, but a failure of the booster in a September 1998 launch, which destroyed twelve satellites aboard, has raised questions about the Zenit's future both as a separate booster and as a component in the Boeing project.[32]

As these last two examples illustrate, there has been a fair amount of collaboration among Ukrainian and Russian defense firms to produce for the world market and even for domestic use. This cooperation has taken time to develop, as Russia originally bridled at Ukraine's competition for business previously held by Russian firms. When the tank deal with Pakistan was originally announced, for example, Russia announced that the deal would not be able to go through because the main turret and gun assemblies were produced in Russia, which would not supply them. Rather than scuttling the deal, the move prompted Ukrainian firms to begin developing their own gun for the tank, and Ukraine is now able to build the entire tank without parts from Russia. Because so many firms in the Soviet Union spread facilities across what are now state boundaries, both Ukrainian and Russian firms will find it much easier to cooperate to conquer the world market than to compete with one another.

The increased efforts at arms exports have certainly had a substantial effect. Ukraine exported approximately $760 million worth of arms in 1995–1997, not including illegal sales, which appear to be much larger.[33] That good news for Ukraine is tempered, however, by the extraordinary corruption that accompanies such sales. Despite plans to allocate money from arms sales for troop housing, no money has been forthcoming. Indeed, it appears that only around 10 percent of the money paid for these exports ever arrives in Ukraine, the rest being deposited in foreign bank accounts beyond the government's control.[34] A second related problem is that illegal arms exports to some of the world's less savory actors have damaged Ukraine's reputation. Ukraine traded Iran fifty MiG-29 fighters and 200 tanks out of Soviet surplus for oil. Ukrainian arms are also reported to have shown up in Bosnia, in violation of the arms embargo, as well as in Afghanistan and Ecuador and in the hands of Colombian drug cartels. Both in terms of limiting undesirable sales and bringing revenue from such sales into state coffers, the Ukrainian government has a lot of work to do before the resurgence of the Ukrainian arms business can be considered a success.

CIVIL-MILITARY RELATIONS

Civil-military relations constitute one of the most significant problems for new states. Many new democracies through the years have reverted to authoritarianism when the military has taken over, a threat that is still mentioned concerning Russia every time a new crisis emerges there. In Ukraine, issues of civilian control of the military persist, but the most serious dangers have never even arisen. For various reasons that will be detailed below, the Ukrainian military has never had the political influence of its Russian counterpart and has never even insinuated that it might intervene in politics. Nor is there any evidence that civilian authorities have seriously contemplated asking for military intervention. The main point here is that the military has been passive rather than active and that the main civilian-military political conflicts have come over military resistance to its own reform. In other words, civil-military conflicts remain limited to issues of direct concern to the military rather than spilling over into politics more broadly.

The role of civil-military relations in a new democracy is important for three related reasons. First, as Jon Elster, Claus Offe, and Ulrich Preuss discuss, many new democracies are formed through the direct intervention of the military in politics, either through the military defeat of the old regime or through the defeat of a previously ruling military regime.[35] Thus, many democracies begin with the military already active in politics. Second, as discussed above, the military can play an important role in state building, both symbolically, as the emblem of the will of the state, and quite prosaically, as the embodiment of the monopoly on violence, which is the state's defining factor and occasionally has to be demonstrated. Third, the military can be one of the most substantial obstacles to the consolidation of democracy. Because technically the military, not the government, possesses the means of violence, it can seek to influence the political process, to replace the government, or even to overthrow the democracy entirely. One recent example is Turkey, where in defense of Turkey's secular tradition, the Turkish military forced the democratically elected government to resign. This did not mean the end of democracy in Turkey, but it certainly eroded the notion of Turkish democracy. The goal, then, in discussions of civil-military relations is typically described as "civilian control of the military." The idea is that the military should retain its expertise about *how* to conduct military operations but that the government controls *what* missions should be performed and *when* the military will go into action and, more broadly, assures that military influence will not stray into nonmilitary affairs. Although the Ukrainian military is plagued with problems, these most fundamental ones have not been among them.

The "conspicuous absence" of military conflict in the transition is shared by almost all of the post-Communist states but stands in contrast to previous examples in Latin America and Africa.[36] Because the military was not involved from the beginning in Ukraine, it was much less likely that it would become politically active later. Instead, the genesis of the Ukrainian state in 1990–1992 transpired in several ways that tended to keep the military out of the process. First, in separating the Ukrainian military from the Soviet military, Ukraine created a military without a head, that is, without the strong leadership that would facilitate a role in politics. Prior to 1991, there was no Ukrainian general staff, no independent organizational capacity, no Ukrainian command structure. These were created by the newly independent state and for its purposes. While the state was at its weakest, the military, too, had been thrown into complete disarray. Moreover, there was from the beginning vigilance toward the military, stemming from the fact that few of the officers were actually native Ukrainians. Maintaining control was therefore a priority from the beginning, but it could succeed because of the previous point: The military started with no "head." Symbolically and practically, the military became a means for establishing Ukrainian independence from Russia and hence for building the state.

In the longer term, the military has generally continued to stay out of politics, though the institutional mechanisms for this are still developing. One of the most widely used indicators of "civilian control" in the West is having a civilian defense minister. This is one of the major requirements for a state to be considered for admission into NATO, thus it was regarded as a major advance when Kuchma appointed Shmarov, a civilian, in 1994. Prior to that time, and since his firing as well, Ukraine has had a military officer as minister of defense. Yet a civilian minister of defense is only one person, and while useful as an overall indicator, this does not say much about how politics actually works. In fact, there has been little variation in civilian control under Shmarov compared to his predecessors and successors.

The two significant attempts by the military to involve itself in politics demonstrate that such involvement is insignificant in Ukraine. In the first, Defense Minister Morozov (a general) publicly denounced the agreements reached between Ukraine and Russia at the Massandra Summit in September 1993. The Massandra agreements would have ceded the Black Sea Fleet to Russia in return for debt forgiveness. Morozov, a strong Ukrainian nationalist despite his Russian roots, denounced the deal, as did most of the Parliament. The deal was never ratified or implemented, but Morozov played a minimal role in its overall defeat. Rather he sought to influence the process, was largely irrelevant, and for his effort was forced to resign shortly thereafter. Early on, then, it was demonstrated that even when the defense minister's position is widely shared by the elite, intervening in what was deemed a political decision was viewed as unacceptable. Equally important, in contrast to several generals in Russia (i.e., Lev Rokhlin and Aleksandr Lebed) who were forced out of government service and became leading politicians themselves, Morozov has not taken a leading role in the country's politics.

PHOTO 8.2   Presidents Leonid Kuchma and Boris Yeltsin sign agreement on Black Sea Fleet, Sochi, summer 1995

The second major dispute between military and civilian authorities concerned Shmarov's reform plan, the debate over which was outlined above. Here, the military took exception to the reform plan devised by the civilian defense minister, an occurrence with which even societies with quite solid civilian control are familiar. The issue, however, was not outside the military's expertise. Nor was it clearly outside the military's authority (General Lopata complained that the lines of authority between the general staff and the ministry were not sufficiently elaborated, but several attempts to delineate functions led nowhere).[37] And though a compromise was reached, the military officer leading the resistance and the defense minister were both fired.

Although he found it necessary to return to a military officer as minister of defense, Kuchma also developed a different mechanism of civilian control, forming the General Military Inspectorate in August 1995. The inspectorate was staffed equally with civilians and officers, but more important, it was subordinated directly to the presidential administration rather than the general staff, the intent being to shift its bureaucratic interest from the military to the president.[38]

A substantial explanation for the difficulty of maintaining a civilian in the role of defense minister, which explains why even the General Military Inspectorate has to be staffed largely with officers, is the lack of civilian expertise on defense and military matters in Ukraine. In the Soviet Union, military expertise was largely monopolized by the military itself, and what civilian expertise did exist was concentrated in Moscow. Ukraine thus began its independence with no real capacity for civilian control. This was clearly a problem for Shmarov, who, though he came from the military-industrial complex, had to learn about military issues on the job. Moreover, there was little trained civilian staff to help him. "When Shmarov arrived in the Defense Ministry in August 1994, he found there only a handful of civilian experts and none of them in a position of any influence."[39] It will take time for such civilian expertise to develop and for this staff to gain experience. Thus, efforts to improve civilian control have had to use military officers rather than replacing them with civilians. In addition to the creation of the General Military Inspectorate, a second factor promoting civilian control is division within the military itself. Because the military is not unified for or against any particular plan, it is easier to resist.

In sum, then, the military has maintained some ability to resist calls from outside to change the way it does business. There has been stiff resistance both to downsizing in general and to more specific plans to reform the army. However, this resistance is hardly unique to Ukraine, as President Clinton found in the United States when he attempted to change policy toward homosexuals in the military. It is also significant that the military has rarely sought to involve itself in issues outside its acknowledged realm of competence, in part perhaps due to the need to focus all of its effort on survival. In those few cases where the military has attempted to assert itself in broader foreign policy issues, such involvement has been rejected and the officers linked to it have been fired. In that sense, although it has not pursued civilian control in an orthodox fashion, Ukraine nonetheless has achieved the goal somewhat effectively. As civilian expertise develops over time and provides the human resources necessary for more regularized civilian control, that control will likely emerge, for the goal is widely shared in Ukraine, even if the first civilian defense minister did not last long.

TOWARD THE FUTURE: DETERMINING A SECURITY DOCTRINE

One of the most difficult tasks for Ukraine's security and military policy is the development of an overall conception of the role of military vis-à-vis other tools in security policy and the question of ends and means in security policy itself. These questions are intimately intertwined with the broader questions of foreign policy discussed in the preceding chapter, and that discussion will not be repeated here. However, it is necessary to discuss the primarily military and security issues that go beyond the questions of foreign policy.

The biggest problem for Ukraine, as for many states in the post–cold war world, is finding a threat. It is good news, of course, that Ukraine faces no imminent or serious military threat to its security. At the same time, however, the absence of such a threat creates some unique dilemmas for the military and for security policy more broadly. As was argued in the preceding chapter, since Ukraine has come to view economic threats as much more immediate than military threats, the military tool in security policy will play a different role than typically envisioned, with important effects for the military. The evolution of Ukrainian debates on the goals and means of national security policy highlights the dilemmas for the military, even if the overall implication for national security is positive. Three trends should be noted: First, the idea of basing security on nuclear deterrence, never widely held, was completely abandoned. Second, Ukraine's security posture toward Russia has softened in several ways. Third, an increasingly close relationship with NATO has raised questions both about Ukraine's declared neutrality and about specific military-technical issues.

During the early period in Ukraine's independence, when many Ukrainian leaders felt the state was insecure in its position between Russia's increasing assertiveness and the West's indifference, a variety of solutions were discussed. At this point, the military was seen as a guarantor of Ukraine's independence. It was only logical for some to point out that the most reliable source of military deterrence was the nuclear arsenal that Ukraine already possessed. Although the technical barriers to making the arsenal usable were formidable, they could be overcome with time. Retaining the arsenal had a second, symbolic benefit as well: It reasserted Ukraine's right to all property of the Soviet Union on its territory, as well as Ukraine's juridical equality with Russia.

The idea of basing security on nuclear weapons was grounded on a variety of military and political factors, as discussed in the previous chapter. In addition to the changes in the diplomatic climate caused by the decision, this strategy also contributed to the ongoing process of refocusing Ukraine's security policy away from narrow military means—the use or threat of force—and toward the diplomatic realm, working to ensure that conflicts with Russia (and within Ukraine) were contained in the diplomatic realm. Military leaders were never among the strongest proponents of a nuclear Ukraine (nationalist politicians were), and they tended to regard the weapons as a security liability (both as targets and as systems requiring immense investment in upkeep and safety) rather than as an asset.

This shift away from a strictly military security posture was evident in the more general debates on the subject. The Military Doctrine adopted in October 1993 concentrated on a central perceived threat: the palpable danger of intervention in Ukrainian affairs by Russia (which was not mentioned by name but was unmistakably the subject of much of the doctrine). Nor was the threat elaborated in great detail, which probably obscured the differences between two separate emphases. Some Ukrainian leaders still believed in the possibility of an outright military attack by Russia aimed at bringing Ukraine back into Russian control. More widely feared was Russian support, covert or otherwise, for separatist movements in Ukraine, particularly involving Crimea. The role of Russia in prompting and supporting Abkhaz separatism in Georgia and Trans-Dniester separatism in Moldova provided clear evidence of what was possible and probably prompted the reference in the doctrine to the unacceptability of basing foreign troops on Ukrainian soil.[40] In sum, the threat was clear, and it was military. What remained unclear was the military parameters of the threat. If a massive attack was likely, then the large-scale battle format inherited from the Soviet Union would best be preserved, if re-aimed. This threat also motivated some who argued for Ukraine to adopt permanent nuclear status. In any event, there was little funding to be had either to completely restructure the force or to reorient its basing from west to east, but this situation left one question clear and another up for debate. It was clear that Russia would be the focus of military policy, but it was unclear what the implication was for military reform. This uncertainty therefore played itself out in the debate over military reform between Shmarov and Lopatin.

By 1995, perspectives on security had changed due to the economic crisis and to progress on the diplomatic front, and change has continued. The economic crisis, which seemed to peak in 1994, combined with Kuchma's ascension to the presidency, led to a shift in threat perception away from external security threats and toward internal security threats. At the same time, two issues raised the possibility of cooperating with Russia in the security sphere, though the categorical rejection of CIS military integration was maintained. First, over time, the clear joint interest in cooperation in arms production for the export market has become more salient, as discussed above. Related to this, a certain amount of cooperation is required for both militaries to maintain equipment that was produced jointly in the Soviet Union. For example, the major facilities for tank maintenance were concentrated in Ukraine. Also over time, the "danger" of cooperating with the "enemy" has been replaced by the opportunity of putting unemployed defense workers back to work and bringing badly needed revenue into the military-industrial complex. Second, Ukraine has recognized the desirability of cooperating in the area of air defense. The single perimeter of radar systems and interceptors built by the Soviet Union left none of its successors with a separate viable system. After a period of rejecting any cooperation in this area, the Ukrainian leadership has embraced the project, in large part because Russia agreed to fund the upkeep of the relevant facilities. Most broadly, the foreign policy of the Kuchma administration, while surprising some by continuing Ukraine's anti-integrationist policies, completely shifted the tone of relations with Russia to focus on "strategic partnership" rather than rivalry.

At the same time, internal threats were seen to be growing because economic chaos was leading to increasing dissatisfaction in general and was feeding growing separatist movements in Crimea and the Donbas. The combination of economic decline and ethnic/regional conflict had the potential to be explosive.[41] The shift in emphasis was confirmed by a surprisingly frank interview given by Volodymyr Horbulin, secretary of the National Security and Defense Council, in May 1998: "[P]olitical security ... can be internal and external. The current situation in our country is determined by internal problems; therefore, let us limit ourselves to the topic of our internal political security."[42] For this reason, the internal security forces of Ukraine have continued to grow, even as the regular military is downsized.

The most significant evolution in Ukraine's security situation since independence has been the burgeoning relationship with NATO. Diplomatically, the end of Ukraine's isolation from the West, beginning in

1994, has opened up a series of new policy options. Militarily, the opportunity to work closely with NATO has provided its own opportunities and challenges. However, the desired goal of all this activity has yet to be decided upon. Although there is widespread support in Ukraine for increased contacts with NATO, there is no consensus either in Ukraine or in the West about what the goal of this is or about how it should affect Ukraine's relations with Russia. Some "Western-oriented" individuals support an unequivocal pro-NATO policy, with the goal of obtaining as much support as possible from NATO in a possible future conflict with Russia. This "balance-of-power view" characterized the policy of Kravchuk's government, which enthusiastically supported NATO expansion and Ukraine's increased interaction with the alliance. In this view, NATO expansion to Ukraine's borders put Ukraine one step closer to membership and provided that much more latitude for Ukraine in its relations with Russia. The second widespread view might be called the "neither East nor West" view and has characterized Kuchma's policy. From this view, Ukraine should interact with NATO as much as possible to gain technical advice and to be accepted as part of Europe. But in this perspective, Ukraine's relations with NATO are not seen as an alternative

PHOTO 8.3   Ukrainian and U.S. troops in a NATO Partnership for Peace exercise, Yavoriv training ground, western Ukraine, 1997

to good relations with Russia, but rather as a complement. Hence, Kuchma's government has been much less enthusiastic about NATO enlargement, insisting that it be carried out only after an agreement between NATO and Russia, rather than over Russia's objections. From this "neither East nor West" perspective, the possibility of Ukraine joining NATO is at best far in the future and at worst would cause conflict both within Ukraine and between Ukraine and Russia.

In sum, then, we see evolution in Ukraine's security policy, as in its foreign policy more generally, away from a confrontation with Russia and toward a defensive cooperation. Yet opinion remains divided. Some see relations with Russia as inherently conflictual and hence see the military and links with NATO in terms of the need for assets to use against Russia. Others see relations with Russia in terms of the need to avoid conflict, and they condition security policies and links with NATO on that premise. In the former view, whether Russia approves of NATO expansion or Ukraine's ties with NATO (or eventual membership) is irrelevant. In the latter view, Russia's views are essential, because in this view conflict with Russia should be avoided where possible. In the short term, NATO expansion is a given, Ukrainian membership in NATO is a nonstarter, and the parameters of Ukraine's involvement with NATO are largely determined in Brussels and Washington, not in Kyiv. So most of the serious debates have not had to be resolved in Ukraine, because they have been resolved for Ukraine by others.

SUMMARY

Overall, Ukrainian security policy since independence has been characterized above all by transition, and this transition will continue at least for the next decade, even if at a slower pace. In many ways, one can say that the transition has been in a positive direction for the Ukrainian state: The military was used as a means for reinforcing Ukraine's separation from the former Soviet Union; it has been transformed into a Ukrainian institution with loyalty to the Ukrainian state; and it has been reduced in size faster than most thought possible. It is most significant that the military has largely kept out of politics, avoiding one of the primary pitfalls of new democracies. Security policy more broadly has seen a shift from a combination of conflict with Russia and isolation from the West to an accommodation with Russia and partnership with the West. In light of the enormous tasks that existed in August 1991, the accomplishments are substantial. Three shortcomings, however, threaten to undermine much of this success. First, the lack of the political consensus and political will to develop and implement a genuine reform plan will leave the military increasingly irrelevant to the security tasks faced by the state. Second, ongoing corruption in the military undermines its effectiveness both by diverting the materials and funds allocated by the government away from their intended purposes and by diverting proceeds from the sales of equipment on the world market away from the state's coffers. Finally, the miserable living and training conditions of much of the military are making it increasingly unlikely that the forces can be used constructively and make it correspondingly likely that corruption and crime emanating from the military will grow.

The next decade will see an effort to complete the downsizing of the military as well as renewed efforts to reform it in terms of its composition and orientation. Debates on the optimal form and size of the military and on the question of professionalization will continue. There is little reason to believe that these debates will be decisively resolved. It is even more significant that the major shortcomings in Ukraine's military all stem in one way or another from the collapse of the country's economy and the failure to rebuild it. Since economic reform and growth look set to come slowly, if at all, in Ukraine (see Chapter 6), the problems of the military will persist. Whether they grow in size and in scope (for example, whether civilian control begins to weaken) will be determined by just how bad the economy gets and by the strength of civilian control, which is difficult to estimate until it is tested. Thus, problems for the military will continue, but the broader prospects for security remain good, due to the successes of Ukraine's foreign policy, which has helped provide a security environment that has become considerably more congenial and looks set to remain that way.

▪ NINE ▪

Conclusion: Problems and Prospects for Ukraine in the Twenty-First Century

There is an old joke in Ukraine that goes like this: A pessimist is one who thinks things are going to get worse, and an optimist is one who thinks things cannot possibly get any worse. These seem to be the two prevalent attitudes about the experience of the country over the last ten years and the prospects for the next ten. Many of the hopes that accompanied Ukrainian independence in 1991 have been frustrated in the years since, but the accomplishments of the last decade should not be underestimated: Ukraine has gained its independence and has established it securely in the face of numerous potential threats. Ukraine has transformed its political system from the Soviet totalitarian system to one that in many respects is democratic. And it has seen an end to the command economy that brought the country to ruin in the Soviet era. That much has been accomplished, but much more remains to be done in order for Ukraine's transition to be regarded as complete or regarded as a success either by Ukrainians themselves or by outside observers. The previous chapters of this book have assessed both the success and failures of Ukrainian politics in the past decade. The purpose of this conclusion is to review and summarize those findings and to ask about the prospects for the future. Will Ukraine continue to move toward liberal democracy and the market, or is that process somehow stalled?

This conclusion begins then by reviewing the substantive findings of the book and by highlighting the problems that have arisen in the main areas of Ukrainian politics. We then move into a series of broader questions concerning the future. How is this story likely to turn out? And what measures or programs by the government might lead to a happy ending? Finally, we consider the lessons of the Ukrainian experience in light of the other recent cases of post-Communist transformation. What can we learn from those cases that helps us understand Ukraine? What does Ukraine's experience tell us about broader problems of transformation?

REVIEW OF THE FINDINGS

Before discussing the problems and failures of post-Soviet Ukraine, it is necessary to recall the politics of the Soviet Union, which, as we showed in Chapter 1, left a legacy of obstacles for the development of an independent, democratic, market-oriented Ukraine. As the Soviet Union evolved and then collapsed under Gorbachev, Ukraine was able to gain a bit of experience with reform but was nonetheless essentially unprepared for the tasks that arose upon independence. The legacy of Soviet rule, as much as any factors inherent to Ukrainian society or arising since independence, explains much of Ukraine's failure to forge a successful transformation. A few of these points are worth reviewing. First, the Soviet economy was formed in such a way that it is very hard to reform, even with the best of intentions. The tendency toward monopolies, in particular, means that it is not enough simply to privatize firms. Demonopolization—a much more complex task—is needed if market forces are to drive prices and allocation of resources. Second, the trade-off made at the time of independence—that nationalists would not seek to remove the existing elite if that elite supported independence—continues to influence politics. Ukraine did not, in that sense, have a revolution, a profound change in which the prevailing order would have been completely overthrown. At the micro level, much in fact remained constant and has been resistant to change. Rather than starting out with a clean slate in 1991, Ukraine saw a great deal of institutional continuity from the Soviet to the post-Soviet era. As we see in the case of economic reform, it is quite difficult for old institutions to perform new functions, and it is often difficult to persuade the people staffing those institutions to adopt new goals. In sum, though we think of 1991 as a "break" in Ukrainian politics, we need to recall that as profound as the break was in some respects, there was much more continuity in others.

Among the most vexing problems faced by Ukraine is the fragmented nature of its society, which we highlighted in Chapter 2 on national identity. Again, the legacy of the past weighs heavily. Ukraine has been united geographically only since 1939, before which the western one-third of the country had never been connected with Russia, whereas the eastern portion had been subject to "Russification" campaigns under both the tsars and the Soviets. There is little consensus, therefore, on what it means to be Ukrainian and on what the nature of the Ukrainian national identity is and should be. Similarly, the populace is heterogeneous linguistically, with some using primarily Ukrainian, others Russian, and others using both. Differences in the most fundamental notions of identity influence almost every other issue in the country. Most fundamentally, the absence of a coherent national identity undermines efforts to build a civil society in Ukraine. Politically, the different experiences and outlooks make it less likely that a powerful political center will develop. In education, the question of language of instruction has become a hotly contested one. In economics, different traditions lead to vastly different views of the proper roles for state and market in the economy. And in foreign policy, different conceptions of national identity lead to differences over whether the future "belongs" with Russia or with the West.

The state and nationalist politicians face a troublesome dilemma in the area of national identity. On the one hand, it appears that without a more unified notion of Ukrainian national identity, the problems just mentioned will never be resolved. There is therefore a powerful incentive to engage in "nationalizing" programs, such as promoting the adoption of the Ukrainian language by more Ukrainian citizens and supporting the view that Ukraine is culturally, historically, and politically distinct from Russia. On the other hand, those policies may engender exactly the opposite response to that intended. To the extent that Russian speakers feel that their civil liberties or economic prospects are being infringed by nationalizing policies, there may be more ethnic strife, not less, and rather than bringing the country together, a wedge may be driven between Ukrainians and Russians. Ukraine's own experience under the Russian Empire and the Soviet Union demonstrates both effects: Russification policies certainly had powerful effects, decreasing the use of the Ukrainian language and the level of Ukrainian national sentiment, but they never completely achieved Russification, despite being applied extremely coercively over decades; and indeed, those policies spurred the resentment that helped promote the movement for Ukrainian independence.

So far, Ukraine has adopted much more liberal nationality policies than many other states in the region, and despite many fears, it has not collapsed. The combination of liberal nationality policies and an open political system has given minorities (most notably ethnic Russians) powerful incentives to participate in the political system rather than rebel against it, choosing "voice" over "exit."[1] Perhaps the development of civil society can lead to a more coherent notion of national identity, but until that happens, the policy dilemma remains, and divisions in national identity hamper progress in political and social transformation.

In one narrower dimension of national identity, Ukraine has been more successful at limiting, if not eliminating, conflict. There remain important religious cleavages in Ukraine, linked to broader national identity cleavages, but religion itself has not become a significant axis of conflict in post-Soviet Ukraine. This religious peace can in large part be attributed to the decision not to establish a state religion. Putting aside the civil liberties arguments against state religions, seeking to establish one in a multiconfessional setting such as Ukraine would potentially empower some religious groups at the expense of others, hence becoming the arena for intense political conflict and perhaps even violence. Here is one clear case in which refraining from seeking to build a single homogeneous national identity has probably furthered that goal, by removing a potential source of conflict between the groups the state hopes to homogenize. Religious tensions remain, particularly between different factions of the Orthodox Church, but they are largely confined to religious and church issues and have not poisoned the broader political arena. A brief look at Yugoslavia indicates how significant an achievement this is.

Largely because of Ukraine's weak national identity, Ukraine has yet to develop what political scientists call a "civil society," in which there is widespread commitment to the use of democratic processes for the resolution of society's debates. The problem is not that support for democracy is weak. On the contrary, virtually all indicators show that the basic belief in democracy is strong in Ukraine, and there are very few who advocate authoritarianism as a way forward. Instead, national identity, ideology, and public opinion are so badly fragmented that finding workable compromises has been nearly impossible in Ukraine. At the broadest level of national identity, there are vast differences in how people see the Ukrainian state and nation. On more concrete issues such as economic reform, atomization becomes even more clear: Opinion is spread across the spectrum from those advocating radical free market solutions to those advocating social democracy on the Swedish model to those advocating a return to communism and central planning. Many people remain at the poles in these debates, such that it has been impossible to build a strong working coalition at the center of the spectrum. We will discuss shortly the institutional barriers to formation of a civil society, but even with perfectly designed institutions, it would be difficult to build effective compromise in a system where attitudes diverge so widely.

Societal fragmentation has been compounded by institutional shortcomings in preventing effective democratic governance. Within society, there is a serious dearth of intermediate institutions that help organize and aggregate public opinion and channel it into the decisionmaking process. Most important, as we discussed in Chapter 5, political parties have yet to consolidate to the point where they are meaningful transmission belts of opinion from society to the state. The weakness of the party system is caused as well by institutional deficiencies in the constitution and election law. The 4-percent threshold in the party-list portion of parliamentary elections has not been enough to prompt serious party consolidation. The runoff system for the single-member district seats in Parliament, and for the presidency, also reduces incentives to consolidate. In sum, societal and institutional factors mutually reinforce one another in preventing the consolidation of political opinion and political power in Ukraine.

All of these problems manifest themselves in the utter failure of Ukraine to address its most pressing problem: economic reform. Western economists as well as Ukrainians debate the ideal ultimate goal of economic reform as well as the ideal means of getting there. But no one would advocate the inertia and decay that have taken place in the absence of a real policy. A less-than-perfect policy, competently executed, would be far preferable to the lack of direction and self-contradiction that accompany Ukrainian economic policy. As we pointed out in Chapter 6, there have been some real successes in Ukrainian economic policy, most notably the establishment of a stable currency beginning in late 1996. Any benefits, however, have been wiped out by the inability to pursue other legs of economic reform, the most important among them being privatization. The failure to reform the economy and the concomitant economic collapse have substantial feedback effects on the society, exacerbating eastern-western, Ukrainian-Russian, and left-right cleavages. How far these effects will go remains to be seen, but they must raise concerns for the future political stability in the country.

Ukraine's greatest political accomplishments since 1991 have been in the realm of foreign policy (Chapter 7), but in the future, we can expect that domestic problems will increasingly undermine foreign policy objectives. Given the lack of enthusiasm for Ukrainian independence in the world community as well as the active opposition in the Soviet Union and the Russian Federation, it was a considerable achievement for Ukraine to have managed to establish and consolidate its independence. It accomplished this both in the international legal realm, by attaining diplomatic recognition and UN membership, and in the context of the former Soviet Union, by actively separating its economy from the others in 1992. The March 1992 economic plan that proved completely ineffective in terms of reform did have the intended effect of separating Ukraine's economic ties with Russia. That tension—between political independence from Russia and economic interdependence with Russia—is inherent in Ukraine's foreign policy and will continue to create problems. Ukraine's other major success in foreign policy was shifting the geometry of the Ukrainian-Russian-U.S. triangle, so that Ukraine, rather than Russia, became the main ally of the United States in the region.

The problem of economic interdependence can be expected to get worse before it gets better, for reasons both internal and external to Ukraine. Internally, as the momentum for reform has slowed, the prospects for a domestic solution to the "economic crisis" are diminishing. That will prompt some to look harder at increasing integration with Russia as a solution to problems. There is little evidence to indicate that integration with Russia would somehow boost Ukraine's economy in the absence of reform, but the idea is nonetheless frequently mentioned by leftist politicians. Externally, Ukraine's room for maneuver is likely to decrease as a result of the European Union's expansion to include Poland, Hungary, and the Czech Republic. Rather than connecting Ukraine's economy to the EU, this process will likely cut it off from Poland and Hungary, two major trade partners and corridors to the West. The EU, though free internally, has substantial external barriers to trade and to the movement of people. It is likely, therefore, that it will be more difficult for Ukrainian firms to sell in Poland and more difficult for traders to move freely between Ukraine and Poland, a major source of income in western Ukraine. To the extent that this occurs, there will be even more desire to increase trade with the other post-Soviet states. Moreover, if the United States and IMF begin to suffer "donor fatigue," Ukraine's economic position could suffer even more. In short, although Ukraine has successfully completed the foreign policy tasks related to separation from Russia, it is having a more difficult time completing the tasks of an independent state. To the extent that a successful foreign policy will rest upon effective reform of the economy, the future looks less bright for Ukraine.

The armed forces and military-industrial complex have had great difficulty adjusting to the collapse of funding. An increasingly savvy approach to global arms markets has helped boost some sectors of the military-industrial complex, but others remain in collapse, and the level of corruption in exports means that little of the proceeds goes toward military or government purposes. Despite cutting military personnel by nearly 50 percent, the forces that remain are underfunded to the point where they must become entrepreneurs to sustain themselves, with profoundly deleterious effects on morale and readiness. The absence of an agreed reform program leaves Ukraine with a military that is largely inappropriate to its defense needs. Despite this bleak situation, there are two bright spots in the defense picture. First, Ukraine is not likely to be hurt by its lack of military readiness and lack of appropriate force structure because there are currently no foreseeable military threats to the country. Second, the military has stayed almost completely out of politics, establishing one of the more important bases for the consolidation of democracy.

Taken in total, then, we see a picture of Ukrainian politics and society that is somewhat bleak, but it could be a lot worse. The few successes to date seem to be outweighed by the large number of important failures, but perhaps the biggest success is the absence of even larger failures, such as a military takeover, widespread ethnic unrest, or a serious move to reunite the country with Russia.

QUESTIONS FOR THE FUTURE

If we summarize the state of Ukraine in 1999 by looking at the questions that remain to be answered in the coming years, we find the list is daunting: Will the state survive, or will it collapse in one way or another? Can corruption be curtailed and a functioning state develop? Will the economy improve? Will there emerge a unified national identity? Can a functioning party system develop? Will the state gravitate toward Russia, toward the West, or remain in between? Can democracy consolidate in Ukraine? Those who study the region have learned the hard way not to make predictions, but it is worth sketching out how one might think about these daunting questions.

Despite the depth of the problems Ukraine faces, there is little reason to believe that the state as an independent, unified, and sovereign actor will not persist for some time to come. The simple reason is that there is no one in Ukraine with any incentive to challenge that basic fact. To reintegrate Ukraine with Russia would lower Ukraine's leaders from being officials of an independent state, with all the prestige, power, and wealth that carries, to being minor provincial officials. There is little incentive for that, and indeed, the incentive for even antireform Ukrainian elites to support independence was demonstrated by the behavior of most Communist Party members in 1991 and since then. Internally, there is also little reason to seek to destroy the state. Instead, the incentive for actors powerful enough to make such a challenge is to capture the state, thereby capturing the attendant privileges. The most serious threats to the state come from potential secession, either in Crimea or eastern Ukraine, but again, the elites in these regions have found they have much more say in Kyiv than they would in Moscow. Thus, although the pressure on the state is severe, the mechanism by which the state would collapse and the actors who would initiate its downfall are hard to imagine.

The much more real question is whether the state will become effective, and we emphasize "become" because currently the Ukrainian government must be regarded as extremely weak. If one looks at any of the canonical measures of state strength, such as a monopoly on violence or ability to extract taxes from the populace, Ukraine looks pathetic. Extreme corruption, combined with inexperience, makes it impossible for people at the top of the Ukrainian state to expect that their orders or laws will be implemented in society. Tax collection, discussed in Chapter 4, is the clearest example. A combination of inexperience and incompetence gives Ukraine a tax code that is both hopelessly complex and ruinous to business if followed. Corruption leaves open an easier solution: Tax inspectors take bribes rather than closing down businesses and charging owners. When the state cannot collect taxes, it cannot run schools, hospitals, or the military, nor can it pay off its debts. What is the prospect for serious change here? In the summer of 1998, Prime Minister Pustovoitenko actually locked a number of industrial tax delinquents in a Kyiv palace, refusing to let them go until they paid taxes. This sort of heavy-handed measure earned Pustovoitenko wide praise but did not substantially increase tax revenues. Surely a more streamlined and moderate tax code would both raise the incentives to pay and make enforcement easier, but corruption would remain a problem, and the prospects for drastic improvement appear dim.

Because the state is so ineffective and because the society is divided, the prospects for economic reform must be regarded as slim. Three distinct obstacles exist. First, it is not clear what the best way to proceed is. Not only Ukrainians, but Westerners as well, disagree on how to reform centrally planned economies. The legacy of the Soviet Union makes this task much more complex than in Central Europe, and the fact that the job is being carried out by a brand new government further complicates the task. Second, the society and elite are badly divided over what is desirable and what is acceptable. Finally, even if the first two obstacles were removed, it remains doubtful whether the Ukrainian government could effectively implement the necessary measures, such as regulation of securities markets, reliable enforcement of contracts, and so on.

There is perhaps more reason for optimism regarding the development of a more coherent national identity. Although it remains unlikely that all Ukrainian citizens will use the Ukrainian language anytime soon, there does seem to have been an increasing identification of Ukraine's ethnic and linguistic Russians with the Ukrainian state. In other words, the "ethnic nation" is emerging only very slowly, but the "civic nation" is moving more rapidly. The process remains geographically uneven, with Ukrainian language use and national identity higher in the west than in the east. But the possibility of ethnic violence has receded, and since the parliamentary elections of 1998, typical left-right cleavages have tended to dominate Ukrainian political debates, while east-west cleavages have tended to recede in political salience, though they clearly still exist.

However, the political spectrum remains fragmented, and there is no evidence that political parties will consolidate in the near future, making it easier to achieve a working coalition in Parliament. The proportional representation system has only been in effect for one election cycle, and it may take longer for its full effects to be felt, but so far, those effects have been meager. On the left, the center, and the right, there remain a multitude of different parties with similar platforms. As Chapter 5 showed, many parties are dominated by single individuals whose ambitions do not permit merging with other parties. The regional divide remains salient as well, with no single party able to span the whole country.

Finally, with a relatively low threshold (4 percent) for admittance to Parliament, there is some incentive to go it alone rather than merge. In Poland, raising the threshold from 3 to 5 percent had a significant consolidating effect, and Ukraine, too, may find it necessary to raise its barrier.

In foreign policy, the questions are equally pressing. Ukraine has been somewhat successful in finding a political position that allows it simultaneous cordial relations with both the West and Russia. This position is under pressure both internally and externally. Internally, the current position is not widely popular but represents a compromise between pro-Western and pro-Russian forces. Both of these groups would strive to shift that policy if they gained sufficient power. For the Western-oriented group, the goal is membership in the EU and NATO. Even though those objectives are not currently realistic, pursuing them would mean turning away decisively from Russia. At the other end of the spectrum are those who seek to abandon the Western orientation entirely and throw Ukraine's lot in with that of Russia. They advocate a much more powerful CIS with Ukraine playing a prominent role and a clearer foreign policy alliance with Russia against the West. Such a policy would include opposition to NATO expansion; greater support of Iran, Iraq, and Serbia against U.S.-led sanctions; and a general return to the cold war mistrust of the United States. It is difficult to make predictions here, but the direction of Ukraine's foreign policy will depend in large part on who wins the 1999 presidential election. However, we should not overestimate the president's ability to change foreign policy. Kuchma ran in 1994 advocating much closer relations with Russia but found after election that both internal and external realities made this an unwise move, and his positions have not differed fundamentally from those of Kravchuk. The current compromise may be more robust than politicians' rhetoric indicates.

Overall, then, this sketch of the future sees Ukraine continuing to "muddle through," not decisively resolving any of its bigger problems but not collapsing into authoritarianism or civil war, either. The government's inability to reform the economy is partially offset by the "shadow economy," which provides much of what the official one cannot. The continuing weakness of Ukrainian national identity has been accompanied by a moderation that will likely prevent nationality issues from getting out of control. Democracy will not function fully in Ukraine anytime soon, but neither will it vanish. If we focus on the hope of Ukraine's achieving a transition comparable to those of Poland and Hungary, pessimism is in order. But if we focus on the fear of civil war (as in Russia over Chechnya) or authoritarianism (as in Belarus), optimism is in order. Ukrainians characterize themselves as survivors, and Ukraine will survive, even though times will remain difficult.

If a prediction is to be made, then, it must be one of continuity. Two key aspects of Ukraine's politics reinforce one another in a cycle that will be hard to break. If Ukraine's main political problem is the ineffectiveness of its state, that weakness is both a cause and a result of corruption. Corruption and state weakness reinforce each other, such that there is no obvious way to break the cycle. Because the state cannot collect taxes, it cannot muster the resources to crack down on corruption and crime. Because it cannot eradicate that corruption, tax collection becomes impossible, as firms and individuals evade, threaten, or bribe their way out of paying their taxes. Only when the state has enough money to pay tax collectors enough so that taking bribes is no longer so enticing, and only when enough honest officials can be found who will resist taking bribes even when they know they can get away with it, will the cycle be broken. There is no reason to believe this will happen in Ukraine anytime soon.

Some would argue that the only way to break this cycle is through authoritarianism. In this view, only by suspending suspects' rights, due process, and so on can the state avoid the many loopholes that corrupt officials and organized criminals use to evade prosecution. In a system where the process of gathering evidence is ill formed and where accounting standards make gathering evidence difficult in financial cases, a much lower burden of proof might be necessary to bring miscreants to justice. The authoritarianism argument is linked to that concerning "stages" of reform, in which some contend that it is necessary to have a strong state *before* one can have a democratic state. In this view, weak democracies end up permanently hobbled and prevented from becoming strong consolidated democracies. Once the state has achieved a considerable amount of authority in the society, it can then turn to democratization. The models that support this argument are those in Chile, South Korea, and Southeast Asia.

This argument has its problems, however. Most notably, there is no clear connection between democracy and corruption or between authoritarianism and the lack of corruption. The developing world is full of countries that are very authoritarian and at the same time monumentally corrupt (as was the Soviet Union in its last few decades). Corruption can breed even more readily where there is no freedom of expression and no democratic oversight than where those checks are quite imperfect, as they are in Ukraine. Recent experience in Indonesia, Malaysia, and South Korea has cast those models of authoritarian development in a much less positive light than they were regarded a few years ago: Rampant corruption has undermined the economic progress that the "strong hand" was supposed to have provided.

So if democracy does not seem conducive to state building, and authoritarianism is suspect both on normative and practical grounds, what path could Ukraine and other states like it follow to economic and political reform? The answer is not clear. To the extent that we have a clear notion of where Ukraine is now and where it is going, it is still quite unclear what path connects the two points. Most solutions to the problems of Ukraine (and Russia, for that matter) involve some sort of deus ex machina in which a strong and popular leader somehow comes to power democratically and convinces the people and the elite to feel enough trust so the new leader can undertake the painful measures needed to fundamentally reorder society. There is no reason to believe that such an individual could exist in Ukraine, that there is any individual, real or imaginary, who would command widespread confidence across this atomized country.

If Ukraine is to emerge from its current morass, we contend, it will do so only slowly, and the process will have to begin institutionally in the Ukrainian Parliament. The first important step would be the establishment of a clear working majority and opposition in Parliament. In the short term, it appears that only the left has much of a chance of mustering such a majority, and though that prospect is not appetizing to many, it might lead to long-term progress. In the political realm, establishment of a majority would likely help both the left and right parties consolidate out of necessity—the left to maintain its coalition, the right to oppose the left effectively. Such a leftist majority would no doubt pass a great deal of retrograde legislation. But people would have an ability to see how the left ruled and either accept it or reject it. Only then is there a real chance for a reformist majority in Ukraine's Parliament and society. In other words, reform in Ukraine is obstructed as much by the ineffectiveness of the Parliament as an institution as it is by the policies of leftists. One cannot have parliamentary democracy without a functioning Parliament.

The success of democracy is based both on societal and institutional factors. It requires both a society that is broadly supportive of democratic norms and willing to make some sacrifices for them and political institutions that manage to take millions of individual opinions and channel them into policies that are both effective and palatable. Ukraine is defective on both scores. The unfortunate fact of the matter is that popular support for reform in Ukraine is weak and that Ukraine's institutions tend to fragment rather than concentrate that support. Ironically, this is linked to the fact that as bad as things are in Ukraine, they could be a lot worse, and in fact they have been much worse in the earlier decades of the twentieth century. As long as people can scrape by working extra jobs and growing their own food, they are unlikely to divert time from those activities into active protest aimed at reforming the government. It is often the case that real reform happens only after a catastrophe has concentrated people's attention on a problem and a solution. The good news in Ukraine is that such a catastrophe has not occurred, but that will mean that Ukraine will continue to muddle through rather than decisively change.

Notes

INTRODUCTION

1. Zbigniew Brzezinski, "The Premature Partnership," *Foreign Affairs*, vol. 73, no. 2 (March–April 1994): 80.
2. Omar G. Encarnacin, review article, "The Politics of Dual Transitions," *Comparative Politics*, vol. 28, no. 4 (July 1996): 477–492.
3. Stephan Haggard and Steven B. Webb, eds., *Voting for Reform: Democracy, Political Liberalization, and Economic Adjustment* (New York: Oxford University Press, 1994).
4. Leslie Elliot Armijo, Thomas J. Biersteker, and Abraham F. Lowenthal, "The Problems of Simultaneous Transitions," *Journal of Democracy*, vol. 5, no. 4 (October 1994): 161–175.
5. Ross E. Burkhart and Michael S. Lewis-Beck, "Comparative Democracy: The Economic Development Thesis," *American Political Science Review*, vol. 88, no. 4 (December 1994): 903–910.
6. Adam Przeworski, *Democracy and the Market* (Cambridge: Cambridge University Press, 1991).
7. Paul Kubicek, "Post-Soviet Ukraine: In Search of a Constituency for Reform," *Journal of Communist Studies and Transition Politics*, vol. 13, no. 3 (September 1997): 103–126.
8. Mancur Olson, *The Logic of Collective Action* (Cambridge: Harvard University Press, 1965).
9. Stephan Haggard and Robert Kaufman, *The Political Economy of Democratic Transitions* (Princeton: Princeton University Press, 1995).
10. Juan J. Linz and Alfred Stepan, *Problems of Democratic Transition and Consolidation: Southern Europe, South America, and Post-Communist Europe* (Baltimore: Johns Hopkins University Press, 1996).
11. See William Zimmerman, "Is Ukraine a Political Community?" *Communist and Post-Communist Studies*, vol. 31, no. 1 (1998): 43–55. On regionalism, see Lowell Barrington, "The Geographic Component of Mass Attitudes in Ukraine," *Post-Soviet Geography and Economics*, vol. 38, no. 10 (December 1997): 601–614; and Jane I. Dawson, "Ethnicity, Ideology, and Geopolitics in Crimea," *Communist and Post-Communist Studies*, vol. 30, no. 4 (1997): 427–444.
12. Claus Offe, "Capitalism by Democratic Design? Democratic Theory Facing the Triple Transition in East Central Europe," *Social Research*, vol. 58, no. 4 (Winter 1991): 871.

13. See Alexander Motyl, *Dilemmas of Independence: Ukraine After Totalitarianism* (New York: Council on Foreign Relations, 1993), p. 67; and Barnett R. Rubin, "Conclusion: Managing Normal Instability," in Barnett R. Rubin and Jack Snyder, eds., *Post-Soviet Political Order: Conflict and State Building* (London: Routledge, 1998), p. 177.

14. Alexander J. Motyl, "Structural Constraints and Starting Points: The Logic of Systematic Change in Ukraine and Russia," *Comparative Politics*, vol. 29, no. 4 (July 1997): 433–447; and Taras Kuzio, "Ukraine: A Four-Pronged Transition," in Taras Kuzio, ed., *Contemporary Ukraine: Dynamics of Post-Soviet Transformation* (Armonk, NY: M. E. Sharpe, 1998), pp. 165–180.

15. This point is made in the clearest fashion by Armijo, Biersteker, and Lowenthal, "The Problems of Simultaneous Transitions," p. 165.

16. See Motyl, *Dilemmas of Independence*, p. 67.

17. Kuzio, "Ukraine: A Four-Pronged Transition," p. 170.

18. Ibid.

19. See the chapters by Paul Kubicek and Roman Zyla in Taras Kuzio, Robert S. Kravchuk, and Paul D'Anieri, eds., *State and Institution Building in Ukraine* (New York: St. Martin's Press, 1999).

20. Beverly Crawford and Arend Lijphart, "Explaining Political and Economic Change in Post-Communist Eastern Europe: Old Legacies, New Institutions, Hegemonic Norms, and International Pressures," *Comparative Political Studies*, vol. 28, no. 2 (July 1995): 171–199.

CHAPTER 1

1. The treaty was ratified by the Russian State Duma in December 1998 and the Russian Federation Council in February 1999.

2. These starting points are discussed in Alexander Motyl, "State, Nation, and Elites in Independent Ukraine," Roman Solchanyk, "The Post-Soviet Transition in Ukraine: Prospects for Stability," and Marc Nordberg, "State and Institution Building in Ukraine," in Taras Kuzio, ed., *Contemporary Ukraine: Dynamics of Post-Soviet Transformation* (Armonk, NY: M. E. Sharpe, 1998), pp. 1–56. See also T. Kuzio, R. S. Kravchuk, and P. D'Anieri, eds., *State and Institution Building in Ukraine* (New York: St. Martin's Press, 1999).

3. A good framework for the study of Ukraine is found in Paul Robert Magosci, "The Ukrainian National Revival: A New Analytical Framework," *Canadian Review of Studies in Nationalism*, vol. 16, nos. 1–2 (1989): 45–62. For historical background, see Bohdan Krawchenko, *Social Change and National Consciousness in Twentieth-Century Ukraine* (New York: Macmillan, 1985); Orest Subtelny, *Ukraine: A History* (Toronto: University of Toronto Press, 1994); P. R. Magosci, *A History of Ukraine* (Toronto: University of Toronto Press, 1996); Andrew Wilson, *Ukrainian Nationalism in the 1990s: A Minority Faith* (Cambridge: Cambridge University Press, 1997); and A. Wilson, "Ukraine: Between Eurasia and the West," in Thomas G. Fraser and Seamus Dunn, eds., *Europe and Ethnicity: The Legacy of World War I* (London: Routledge, 1996), pp. 110–137.

4. See Stephen Velychenko, "Empire Loyalism and Minority Nationalism in Great Britain and Imperial Russia, 1707–1914: Institutions, Law, and Nationality in Scotland and Ukraine," *Comparative Studies in Society and History*, vol. 39, no. 3 (July 1997): 413–441; David Saunders, "What Makes a Nation a Nation? Ukrainians Since 1600," *Ethnic Groups*, vol. 10 (1993): 101–124; D. Saunders, "Russia and Ukraine Under Alexander II: The Valuev Edict of 1863," *International History Review*, vol. 17, no. 1 (February 1995): 23–50; D. Saunders, "Russia's Ukrainian Policy (1847–1905): A Demographic Approach," *European History Quarterly*, vol. 25, no. 2 (April 1995): 181–208; Arthur Takach, "In Search of Ukrainian National Identity: 1840–1921," *Ethnic and Racial Studies*, vol. 19, no. 3 (July 1996): 640–659; and John-Paul Himka, "Young Radicals and Independent Statehood: The Idea of a Ukrainian Nation-State, 1890–1895," *Slavic Review*, vol. 41, no. 2 (Summer 1982): 219–235.

5. See Ivan Rudnytsky, "The Ukrainian National Movement on the Eve of the First World War," *East European Quarterly*, vol. 11, no. 2 (1977): 141–154; I. Rudnytsky, "The Role of the Ukraine in Modern History," *American Slavic and East European Review*, vol. 22, no. 2 (Summer 1963): 199–216; and Omeljan Pritsak and John S. Reshetar, "The Ukraine and the Dialectics of Nation-Building," *American Slavic and East European Review*, vol. 22, no. 2 (Summer 1963): 224–255.

6. On tsarist nationality policies, see Theodore R. Weeks, *Nation and State in Late Imperial Russia: Nationalism and Russification on the Western Frontier, 1863–1914* (De Kalb: Northern Illinois University Press, 1998), and Richard Pipes, "Peter Struve and Ukrainian Nationalism," *Harvard Ukrainian Studies*, vols. 3–4, pt. 2 (1979–1980): 675–683.

7. See Jurij Borys, *The Sovietization of Ukraine, 1917–1923: The Communist Doctrine and Practice of National Self-Determination* (Edmonton: Canadian Institute Ukrainian Studies, 1980), and Susan Procyk, *Russian Nationalism and Ukraine: The Nationality Policy of the Volunteer Army During the Civil War* (Edmonton: Canadian Institute Ukrainian Studies, 1995).

8. See Bohdan Budurowycz, "Poland: The Ukrainian Problem, 1921–1939," *Canadian Slavonic Papers*, vol. 25, no. 4 (December 1983): 473–500, and J.-P. Himka, "Western Ukraine in the Interwar Period," *Nationalities Papers*, vol. 22, no. 2 (Fall 1994): 347–363.

9. See chap. 4, "Nationalizing States in the Old 'New Europe'—and the New," in Rogers Brubaker, *Nationalism Reframed: Nationhood and the National Question in the New Europe* (Cambridge: Cambridge University Press, 1996), p. 100.

10. On the strength of the nationalist underground, see Jeffrey Burds, "AGENTURA: Soviet Informants' Networks and the Ukrainian Underground in Galicia, 1944–48," *East European Politics and Society*, vol. 11, no. 1 (Winter 1997): 89–130.

11. For a comparison on how this affected Soviet nationality policies in western Ukraine in relation to western Belarus, see Roman Szporluk, "West Ukraine and West Belarussia: Historical Tradition, Social Communication, and Linguistic Assimilation," *Soviet Studies*, vol. 31, no. 1 (January 1979): 76–98.

12. See James E. Mace, *Communism and the Dilemmas of National Liberation: National Communism in Soviet Ukraine, 1918–1933* (Cambridge: Harvard University Press, 1983), and George O. Liber, *Soviet Nationality Policy, Urban Growth, and*

Identity Change in the Ukrainian SSR, 1923–1934 (Cambridge: Cambridge University Press, 1992).

13. Christine D. Worobec, "Galicians into Ukrainians: Ukrainian Nationalism Penetrates Nineteenth-Century Rural Austrian Galicia," *Peasant Studies*, vol. 16, no. 3 (Spring 1989): 198–209; Ivan L. Rudnytsky, "The Ukrainians in Galicia Under Austrian Rule," *Austrian History Yearbook*, vol. 3, pt. 2 (1967): 394–429, and J. P. Himka, "Priests and Peasants: The Greek Catholic Pastor and the Ukrainian National Movement in Austria, 1867–1900," *Canadian Slavonic Papers*, vol. 21, no. 2 (June 1979): 1–14.

14. See P. R. Magosci, "A Subordinate or Submerged People: The Ukrainians of Galicia Under Hapsburg and Soviet Rule," in David F. Good and Richard L. Rudolph, eds., *Nationalism and Empire: The Hapsburg Empire and the Soviet Union* (New York: St. Martin's Press, 1992), pp. 95–107.

15. See T. Kuzio, "The Polish Opposition and the Ukrainian Question," *Journal of Ukrainian Studies*, vol. 12, no. 23 (Winter 1987): 26–58.

16. See the three chapters on Ukraine in Ilya Prizel, *National Identity and Foreign Policy: Nationalism and Leadership in Poland, Russia, and Ukraine* (Cambridge: Cambridge University Press, 1998), pp. 300–403.

17. See Robert Conquest, *The Harvest of Sorrow: Soviet Collectivization and the Terror Famine* (London: Hutchinson, 1986).

18. P. R. Magosci, *A History of Ukraine*, p. 669.

19. See T. Kuzio and M. Nordberg, "Nation and State Building, Historical Legacies, and National Identities in Belarus and Ukraine: A Comparative Analysis," *Canadian Review of Studies in Nationalism*, vol. 26, nos. 1–2 (forthcoming 1999).

20. H. V. Kas'ianov, "Ukraiins'kyi natsionalizm: Problema naukovoho pereosmyslennia," *Ukraiins'kyi Istorychnyi Zhurnal*, no. 2 (1998): 40. See also his "Ukraiins'kyi natsionalizm: Sproba pereosmyslennia," *Viche*, no. 1 (1997): 135, 136, 141.

21. See Robert S. Sullivant, *Soviet Politics and the Ukraine, 1917–1957* (New York: Columbia University Press, 1962), and Borys Lewytzkyj, *Politics and Society in Soviet Ukraine, 1953–1980* (Edmonton: Canadian Institute Ukrainian Studies, 1984).

22. See Peter J. Potichnyj, ed., *Ukraine in the Seventies* (Oakville, Ontario: Mosaic Press, 1975), and B. Krawchenko, ed., *Ukraine After Shelest* (Edmonton: Canadian Institute Ukrainian Studies, 1983).

23. See T. Kuzio, *Ukraine: Perestroika to Independence*, 2d ed. (London: Macmillan, 1999).

24. See Roman Szporluk, "Ukraine: From an Imperial Periphery to a Sovereign State," *Daedalus*, vol. 126, no. 3 (Summer 1997): 85–120; T. Kuzio, *Ukraine: State and Nation-Building* (London: Routledge, 1998); and T. Kuzio, "The National Factor in Ukraine's Quadruple Transition," paper prepared for the conference "Soviet and Post-Soviet Ukraine: A Century in Perspective," Yale University, 23–24, April 1999.

25. *Pravda*, 24 September 1989.

26. See the comments by Galina Starovoitova in David Remnick, "Letter from Russia: Gorbachev's Last Hurrah," *New Yorker*, 11 March 1996, p. 77.

27. Bohdan Nahaylo and Victor Svoboda, *Soviet Disunion: A History of the Nationalities Problem in the USSR* (London: Hamish Hamilton, 1990), p. 354.

28. Alexander J. Motyl, "From Imperial Decay to Imperial Collapse: The Fall of the Soviet Empire in Comparative Perspective," in Good and Rudolph, *Nationalism and Empire*, p. 19. On the collapse of the USSR in historical perspective, see Karen Dawisha and Bruce Parrott, eds., *The End of Empire? The Transformation of the USSR in Comparative Perspective* (Armonk, NY: M. E. Sharpe, 1997), and Karen Barkey and Mark Von Hagen, eds., *After Empire: Multiethnic Societies and Nation-Building: The Soviet Union and the Russian, Ottoman, and Hapsburg Empires* (Boulder: Westview Press, 1997).

29. For a complete survey of this period, see Taras Kuzio and Andrew Wilson, *Ukraine: Perestroika to Independence* (London: Macmillan, 1994), chaps. 6–9.

30. "Inside Ukrainian SSR Politics: Interview with Dmytro Pavlychko," *Ukrainian Weekly*, 5 August 1990.

31. *Leninska Zmina* (no. 103), 1990.

32. Radio Ukraine World Service, 19 August 1993.

33. Radio Ukraine World Service, 1 September 1993.

34. Andrew Wilson, *Ukrainian Nationalism in the 1990s: A Minority Faith* (Cambridge: Cambridge University Press, 1997), p. 107.

35. Kravchuk recalled how during the August 1991 putsch, Hurenko telephoned him full of confidence, believing that power had shifted back to the KPU away from the radical and increasingly nationalistic Parliament. See Serhei Kychyhyn, ed., *Leonid Kravchuk: Ostanni dni imperii . . . pershi roky nadii* (Kyiv: Dovira, 1994), p. 49.

36. Oliynyk was not a member of the 1990–1994 Parliament. He was elected as a KPU deputy from Zaporizhzhya in 1994 and became head of the Parliamentary Committee on Foreign and CIS Affairs. He remains a national Communist, believing that "independence is historically necessary and our people earned this independence. I think that every normal Ukrainian, no matter to what faction he belongs, has only one fatherland. Its name is Ukraine." See "Nezalezhnist' ochyma chotyr'iokh," *Ukrains'ka Hazeta*, 26 September 1996, and his memoirs about his period as an adviser to Gorbachev, published as *Dva roky v kremli* (Kyiv: Sil's'ki Visti, 1992).

37. Interview with Ivan Pliushch, Kyiv, 13 March 1996.

38. *Economist*, 7 May 1994.

39. V. Zhmyr, *Na shliakhu do sebe (Ethno-sotsiolohichna-rozvidka)* (Kyiv: Democratic Initiatives, 1995), p. 112.

40. National minorities largely backed independence because they saw their national rights improving in a democratic Ukraine. They also understood the justice of the vote for Ukrainian national rights. See Oleh Rudakevych, "Suverenitet ukraiins'koii natsii—holovna politychna problema postkomunistychnoii Ukraiiny," *Rozbudova Derzhava*, no. 5 (May 1996): 14.

41. See the appeal "K Russkim, grazhdanam Ukrainy" (*Literaturna Ukraiina*, no. 47, 1991), calling upon Russians to vote for independence. The "Russians for Independence" movement also appealed for support (*Literaturna Ukraiina*, 24 October 1991), as did representatives of the coal-mining region of the Donbas (*Robitnycha Hazeta*, 1 November 1991). The Odesa branch of the Russian Christian Democratic Movement called for a "no" vote (*Molod' Ukraiiny*, 12 November 1991). One Western diplomat observed that "the vote among Russians was apathetic, and that

they may be open to a swing in their views" (*Financial Times*, 3 December 1991). A Russian from central Ukraine, P. Zhuk, wrote to *Demokratychna Ukraiina* (3 December 1991) that he and his Russian friends all supported independence because: "We, like the entire Ukrainian people, are for independence, the self-determination of the Ukrainian state. We don't need any new slavery."

42. *Demokratychna Ukraiina*, 5 December 1991.

43. See the statement by the Independent Trade Unions of Ukraine in *Vechirnyi Kyiv*, 29 November 1991.

44. Kravchuk recalled his discussion with Gorbachev: "'They won't vote for independence, Leonid Makarovych!' 'They'll vote!' 'Well there won't be 50 percent.' And I to him: 'There'll be 75–76'" (*Chas-Time*, 22 August 1995).

45. Yet in prereferendum polls, the level of support for independence remained high at between 70 and 85 percent. See *Vechirnyi Kyiv*, 11 October and 26 November 1991. In Kyiv the level of support was 83 percent (*Vechirnyi Kyiv*, 28 November 1991). This was up from 63 and 71 percent in August and October, respectively (*Vechirnyi Kyiv*, 31 October 1991).

46. Kychyhin, *Leonid Kravchuk*, p. 98. In an interview a number of years later, Kravchuk quoted Gorbachev as saying: "It's not going to work. People won't cast their votes for independence" (*Panorama*, vol. 1, 1996), p. 67.

47. Interview with Leonid Kravchuk, Kyiv, 28 November 1995.

48. Kychyin, *Leonid Kravchuk*, p. 21.

49. Interview with Leonid Kravchuk, Kyiv, 28 November 1995.

50. Three referenda were held in March 1991 in Ukraine. In the three Galician oblasts of L'viv, Ternopil', and Ivano-Frankivs'k, a referendum obtained high support for independence. Gorbachev's referendum called for a "renewed federation" and obtained less than Kravchuk's referendum ballot, which called for the USSR to be transformed into a confederation of sovereign states.

51. Interview with Leonid Kravchuk, Kyiv, 28 November 1995.

52. Interview with Levko Lukianenko, Kyiv, 2 October 1995.

53. Presidential elections were held on the same day as the referendum on independence (1 December 1991).

54. *Sunday Telegraph*, 1 December 1991. The editor of *Vechirnyi Kyiv* (10 December 1991) also wrote that "this person [Kravchuk] who won the presidential elections has based himself largely on the main ideas of Rukh."

55. Interview with Leonid Kravchuk, Kyiv, 28 November 1995.

56. The results of the referendum by oblast and autonomous republic are given in *Pravda Ukrainy*, 7 December 1991.

57. "I Play Only White," *Panorama*, vol. 1, 1996, p. 67.

58. Interview with Levko Lukianenko, Kyiv, 2 October 1995. All levels of the establishment and opposition were united in their support for independence during August–December 1991. See the interview with Vitaliy Vrablevskyi, Institute of Sociology, "Elita vyrishuye vse," *Demokratychna Ukraiina*, 13 May 1996. Vrablevskyi was an adviser to Ukrainian Communist Party leader Shcherbyts'kyi for eighteen years.

59. *Literaturna Ukraiina*, 24 October 1991.

60. Alexander J. Motyl, "The Conceptual President: Leonid Kravchuk and the

Politics of Surrealism," in Timothy J. Colton and Robert C. Tucker, eds., *Patterns in Post-Soviet Leadership* (Boulder: Westview, 1995), pp. 105, 111.

61. Times, 2 December 1991.
62. *Times*, 2 December 1991. A pensioner from near Kyiv, Maria Sniher, echoed similar views: "I remember how they caught children and ate them during the famine. We saw little that was good in our lives and I pray that our grandchild will live better" (*Times*, 2 December 1991).
63. *Der Spiegel*, 1 March 1993.
64. *Vechirnyi Kyiv*, 31 October 1991, and *Holos Ukraiiny*, 1 November 1991.
65. *Holos Ukraiiny*, 19 January 1993.
66. *Independent*, 7 December 1991.
67. *Financial Times*, 3 December 1991.
68. *Independent*, 7 December 1991.
69. Radio Ukraine World Service, 3 April 1993.
70. *Financial Times*, 17 December 1991.
71. See M. S. Gorbachev, *Dekabr'-91: Moia pozitisiia* (Moscow: Novosti, 1992).
72. *Nezavisimaya Gazeta*, 25 December 1996.
73. Remnick, "Letter from Russia."
74. Ibid.
75. *Reuters*, 6 December 1996.
76. *Kyivs'ka Pravda*, 7 July 1995.
77. Igor Kliamkin, "Russian Statehood, the CIS, and the Problem of Security," in Leon Aron and Kenneth M. Jensen, eds., *The Emergence of Russian Foreign Policy* (Washington, DC: United States Institute of Peace, 1994), pp. 107–118. Roman Szporluk makes the same point when he argues that the disintegration of the USSR enabled Russians to redefine themselves as different from the Soviet Union. See his "After Empire: What?" *Daedalus*, vol. 123, no. 3 (Summer 1994): 27.
78. *Reuters*, 16 December 1996.
79. Rogers Brubaker, "Nationhood and the National Question in the Soviet Union and Post-Soviet Eurasia: An Institutionalist Account," *Theory and Society*, vol. 23, no. 1 (February 1994): 62.
80. *Reuters*, 6 December 1996.
81. Conversation with David Marples, University of Alberta, Edmonton, Canada, 11 March 1997. Marples based this analysis on interviews he had conducted with Shushkevych in Minsk the year before.
82. Interview with Leonid Kravchuk, London, 12 June 1996.
83. Vladimir Radyuhin, "Collapse of USSR: A Tale of Intrigue and Deceit," *Johnson's Russia List*, 8 December 1996.
84. Peter Rutland, "How the Soviet Union Ended: Yegor Gaidar Reflects on the Events of Fall 1991," *OMRI Analytical Brief*, no. 453 (11 November 1996).
85. *Kyivski Vidomosti*, 22 March 1996.
86. Ibid.
87. *Reuters*, 6 December 1996.
88. Ibid. Yegor Gaidar agrees: "It was a question of liquidating de jure a nuclear superpower which had already disintegrated de facto" (*Itogi*, 5 November 1996).
89. Kychyhin, *Leonid Kravchuk*, p. 18.

90. "Belovezhskaya pushcha: Kak eto byilo," *Pravda Ukrainy*, 14 January 1997. Prior to the putsch only 13 percent of Ukrainians, according to Valeriy Khmelko, one of Ukraine's leading sociologists, supported independence. This number grew rapidly after the putsch, largely as a territorial argument for independence from the collapsing Soviet center.

91. Ibid.

92. Kychyhin, *Leonid Kravchuk*, p. 27.

93. *Reuters*, 6 December 1996.

94. See L. Kravchuk's views in *Kyivs'ka Pravda*, 7 July 1995. Roman Laba argues that "[t]he assumption was that Russia and Yeltsin would rule. There were two possibilities: Russia would encompass the union, or Russia would dominate through the facade of a union." This, to the non-Russians, "signified an open Russian hegemony over the nations of the multinational country which they all lived in." See his "How Yeltsin's Exploitation of Ethnic Nationalism Brought Down an Empire," *Transition*, vol. 1, no. 2 (12 January 1996): 10.

95. On the blurring of identity between Russia, the Soviet Union, and the CIS, see Paul D'Anieri, *Economic Interdependence in Ukrainian-Russian Relations* (Albany: State University of New York Press, 1999), chap. 6.

96. *Pravda Ukrainy*, 16 January 1997.

97. Kychyhin, *Leonid Kravchuk*, p. 32.

98. This section draws upon Taras Kuzio, "Ukraine: Coming to Terms with the Soviet Legacy," *Journal of Communist Studies and Transition Politics*, vol. 14, no. 4 (December 1998): 1–27.

99. Liber, *Soviet Nationality Policy*, p. 182.

100. Ibid., p. 181.

101. Ibid.

102. The proportion of Ukrainians giving Ukrainian as their "native language" in Soviet censuses declined from 93.5 percent in 1959 to 91.4 and 60 percent in 1970 and 1989, respectively. This was part of a general trend toward greater bilingualism, on the one hand, and greater Russian-language proficiency, on the other. See Ivan Dziuba, *Internationalism or Russification? A Study in the Soviet Nationalities Problem* (London: Weidenfeld and Nicholson, 1968). Reprinted with the same title by KM Akademia, Kyiv, 1998.

103. Victor Zaslavsky, "Nationalism and Democracy: Transition in Postcommunist Societies," *Daedalus*, vol. 121, no. 2 (Spring 1992): 97–122. See also Yuri Slezkine, "The USSR as a Communal Apartment, or How a Socialist State Promoted Ethnic Particularism," in Geoff Eley and Ronald Grigor Suny, eds., *Becoming National* (New York: Oxford University Press, 1996).

104. Ronald G. Suny, *The Revenge of the Past: Nationalism, Revolution, and the Collapse of the Soviet Union* (Stanford: Stanford University Press, 1993), pp. 100–101.

105. On this question, see Carol Barner-Barry and Cynthia A. Hody, *The Politics of Change: The Transformation of the Former Soviet Union* (New York: St. Martin's Press, 1995), pp. 85–91.

106. Brubaker, "Nationhood and the National Question," p. 58.

107. See Kuzio, *Ukraine: State and Nation-Building*.

108. *Ukraiins'ka Hazeta*, 4 January 1996.

109. *Financial Times*, 17 December 1991.
110. Mykola Ryabchuk, "Between Civil Society and the New Etatism: Democracy in the Making and State Building in Ukraine," in Michael D. Kennedy, ed., *Envisioning Eastern Europe: Post-Communist Studies* (Ann Arbor: University of Michigan Press, 1994), p. 129.
111. Brubaker, "Nationhood and the National Question," p. 52.
112. The Russian Federation is an exception to the remainder of the USSR. It inherited many of the institutions of the Soviet outer empire. Nevertheless, these institutions and personnel were top-heavy, dominated heavily by the security forces and inculcated with Soviet great power ideology.
113. See Taras Kuzio, "National Identity and Foreign Policy: The Eastern Slavic Conundrum," in Kuzio, ed., *Contemporary Ukraine*, pp. 221–244.
114. *Argumenty i Fakty*, no. 27 (July 1997). This compared to 75 and 40 percent of Russians who supported union with Belarus and Kazakhstan, respectively.
115. See Taras Kuzio, "National Identity in Independent Ukraine: An Identity in Transition," *Nationalism and Ethnic Politics*, vol. 2, no. 4 (December 1996): 582–608.
116. Motyl, "The Conceptual President," p. 105.
117. Ivan L. Rudnytsky, "The Soviet Ukraine in Historical Perspective," *Canadian Slavonic Papers*, vol. 14, no. 2 (1972): 240.
118. Dominique Arel, "A Lurking Cascade of Assimilation in Kiev?" *Post-Soviet Affairs*, vol. 12, no. 1 (January–March 1996): 73–90.
119. Roman Szporluk, "The Soviet West—or Far Eastern Europe," *East European Politics and Society*, vol. 5, no. 3 (Fall 1991): 480.
120. Roman Szporluk, "Nation Building in Ukraine: Problems and Prospects," in J. W. Blaney, ed., *The Successor States to the USSR* (Washington, DC: Congressional Quarterly, 1995), p. 177.
121. See Taras Kuzio, *Ukraine Under Kuchma: Political Reform, Economic Transformation, and Security Policy in Independent Ukraine* (London and New York: Macmillan and St. Martin's Press, 1997).
122. *Interfax*, 30 October 1997.
123. *Den'*, 13 June 1997.

CHAPTER 2

1. Walker Connor, "Nation-Building or Nation-Destroying?" *World Politics*, vol. 24, no. 1 (April 1972): 320.
2. Omeljan Pritsak and John S. Reshetar, "The Ukraine and the Dialectics of Nation-Building," *Slavic Review*, vol. 22, no. 2 (Summer 1963): 227.
3. Hugh Seton-Watson, *Nations and States: An Enquiry into the Origins of Nations and the Politics of Nationalism* (London: Methuen, 1982), p. 5.
4. See Ernest Gellner, *Nations and Nationalism* (Ithaca: Cornell University Press, 1983).
5. Anthony D. Smith, "The Origins of Nations," *Ethnic and Racial Studies*, vol. 12, no. 3 (July 1989): 343.

6. Jaroslaw Krejci and Vitezslav Velimsky, "Ethnic and Political Nations in Europe," in John Hutchinson and Anthony D. Smith, eds., *Ethnicity* (Oxford: Oxford University Press, 1996), p. 209.

7. Anthony D. Smith's definition of a "nation" includes these two additional attributes. See his *National Identity* (London: Penguin Books, 1991), p. 14. See also Jack S. Plano and Roy Olton, *The International Relations Dictionary* (New York: Holt, Rinehart and Winston, 1969), p. 119.

8. Juan J. Linz, "State Building and Nation-Building," *European Review*, vol. 1, no. 4 (1993): 356.

9. See Taras Kuzio, "Defining the Political Community in Ukraine: State, Nation, and the Transition to Modernity," in Taras Kuzio, Robert S. Kravchuk, and Paul D'Anieri, eds., *State and Institution Building in Ukraine* (New York: St. Martin's Press, 1999). Linz argues that "[t]he nation, as such, does not have any organized character comparable with those of the state. It has no autonomy, no agents, no rules but only the resources derived from the psychological identification of the people that constitute it. A state can exist on the basis of external conformity with its rules. A nation requires some internal identification." See Linz, "State Building and Nation-Building," pp. 359–360.

10. See Colin Williams and Anthony D. Smith, "The National Construction of Social Space," *Progress in Human Geography*, vol. 7, no. 4 (December 1983): 502–518. Williams and Smith believe that "nationalism is always a struggle for control of land, whatever else the nation may be, it is nothing if not a mode of constructing and interpreting social space" (p. 502). See also Taras Kuzio, "Borders, Symbolism, and Nation-State Building: Ukraine and Russia," *Geopolitics and International Boundaries*, vol. 2, no. 2 (Autumn 1997): 36–56.

11. See Taras Kuzio, "Ukraine: Coming to Terms with the Soviet Legacy," *Journal of Communist Studies and Transition Politics*, vol. 14, no. 4 (December 1998): 1–27.

12. See Kuzio, Kravchuk, and D'Anieri, *Ukraine: State and Institution Building*.

13. Robert H. Jackson, *Quasi-States: Sovereignty, Iinternational Relations, and the Third World* (Cambridge: Cambridge University Press, 1990), p. 41.

14. See Kuzio, "Ukraine: Coming to Terms with the Soviet Legacy."

15. William Zimmerman, "Is Ukraine a Political Community?" *Communist and Post-Communist Studies*, vol. 31, no. 1 (1998): 43–55; George Liber, "Imagined Ukraine: Regional Differences and the Emergence of an Integrated State Identity," *Nations and Nationalism*, vol. 4, no. 2 (April 1998): 187–206; Catherine Wanner, *Burden of Dreams: History and Identity in Post-Soviet Ukraine* (Pittsburgh: Pennsylvania State University Press, 1998); and Taras Kuzio, *Ukraine: State and Nation-Building* (London: Routledge, 1998). For a more pessimistic view, see Andrew Wilson, *Ukrainian Nationalism in the 1990s: A Minority Faith* (Cambridge: Cambridge University Press, 1997); A. Wilson and Valeriy Khmelko, "Regionalism and Ethnic and Linguistic Cleavages in Ukraine," in Taras Kuzio, ed., *Contemporary Ukraine: Dynamics of Post-Soviet Transformation* (Armonk, NY: M. E. Sharpe, 1998), pp. 60–80; and Ilya Prizel, "Redefining Ethnic and Linguistic Boundaries in Ukraine: Indigenes, Settlers, and Russophone Ukrainians," chap. 6 in Graham Smith et al., *Nation-Building in the Post-Soviet Borderlands: The Politics of National Identities* (Cambridge: Cambridge University Press, 1998), pp. 119–138.

16. Linz, "State Building and Nation-Building," p. 361.

17. Jim MacLaughlin, "The Political Geography of 'Nation-Building' and Nationalism in Social Sciences: Structural Versus Dialectical Accounts," *Political Geography Quarterly*, vol. 5, no. 4 (October 1986): 299–329.

18. Arnold van Gennep, *The Rites of Passage* (Chicago: University of Chicago Press, 1961), quoted in Ilya Prizel, *National Identity and Foreign Policy: Nationalism and Leadership in Poland, Russia, and Ukraine* (Cambridge: Cambridge University Press, 1998), p. 340.

19. This is covered in an excellent manner in Prizel, *National Identity and Foreign Policy*, pp. 300–403. See also Zenon E. Kohut, "The Development of a Little Russian Identity and Ukrainian Nation-Building," *Harvard Ukrainian Studies*, vol. 10, nos. 3–4 (December 1986): 559–576, and Frank E. Sysyn, "The Khmelnytsky Uprising and Ukrainian Nation-Building," *Journal of Ukrainian Studies*, vol. 17, nos. 1–2 (Summer–Winter 1992): 141–170.

20. Zenon E. Kohut, *The Question of Russo-Ukrainian Unity and Ukrainian Distinctiveness in Early Modern Ukrainian Thought and Culture*, Edmonton, Canadian Institute Ukrainian Studies, p. 19.

21. Ihor Sevcenko, *Ukraine Between East and West* (Edmonton: Canadian Institute Ukrainian Studies, 1996), pp. 187, 193–194.

22. See David Saunders, "What Makes a Nation a Nation?" *Ethnic Studies*, vol. 10 (1993): 114.

23. Ibid., p. 109.

24. Miroslav Hroch, "From National Movement to the Fully Formed Nation: The Nation-Building Processes in Europe," in Geoff Eley and Ronald G. Suny, eds., *Becoming National: A Reader* (New York: Oxford University Press, 1996), p. 62.

25. Paul R. Magosci, *A History of Ukraine* (Seattle: University of Washington Press, 1996), p. 456.

26. Stephen Velychenko brings this difference out very clearly in his fascinating comparative study of the Scottish-English and Ukrainian-Russian unions. See his "Empire Loyalism and Minority Nationalism in Great Britain and Imperial Russia, 1707–1914: Institutions, Law, and Nationality in Scotland and Ukraine," *Comparative Studies in Society and History*, vol. 39, no. 3 (July 1997): 413–441.

27. John-Paul Himka, "The Greek-Catholic Church and Nation-Building in Galicia, 1772–1918," *Harvard Ukrainian Studies*, vol. 8, nos. 3–4 (December 1984): 440, 452.

28. David Saunders, "Russia's Ukrainian Policy (1847–1905): A Demographic Approach," *European History Quarterly*, vol. 25, no. 2 (April 1995): 189.

29. Vasyl' Kremen', Dmytro Tabachnyk, Vasyl' Tkachenko, *Ukraiina: Alternatyvy postupu. Krytyka istorychnoho dosvidu* (Kyiv: ARC-Ukraine, 1996), p. 139.

30. See Ivan Lysiak-Rudnytskyi, "Rusyfikatsiya chy malorosianizatsiya?" *Journal of Ukrainian Studies*, vol. 3, no. 1 (Spring 1978): 78–84.

31. Magosci, *A History of Ukraine*, p. 669.

32. See Dominique Arel and Valeriy Khmelko, "The Russian Factor and Territorial Polarization in Ukraine," *Harriman Review*, vol. 9, nos. 1–2 (March 1996): 81–91.

33. Kremen', Tabachnyk, and Tkachenko, *Ukraiina*, pp. 200–201, 206–207.

34. *Uriadovyi Kurier*, 25 December 1997.

35. Figures extracted from a speech given by Zenoviy Kulyk, minister of information, to the Presidential Council on Language Questions, 19 October 1998 (*Uriadovyi Kurier*, 27 October 1998).

36. While on a state visit to Budapest, Kuchma complained that some Western countries lumped Ukraine in the same "gray zone" as Russia and Belarus (*Intelnews*, 27 October 1998).

37. Interview with a member of the National Security and Defense Council, Odesa, 26 September 1998.

38. On the Orthodox Church in Ukraine, see Taras Kuzio, "In Search of Unity and Autocephaly: Ukraine's Orthodox Churches," *Religion, State, and Society*, vol. 25, no. 4 (December 1997): 393–415.

39. Paul Kubicek, "Dynamics of Contemporary Ukrainian Nationalism: Empire-Breaking to State Building," *Canadian Review of Studies in Nationalism*, vol. 23, nos. 1–2 (1996), p. 45.

40. *Literaturna Ukraiina*, 17 December 1992.

41. See Volodymyr Kulyk, "The Search for Post-Soviet Identity in Ukraine and Russia and Its Influence on the Relations Between the Two States," *Harriman Review*, vol. 9, nos. 1–2 (Spring 1996): 16–27.

42. Kravchuk said that the Ukrainian language "should be assigned absolute priority as a state language." Ukraine needed to revive its "historical memory." See Mykola Shpakovaty, ed., *Leonid Kravchuk: Our Goal—A Free Ukraine* (Kyiv: Globus, 1993), p. 116.

43. Orest Subtelny, "Imperial Disintegration and Nation-State Formation," in John W. Blaney, ed., *The Successor States to the USSR* (Washington, DC: Congressional Quarterly Press, 1995), p. 189.

44. One commentator complained that Kravchuk lost the elections because he "did not use all the possibilities open to him within the state for the derussification and national revival of Ukraine." Instead, he played "diplomatic games" with Ukrainophobe forces who still regarded him as a "nationalist" and eventually turned against him. See Heohriy Bachynskyi, "Chy zalyshytsia Ukraiina ukraiins'koho?" *Universum*, nos. 9–10 (September–October 1995): 6.

45. See Rogers Brubaker, "National Minorities, Nationalizing States and External National Homelands in the New Europe," *Daedalus*, vol. 124, no. 2 (Spring 1995): 107–132, and Juan J. Linz and Alfred Stepan, *Problems of Democratic Transformation and Consolidation: Southern Europe, Southern America, and Post-Communist Europe* (Baltimore: Johns Hopkins University Press, 1996), pp. 35–37.

46. There is a considerable literature on the dilemmas concerning nationalization in Ukraine. See Dominique Arel, "Ukraine: The Temptation of the Nationalizing State," in Vladimir Tismaneanu, ed., *Political Culture and Civil Society in Russia and the New States of Eurasia* (Armonk, NY: M. E. Sharpe, 1995), pp. 157–188, and the Ukrainian criticism by Taras Marusyk, "Pro odyn zakhidnyi 'retsept' oduzhannia vid natsionalizmu," *Vechirnyi Kyiv*, 16 July 1996. See also Louise Jackson and Kataryna Wolczuk, "Defining Citizenship and Political Community in Ukraine," *Ukrainian Review*, vol. 44, no. 2 (Summer 1997): 16–27; Graham Smith and Andrew Wilson, "Rethinking Russia's Post-Soviet Diaspora: The Potential for Political Mobilization in Eastern Ukraine and North-East Estonia," *Europe-Asia Studies*, vol. 49, no. 5 (July 1997): 845–864; and Smith et al., *Nation-Building in the Post-Soviet Borderlands*, pp. 119–138.

47. Vasily Kremen', "The East Slav Triangle," in Vladimir Baranovsky, ed., *Russia and Europe: The Emerging Security Agenda* (Oxford: Oxford University Press, 1997), p. 275.

48. See T. Kuzio, "Europe or Eurasia? The Ideology of 'Kuchmism,'" *Journal of Ukrainian Studies*, vol. 22, nos. 1–2 (Summer–Winter 1997): 134–163.

49. Wanner, *Burden of Dreams*, p. xix.

50. Kremen', Tabachnyk, and Tkachenko, *Ukraiina*, p. 198.

51. *Uriadovyi Kurier*, 25 December 1997.

52. See Kuchma's Independence Day speech, which called for regions to have greater autonomy in developing their cultural, educational, and linguistic policies (*Holos Ukraiiny*, 28 August 1995).

53. See Kuchma's speech on the anniversary of the referendum on independence (*Ukrainian Weekly*, 22 December 1996).

54. Kuchma's ideologues talked of a "strong state" and a "national" state rather than a nation-state. This is closer to Tilly's "national state" or Linz's "state-nation." See Vasyl' Tkachenko and Vasyl' Holovatiuk, "Vid natsional'noho romantyzmu do natsional'noii derzhavnosti," *Demokratychna Ukraiina*, 30 January 1996. This concept of a "state-nation" is also developed by Vasyl Kremen' in his "Konstytutsiia provela istorychnu mezhu," *Uriadovyi Kurier*, 21 June 1997.

55. V. Kremen', "Ukraiina: Shliakh do sebe," *Uriadovyi Kurier*, 28 March 1998.

56. See Taras Kuzio, "Europe or Eurasia? National Identity, Transformation, and Ukrainian Foreign Policy," *Journal of Communist Studies and Transition Politics*, forthcoming 1999.

57. See the critical remarks of an MP from the 1994–1998 *Rada*, Volodymyr Alekseyev, who supported two state languages in his "Osoblyvyi poriadok dlia movy: Rosiys'koii," *Holos Ukraiiny*, 20 February 1997.

58. See the poll quoted by Valeriy Khmelko of the Kyiv International Institute of Sociology in "Ukraiina mezhie do livoho tsentru," *Den'*, 12 August 1997.

59. Article 11 of the Constitution made Ukrainians the first among equals as the core nation. At the same time, all of the remaining national minorities belonged to the Ukrainian political nation (*Holos Ukraiiny*, 13 July 1996). The National Security Concept supported the "development of the Ukrainian nation, the historical consciousness and national pride of Ukrainians" and went on to add that support would be given to the ethnic, cultural, linguistic, and religious identities of all other remaining Ukrainian citizens (*Holos Ukraiiny*, 4 February 1997). See also Leonid Kistersky and Serhiy Pirozhkov, "Ukraine: Policy and Analysis," in Richard Smoke, ed., *Perceptions of Security: Public Opinion and Expert Assessments in Europe's New Democracies* (Manchester, England: Manchester University Press, 1996), p. 215.

60. See the presidential decree on the annual anniversary of Ukrainian independence (*Uriadovyi Kurier*, 7 June 1997).

61. Interview with Kuchma in *Algemeen Dagblad*, 29 November 1997.

62. *Holos Ukraiiny*, 23 May 1998.

63. See Oleh Hryniv, "Natsional'na hidnist u nedodekolonizovaniy malorosii," *Molod' Ukraiiny*, 11 August 1995; Bachynskyi, "Chy zalyshytsia Ukraiina Ukraiins'koiu?" pp. 2–6; and the interview with Petro Zhuk of the National Academy of Sciences in *Za Vilnu Ukraiinu*, 8 April 1997.

64. See the editorial on the Second World Congress of Ukrainians in *Vechirnyi Kyiv*, 2 September 1997.

65. Nikolay Churhivov and Tatyana Koshechkina, "Public Attitudes in Ukraine," in Smoke, *Perceptions of Security*, p. 194; Natalija Lazika-Sachuk and Natalie Melnyczuk, "Ukraine After Empire: Ethnicities and Democracy," in Leokadia Drobizheva et al., eds., *Ethnic Conflict in the Post-Soviet World: Case Studies and Analysis* (Armonk, NY: M. E. Sharpe, 1998), pp. 111–112.

66. "It is time to halt the horrible process of the denationalization of Ukrainians!" Vasyl' Balushok demanded. See his "Khto my, Ukraiintsi: Kolonial'na narodnist' chy taky natsiia?" *Vechirnyi Kyiv*, 25 October 1996.

67. Ihor Kharchenko, "Kul'tura iak natsional'na meta," *Viche*, no. 2 (February 1995): 138.

68. Oleksandr Maiboroda, "Khochemo Evropu—Vykoniumo zakon pro movy," *Den'*, 29 May 1997.

69. See Taras Kuzio, "The Crimea and European Security," *European Security*, vol. 3, no. 4 (Winter 1994): 734–774, and Kuzio, *Ukraine Under Kuchma*, pp. 67–89.

70. Interview with Tolochko in *Den'*, 22 August 1998.

71. Wanner, *Burden of Dreams*, p. 103.

72. Ibid., p. xxiv.

73. *Uriadovyi Kurier*, 2 December 1997.

74. See Kuzio, "Borders, Symbolism, and Nation-State Building."

75. *Istoriia v Shkoli*, nos. 7–8 (July–August 1998), p. 2.

76. Liudmilla Kalinina and Olena Pometun, "Na shliakhu do vzaiemorozuminnia: Zahal'no evropeis'kiy kontekst shkil'noii istorii," *Istoriia v Shkoli*, no. 1 (1998), p. 24.

77. See Kuzio, *Ukraine: State and Nation-Building*, pp. 198–229.

78. Quoted from L. Kuchma's preface to *Mykhailo Hrushevs'kyi* (Kyiv: Ukraiina, 1996).

79. Kremen', Tabachnyk, and Tkachenko, *Ukraiina*, p. 42.

80. Roman Szporluk, "The Ukraine and Russia," in Robert Conquest, *The Last Empire: Nationality and the Soviet Future* (Stanford: Stanford University, 1986), pp. 160–162.

81. *Sovetskaya Rossiya*, 12 November 1996.

CHAPTER 3

1. Andriy Yunash, "Suchasnyi riven' relihiynoii aktyvnosti v Ukraiini," *Heneza-Ekspert* (March 1996): 33.

2. See Andriy Sayenko, "Relihiynyi svitohliad molodi: Sotsiolohichnyi analiz," *Respublikanets*, vol. 4, nos. 3–4 (1994): 108–110.

3. *Den'*, 12 April 1997.

4. See Bohdan R. Bociurkiw, *The Ukrainian Catholic Church and the Soviet State, 1939–1950* (Edmonton and Toronto: Canadian Institute Ukrainian Studies, 1996).

5. On this question, see Petro Yarotskyi, "Ukraiinskyi protestantizm: Uchora i s'ohodni," *Viche* (November 1994): 147–157.

6. On the implementation of this law, see Mykhailo Kosiv, head of the Parliamentary Committee on Culture and Spirituality, "Zakon—tse dyshlo? Dyshlo!" *Holos Ukraiiny*, 10 July 1996.

7. *Holos Ukraiiny*, 6 June 1991.
8. *Post Postup*, no. 5 (1991).
9. *Viche*, August 1993, p. 88.
10. *Heneza Ekspert*, March 1996, p. 32.
11. Jaroslaw Martyniuk, "Religious Preferences in Five Urban Areas of Ukraine," *RFE/RL Research Report*, vol. 2, no. 15 (9 April 1993).
12. *Vechirnyi Kyiv*, 13 July 1993.
13. Vitaly Zhuravskyi, "Tserkva i derzhava," *Vechirnyi Kyiv*, 19 July 1996.
14. *Vechirnyi Kyiv*, 13 July 1993.
15. *Informatsynyi Biuletyn, Ministerstvo Ukraiiny u Spravakh Natsionaln'stey, Mihratsii ta Kultiv*, no. 1 (March 1995), p. 51, and Jaroslaw Martyniuk, "The State of the Orthodox Church in Ukraine," *RFE/RL Research Report*, vol. 3, no. 7 (18 February 1994). See also Andriy Yurash, "Pravoslavna tserkva v Ukraiini," *Heneza*, no. 1 (1994): 237–247.
16. Interview with official of the Ministry of Nationalities who wished to remain anonymous, *Migration and Cults*, Kyiv, 31 August 1995.
17. Figures provided by Patriarch Filaret in *Kyivski Vidomosti*, 26 April 1996.
18. *Informatsynyi Biuletyn*, p. 52.
19. *Demos*, no. 14, 1995, p. 15.
20. *Ukrains'ke Slovo*, 4 December 1994.
21. A bit of terminological clarification might be helpful here: The terms "Greek Catholic," "Ukrainian Catholic," and "Uniate," as well as the abbreviation "UHKTs," all refer to the same thing, the uniquely Ukrainian blend of subservience to the pope and the Eastern Rite that emerged as a political compromise in 1596. This hybrid is in many respects emblematic of Ukraine's history between Poland and Russia. The maintenance of the Eastern Rite distinguishes the Ukrainian Catholic Church from the Roman Catholic.
22. Mykhailo Dymyd, "Hreko-Katolyky: Stanovlennia pislia katakomb," *Holos Ukraiiny*, 3 November 1992.
23. See P. Yarotskyi, "Beresteys'ka uniya: Pro shcho svidchat' i ii uroky," *Viche* (June 1994): 140–153, and Ivan Paslavs'kyi, "Slovo pro beresteys'ku uniu," *Khrystos—Nasha Syla*, no. 4 (March 1996).
24. See Yuriy Shukhevych, "Novyi krok do kanonichnosti ukraiins'koho patriarchatu," *Khrystos—Nasha Syla*, no. 6 (May–June 1996).
25. See Rev. Dr. Ivan Dacko, "Spivvidnosyny UHKTs z inshymy konfesiyamy Ukraiiny," *Za Vilnu Ukraiinu*, 24 December 1992.
26. On the situation of the UHKTs Church in Trans-Carpathia, see the open letter from the chairman of the Trans-Carpathian branch of the A. Sheptyskyi UHKTs Union, Rev. Vasyl' Danylash, to the prime minister of Ukraine (*Khrystos—Nasha Syla*, no. 7 [July 1996]).
27. See Chris Hann, "Ethnic Cleansing in Eastern Europe: Poles and Ukrainians Beside the Curzon Line," *Nations and Nationalism*, vol. 2, pt. 3 (November 1996): 389–406.
28. Rostislav Khotyn, "Cleric Says Pope to Visit Ukraine Next Year," *Reuters*, 3 October 1996.
29. See the comments by Metropolitan Kiril of Smolensk and Kaliningrad, one of the 17 hierarchs of the Russian Orthodox Church (*Reuters*, 28 November 1996).

30. Serhiy Plokhy, "Derzhavna tserkva v Ukraiini: Ideii, modeli, realii," *Suhcasnist'*, nos. 7–8 (July–August 1995): 110.
31. Iryna Lukoms'ka, "Moskovs'kyi Patriarkhat Rozirvav Stosunky iz vselens'kym," *Vechirnyi Kyiv*, 13 March 1996.
32. *Reuters*, 5 March 1996.
33. On the language question, see the open letter to President Kuchma by Oleksandr Hudyma, a member of Parliament and chairman of the Ukrainian Orthodox Brotherhood: "Zaporuka vidrodzhennia," *Molod' Ukraiiny*, 15 March 1996.
34. See Deacon Viktor (Sotnychenko), chairman of the Union of Orthodox Brotherhoods of Ukraine (UPTs), "Pravoslaviye na Ukraine," *Tovarysh*, no. 21 (May 1995), and the press release by the same organization in *Tovarysh*, nos. 23–24 (June 1995).
35. *Uriadovyi Kurier*, 23 May 1996.
36. *Holos Ukraiiny*, 13 July 1996.
37. See the appeal of the Synod of the UPTs–KP in *Ukrains'ke Slovo*, 7–14 April 1996, and analysis in *Kyivski Vidomosti*, 15 March 1996.
38. Viktor Slizko, "Konstaninople uzhe teper hotovyi nadaty avtokefaliu chastyni ukraiins'koho pravoslav'ia," *Kyivski Vidomosti*, 26 April 1996, and Taras Abrakhov, "Chy bude vselens'kyi Patriarch Varfolomyi ob'iednuvaty pravoslavni tserkvy v Ukraiini?" *Kyivski Vidomosti*, 19 June 1996.
39. *Ukrains'ke Slovo*, 4 December 1994.
40. See "Kudy priamuye UAPTs?" *Ukrains'ke Slovo*, 17–24 November 1996.
41. *Kyivski Vidomosti*, 27 September 1996; *Vechirnyi Kyiv*, 2 and 23 October 1996; and *Den'*, 22 October 1996.
42. Iryna Lukoms'ka, "Patriarch UAPTs Dymytriy harantue srechennia patriarshoho prestolu," *Vechirnyi Kyiv*, 20 October 1995; and Tytiana Sylina, "Ob'iednannia chy rozkol ... Chy zmozhut' pereplestysia try hilky ukraiinskoho pravoslav'ia," *Kyivski Vidomosti*, 27 October 1995.
43. Hryhoriy Melanchenko, "U nas odyn Boh i odna Ukraiina," *Ukrainska Hazeta*, 1–4 January 1996.
44. See the interviews with Patriarch Dymytriy in *Vechirnyi Kyiv*, 2 August 1994; *Kyivski Vidomosti*, 24 January 1996; *Molod' Ukraiiny*, 7 and 26 March 1996; and *Kyivski Vidomosti*, 12 April 1996. An appeal by Patriarch Dymytriy to members of Parliament and Orthodox believers in Ukraine was published in *Uspens'ka Vezha*, no. 2 (February 1996).
45. *Za Vilnu Ukraiinu*, 24 December 1992.
46. See Bohdan Bociurkiw, "Politics and Religion in Ukraine: The Orthodox and the Greek Catholics," in Michael Bourdeaux, ed., *The Politics of Religion in Russia and the New States of Eurasia* (Armonk, NY: M. E. Sharpe, 1995), pp. 150–153.
47. M. P. Novychenko, "Relihiyna karta Ukraiiny," *Informatsiynyi Biuleten'*, *Ministerstvo Ukraiiny u Spravakh Natsional'nostei, Mihratsii ta Kul'tiv*, no. 4 (December 1995), p. 38.

CHAPTER 4

1. See Anders Åslund, *How Russia Became a Market Economy* (Washington, DC: Brookings Institution, 1995); Leszek Balcerowicz, *Socialism, Capitalism, Transforma-*

tion (Budapest: Central European University Press, 1995); and Marie Lavigne, *The Economics of Transition* (New York: St. Martin's Press, 1995).

2. See Chester A. Newland, "Transformational Challenges in Central and Eastern Europe and Schools of Public Administration," *Public Administration Review*, vol. 56, no. 4 (July–August 1996): 382–389.

3. See Salvatore Schiavo-Campo, ed., *Institutional Change and the Public Sector in Transitional Economies*, World Bank Discussion Paper no. 241 (Washington, DC: World Bank, 1994), p. 6.

4. See, for instance, Nicolas Spulber, *Restructuring the Soviet Economy: In Search of the Market* (Ann Arbor: University of Michigan Press, 1991); Graham Allison and Grigory Yavlinsky, *Window of Opportunity: The Grand Bargain for Democracy in the Soviet Union* (New York: Pantheon Books, 1991); Olivier Blanchard et al., *Reform in Eastern Europe* (Cambridge: MIT Press, 1992); Jeffrey Sachs, *Poland's Jump to the Market Economy* (Cambridge: MIT Press, 1993). A notable exception is Åslund, *How Russia Became a Market Economy*.

5. Arturo Israel, *Institutional Development* (New York: Oxford University Press, 1987), p. 118.

6. See World Bank, *Sub-Saharan Africa—From Crisis to Sustainable Growth: A Long-Term Perspective* (Washington, DC: World Bank, 1989); Stephan Haggard, *Pathways from the Periphery: The Politics of Growth in Newly Industrializing Countries* (Ithaca: Cornell University Press, 1990); Schiavo-Campo, *Institutional Change and the Public Sector;* Leila L. Frischtak, *Governance Capacity and Economic Reform in Developing Countries*, World Bank Technical Paper no. 254 (Washington, DC: World Bank, 1994); Paul Aligica, "The Institutionalists Take on Transition," *Transition*, 7 March 1997, pp. 46–49.

7. World Bank, *World Development Report—1997: The State in a Changing World* (Washington and New York: World Bank and Oxford University Press, 1997).

8. See Clifford G. Gaddy, *The Price of the Past* (Washington, DC: Brookings Institution, 1996).

9. See Gijsbertus van Selm, "The Economics of the Soviet Breakup," *Ukrainian Economic Review*, vol. 1, nos. 1–2 (1995): 79–95.

10. See Desmond F. McCarthy et al., "External Shocks and Performance Responses During Systemic Transition: The Case of Ukraine," *Ukrainian Economic Review*, vol. 1, nos. 1–2 (1995): 27–48.

11. Marcin Luczynski and Oleg Novoselsky, "Ukraine in Numbers, Year-end 1996 Review," *Ukrainian Legal and Economic Bulletin* (March 1997), table 4, p. 36.

12. See Robert S. Kravchuk, "Budget Deficits, Hyperinflation, and Stabilization in Ukraine, 1991–96," *Public Budgeting and Finance*, forthcoming, April 1999.

13. See Robert S. Kravchuk, "The Challenge of Fiscal Reform in Ukraine, 1991–97," paper presented at the International Conference "Institutional Reform in Ukraine: Exploring Links Between the Market and the State," sponsored by the Yale Ukrainian Initiative, Center for Russian and East European Studies, Yale University, New Haven, Connecticut, 1998 April 24–25. See also Jack Strauss, "The Role of Money and Credits in Explaining Inflation and Movements in the Karbovanets," *Ukrainian Legal and Economic Bulletin* (June 1995): 6–16.

14. Douglass C. North, *Structure and Change in Economic History* (New York: W. W. Norton, 1981), p. 201.

15. Douglass C. North, *Institutions, Institutional Change, and Economic Performance* (New York: Cambridge University Press, 1990), pp. 3–6.

16. Larry L. Kiser and Elinor Ostrom, "The Three Worlds of Action: A Metatheoretical Synthesis of Institutional Approaches," in Elinor Ostrom, ed., *Strategies of Political Inquiry* (Beverly Hills, CA: Sage Publications, 1982), p. 179.

17. Schiavo-Campo, *Institutional Change and the Public Sector*.

18. Thrainn Eggertsson, "The Economics of Institutions in Transition Economies," chap. 2 in Schiavo-Campo, *Institutional Change and the Public Sector*, p. 25.

19. See Oliver Williamson, *Markets and Hierarchies* (New York: Free Press, 1975), and *The Economic Institutions of Capitalism* (New York: Free Press, 1985).

20. See Ronald Coase, "The Problem of Social Cost," *Journal of Law and Economics*, vol. 3 (1960): 1–44.

21. Eggertsson, "The Economics of Institutions in Transition Economies," p. 22.

22. Schiavo-Campo, *Institutional Change and the Public Sector*, p. 5; emphasis in original.

23. David Held, *Models of Democracy* (Berkeley: University of California Press, 1989), p. 165.

24. See Dietrich Rueschemeyer and Peter B. Evans, "The State and Economic Transformation," chap. 2 in Peter B. Evans, Dietrich Rueschemeyer, and Theda Skocpol, eds., *Bringing the State Back In* (New York: Cambridge University Press, 1985), p. 51.

25. Ibid., p. 52; emphasis in original.

26. Haggard, *Pathways from the Periphery*, p. 44.

27. Joan Nelson, "The Political Economy of Stabilization: Commitment, Capacity, and Public Response," chap. 3 in Robert H. Bates, ed., *Toward a Political Economy of Development* (Berkeley: University of California Press, 1988), p. 101.

28. See Arturo Israel, *Institutional Development* (New York: Oxford University Press, 1987), p. 48.

29. Most of the developed literature on governmental capacity concerns U.S. states and municipalities. Although there are obvious institutional differences (in the most *general* sense) between U.S. subnational governments and those in transition economies, the authors maintain that there is a certain internal integrity to the concept of *capacity*, which transcends time and space. For instance, all governments levy and collect taxes, print money and regulate its value, administer programs, and so on. In this regard, we will employ the terms "governance capacity," "managerial capacity," and "administrative capacity" interchangeably.

30. Timothy D. Mead, *Measuring the Management Capacity of Local Governments*, Report to the Office of Policy Development and Research, U.S. Department of Housing and Urban Development (Washington, DC: Academy for Contemporary Problems, 1979), p. 1.

31. Beth Walter Honadle, "A Capacity-Building Framework: A Search for Concept and Purpose," *Public Administration Review* (September–October): 578.

32. See Terry M. Moe, "The Politicized Presidency," in John E. Chubb and Paul E. Peterson, eds., *The New Direction in American Politics* (Washington, DC: Brookings Institution, 1985), pp. 235–271.

33. See John J. Gargan, "Consideration of Local Government Capacity," *Public Administration Review* (November–December 1981): 652.
34. Much the same perspective is adopted by Weaver and Rockman in their study of government institutions. See R. Kent Weaver and Bert A. Rockman, "Assessing the Effects of Institutions," in Weaver and Rockman, eds., *Do Institutions Matter? Government Capabilities in the United States and Abroad* (Washington, DC: Brookings Institution, 1993), pp. 1–41.
35. See Paul Collins, "Civil Service Reform and Retraining in Transitional Economies: Strategic Issues and Options," *Public Administration and Development*, vol. 13 (1993): 323–344.
36. See Beth Honadle, "Identifying Management Capacity Among Local Governments," *Urban Affairs Papers*, vol. 3 (Winter 1981): 1–12, as well as her "Issues in Defining Local Management Capacity," chap. 2 in Beth Walter Honadle and A. M. Howitt, eds., *Perspectives on Management Capacity Building* (Albany: State University of New York Press, 1986), pp. 24–46.
37. Israel, *Institutional Development*, pp. 11–12.
38. Leila Frischtak, *Governance Capacity and Economic Reform*, terms it more broadly as "the paradox of the adjusting state."
39. See Stephan Haggard and Robert Kaufman, "The Politics of Stabilization and Structural Adjustment," in Jeffrey D. Sachs, ed., *Developing Country Debt and Economic Performance*, vol. 1, *The International System* (Chicago: University of Chicago Press, 1989), pp. 232–239. See also Frischtak, *Governance Capacity and Economic Reform*.
40. Traditional "heterodox" stabilization measures prescribed by the World Bank and the International Monetary Fund call for making serious reductions in the size of the state, backing away from extensive social security commitments, reducing numbers of public employees, initiating mass privatization, and weaning enterprises from their appetite for budgetary credits and other subsidies.
41. See James M. Buchanan, "Rent-Seeking and Profit-Seeking," in James M. Buchanan, Richard D. Tollison, and Gordon Tullock, eds., *Towards a Theory of the Rent-Seeking Society* (College Station: Texas A&M University Press, 1980).
42. Frischtak, *Governance Capacity and Economic Reform*, p. 8.
43. For a recent review of the literature and summary of the critical points, see Herbert A. Werlin, *The Mysteries of Development* (Lanham, MD: University Press of America, 1998).
44. For the complete text, see Ukrainian Legal Foundation, *International Symposium on the Draft Constitution of Ukraine* (Kyiv: Ukrainian Legal Foundation and Council of Advisers to the Parliament of Ukraine, 1993).
45. See the various useful and interesting commentaries provided by U.S. jurist Bohdan A. Futey: "Analysis: Proposed Draft of Ukraine's Constitution," *Ukrainian Weekly*, 14 November 1993, p. 8; "The Proposed Constitution of Ukraine: A Legal Perspective," *Demokratizatsiya*, vol. 2, no. 4 (1994): 642–650; and "Comments on the Constitution of Ukraine: Achievements and Shortcomings of the New Fundamental Law," *East European Constitutional Review*, vol. 5, nos. 2–3 (Spring–Summer 1996): 29–34.
46. See Petro Matiaszek, "An Overview of Ukraine's New Constitution,"

Ukrainian Quarterly, vol. 52, nos. 2–3 (Summer–Fall 1996): 174–179, and "Analysis: A Closer Look at Ukraine's Constitution," *Ukrainian Weekly*, 4 August 1996, pp. 2, 18–19.

47. For a definition of "semipresidentialism" and a typology of regimes, see Philip G. Roeder, "Varieties of Post-Soviet Authoritarian Regimes," *Post-Soviet Affairs*, vol. 10 (1994): 61–101.

48. See Juan Linz, "The Perils of Presidentialism," *Journal of Democracy*, vol. 1, no. 1 (Winter 1990): 51–69, and Matthew Shugart and John M. Carey, *Presidents and Assemblies* (Cambridge: Cambridge University Press, 1992).

49. See Roeder, "Varieties of Post-Soviet Authoritarian Regimes," and Ray Taras, ed., *Postcommunist Presidents* (Cambridge: Cambridge University Press, 1997).

50. See Charles R. Wise and Vladimir Pigenko, "The Separation of Powers Puzzle in Ukraine: Sorting Out Responsibilities and Relationships Between President, Parliament, and the Prime Minister," in Taras Kuzio, Robert S. Kravchuk, and Paul D'Anieri, eds., *State and Institution Building in Ukraine* (New York: St. Martin's Press, 1999).

51. Charles Wise and Trevor Brown, "Laying the Foundations for Institutionalization of Democratic Parliaments in the Newly Independent States: The Case of Ukraine," *Journal of Legislative Studies*, vol. 2, no. 3 (Autumn 1996): 216–244.

52. For a period, former President Leonid Kravchuk appointed so-called presidential representatives in the capital cities of the 27 oblasts (administrative territories) of Ukraine, including the cities of Kyiv and Sevastopol. Modeled after the French "prefect," the president's representative was to be the titular head of the oblast administration, acting in the name of the president. The subject of much controversy, Kravchuk's move was seen as an attempt to reestablish the old Communist system of "government by telephone," operating through a network of officials who were personally loyal to the head man. The former president also apparently envisioned this system as the core of his regional reelection organization. At the climax of an intense political battle with the president, Parliament on 12 February 1994 passed the new "Law on Formation of Local Government Bodies of Ukraine," which eliminated the office of president's representatives, coincident with the presidential and local government elections, on 26 June 1994.

53. President Kuchma responded to the previous state of affairs early in his administration with an August 1994 decree that declared that the Cabinet of Ministers is wholly subordinated to the president, especially as regards the most important economic issues on the government's agenda. Further, the president declared his right to set the government's calendar of business and to determine almost all staff appointments within the government and its subordinate bodies. This issue was largely resolved in a constitutional deal struck with Parliament on 7 June 1995. It is now completely resolved in the 1996 Constitution.

54. The Autonomous Republic of Crimea and the strategically important cities of Kyiv and Sevastopol are accorded special status in the Constitution. They are herein counted among the 27 regions of Ukraine, including the 24 oblasts.

55. See Robert S. Kravchuk, "The Quest for Balance: Regionalism and Sub-National Fiscal Policy in Ukraine," in Kuzio, Kravchuk, and D'Anieri, eds., *State and Institution Building in Ukraine*.

56. This practice has been banned under Article 142 of the Constitution, which requires compensation for local expenditures "arising from the decisions taken by bodies of state power." Much to the frustration of regional authorities, this provision has largely been ignored.

57. See Law of Ukraine, "On Local Radas of People's Deputies and Local and Regional Self-Government," no. 51-92-VR, 7 February 1992; Law of Ukraine, "On Formation of Local Government Bodies," 13 February 1995, VR-3917-12; Law of Ukraine, "On Local Self-Governments in Ukraine," 28 May 1997, no. 280-97-VR.

58. Law of Ukraine, "On Formation of Local Government Bodies," 13 February 1995, VR-0-3917-12.

59. See Robert S. Kravchuk, "The Challenge of Fiscal Reform in Ukraine, 1991–97."

60. Presidential Decree, "On Ways to Ensure Appropriate Management of Local Structures of State Executive Authorities," reprinted in *Holos Ukraiiny*, 11 August 1994.

61. For instance, one of the authors observed during 1993–1994, a two-year period during which he worked in the Ministry of Finance in Kyiv, that the minister himself often assigned offices, office equipment, and even telephone numbers. In the absence of adequate levels of monetary compensation, such perquisites take on much greater symbolic importance to employees.

62. See World Bank, *World Development Report—1997: The State in a Changing World* (Washington, DC, and New York: World Bank and Oxford University Press, 1997).

63. Judy Hague, Aidan Rose, and Marko Bojcun, "Rebuilding Ukraine's Hollow State: Developing a Democratic Public Service in Ukraine," *Public Administration and Development*, vol. 15 (1995): 417–433.

64. Ibid.

65. From remarks by Dr. Bohdan Krawchenko, delivered at the International Conference "Institutional Reform in Ukraine: Exploring Links Between the Market and the State," sponsored by the Yale Ukrainian Initiative, Center for Russian and East European Studies, Yale University, New Haven, Connecticut, 24–25 April 1998.

66. From an interview with Dr. Bohdan Krawchenko, associate director of the Academy of Public Administration in Kyiv. According to Krawchenko, this figure excludes uniformed personnel of the Ministry of Defense, border guards, and postal employees. The 12,000 figure expands to 47,000 if the 35,000 workers of the State Tax Inspectorate based in the various regional and raion tax offices across Ukraine are included. (Note: In October 1996, the Tax Inspectorate was elevated to the status of a cabinet ministry, albeit taking the form of a "state commission.") At all levels of government, approximately 428,000 bureaucrats are employed, a paltry number for a nation of 51 million souls. These statistics are from a 1997 interview with Vasyl Durdynets, director of the National Bureau of Investigation of Ukraine, that appeared in *Uriadovyi Kurier*, 18 September 1997, p. 5, FBIS-SOV-97-269 (original in Ukrainian).

67. See, for instance, the characterization of Ukraine's bureaucracy by Markian Bilynskyj, "News Analysis: Ukraine May Be Getting Serious About Reforms (Again)," *Ukrainian Weekly*, 30 March 1997, p. 2.

68. See John P. Willerton, *Patronage and Politics in the USSR* (New York: Cambridge University Press, 1992).

69. See Eric M. Rice, "Public Administration in Post-Socialist Eastern Europe," *Public Administration Review* (March–April 1992): 116–124.

70. Decree of the President of Ukraine, "On Measures to Improve Work of the State Executive Bodies," no. 459, 15 October 1993. The decree also included a vague directive that the government base the selection of state employees "on a competitive basis" but did not elaborate further.

71. International Monetary Fund, *Ukraine: Economic Review* (Washington, DC: International Monetary Fund, October 1997).

72. Israel, *Institutional Development*.

73. Decree of the President of Ukraine, "On Measures to Improve the System and Organization of State Executive Bodies," 19 January 1994. The stated objective of the decree was to reduce the number of employees of national, regional, and local governmental units to their levels of 1 January 1992.

74. *Molod Ukrayinu*, 2 June 1995.

75. See Hague, Rose, and Bojcun, "Rebuilding Ukraine's Hollow State." For information concerning the curriculum, see *Informatsiniy Buleten* (Kyiv: Ukrainian Academy of Public Administration, 1998).

76. Released by the government on December 16, 1993, the text of the law was published in the government's official state organ, *Uradoviy Kur'er*, 4 January 1994, pp. 4–6.

77. Decree of the President of Ukraine, "On Development of a Program on Cadre Supplies to the Government Services," no. 381, 19 May 1995. In order to heighten its visibility, Kuchma named as cochairs of the Council on Cadres the head of the Presidential Administration (chief of staff) Dmytro Tabachnyk (since dismissed), and minister of the Cabinet of Ministers (now prime minister) Valeriy Pustovoitenko, two close political allies who were instrumental in his 1994 campaign for the presidency.

78. We characterize this situation as one of "hollow government leading to administrative constipation."

79. See the complaints of economics minister Viktor I. Suslov in *Zerkalo Nedeli*, 30 August 1997, p. 9, FBIS-SOV-97-253, 10 September 1997 (original in Russian).

80. Krawchenko, remarks at Yale conference.

81. This problem plagues all of the former Soviet states, albeit in varying degrees. See Stanley Vanagunas, "The Influence of the Nomenklatura on Post-Soviet Administration," *International Journal of Public Administration*, vol. 18, no. 12 (1995): 1815–1839.

82. See Michael Voslensky, *Nomenklatura: The Soviet Ruling Class, An Insider's Report* (New York: Doubleday and Company, 1984).

83. No complete statistics are available concerning the rate and extent of official corruption. However, polls of businessmen and others who must deal with government licensing requirements, tax officials, customs, and so on regularly cite official corruption as a major obstacle to doing business in Ukraine. In addition, it is significant that President Kuchma has made fighting organized crime and corruption a chief objective of his administration.

84. "Constitution Watch—Ukraine," *Eastern European Constitutional Review*, vol. 4, no. 2 (Spring 1995): 32–34.

85. See Roman Woronowycz, "Kuchma Removes Lazarenko as Prime Minister," *Ukrainian Weekly*, 22 June 1997, p. 1; and Oxford Analytica, "Ukraine: Lazarenko Removal," *East Europe Daily Brief*, 4 July 1997.

86. See Roman Woronowycz, "Lazarenko Arrested by Swiss Authorities," *Ukrainian Weekly*, 13 December 1998, p. 1.

87. For more on Kuchma's short-lived "Clean Hands" anti-corruption program, see Geoffrey A. Dubrow, "Ukraine's 'Operation Clean Hands' Runs into Hot Water," *Governance*, vol. 1, no. 1 (January 1998): 40–45.

88. See the discussion in Chapter 6. The paradigm case of "shock therapy" is Poland. See David Lipton and Jeffrey Sachs, "Creating a Market Economy in Eastern Europe: The Case of Poland," *Brookings Papers on Economic Activity*, vol. 1 (1990): 75–133; Jeffrey Sachs, *Poland's Jump to the Market Economy* (Cambridge: MIT Press, 1993); Ben Slay, *The Polish Economy* (Princeton: Princeton University Press, 1994); and Balcerowicz, *Socialism, Capitalism, Transformation*.

89. See Eggertsson, "The Economics of Institutions in Transition Economies."

90. See Israel, *Institutional Development*, p. 19.

91. Eggertsson elaborates further that "[a]s organizations are partly country specific (in a way that is little understood), it is not possible to import techniques of organization as easily as production technology" ("The Economics of Institutions in Transition Economies," p. 34).

92. See Collins, "Civil Service Reform."

93. See J. J. Hesse, "Introduction," in J. J. Hesse, ed., *Administrative Transformation in Central and Eastern Europe: Towards Public Sector Reform in Post-Communist Societies* (London: Macmillan, 1993), pp. 1–12.

94. Newland, "Transformational Challenges," p. 385.

95. See Christopher Hood, "A Public Management for All Seasons?" *Public Administration*, vol. 69 (Spring 1991): 3–19.

96. See Hague, Rose, and Bojcun, "Rebuilding Ukraine's Hollow State."

97. Roeder, "Varieties of Post-Soviet Authoritarian Regimes," pp. 61–101.

98. See Wise and Brown, "Laying the Foundations," p. 231.

99. See Alexander J. Motyl, "The Conceptual President: Leonid Kravchuk and the Politics of Surrealism," in Timothy J. Colton and Robert C. Tucker, eds., *Patterns in Post-Soviet Leadership* (Boulder: Westview Press, 1995), pp. 103–121; and Andrew Wilson, "Ukraine: Two Presidents and Their Powers," in Taras, ed., *Post-communist Presidents*, pp. 67–105.

100. Wise and Brown, "Laying the Foundations."

101. In the Ukrainian legislative process, a bill must be voted on and approved twice by Parliament before it may be presented to the president for his signature or veto.

102. See "Kuchma, Deputies to Coordinate Political Reforms," Moscow INTERFAX News Service, 16 December 1994, FBIS-SOV-94-243 (original in English).

103. Implementation of the Law on Power required the suspension of some 60 of the 170 articles of the Constitution of 1978, as well as changes in certain other laws. See Taras Kuzio, *Ukraine Under Kuchma* (London: Macmillan, 1997), p. 101.

104. Decree of the President of Ukraine, "On Holding Plebiscite to Ascertain the Trust Citizens of Ukraine Place in the President of Ukraine and the Verkhovna

Rada of Ukraine," 31 May 1995, no. 413-95. See also "Kuchma Interviewed on Parliament Session," Moscow INTERFAX News Service, 14 May 1995, FBIS-SOV-95-093 (original in English).

105. Marta Kolomayets, "Ukraine's Parliament Passes Law on Powers," *Ukrainian Weekly*, 28 May 1995, p. 1. See the text of the law in *Holos Ukraiiny*, 6 June 1995, p. 2.

106. The text of the Constitutional Accord was published in English translation by *IntelNews*, "On the Books," 7 June 1995. It can also be found in English on the World Wide Web. Available: www.kiev.sovam.com: 70/00/UPRESA/WEEKLY/06.07.95-06.12.95/Documents. For a summary of the major points, see "Some Aspects of the Constitutional Agreement Between the Supreme Council and the President," *Ukrainian Economic Monitor*, vol. 2, no. 4 (1995): 20. For its political implications, see Chrystyna Lapychak, "Showdown Yields Political Reform," *Transition*, 28 July 1995, pp. 3–7.

107. Both of these provisions were to be incorporated into the executive authority of the president in the June 1996 Constitution of Ukraine.

108. For various commentaries on the 1996 Ukrainian constitutional adoption process, see Kataryna Wolczuk, "The New Ukrainian Constitution: In Pursuit of a Compromise," CERT Discussion Paper no. 97/10, Centre for Economic Reform and Transformation, Department of Economics, Heriot-Watt University, Edinburgh, Scotland, March 1997; Kuzio, *Ukraine Under Kuchma*; and Oliver Vorndran, "The Constitutional Process in Ukraine: Context and Structure," Research Paper no. REES97/3, Centre for Russian and East European Studies, University of Birmingham, December 1997.

109. Wise and Brown, "Laying the Foundations," p. 221.

110. David M. Olson and Peter Norton, "Legislatures in the Democratic Transformation: The Paradox of Opportunity and Capability," paper presented at the Parliaments in Central and Eastern Europe Conference, Prague, Czech Republic, August 1994. Cited in Charles R. Wise and Trevor L. Brown, "The Internal Development of the Ukrainian Parliament," *Public Administration and Development*, vol. 16 (1996): 265–279. (The reference to "rebuilding the ship at sea" is taken from the subtitle of Jon Elster, Claus Offe, and Ulrich K. Preuss, *Institutional Design in Post-Communist Societies* [Cambridge: Cambridge University Press, 1998].)

111. Wise and Brown, "Laying the Foundations," p. 242.

112. See Constitution of Ukraine, 28 June 1996, Article 93.

113. Law of Ukraine, "On the Status of People's Deputies of Ukraine," as amended 7 July 1995, Article 11.

114. See Rules of the Verkhovna Rada of Ukraine, 27 July 1994, chap. 6. (Note that the 10-day return requirement is in direct contradiction to the constitutional requirement of 15 days.)

115. Once signed, the law goes into effect only upon its publication in an official source, such as *Holos Ukraiiny*, the official newspaper of Parliament; *Uriadovyi Kurier*, the newspaper of the executive branch; or *Parliamentary News*. These three published versions are considered to be "official texts" of the law.

116. Law of Ukraine, "On Local Self-Governments in Ukraine," 28 May 1997, no. 280-97-VR.

117. Wise and Brown, "Laying the Foundations."

118. Law of Ukraine, "On the Budget System," as amended 28 May 1995.
119. Law of Ukraine, "On Local Radas of People's Deputies and Local and Regional Self-Government," 7 February 1992. The legislative basis for local self-government in Ukraine can be traced from the Soviet period. For a fuller enumeration of the legislative basis for local government in Ukraine, see Yuriy Sayenko, Anatoliy Tkachuk, and Yuriy Privalov, *Misetsve samovryaduvannyah v Ukraiini: Problemi i prognozi* (Kyiv: Institute of Sociology of the Ukrainian Academy of Sciences, 1997).
120. In the act, "local" is understood also to mean "regional."
121. Law of the Ukrainian SSR, "Law on the Budget System," 5 December 1990, VR-513-12.
122. Law of Ukraine, "On Amendments to the Law of the Ukrainian SSR, 'On the Budget System of Ukraine,'" 19 April 1995.
123. The current tax and revenue assignments are quite restrictive. See the Law of Ukraine, "On the Introduction of Amendments to the Law of Ukraine, 'On the System of Taxation,'" 18 February 1997, 77-97-VR (see *Golos Ukrainy*, 25 March 1997, pp. 6–7, FBIS-97-070 [original in Russian]).
124. Decree of the President of Ukraine, "On the Representatives of the President of Ukraine," 20 March 1992. (The text of the decree was published in *Holos Ukraiiny*, 20 March 1992.)
125. Decree of the President of Ukraine, "On Regulations Concerning Local State Administration," 14 April 1992.
126. Decree of the President of Ukraine, "On Subordination of Local State Administrations," 27 October 1992.
127. 5 March 1992.
128. Enacted November 29, 1993, the eastern oblasts affected were Dnipropetrovs'k, Donets'k, Luhans'k, and Zaporizhzhya. See *Ukrainian Weekly*, 19 December 1993, p. 2; and *IntelNews*, 28 February 1994, p. 1.
129. So frustrated with direct presidential rule were officials in the Crimean City of Sevastopol that on November 4, 1993, the City Council asked the Ukrainian president and Parliament to eliminate the presence of president's representatives in the city. The council expressed its desire to manage and control local executive powers unimpeded by interference from above. The council's letter to President Kravchuk indicated that it would take preliminary steps toward regaining control of the municipal state administration within a month if it failed to receive a response from Kyiv. See *IntelNews*, "In Brief," 5 November 1993, p. 4.
130. Law of Ukraine, "On the Formation of Local Power and Self-Governing Bodies," 3 February 1994, VR-3917-12.
131. Will Ritter, "Elections to Local Radas Set for June 26," *IntelNews*, 6 February 1994, p. 1.
132. Decree of the President of Ukraine, "On Additional Measures for Delegating More Powers for Dnipropetrovs'k, Donets'k, Zaporizhzhia, and Luhans'k Regional State Administrations in Managing All-State Property," 21 February 1994. See also "Decentralization on the Way," *IntelNews*, 28 February 1994, p. 1.
133. Decree of the President of Ukraine, "On the Strengthening of the Economic Basis of the Municipal Self-Government in Ukraine," 12 March 1994. See the text in *Uriadoviy Kur'er*, 15 March 1994.

134. Victor Zubaniuk, "Kravchuk Signs Decentralization Decree," *IntelNews*, 17 March 1994, p. 3.

135. Decree of the President of Ukraine, "On Ways to Ensure Appropriate Management of Local Structures of State Executive Authorities," 9 August 1994. See also "Ukraine's Leader Issues Decrees to Expand Hold on Parliament," *New York Times* (late New York edition), 11 August 1994.

136. The Council of Regions was formally established on September 20, 1994. See *Holos Ukraiiny*, 23 September 1994.

137. Some saw the Council of Regions as the basis for the formation of an upper house in a new bicameral parliament. In fact, Kuchma was to place the regional leaders in the core of a "Senate" in the draft constitution of Ukraine that the president submitted to Parliament on 17 November 1995.

138. For a chronicle of the evolution of the 1995 Law on Power, see Viktor Tkachuk, "President Pushes for Real Power," *UPressA Weekly*, Ukrainian Press Agency, 6–12 November 1995.

139. Draft Law of Ukraine, "On the State Powers and Local Self-Government," introduced 2 December 1994. See the text in *Uriadoviy Kur'er*, 6 December 1994.

140. Draft Law of Ukraine, "On Local Councils of People's Deputies," 10 November 1994. See the text translated from *Kiev MOST*, 10 November 1994, FBIS-USR-94-131, 5 December 1994, p. 34 (original in Russian). According to the draft, enterprises were to be under the control of and accountable to the Soviets in the territory where they were located.

141. Decree of the President of Ukraine, "On the Basic Organization and Functioning of State Power and Local Self-Government in Ukraine in the Period Until Adoption of a New Constitution of Ukraine," 8 August 1995, and Decree of the President of Ukraine, "On the Status of Oblast, Kyiv and Sevastopol and Regional Government Administrations," 21 August 1995. The purpose of holding new elections in the case of dismissal of a council chair was to preserve their dual roles as head of the local administration and chair of their respective councils.

142. Kuchma has referred to the president as the "guarantor of the constitution" on a number of occasions. For instance, see the text of his speech before the Ukrainian Association of Local and Regional Authorities on 19 June 1997 in *Urayadovyy Ku'rer*, 21 June 1997, pp. 3–4, FBIS-SOV-97-147-S (original in Ukrainian); see also Kuchma's Message to Parliament concerning his veto of the enacted "Law on Local State Administrations," in *Urayadovyy Ku'rer*, 14 August 1997, p. 3, FBIS-SOV-97-266 (original in Ukrainian).

143. Despite the conflict of laws, it seems that Parliament was more concerned that Kuchma's innovation might set the precedent for a new two-house parliament, with the upper chamber being a "Council of Regions," represented by the elected chairmen of regional councils, all accountable to the president.

144. Decree of the President of Ukraine, "On Delegating State Executive Authority Powers to Chairmen and Executive Committees Headed by Them of Village, Settlement and City Councils," 4 January 1996. See "Kuchma Issues Decree Delegating State Executive Authority," Moscow INTERFAX News Service, 4 January 1996, FBIS-SOV-96-004 (original in English).

145. According to former President Leonid Kravchuk, Kuchma's bicameral legislature failed for two reasons. First, leftist forces feared that a proexecutive upper

chamber would dilute their power. The Council of Regions at the time was functioning as an "embryo Senate," with a proreform membership. Second, eastern Ukraine eventually withdrew support for an upper house, fearing that equal representation of all oblasts in the proposed Senate would shift dominance of national policymaking away from the east. At the end, the only faction that supported a two-chamber Rada was Statehood, a center-right faction from western Ukraine. Kravchuk made his remarks to Taras Kuzio at the conference "Soviet to Independent Ukraine: A Troubled Transformation," University of Birmingham, 13–15 June 1996.

146. An official English-language translation of the June 1996 Constitution of Ukraine has been published in *Ukrainian Quarterly*, vol. 52, nos. 2–3 (Summer–Fall 1996): 223–289. The text also appears in an official English-language translation over the World Wide Web. Available: www.Rada.Kiev.UA/const/conengl.htm. Also, the Ukrainian (CP1251 Cyrillic Coding) version is available: www.Rada.Kiev.UA/const/const1.htm. A broad overview of the highlights of the new basic law of Ukraine is provided in *Ukrainian Economic Monitor*, vol. 3, nos. 8–9 (15–16) (August–September 1996): 30.

147. See Sarah Birch and Ihor Zinko, "Ukraine: The Dilemma of Regionalism," *Transition*, vol. 1 (November 1996): 24.

148. See Kuchma's remarks before a meeting in Kyiv of the Association of Towns of Ukraine, "President Kuchma on Local Self-Government Law," Kyiv UT-1 Television Network, 19:00 GMT, 25 January 1997, translated in FBIS-SOV-97-017 (original in Ukrainian).

149. Law of Ukraine, "On Local Self-Governments in Ukraine," 28 May 1997, no. 280-97-VR.

150. See Robert S. Kravchuk, "The Quest for Balance: Regionalism and Sub-National Fiscal Policy in Ukraine," in Kuzio, Kravchuk, and D'Anieri, eds., *State and Institution Building in Ukraine*.

151. The turnover statistics are from Ukrainian Center for Peace, Conversion, and Conflict Resolution Studies, "Sociological Portrait of Ukrainian Government, 1990–97," Occasional Paper 51, 1 May 1998.

152. See *Economist*, "Dream On," 17 October 1992, p. 56.

153. For more detail, see Chapter 6.

154. See *Economist*, "Man of Iron," 26 December 1992–8 January 1993, p. 62.

155. See *Ukrainian Weekly*, "'Red Directors' Block Reforms," 17 January 1993.

156. For an analysis of the effects of the 1989 miners' strikes, see David Marples, *Ukraine Under Perestroika: Ecology, Economics, and the Workers' Revolt* (New York: St. Martin's Press, 1991).

157. Decree of the President of Ukraine, "On Urgent Measures for the Stabilization of the Economic and Political Situation in Ukraine," reprinted in *Ukrainian Weekly*, 20 June 1993, p. 3.

158. Unable to secure consistent sources of working capital, many state enterprises and other firms simply ignored the central directives, instead producing for the open market.

159. The main tenets of the program are summarized in Chapter 6. See also the unofficial English translation of the complete text of the program by the Council of Advisors to Parliament, published in two parts, in *Ukrainian Legal and Economic Bulletin*, November and December 1994 issues.

160. From commentary by Ihor Sharov, deputy minister of the Cabinet of Ministers, in *Uriadovyi Kurier*, 1 September 1998, p. 7, FBIS-SOV-98-275 (original in Ukrainian).

161. See Jack H. Knott and Gary J. Miller, *Reforming Bureaucracy: The Politics of Institutional Choice* (Englewood Cliffs, NJ: Prentice-Hall, 1987).

162. Mancur Olson sees the problem of economic policymaking and its execution as a problem of *collective action*. Institutional arrangements linking the state to the social economy are critical in this regard. To the extent that powerful groups are able to penetrate the state and exert influence over economic policymaking, their short-run interests will tend to turn policy into a *distributional game*. Policy options will be constrained and analysis of options prematurely foreclosed. See Mancur Olson, *The Rise and Decline of Nations* (New Haven: Yale University Press, 1982).

163. For a basic introduction to the relevant literature, see James G. March and Johan P. Olsen, "Organizing Political Life: What Administrative Reorganization Tells Us About Government," *American Political Science Review*, vol. 77, no. 1 (1983): 281–296; "The New Institutionalism: Organizational Factor in Political Life," *American Political Science Review*, vol. 78, no. 3 (1984): 734–649; and *Rediscovering Institutions: The Organizational Basis of Politics* (New York: Free Press, 1989). See also Harold Seidman and Robert Gilmour, *Politics, Position, and Power*, 4th ed. (New York: Oxford University Press, 1986); Terry Moe, "The Politics of Structural Choice: Toward a Theory of Public Bureaucracy," in Oliver Williamson, ed., *Organization Theory* (New York: Oxford University Press, 1990); and Eggertsson, "The Economics of Institutions in Transition Economies."

164. See Haggard, *Pathways from the Periphery*, especially p. 44. See also Werlin, *The Mysteries of Development*.

165. See Roberto Mangabeira Unger, *Law in Modern Society* (New York: Free Press, 1976); David Held, *Political Theory and the Modern State* (Stanford: Stanford University Press, 1989); and Robert S. Kravchuk, "Public Administration and the Rule of Law," *International Journal of Public Administration*, vol. 14, no. 3 (Spring–Summer 1991): 265–302.

166. See Daniel Kaufmann, "Market Liberalization by Stealth: Curse or Blessing in Disguise?" *Ukrainian Legal and Economic Bulletin*, vol. 3, nos. 1–2 (January–February 1995): 13–30.

167. From a statement by Viktor M. Penzenyk, deputy prime minister, in an interview with Fedir Storozhenko, *IntelNews*, 7 October 1994.

168. For instance, see some of the analyses in the collection of essays by the editors and contributors to the Ukrainian journal *Politichna Dumka, the Political Analysis of Postcommunism* (Kyiv: Political Thought, 1995).

CHAPTER 5

1. *Uriadovyi Kurier*, 3 November 1998.

2. One poll in Kyiv found that 90 percent of those who backed Ukrainian statehood also had "liberal" (i.e., proreform) views. Meanwhile, only 43 percent of the left backed statehood (*Uriadovyi Kurier*, 18 February 1996).

3. *Kievskiye Vedomosti*, 8 July 1997.

4. Valerie Bunce, "Comparing East and South," *Journal of Democracy*, vol. 6, no. 3 (October 1995): 91–92.

5. Adam Przeworski, "Some Problems in the Study of the Transition to Democracy," in Guillermo O'Donnell, Philippe C. Schmitter, Lawrence Whitehead, eds., *Transitions from Authoritarian Rule: Prospects for Democracy* (Baltimore: Johns Hopkins University Press, 1986), p. 61.

6. Andreas Schedler, "What Is Democratic Consolidation?" *Journal of Democracy*, vol. 9, no. 2 (April 1998): 94.

7. Giovani Sartori, *Parties and Systems: A Framework for Analysis* (Cambridge: Cambridge University Press, 1976).

8. Samuel Huntington, *Political Order in Changing Societies* (New Haven: Yale University Press, 1968).

9. Jack Snyder, "Averting Anarchy in the New Europe," *International Security*, vol. 14, no. 4 (Spring 1990): 5–37.

10. Paul Kubicek, "Delegative Democracy in Russia and Ukraine," *Communist and Post-Communist Studies*, vol. 27, no. 4 (December 1994): 424.

11. Gabriel A. Almond and Sidney Verba, *The Civic Culture: Political Attitudes and Democratization in Five Nations* (Princeton: Princeton University Press, 1963), p. 1011.

12. Andreas Schedler, "Concepts of Democratic Consolidation," paper presented to the Latin American Studies Association, Guadalajara, Mexico, 17–19 April 1997.

13. Quoted in Heinz Eulau, Samuel J. Eldersveld, and Morris Janowitz, eds., *Political Behavior: A Reader in Theory and Research* (Glencoe, IL: Free Press, 1956), pp. 34–42.

14. Lucian W. Pye, introduction to Lucien W. Pye and Sidney Verba, eds., *Political Culture and Political Development* (Princeton: Princeton University Press, 1965), pp. 3–26.

15. Andrew Wilson and Artur Bilous, "Political Parties in Ukraine," *Europe-Asia Studies*, vol. 45, no. 4 (1993): 696.

16. Almond and Verba, *The Civic Culture*, p. 500.

17. Ibid, p. 7.

18. Edward Shils, "The Virtue of Civil Society," *Government and Opposition*, vol. 26, no. 1 (Winter 1991): 3.

19. For more on this alliance, see Taras Kuzio and Marc Nordberg, "Nation and State Building, Historical Legacies, and National Identities in Belarus and Ukraine: A Comparative Analysis," *Canadian Review of Studies in Nationalism*, vol. 26, nos. 1–2 (1999).

20. Samuel Huntington, "Will More Countries Become Democratic?" *Political Science Quarterly*, vol. 99, no. 2 (1984): 212–213.

21. On political pluralism in Ukraine, see *Molod' Ukraiiny*, 23 December 1990; *Kommunist Ukraiiny*, no. 12 (1990); *Kul'tura i Zhyttia*, 5 January 1991; *Visti z Ukraiiny*, no. 15 (1991); *Literaturna Ukraiina*, 20 June 1991; *PostPostup*, no. 6 (1991); *Volia*, nos. 15–16 (1991); *Slovo*, May 1991; *Radianska Ukraiina*, 22 May 1991; *Samostiina Ukraiina*, no. 29 (July 1992); and *Uriadovyi Kurier*, 31 July 1992. A roundtable of political parties was covered in *Za Vilnu Ukraiinu*, 30 April 1991. See also the surveys by Oleksiy Haran in *Zoloti Vorota*, no. 1 (1991): 48–57.

22. On the period in Ukraine between 1985 and 1990, see Taras Kuzio, "Ukraine Under Gorbachev," *Uncaptive Minds*, vol. 1, no. 3 (September–October 1988): 17–19, and "Unofficial Groups and Publications in Ukraine," *Report on the USSR*, no. 47 (1989): 10–21.

23. See the article by Artur Bilous in *Suchasnist*, no. 6 (June 1992): 108–119.

24. The programs are reprinted in A. H. Slyusarenko and M. V. Tomenko, *Novi politychni partii Ukrainy: Dovidnyk* (Kyiv: Tovarystvo "Znannya" Ukrainskoi RSR, 1990), and Oleksa Haran, ed., *Ukraina bahatopartiina: Prohramni dokumenty novykh partii* (Kyiv: MP "Pamiatky Ukrainy," 1991). Haran's introductory essay is expanded upon in *Vid stvorennia Rukhu do bahatopartiinosti* (Kyiv: Znannia, 1992).

25. *Den'*, 28 October 1998.

26. *Nezalezhnyj Ohliadach*, August–September 1991.

27. On political parties in Galicia, see the article by Yevhen Boltarovych in *Respublikanets*, no. 2 (November–December 1991): 21–40.

28. Text in the authors' possession, entitled "Our Aspirations," by Levko Lukianenko (no date or place of publication).

29. *Ukrainian Weekly*, 3 March 1991.

30. *Vechirnyi Kyiv*, 3 December 1991, and *Suchasnist*, no. 6 (June 1992): 114.

31. *Filosophska i Sotsiolohichna Dumka*, no. 1 (1991): 21.

32. Several parties began a campaign to broaden their access to a mass media still dominated by national Communists, including the demand for an independent television channel. See *Samostiina Ukraiina*, no. 29 (July 1992). See also the survey of viewing levels of Ukrainian television in *Demokratychna Ukraiina*, 18 July 1992; and a critical survey of the state of Ukrainian television by Volodymyr Ruban in *PostPostup*, no. 28 (1992).

33. *Narodna Hazeta*, no. 12 (April 1992).

34. The combined left had 27.3, national democrats 12–16 percent, and centrist parties 8–12 percent (data provided by the Ukraine-U.S. Strategic Communications Center in *Den'*, 10 November 1998). A striking 50 percent simply did not care!

35. Steven Fish, "The Emergence of Independent Associations and the Transformation of Russian Political Society," *Journal of Communist Studies*, vol. 7, no. 3 (September 1991): 321.

36. The Agrarians were established to take away votes from the left in rural constituencies (*Vysokyi Zamok*, 22 April 1998).

37. *Ukraiina Moloda*, 28 September 1998.

38. *Moloda Halychyna*, 14 March 1991, and *Ukraiinski Visti*, 28 April 1991.

39. *Ukraiinskyi Ohliadach*, no. 7, 1992.

40. *Ukraiina Moloda*, 18 October 1997.

41. Giovanni Sartori, *Parties and Party Systems: A Framework for Analysis*, vol. 1 (New York: Free Press, 1976).

42. Victor Chudowsky, "The Ukrainian Party System," in John S. Micgiel, ed., *State and Nation Building in East Central Europe: Contemporary Perspectives* (New York: Institute on East Central Europe, Columbia University, 1996), pp. 331–350.

43. Maurice Duverger, *Party Politics and Pressure Groups: A Comparative Introduction* (New York: Thomas Y. Crowell Company, 1972), p. 20.

44. See Taras Kuzio, "The 1994 Parliamentary Elections in Ukraine," *Journal of Communist Studies and Transition Politics*, vol. 11, no. 4 (December 1995): 335–361.
45. Duverger, *Party Politics and Pressure Groups*, pp. 27–32.
46. Scott Mainwaring, "Politicians, Parties, and Electoral Systems: Brazil in Comparative Perspective," *Comparative Politics*, vol. 24, no. 1 (1991): 26–27.
47. John Lowenhardt, *The Reincarnation of Russia* (Durham, NC: Duke University Press, 1995), p. 40.
48. The list of those deputies who supported Moroz's removal was published in *Tovarystvo* (June 1996).
49. Only 14 members of the socialist faction were members of the Socialist Party of Ukraine (*Ukraiina Moloda*, 15 November 1996).
50. But not in the final voting procedures.
51. Artur Bilous, "Verkhovna Rada Ukraiiny: Roztashuvannia syl i perspektyvy partiy," *Nova Polityka* (June–July 1995): 35.
52. *Ukraiina Moloda*, 15 November 1996.
53. *Ukraiina moloda*, 6 August 1996.
54. The most common phenomenon for this is the refusal to register for a plenary session of the *Verkhovna Rada* (for example, when the accession to the CIS Interparliamentary Assembly was tabled or in the constitutional process).
55. Angelo Panebianco, *Political Parties: Organization and Power* (Cambridge: Cambridge University Press, 1988), p. 50. Panebianco calls this territorial diffusion. It occurs in democratizing countries when the center lacks the power to create its own party structure throughout the country (territorial penetration). Because of the strength at independence of both nationalist and Communist organizations, we also see territorial diffusion of parties in Ukraine.
56. Ottorino Cappelli, "The Short Parliament, 1989–91: Political Elites, Societal Cleavages, and the Weakness of Party Politics," *Journal of Communist Studies*, vol. 9, no. 1 (1993): 112.
57. Ibid.
58. See Taras Kuzio, "A Four-Pronged Transition," in Taras Kuzio, ed., *Contemporary Ukraine: Dynamics of Post-Soviet Transformation* (Armonk, NY: M. E. Sharpe, 1998), pp. 165–180.
59. Dankwart A. Rustow, "Transitions to Democracy: Toward a Dynamic Model," *Comparative Politics*, vol. 2, no. 3 (1970): 358–361.
60. *Vechirnyi Kyiv*, 25 September 1996.
61. For example, see Dominique Arel and Valeri Khmelko, "The Russian Factor and Territorial Polarization in Ukraine," *Harriman Review*, vol. 9, nos. 1–2 (March 1996): 81–91; and Sven Holdar, "Torn Between East and West: The Regional Factor in Ukrainian Politics," *Post-Soviet Geography*, vol. 36, no. 2 (February 1996): 112–132. Louise Jackson argues against this view. See her "Identity, Language, and Transition in Eastern Ukraine: A Case Study of Zaporizhzhia," in Kuzio, *Contemporary Ukraine*, pp. 99–114.
62. Herbert Kitschelt, "The Formation of Party Systems in East Central Europe," *Politics and Society*, vol. 20, no. 1 (1992): 25.
63. See Taras Kuzio, *Ukraine: The Unfinished Revolution* (London: Institute for European Defence and Strategic Studies, 1992), pp. 17–20.

64. On this connection, see Taras Kuzio, "Belarus and Ukraine: Democracy Building in a Grey Security Zone," in Jan Zielonka and Alex Pravda, eds., *Democratic Consolidation in Eastern Europe: International and Transnational Factors* (Florence: European University Institute, forthcoming).
65. *Ukraiina Moloda*, 27 October 1998.
66. Juan J. Linz and Alfred Stepan, *Problems of Democratic Transformation and Consolidation: Southern Europe, Southern America, and Post-Communist Europe* (Baltimore: Johns Hopkins University Press, 1996), pp. 3–86, cited in Schedler, "What Is Bureaucratic Consolidation?" pp. 98–99.

CHAPTER 6

1. See World Bank, *World Development Report, 1996: From Plan to Market* (Washington, DC, and New York: World Bank and Oxford University Press, 1996), pp. 9–21. See especially Figure 1.2, p. 14.
2. See World Economic Forum, *Global Competitiveness Report* (Washington, DC: World Economic Forum, 1997).
3. See János Kornai, *The Socialist System* (Princeton: Princeton University Press, 1992), pp. 361, 387–392.
4. According to former Polish finance minister Leszek Balcerowicz, the designer of Poland's "shock therapy" program, "A pure shock-type, or radical transition to a private market economy may be defined as a transition whereby all constituent processes are implemented with the maximum possible speed." The rationale is that radical reform is painful and tests the people's patience and therefore must be implemented before political support erodes. See Leszek Balcerowicz, *Socialism, Capitalism, Transformation* (Budapest: Central European University Press, 1995), p. 179.
5. See James R. Millar, "The Failure of Shock Therapy," *Problems of Post-Communism* (Fall 1994): 21–25.
6. See Ben Slay, "Rapid Versus Gradual Economic Transition," *RFE/RL Research Report*, vol. 3, no. 31 (12 August 1994): 31–42, and Amanda Rose, "Sachs Was Right: Economic Assessments Under Rapid and Gradual Reform in Central and Eastern Europe," paper presented at the Annual Meeting of the American Political Science Association, San Francisco, California, 29 August 1996.
7. See David Lipton and Jeffrey Sachs, "Creating a Market Economy in Eastern Europe: The Case of Poland," *Brookings Papers on Economic Activity 1* (Washington, DC: Brookings Institution, 1990); David Lipton and Jeffrey Sachs, "Privatization in Eastern Europe: The Case of Poland," *Brookings Papers on Economic Activity 2* (Washington, DC: Brookings Institution, 1990); and Peter Murell, "What Is Shock Therapy? What Did It Do in Poland and Russia?" *Post-Soviet Affairs*, vol. 9, no. 2 (April–June 1993): 111–140.
8. See János Kornai, *The Road to a Free Economy* (New York: W. W. Norton, 1990).
9. Murell, "What Is Shock Therapy?"
10. See Ronald McKinnon, *The Order to Economic Liberalization* (Baltimore: Johns Hopkins University Press, 1991).
11. Kornai, *The Road to a Free Economy*.

12. See Tim Carrington, "Efforts to Ease Social Pain of Transition to Market Economy Often Can Backfire," *Wall Street Journal,* 2 May 1994.
13. See John Williamson, ed., *The Political Economy of Policy Reform* (Washington, DC: Institute for International Economics, 1993).
14. See Paul Kubicek, "Post-Soviet Ukraine: In Search of a Constituency for Reform," *Journal of Communist Studies and Transition Politics,* vol. 13, no. 3 (September 1997): 103–126.
15. Ibid., p. 112.
16. See Alexander J. Motyl, "Structural Constraints and Starting Points: The Logic of Systemic Change in Ukraine and Russia," *Comparative Politics,* vol. 29, no. 4 (July 1997): 433–447.
17. Among the postsocialist countries, only Albania and Turkmenistan have suffered worse declines.
18. See Jan Winiecki, "The Inevitability of a Fall in Output in the Early Stage of a Transition to the Market: Theoretical Underpinnings," *Soviet Studies,* vol. 43, no. 4 (1991): 669–676.
19. See World Bank, *World Development Report, 1997: The State in a Changing World* (New York: Oxford University Press, 1997).
20. In purely economic terms, bankruptcy entails reallocation of productive assets to the most efficient uses. It is widely agreed that this serves to increase long-run efficiency. In the short run, however, bankruptcy and plant closings will also have demand-reducing effects, insofar as redundant labor is shed and demand for input materials is curtailed. This contributes to the general output fall.
21. Kornai sees this as "possibly the main cause behind the recession" in formerly socialist countries. See *The Road to a Free Economy,* p. 44.
22. See Razumkov et al., Report of the Ukrainian Center for Economic and Political Studies, "The Shadow Economy and Organized Crime in Ukraine," *Zerkalo Nedeli* (Kiev), 10 February 1996, p. 6, FBIS-SOV-96-094-S (original in Russian).
23. Based on estimates of changes in electric power consumption in Ukraine, the real output decline has been far less than the official statistics indicate. The difference is accounted for by movement into the shadow sector, where such activity escapes registration, regulation, taxation, and corruption. For estimates for formerly socialist countries in transition, see Istvan Dobozi and Gerhard Pohl, "Real Output Decline in Transition Economies—Forget GDP, Try Power Consumption Data," *Transition,* vol. 6, nos. 1–2 (January–February 1995): 17–18.
24. Razumkov et al., "The Shadow Economy and Organized Crime."
25. See Alexander Paskhaver, "The Adaptation of the Ukrainian Economy to the Crash of the Government Management System," *Ukrainian Legal and Economic Bulletin,* vol. 2, no. 3 (March 1994): 37–41.
26. Kyiv UNIAN, 18:30 GMT, 30 January 1995, FBIS-SOV-95-020 (original in Ukrainian).
27. See Alexander Paskhaver, "Ukraine's Shadow Economy During the Period of Transition," *Ukrainian Economic Monitor,* vol. 3, no. 6 (13) (June 1996): 6–11.
28. Cited in Razumkov et al., "The Shadow Economy and Organized Crime."
29. Ibid.
30. See Daniel Kaufmann and Aleksander Kaliberda, "Integrating the Unofficial Economy into the Dynamics of Post-Socialist Economies," chap. 4 in Bart-

lomiej Kaminski, ed., *Economic Transition in Russia and the New States of Eurasia* (Armonk, NY: M. E. Sharpe, 1996), pp. 81–120.

31. Further, Ukraine inherited from the Soviet Union an overly generous social welfare system, which the country could not afford but which its leaders were reluctant to abandon in the face of dramatic falls in the standard of living. For more on these issues, see below.

32. See *Ukrainian Economic Monitor*, no. 3 (32) (March 1998), table 7, p. 3.

33. See Economist Intelligence Unit, *Ukraine Country Forecast—Third Quarter 1998*. Until 1996, Russia implicitly subsidized Ukrainian energy imports, as measured by the spread between the import price and world market prices, to the sum of 30.5 percent of imports, or 1.3 percent of Ukrainian GDP, annually from 1992 to 1995. See Gregory V. Krasnov and Josef C. Brada, "Implicit Subsidies in Russian-Ukrainian Energy Trade," *Europe-Asia Studies*, vol. 49, no. 5 (1997): 825–843.

34. See Oleksandr Bilotserkivets, "Ukraine's Foreign Trade: Structure and Developments," *Ukrainian Economic Monitor*, nos. 6–7 (35–36) (June–July 1998): 23–28.

35. See Taras Kuzio, "Ukraine's Arms Exports Continue to Expand," *Jane's Intelligence Review*, vol. 9, no. 3 (March 1997): 108–111.

36. See Paul D'Anieri, *Economic Interdependence in Ukrainian-Russian Relations* (Albany: State University of New York Press, 1999), especially chap. 6.

37. The CIS Customs Union includes Russia, Belarus, Kazakhstan, and Kyrgyzstan.

38. See German Consultative Group, "Foreign Direct Investment in Ukraine: From a Disappointing Trickle to a Salutary Flow?" *Ukrainian Economic Monitor*, no. 3 (32) (March 1998): 20–26.

39. See "Foreign Investments Inflow Rising, but Slowly," *Kyiv Post*, 21 November 1997, p. 12.

40. German Consultative Group, "Foreign Direct Investment in Ukraine," table 3, p. 25.

41. Significantly, the same survey respondents cited as positive elements the following: worker reliability, education and training levels, and eagerness of personnel to upgrade their performance.

42. See Ukrainian Press Agency, *UPressA*, 27 November 1995, p. 3. See also INTERFAX-Ukraine, "Excess of $20 Billion Transferred Abroad over Four Years," FBIS-TDD-97-001-L, 22 November 1996 (original in English).

43. Alex Sudakov, "Ukraine—International Trade Issues," Kyiv, May 1996.

44. *Ukrainian Economic Monitor* (various issues).

45. See "Ukraine Plans to Increase Foreign Debt," *IntelNews*, 1 February 1998, FBIS-SOV-98-032 (original in English).

46. See Margarita Shalenko, "Labor Market in Ukraine: The Problem of Latent Unemployment," *Kiev Times*, 17–24 September 1993, p. 5.

47. By its nature, official statistics cannot capture the shadow sector. We may infer from what is known about it that it is large and therefore crucial to the livelihood of many Ukrainians, making for a vital "safety valve" for social tensions.

48. A countervailing factor is that unemployment benefits are so low (approxi-

mately 40 HRV per month, or around $18) that many workers do not bother to register with the State Employment Service.

49. See *Ukrainian Economic Monitor,* nos. 1–2 (30–31) (January–February 1998): 6, and no. 8 (37) (August 1998): 6.

50. See Economist Intelligence Unit, *Ukraine Country Forecast—3rd Quarter 1998.*

51. See Robert S. Kravchuk, "Budget Deficits, Hyperinflation, and Stabilization in Ukraine, 1991–96," *Public Budgeting and Finance* (forthcoming, 1999).

52. Ukrainian definitions of money largely correspond to the international conventions, so that interpretations of "narrow money" (M1) and "broad money" (M2) are reasonably straightforward.

53. See Robert S. Kravchuk, "The Challenge of Fiscal Reform in Ukraine, 1991–97," paper presented at the International Conference "Institutional Reform in Ukraine: Implications for Emerging Markets," Yale University, New Haven, Connecticut, 24–25 April 1998.

54. See International Monetary Fund, "Ukraine—Recent Economic Developments," IMF Staff Country Report no. 97/109 (October 1997), p. 45.

55. See Economist Intelligence Unit, *Ukraine Country Forecast—3rd Quarter 1998.*

56. See Ukrainian-European Policy and Legal Advice Centre, "On Privatization in Ukraine," *Ukrainian Legal and Economic Bulletin* (July 1997): 19–26.

57. These statistics are subject to some interpretation. The government's reported privatization statistics tend to overinflate the results in several ways. First, the reported number of privatized enterprises includes those that have initiated the process but are not yet in private hands. Second, many formally privatized entities have had significant blocks of shares retained by the state due to incomplete sale or purchase of all shares. Third, privatization "spin-offs" are counted among the privatized firms, whereas they began the process as a single entity. To overcome some of these statistical reporting issues, starting in the first quarter of 1996, the State Property Fund began to register enterprises as "private" only if all shares were sold.

58. In the wake of President Kuchma's July 1994 electoral victory, the Rada voted overwhelmingly to suspend privatization, enacting a moratorium on concluding new lease-purchase agreements of medium- and large-scale firms. An unanticipated consequence was that when the moratorium was lifted in 1995, there was a burst in privatization activity owing to the more careful preparation of the firms waiting "in the pipeline." See Resolution of the Supreme Council of Ukraine, "On Perfection of the Privatization Mechanism in Ukraine and Intensifying Control of Its Conduct," 29 July 1994.

59. In December 1994, the Rada approved a "negative list" of around 6,000 medium- and large-scale enterprises exempt from privatization, of which some 5,414 were in the energy, transportation, and communications sectors. Others were schools, kindergartens, and other organizations subordinated to the Ministry of Education. There has been considerable movement in the number and composition of the list since then. For instance, on 23 February 1995, the cabinet expanded the list of such entities to 5,600. The parliamentary resolution on 3 March 1995, however, increased this number to 6,102. At the same time, the Rada approved another list of some 90 enterprises in defense, oil, and food industries

that would also be exempt. On 22 November 1996, the first list was expanded again, to 7,111. In early 1997, the list was reduced to 5,125. It was reduced considerably later that year, to 2,850, by removing educational institutions; health, cultural, and sports facilities; and catering firms. At the same time, 219 facilities in machine building, engineering, energy, and food processing industries were added. A lot is at stake in the listing, and the process has been intensely political.

60. See Ukrainian-European Policy and Legal Advice Centre, "On Privatization in Ukraine"; and International Monetary Fund, "Ukraine—Recent Economic Developments," IMF Staff Country Report no. 97/109 (October 1997), especially p. 23.

61. See Lidia Lyakh, "Enterprises in the Post-Privatization Period," *Ukrainian Economic Monitor*, vol. 3, no. 3 (10) (March 1996): 19–20; and Yves G. Van Frausum et al., "Privatization and Industrial Restructuring in Ukraine," *The Ukrainian Legal and Economic Bulletin*, vol. 4, no. 4 (April 1996): 15–27.

62. See Paul Hare et al., in Taras Kuzio, *Contemporary Ukraine* (Armonk, NY: M. E. Sharpe, 1998), p. 194.

63. The proportion of Ukraine's industrial production accounted for by monopolists has grown steadily, from 67 percent in 1990 to 78 percent in 1993, finally reaching 90 percent at the end of 1997. See "Big Monopolies Breaking into Many Smaller Ones," *IntelNews*, 21 January 1994, p. 4; and Anatoliy Revin, "Capital Markets: Who Is the Fairest of Them All?" *Kiyevskiye Vedomosti*, 12 February 1998, p. 9, FBIS-SOV-98-054 (original in Russian).

64. See Dr. Halyna Kozoriz, "Antimonopoly Legislation in Ukraine," *Ukrainian Legal and Economic Bulletin*, vol. 5, no. 5 (May 1997): 9–11.

65. See Gleb Vyshlinskiy, "The President Declared War on Officials," *Kiyevskiye Vedomosti*, 29 December 1997, p. 6, FBIS-SOV-98-013 (original in Russian).

66. See Igor Aksyonov, "How to Improve the Regulatory Conditions for Small Business," *Ukrainian Legal and Economic Bulletin* (April 1997): 9–11.

67. For observations at two points in time, see Kevin Manninen and David Snelbecker, "Obstacles to Doing Western Business in Ukraine," *Ukrainian Legal and Economic Bulletin* (April 1993): 20–30, and Myron Rabij, "Top Twenty Legal Impediments to Doing Business in Ukraine," *Ukrainian Legal and Economic Bulletin* (August–September 1996): 19–20.

68. See Roman Woronowycz, "Kuchma Administration Announces Program to Cut Regulations for Business," *Ukrainian Weekly*, 8 February 1998, p. 1.

69. The authors are grateful to Marek Dabrowski for providing this apt expression.

70. Tragically, in 1992–1994, everyone seemed to understand this except the Ukrainian authorities.

71. Volodymyr Zviglyanich, "Analysis: Stability and Reform Pose Challenges to New President," *Ukrainian Weekly*, 16 October 1994, p. 2.

72. The following events are chronicled in Taras Kuzio, *Ukraine: The Unfinished Revolution*, European Security Study no. 16 (London: Institute for European Defence and Strategic Studies, 1992), chap. 4, pp. 21–25.

73. See Alexei Sekarev, "Ukraine's Policy Structure," *RFE/RL Research Report*, vol. 1, no. 32 (14 August 1992): 60–63.

74. Entitled "Fundamentals of National Economic Policy" and authored principally by Oleksander Yemelyanov, chairman of President Kravchuk's "State Council," this program called for an immediate exit from the ruble zone, coupled with introduction of a new Ukrainian currency, the *hryvnya*. The lack of specific details hampered the Rada's enthusiastic adoption, which considered the program as "preliminary" and subject to further elaboration.

75. The principal author of the plan submitted to the IMF was the reformist minister of the economy, Volodymyr Lanoviy, who was sharply critical of Fokin's program. Lanoviy's alternative plan embraced monetary stabilization, sharp reductions in expenditures (especially for enterprise and consumer subsidies), tax system reform, reduced budget deficits, price liberalization, rapid privatization, and a freeing of external trade. It would not be too much to say that Ukraine was admitted to IMF membership largely on the strength of Lanoviy's personal credibility.

76. See D'Anieri, *Economic Interdependence in Ukrainian-Russian Relations*, chap. 5.

77. Both the new currency and the price liberalization in early 1992 were the handiwork of the young reform economist Volodymyr Lanoviy. Known in the West as the "Ukrainian Gaidar," Lanoviy served as deputy prime minister and minister of the economy until he was dismissed on 11 July 1992. See Thomas Gregory, "The Trembling Hand of Economic Reform," *East European Reporter* (September–October 1992): 32–34.

78. Fokin's resignation coincided with a parliamentary vote of no confidence in the Cabinet of Ministers on 30 September 1992. See Council of Advisors to the Rada of Ukraine, "Political Developments," 14 October 1992 (prepared by Laura Szkrybalo).

79. Alexander J. Motyl, *Dilemmas of Independence: Ukraine After Totalitarianism* (New York: Council on Foreign Relations Press, 1993).

80. See "Dream On," *Economist*, 17 October 1992, pp. 56–57.

81. See "Kuchma Outlines Recovery Plan," *Ukrainian Weekly*, 31 January 1993, p. 2.

82. See "Kuchma Granted Sweeping Powers for Six Months to Set Economy Right," *Ukrainian Weekly*, 22 November 1992, p. 1.

83. Prominent reformers in the new team included: Ihor Yukhnovsky, first deputy prime minister; Viktor Pynzenyk, deputy prime minister for economic reform and minister of the economy; Roman Shpek, minister of destatization of property and demonopolization of industry.

84. See Konstantin Vronsky, "Decrees Adopted by the Ukrainian Government in December 1992," *Kiev Legal and Economic Bulletin*, vol. 1, no. 2 (February 1993): 13–14.

85. Kuchma's program was ratified by the Rada on 7 February 1993. See Borys Klymenko, "The Rada Oks Kuchma Government's Plan for National Economic Policy," *Ukrainian Weekly*, 7 February 1993, p. 1.

86. See "Man of Iron," *Economist*, 26 December 1992–January 8, 1993, pp. 62–63.

87. See "Tough Enough," *Economist*, 13 March 1993, pp. 38–39.

88. See Marta Kolomayets, "Kuchma Supports Introduction of Emergency State in Ukraine," *Ukrainian Weekly*, 11 July 1993, p. 1.

89. Decree of the President of Ukraine, "On Urgent Measures for the Stabilization of the Economic and Political Situation in Ukraine," no. 215-93, 16 June 1993, translated and reprinted in the *Ukrainian Weekly*, 20 June 1993, p. 3.

90. The parliamentary elections were held at the end of March 1994, and the presidential elections in July 1994.

91. See Marta Kolomayets, "Kuchma Unveils New Measures to Speed Market-Oriented Reform," *Ukrainian Weekly*, 27 June 1993, p. 1.

92. See Council of Advisors to the Rada of Ukraine, "Update on Ukraine," no. 9, 29 September 1993 (prepared by Myron Wasylyk).

93. See Serhiy Dmytrychenko, "From Troubled Seas to the Storm Ahead: The Rada Waiting to Die Proves It Still Has Life," *IntelNews*, 26 December 1993, pp. 3–4.

94. See Roman Solchanyk, "Ukraine: A Year of Crisis," *RFE/RL Research Report*, vol. 3, no. 1 (7 January 1994).

95. See Marta Kolomayets, "Kravchuk Names Zviahilskiy Acting Prime Minister," *Ukrainian Weekly*, 26 September 1993, p. 4.

96. In addition to fueling inflation, the ongoing credit emissions had the effect of wiping out existing interenterprise debts as well as tax liabilities to the government, making it impossible to identify loss-making enterprises from among the others.

97. Editors of the *Economist* at the time facetiously referred to Zviahils'kyi's statement as "a breakthrough in economic thinking," 16 October 1993, p. 33.

98. Decree of the President of Ukraine, "On Additional Measures Concerning Currency Regulation," no. 502-93, 2 November 1993.

99. The official rate was raised to 7090 KBV per U.S. dollar as of 30 November 1993, and again to 12,610 on 1 January 1994, but this was still less than half the black market rate at that time.

100. Resolution of the Cabinet of Ministers of Ukraine, "On a Procedure for Implementing the Law of Ukraine 'On Amendments to the Decrees of the Cabinet of Ministers of Ukraine on Currency Regulation,'" 25 November 1993, and Resolution of the Cabinet of Ministers of Ukraine, "On Cancellation of Exemptions Granted to Enterprises and Organizations Regarding Sale of Hard Currency Revenues," 26 November 1993. These decrees canceled citizens' rights to maintain hard currency accounts abroad and canceled all previous exemptions from the standing requirement that 50 percent of all hard currency earnings be surrendered to the state at the official (i.e., undervalued) exchange rate.

101. Joint Resolution of the Cabinet of Ministers of Ukraine and the National Bank of Ukraine, "On Implementation of the Decree of the President of Ukraine of November 2, 1993, 'On Additional Measures Concerning Currency Regulation,'" no. 954, 24 November 1993. The four rates applied to different kinds of transactions: an official rate for all mandatory 50-percent hard currency surrenders, an "auction rate" set at twice the official rate, a noncash rate, and a cash rate that would apply to all street vendors and kiosks.

102. The customary definition of "hyperinflation" is monthly inflation in excess of 50 percent. See Philip Cagan, "The Monetary Dynamics of Hyperinflation," in Milton Friedman, ed., *Studies in the Quantity Theory of Money* (Chicago: University of Chicago Press, 1956).

103. Serhiy Dmytychenko, "The Parliamentary Week in Review," *IntelNews*, 20 December 1993, p. 3.

104. Official telegram, "To Crimean, Republican, and Regional [Oblast] Departments of the National Bank of Ukraine and Commercial Banks," 2 December 1993. The telegram was signed jointly by NBU governor Victor Yushchenko and Acting Prime Minister Yukhim Zviahils'kyi. Document in the authors' possession.

105. According to the telegram, any enterprise failing to return credits would have its hard currency accounts "raided" by the NBU.

106. This amounted to approximately $80 million at December 1993 exchange rates. See "Finance Ministry Ready to Pay Out KBV 23 tn.," *IntelNews*, 5 December 1993, p. 2.

107. See "The Rada Rejects Kravchuk Program," *IntelNews*, 24 December 1993, p. 1.

108. Without controls on credit emissions, policies designed to "insulate" the public from the necessary price adjustment would be doomed to fail. Indeed, in the last four months of 1993, credit emissions accelerated to a level 1.4 times faster than the rate of price increase, pushing Ukraine over the threshold into hyperinflation.

109. See Marta Kolomayets, "President Decrees Signal Return to Command Economy," *Ukrainian Weekly*, 7 November 1993, p. 1.

110. Estimates at the time were that over $20 billion of Ukrainian capital had escaped (or, rather, sought refuge) abroad. See the earlier section, "The Problem of Capital Flight" in this chapter.

111. Including electric energy, oil, gasoline, natural gas, coal, coke, nonferrous metals, grain, vegetable oil, cereals, sugar, textiles, and footwear. See *IntelNews*, "In Brief," 20 November 1993, p. 1.

112. See International Monetary Fund, *Ukraine*, IMF Economic Reviews 1994, no. 17 (Washington, DC: IMF, March 1995).

113. Address of the President of Ukraine to the Supreme Council of Ukraine of 11 October 1994. See "Shlyakhom radikalnykh ekonomichniykh reform," *Holos Ukraiiny*, 13 October 1994, p. 9, unofficial English translation of the Council of Advisors to the the Rada of Ukraine.

114. Address by Michel Camdessus, Managing Director of the International Monetary Fund at the G-7 Conference "Partnership for Economic Transformation in Ukraine," 27 October 1994, Winnipeg, Manitoba, Canada. Transcript in the authors' possession.

115. See Oleh Borsuk, "Kuchma's Economic Proposals—A Point-by-Point Abstract," *IntelNews*, 14 October 1994.

116. See Oleh Borsuk, "Karbovanets Rallies Against Gloomy Prospects," *IntelNews*, 21 October 1994.

117. See Resolution of the Supreme Council of Ukraine, "On Streamlining the Mechanism of Privatization in Ukraine and Strengthening Control over Its Implementation," 22 July 1994. The ban did not apply to small or medium-sized business or to housing privatization. However, the parliamentary resolution prohibited all sale-purchase agreements and those leasing agreements that would result in buyouts. Further, it did not suspend all privatization activities but temporarily

prevented sale-purchase agreements from being consummated. See Jannene MacNeil, "The Rada Halts Privatization," *IntelNews*, 31 July 1994, and Marta Kolomayets, "The Rada Suspends Privatization," *Ukrainian Weekly*, 7 August 1994, p. 2.
118. The ban was lifted on 11 December 1994. The list of objects not to be privatized consisted mainly of large enterprises in the transportation, communications, and energy sectors, as well as bread production and defense industries. See Marta Kolomayets, "The Rada Moves on Privatization," *Ukrainian Weekly*, 11 December 1994, p. 3.
119. See Taras Kuzio, *Ukraine Under Kuchma* (London: Macmillan, 1997): 142–144; Taras Kuzio, "After the Shock, the Therapy," *Transition* (28 July 1995): 38–40; and "Bank Chief Welcomes Marchuk's Appointment," FBIS-SOV-95-042, 2 March 1995.
120. For Kuchma's Economic Address to the Rada, see *Holos Ukraiiny*, 6 April 1995, pp. 3–4.
121. See the discussion on "Correction of Economic Reform" in Kuzio, *Ukraine Under Kuchma*, pp. 144–149.
122. See "Kuchma Issues Edict on Entrepreneurial Activity," Kiev, Radio Ukraine World Service, 17:00 GMT, 30 January 1995, FBIS-SOV-95-020 (original in Ukrainian).
123. See "Kiev Said Ready for Economic Integration with Russia," interview with Presidential Aide Oleksandr Razunko, Moscow INTERFAX News Service, 16:54 GMT, 1 March 1995, FBIS-SOV-95-041 (original in English).
124. See Law of Ukraine, "On Industrial-Financial Groups in Ukraine," 21 November 1995, and *Golos Ukrainy*, 21 May 1996, p. 8 (reprinted in English in FBIS-SOV-124-S [original in Russian]). See also "Political Update on Ukraine," *Ukrainian Legal and Economic Bulletin*, vol. 3, no. 12 (December 1995): 46.
125. A Russian-Ukrainian interstate agreement on basic principles for the establishment of FIGs was signed in July 1995.
126. See Michael Blackman, "An Analysis of Industrial Financial Groups in Ukraine," *Ukrainian Legal and Economic Bulletin* (November 1995), p. 11.
127. The "Law on Power," as it was called, had been introduced on 2 December 1994 and adopted in its first reading on 28 December. The second reading did not take place until April 1995, however, due to delaying tactics of the parliamentary left factions.
128. See Chrystyna Lapychak, "Showdown Yields Political Reform," *Transition*, vol. 1, no. 13 (28 July 1995): 3–7. See also "Political Reform," in Kuzio, *Ukraine Under Kuchma*, pp. 99–109.
129. One of the most significant aspects of the accord is the positioning of the presidential administration at the center of formulation and execution of economic policy and a concomitant decrease in the cabinet's role in the reform process. See "Some Aspects of the Constitutional Agreement Between the Supreme Council and the President," *Ukrainian Economic Monitor*, no. 2 (4) (1995): 20.
130. See Kuzio, *Ukraine Under Kuchma*, p. 109.
131. See "Marchuk Presents Economic Program," transcript of an Address to the Rada of 11 October 1995, Kiev, Radio Ukraine World Service, 19:15 GMT 11 October 1995, FBIS-SOV-95-198 (original in Ukrainian).

132. See Marta Kolomayets, "The Rada Approves Government Program," *Ukrainian Weekly*, 15 October 1995, p. 1.
133. See Danylo Yanevsky, "New Government Program Strikes a Discordant Note," *Transition*, 15 December 1995, pp. 56–58.
134. See Kuzio, *Ukraine Under Kuchma*, p. 148.
135. See Marta Kolomayets, "The Rada Approves Government Program," *Ukrainian Weekly*, 15 October 1995, p. 18.
136. See "Government to Reduce Credits to Industry," *IntelNews*, 27 November 1995.
137. See Hreohoriy Larin, "Nonpayment Crisis Climaxes in a Chain of Bankruptcies," Ukrainian Press Agency, *UpressA*, 7 August 1995.
138. Extended in April 1995, the value of the Standby Loan with the IMF was approximately $1.5 billion.
139. See Hrant Bagratian and Emine Gürgen, *Payments Arrears in the Gas and Electric Power Sectors of the Russian Federation and Ukraine*, IMF Working Paper WP/97/162 (Washington, DC: International Monetary Fund, 1997).
140. Marchuk was formally discharged due to his violation of the law barring government ministers from concurrently serving as members of the Rada. This was a pretext, however, as some 60 other members of the administration also served in the Rada. See "Marchuk Fired Due to Shortcomings in Performance of Cabinet," Moscow INTERFAX, 17:06 GMT, 27 May 1996, FBIS-SOV-96-103 (original in English).
141. See "Marchuk Dismissal Seen Based on Rivalry with Kuchma," Moscow, *Pravda*, 30 May 1996, p. 1, FBIS-SOV-96-106 (original in Russian), and Chrystyna Lapychak, "Power Struggle in Ukraine Reaches Climax with Prime Minister's Dismissal," *OMRI Analytical Brief*, no. 133, 28 May 1996.
142. See Marta Kolomayets, "Kuchma Reaffirms Determination to Stay the Course on Reforms," *Ukrainian Weekly*, 7 April 1996, p. 1.
143. See "New PM Lazarenko Profiled: Statement," Kiev, *Uryadoviy Kur'er*, 30 May 1996, p. 1, FBIS-SOV-96-140-S (original in Ukrainian).
144. "IMF Warns About Consequences of Delayed Budget Approval," Moscow INTERFAX, 17:04 GMT, 28 January 1997, FBIS-SOV-97-019 (original in English). After 1 July 1997, another $3 billion in economic reform loans would be withdrawn. See Roman Woronowycz, "The Rada Passes 1997 Budget After Seven Months of Wrangling," *Ukrainian Weekly*, 6 July 1997, p. 1.
145. See Roman Woronowycz, "Kuchma Removes Lazarenko as Prime Minister," *Ukrainian Weekly*, 22 June 1997, p. 1.
146. See Taras Kuzio, "Ukraine Changes Its Prime Minister—Again," *Oxford Analytica*, East Europe Policy Brief, 4 July 1997.
147. In December 1998, Lazarenko was arrested in Switzerland, accused of money laundering and traveling under a false passport. See Charles Clover, "Swiss Investigate the Profits from Unaccountable Ukrainian Gas Trading," *Financial Times*, 9 December 1998, and Vitaliy Sych, "Lazarenko Faces Trial in Geneva," *Kyiv Post*, 8 December 1998.
148. See Olena Yashchenko, "Pustovoitenko Wins Premiership," *Eastern Economist*, vol. 4, no. 26 (182) (21 July 1997): 1.

149. See Olena Yashchenko, "Profiles in Politics: Valeriy Pustovoitenko—The Compromise Candidate," *Eastern Economist*, vol. 4, no. 26 (182) (21 July 1997): 11.

150. See Economist Intelligence Unit, *Ukraine Country Forecast—3rd Quarter 1998*.

151. The decree was issued pursuant to Article 33 of the "Law on Budget System," which permits the president to order proportional cuts in the event of revenue deficiencies. The decree does not explicitly identify a target deficit level. See Decree of the President of Ukraine, "On Cutting Expenditures for the State Budget of Ukraine for 1998," no. 860-98, 8 August 1998.

152. The majority of cuts were made in just two areas: Chernobyl relief (–43 percent) and aid to local governments (–50 percent). Other expenditures were reduced an average of –12 percent; however, some of the cuts, though minor in magnitude, were painful: Employment Fund (–34 percent); Innovation Fund (–38 percent); Health Care (–25 percent); Culture and Arts (–39 percent); Environmental Protection (–38 percent). Expenditures on Social Protection of the Population were left relatively unchanged. See Fiscal Analysis Office, Rada, "New Presidential Decree on 1998 State Budget," *Second Quarter 1998 Budget and Fiscal Report*, 21 August 1998, pp. 11–17.

153. See "Ukraine's Currency Bond Rating Downgraded," Moscow INTERFAX, 06:24 GMT, 10 September 1998, FBIS-SOV-98-253 (original in English).

154. Olena Bereslavska, "July's Market for Bonds of Internal Government Loan (BIGL)," *Ukrainian Economic Monitor*, no. 8 (37) (August 1998): 11–13.

155. With the blessing of the IMF, which sought to avoid another major default like Russia's, some of the debt service costs were to be "swallowed" by Ukraine's creditors.

156. See Katya Gorchinskaya, "Kuchma Veers from West's Reform Path," *Kyiv Post*, 20 November 1998.

157. See "Ukraine, Finances Ailing, May Print More Money," *New York Times*, 22 November 1998, p. 14.

158. See "Kuchma Addresses the Rada on Crisis," transcript of 19 November 1998 Extraordinary Address to the Rada, "On Measures for Stabilizing the Economy and Stimulating Production," Kyiv, *Uryadoviy Kur'er*, 21 November 1998, pp. 3–5, FBIS-SOV-98-336 (original in Ukrainian).

159. See Katya Gorchinskaya, "IMF, World Bank Freeze Ukraine Loans," *Kyiv Post*, 8 December 1998.

160. For a more thorough discussion, see Dominique Arel, "Ukraine: The Muddle Way," *Current History* (October 1998).

161. Ibid.

CHAPTER 7

1. *Christian Science Monitor*, December 10, 1991.

2. See Paul D'Anieri, "International Cooperation Between Unequal Partners: The Emergence of Bilateralism in the Former Soviet Union," *International Politics*, vol. 34, no. 4 (December 1997): 417–448.

3. See Paul D'Anieri, "Nationalism and International Politics: Identity and Sovereignty in the Russian-Ukrainian Conflict," *Nationalism and Ethnic Politics*, vol. 3, no. 2 (Summer 1997): 1–28.

4. Steven J. Woehrel, "Political-Economic Assessments: Ukraine," in Richard F. Kaufman and John P. Hardt, eds., *The Former Soviet Union in Transition* (Armonk, NY: M. E. Sharpe, 1993).

5. This paragraph is based on Karen Dawisha and Bruce Parrott, *Russia and the New States of Eurasia* (New York: Cambridge University Press, 1994).

6. Alexander Motyl makes a similar argument, contending that given the chaotic nature of economies in the region, larger units of economic administration do not make sense. See Alexander J. Motyl, *Dilemmas of Independence: Ukraine After Totalitarianism* (New York: Council on Foreign Relations Press, 1993), pp. 132–133.

7. INTERFAX, 4 May 1992, translated in FBIS-SOV-92-87, 5 May 1992.

8. Mykhaylo Stasiuk, "Nashi vikhy," *Derzhavnist'*, no. 2 (February 1993): 14.

9. "L. Kravchuk's Report Was a Bombshell," *Komsomolskaya Pravda*, 26 March 1992, pp. 1–2, translated in FBIS-SOV-92-060, 27 March 1992, p. 54. For a critique of the plan, see Mikhail Leontyev, "Couponization at a Faster Rate: The First Concept of Ukrainian Economic Reform," *Nezavisimaya Gazeta*, 1 April 1992, pp. 1, 4, translated in FBIS-USR-92-045, 22 April 1992, pp. 45–47.

10. Woehrel, "Political-Economic Assessments," pp. 966–967; "L. Kravchuk's Report," pp. 54–55.

11. "L. Kravchuk's Report," p. 55.

12. Ukraine's nuclear policy receives more attention in the following chapter. Here, we provide an overview sufficient to demonstrate the problems it caused for relations with the United States and Russia.

13. The crucial role of sovereignty in Ukraine's security policy is discussed in Ustina Markus, "Foreign Policy as a Security Tool," *Transition* (28 July 1995): 12–17, and in Sherman W. Garnett, "The Sources and Conduct of Ukrainian Nuclear Policy," in George Quester, ed., *The Nuclear Challenge in Russia and the New States of Eurasia* (Armonk, NY: M. E. Sharpe, 1995).

14. Jack Snyder, "Containing Post-Soviet Nationalism: International Substitutes for Impotent States," National Council for Soviet and East European Research, contract no. 806-11, 6 July 1992, pp. 33–34, cited in Jason Ellis, "The 'Ukrainian Dilemma' and U.S. Foreign Policy," *European Security*, vol. 3, no. 2 (Summer 1994): 266–267.

15. Quoted in Bohdan Nahaylo, "The Shaping of Ukrainian Attitudes Toward Nuclear Arms," *Radio Free Europe/Radio Liberty Research Report* (19 February 1993): 25.

16. "Kravchuk: Yeltsin Failed to Consult on Arms," *Izvestiya*, 4 February 1992, p. 2, translated in FBIS-SOV-92-025, 6 February 1992, p. 59.

17. See Kravchuk's statement in an interview with TASS, 26 November 1991, translated in FBIS-SOV-91-229, 27 November 1991, p. 59.

18. *Verkhovna Rada* statement on nuclear weapons, Radio Kyiv, 25 October 1991, quoted in Nahaylo, "The Shaping of Ukrainian Attitudes," p. 28.

19. *Arms Control Today*, June 1992, pp. 34–36, cited in Nahaylo, "The Shaping of Ukrainian Attitudes," p. 36. For a Russian view, see Sergei Rogov, "Military

Interests and the Interests of the Military," in Stephen Sestanovich, ed., *Rethinking Russia's National Interest* (Washington, DC: Center for Strategic and International Studies, 1994), p. 71.

20. These problems are discussed in detail in Oles M. Smolansky, "Ukraine's Quest for Independence: The Fuel Factor," *Europe-Asia Studies,* vol. 47, no. 1 (1995): 67–90. On the energy situation in general, see Leslie Dienes, "Energy, Minerals, and Economic Policy," in I. S. Koropeckyj, ed., *The Ukrainian Economy: Achievements, Problems, Challenges* (Cambridge: Harvard Ukrainian Research Institute, 1992); Leslie Dienes, Istvan Dobozi, and Marian Radezki, *Energy and Economic Reform in the Former Soviet Union* (New York: St. Martin's Press, 1994); and *PlanEcon Report,* 15 September 1992, pp. 16, 21.

21. The linkage was made explicit by the Russian ambassador to Ukraine, Leonid Smolyakov, in a press conference on 5 February 1993 and was repeated by Deputy Prime Minister Alexandr Shokin on 8 February, *RFE/RL Daily Report,* 9 and 10 February 1993.

22. *RFE/RL Daily Report,* 22 February 1993. The close ties between Gazprom and the Yeltsin administration were solidified in late 1993 when Gazprom director Viktor Chernomyrdin was named prime minister.

23. Quoted by Reuters, 6 September 1993, in John Morrison, "Pereyaslav and After: The Russian-Ukrainian Relationship," *International Affairs,* vol. 69, no. 4 (1993): 695.

24. For an example of mainstream Ukrainian attitudes toward Russian pressure on energy, see Serhiy Lavreniuk, "Iadernoi zbroi vzhe nema: Mozhe ne buty i hazoprovodiv," *Holos Ukraiiny,* 12 March 1994, p. 2.

25. The agreement and its annex are reprinted in John W. R. Lepingwell, "The Trilateral Agreement on Nuclear Weapons," *RFE/RL Research Report,* vol. 3, no. 4 (28 January 1994): 14–15.

26. Zbigniew Brzezinski, "The Premature Partnership," *Foreign Affairs,* vol. 73, no. 2 (March–April 1994): 80.

27. "Dealing with Ukraine's Gas Arrears," *IMF Survey,* 1 July 1996, p. 227.

28. *Reuters,* 8 February 1996.

29. See D'Anieri, *Economic Interdependence in Ukrainian-Russian Relations* (Albany: State University of New York Press, 1999), chaps. 4 and 5.

30. Volodymyr Diukov, "Shchob vyity z enerhetichnoi kryzy," *Polityka i Chas,* no. 5 (May 1996): 38.

31. O. S. Samodurov, "Z nashym stratehichnym partnerom," *Polityka i Chas,* no. 2 (February 1996): 37. Samodurov was head of the Administration for Bilateral Relations with the Russian Federation at the Ukrainian Ministry of International Economic Relations and Trade.

32. Quoted in *Trud,* 4 November 1994, in FBIS-SOV-94-215, 7 November 1994, p. 2.

33. On bilateralism, see Paul D'Anieri, "International Cooperation Between Unequal Partners."

34. *Financial Times,* 28 May 1997.

35. *Los Angeles Times,* 1 June 1997.

36. President Kuchma expressed this fear following a meeting with European Commission president Jaques Santer on 16 October 1998. See *RFE/RL Newsline,* vol. 2, no. 202, pt. 2, 19 October 1998.

CHAPTER 8

1. See Charles Tilly, "War Making and State Making as Organized Crime," in Peter Evans, Dieterich Rueschmeyer, and Theda Skocpol, eds., *Bringing the State Back In* (Cambridge: Cambridge University Press, 1985); and Charles Tilly, *Coercion, Capital and European States, a.d. 990–1990* (London: Blackwell, 1990).

2. See the concise literature review in Dale R. Herspring, *Russian Civil-Military Relations* (Bloomington: Indiana University Press), 1996, pp. xvi–xx; Roman Kolkowicz, *The Soviet Military and the Communist Party* (Princeton: Princeton University Press, 1967); and Samuel P. Huntington, *The Soldier and the State* (New York: Vintage, 1964).

3. According to the widely used definition that civilian control equals a civilian defense minister, of course, this statement is not true. This indicator, however, is extremely narrow and tells us nothing about the actual processes that determine who controls the armed forces. The issue of civilian control is discussed in more depth later in this chapter.

4. This period is discussed in some detail in Taras Kuzio, "Civil-Military Relations in Ukraine, 1989–1991," *Armed Forces and Society* (Fall 1995): 25–48. See also Andrea Chandler, "Statebuilding and Political Priorities in Post-Soviet Ukraine: The Role of the Military," *Armed Forces and Society* (Summer 1996): 580–581.

5. Bohdan Nahaylo, "The Shaping of Ukrainian Attitudes Towards Nuclear Weapons," *RFE/RL Research Report,* vol. 2, no. 8 (19 February 1993): 23.

6. "Given Ukraine's history of coerced and forced annexation, it is hardly surprising that on the day Ukraine's leaders declared absolute sovereignty and full independence from Moscow, they simultaneously moved to create an armed force capable of defending the new state" (Karen Dawisha and Bruce Parrott, *Russia and the New States of Eurasia* [New York: Cambridge University Press, 1994], p. 245). Similarly, John Morrison states: "Ukraine's political elite has experienced the events of 1990–1993 as a replay of 1917–1920. It is this memory of military defeat which explains the absolute priority given to the creation of independent armed forces at independence" ("Pereyaslav and After: The Russian-Ukrainian Relationship," *International Affairs,* vol. 69, no. 4 [1993]: 680).

7. *Literaturna Ukraina,* 29 August 1991.

8. *RFE/RL Daily Report,* 17 September 1991.

9. Chandler, "Statebuilding and Political Priorities," pp. 580–581.

10. Russian television, 7 September 1991.

11. See Paul D'Anieri, *Economic Interdependence in Ukrainian-Russian Relations* (Albany: State University of New York Press, 1999), chap. 6.

12. See Chandler, "Statebuilding and Political Priorities," for further discussion of this role of the military.

13. Pavel K. Baev and Tor Bukvoll, "Ukraine's Army Under Civilian Rule," *Jane's Intelligence Review* (January 1996).

14. Taras Kuzio, "Ukrainian Security Planning: Constraints and Options," in Roy Allison and Christoph Bluth, eds., *Security Dilemmas in Russia and Eurasia* (London: Royal Institute of International Affairs, 1998), p. 143.

15. Kuzio, "Ukrainian Security Planning," pp. 141–142.

16. See Taras Kuzio, "Crisis and Reform in Ukraine—Part 2," *Jane's Intelligence Review* (November 1996): 496–497.

17. Vyacheslav Pikhovshek and Christopher Pett, "Transformation of the Ukrainain Armed Forces," *NATO Review*, vol. 42, no. 5 (October 1994): 21–25.

18. "When Applied to Crimea, the Word 'Outpost' Sounds Like the Echo of the Cold War" (interview with Oleksandr Kuzmuk), *Krymskaya Pravda*, 5 August 1998, pp. 1–2, in *FBIS Daily Report*, Central Eurasia, 26 August 1998.

19. These figures are from Taras Kuzio, "Crisis and Reform in Ukraine—Part 1," *Jane's Intelligence Review* (October 1996): 448–450; and Kuzio, "Ukrainian Security Planning," pp. 134–141.

20. "Ukrainian Minister Warns Against Budget Cuts," *Jane's Defence Weekly*, 2 September 1998.

21. Kuzio, "Crisis and Reform in Ukraine: Part 1," p. 449.

22. ITAR-TASS news agency, 23 November 1993.

23. Polls by Ukrainian Center for Independent Economic and Political Research in 1996, in the possession of the authors.

24. *Jane's Defence Weekly*, 3 June 1998.

25. Clifford Gaddy, *The Price of the Past: Russia's Struggle with the Legacy of a Militarized Economy* (Washington, DC: Brookings Institution Press, 1996), p. 18.

26. Ustina Markus, "Russia Alarmed over Ukrainian Arms Sales," *Jane's Intelligence Review* (July 1996): 292.

27. "Dumping Arms," *Defense and Foreign Affairs Strategic Policy* (May 1996): 18.

28. See Taras Kuzio, "Ukraine's Arms Sales Continue to Expand," *Jane's Intelligence Review* (March 1997): 108.

29. "Ukraine's International Arms Trading," *Foreign Report*, 15 August 1996.

30. Kuzio, "Ukraine's Arms Sales Continue to Expand."

31. Piotr Butowski, "An-70 Will Be Built Without Western Orders," *Jane's Defence Weekly*, 26 August 1998.

32. Craig Couvault, "Zenit Destroys 12 Globalstars; Failure Threatens Sea Launch," *Aviation Week and Space Technology*, 14 September 1998, p. 60.

33. "Illegal Arms Sales Uncovered in Ukraine," *Jane's Defence Weekly*, 3 June 1998.

34. Markus, "Russia Alarmed over Ukrainian Arms Sales," p. 292.

35. Jon Elster, Claus Offe, and Ulrich K. Preuss, *Institutional Design in Post-Communist Societies: Rebuilding the Ship at Sea* (New York: Cambridge University Press, 1998), p. 6.

36. Ibid.

37. Baev and Bukvoll, "Ukraine's Army Under Civilian Rule," pp. 8ff.

38. Ibid.

39. Ibid.

40. C. J. Dick, *The Military Doctrine of Ukraine* (Fort Leavenworth, KS: Foreign Military Studies Office, 1993), p. 7.

41. See Paul D'Anieri, "The Mitigation of Ethnic Conflict in Ukraine," paper presented at the Annual Meeting of the American Political Science Association, Boston, 31 August–3 September 1998.
42. *Kyivskye Novosti*, 15 May 1998, p. 1, translated in *FBIS Daily Report*, Central Eurasia, 22 May 1998.

CHAPTER 9

1. Paul D'Anieri, "The Mitigation of Ethnic Conflict in Ukraine: The Mysterious Case of the State That Didn't Collapse," paper presented at the Annual Meeting of the American Political Science Association, Boston, 31 August–3 September 1998. See also Albert O. Hirschman, *Exit, Voice, and Loyalty* (Cambridge: Harvard University Press, 1970).

Bibliography of Secondary Sources

GENERAL

Magosci, Paul R. *A History of Ukraine* (Toronto, Buffalo, and London: University of Toronto Press, 1996).
Saunders, David. "Russia and Ukraine Under Alexander II: The Valuev Edict of 1863." *International History Review*, vol. 17, no. 1 (February 1995), pp. 23–50.
_____. "Russia's Ukrainian Policy (1847–1905): A Demographic Approach." *European History Quarterly*, vol. 25, no. 2 (April 1995), pp. 181–208.
Subtelny, Orest. *Ukraine: A History.* Toronto: University of Toronto Press, 1988; revised edition, 1994.
Takack, Arthur. "In Search of Ukrainian National Identity, 1840–1921." *Ethnic and Racial Studies*, vol. 19, no. 3 (July 1996), pp. 640–659.
Velychenko, Stephen. "Empire Loyalism and Minority Nationalism in Great Britain and Imperial Russia, 1707–1914: Institutions, Law, and Nationality in Scotland and Ukraine." *Comparative Studies in Society and History*, vol. 39, no. 3 (July 1997), pp. 413–441.

CHAPTER 1:
THE DEMISE OF THE SOVIET UNION AND THE EMERGENCE OF INDEPENDENT UKRAINE

Dawson, Jane I. *Eco-Nationalism: Anti-Nuclear Activism and National Identity in Russia, Lithuania, and Ukraine.* Durham, NC: Duke University Press, 1996.
Duncan, Peter J.S. "Ukraine and the Ukrainians." Chapter 10 in Graham Smith, ed., *The Nationalities Question in the Post-Soviet States*, pp. 188–209. London and New York: Longman, 1996.
Holmes, Leslie. *Post-Communism: An Introduction.* Durham, NC: Duke University Press, 1997.
Karatnycky, Adrian. "Ukraine at the Crossroads." *Journal of Democracy*, vol. 6, no. 1 (January 1995), pp. 117–130.
_____. "The Ukraine Factor." *Foreign Affairs*, vol. 71, no. 3 (Summer 1992), pp. 90–107.

Krawchenko, Bohdan. "Ukraine: The Politics of Independence." In Ian Bremmer and Ray Taras, eds., *Nations and Politics in the Soviet Successor States*, pp. 75–98. Cambridge: Cambridge University Press, 1993.

Kuzio, Taras. "Ukraine: Coming to Terms with the Soviet Legacy." *Journal of Communist Studies and Transition Politics*, vol. 14, no. 4 (December 1998), pp. 1–27.

_____. "Ukraine: A Four-Pronged Transition." In Taras Kuzio, ed., *Contemporary Ukraine: Dynamics of Post-Soviet Transformation*, pp. 165–180. Armonk, NY: M. E. Sharpe, 1998.

_____. *Ukraine: The Unfinished Revolution*. European Security Studies 16. London: Institute for European Defence and Strategic Studies, 1992.

Kuzio, Taras, and Andrew Wilson. *Ukraine: Perestroika to Independence*. London: Macmillan, 1994.

Lapychak, Chrystyna. "Ukraine's Troubled Rebirth." *Current History*, vol. 92, no. 576 (October 1993), pp. 337–341.

Marples, David R. "'After the Putsch': Prospects for Independent Ukraine." *Nationalities Papers*, vol. 21, no. 2 (Fall 1993), pp. 35–46.

Motyl, Alexander J. *Dilemmas of Independence. Ukraine After Totalitarianism*. New York: Council on Foreign Relations, 1993.

Nahaylo, Bohdan. "The Birth of an Independent Ukraine." RL 420/91, *Report on the USSR*, vol. 3, no. 50 (13 December 1991).

_____. *The Ukrainian Resurgence*. London: Hurst, 1998.

Strayer, Robert. *Why Did the Soviet Union Collapse? Understanding Historical Change*. Armonk, NY: M. E. Sharpe, 1998.

Urban, George. "Ukraine: The Awakening." *National Interest*, no. 27 (Spring 1992), pp. 39–47.

CHAPTER 2: NATION BUILDING AND NATIONAL IDENTITY; AND CHAPTER 3: RELIGION, STATE, AND SOCIETY

Arel, Dominique, and Valeriy Khmelko. "The Russian Factor and Territorial Polarization in Ukraine." *Harriman Review*, vol. 9, nos. 1–2 (March 1996), pp. 81–91.

D'Anieri, Paul. "Nationalism and International Politics: Identity and Sovereignty in the Russian-Ukrainian Conflict." *Nationalism and Ethnic Politics*, vol. 3, no. 2 (Summer 1997), pp. 1–28.

Kuzio, Taras. "Borders, Symbolism, and Nation-State Building: Ukraine and Russia." *Geopolitics and International Boundaries*, vol. 2, no. 2 (Autumn 1997), pp. 36–56.

_____. "National Identity in Independent Ukraine: An Identity in Transition." *Nationalism and Ethnic Politics*, vol. 2, no. 4 (Winter 1996), pp. 582–608.

_____. *Ukraine: State and Nation-Building*. London: Routledge, 1998.

Kuzio, Taras, Paul D'Anieri, and Robert S. Kravchuk, eds. *State and Institution Building in Ukraine*. New York: St. Martin's Press, 1999.

Liber, George O. "Imagining Ukraine: Regional Differences and the Emergence of an Integrated State Identity, 1926–1994." *Nations and Nationalism*, vol. 4, pt. 2 (March 1998), pp. 187–206.

Ozhiganov, Edward. "The Crimean Republic: Rivalries for Control." In Alexei Arbatov et al., eds., *Managing Conflict in the Former Soviet Union: Russian and American Perspectives*, pp. 83–135. Cambridge: MIT Press, 1997.
Pirie, Paul S. "National Identity and Politics in Southern and Eastern Ukraine." *Europe-Asia Studies*, vol. 48, no. 7 (November 1996), pp. 1076–1104.
Prizel, Ilya. *National Identity and Foreign Policy. Nationalism and Leadership in Poland, Russia, and Ukraine.* Cambridge: Cambridge University Press, 1998.
_____. "Redefining Ethnic and Linguistic Boundaries in Ukraine: Indigenes, Settlers, and Russophone Ukrainians." Chapter 6 in Graham Smith et al., *Nation-Building in the Post-Soviet Borderlands: The Politics of National Identities*, pp. 119–138. Cambridge: Cambridge University Press, 1998.
Shulman, Stephen. "Competing Versus Complementary Identities: Ukrainian-Russian Relations and the Loyalties of Russians in Ukraine." *Nationalities Papers*, vol. 26, no. 4 (December 1998), pp. 599–614.
_____. "Cultures in Competition: Ukrainian Foreign Policy and the 'Cultural Threat from Abroad.'" *Europe-Asia Studies*, vol. 50, no. 2 (March 1998), pp. 287–303.
Wanner, Catherine. *Burden of Dreams: History and Identity in Post-Soviet Ukraine.* Pittsburgh: Pennsylvania State University Press, 1998.
Wilson, Andrew. *Ukrainian Nationalism in the 1990s: A Minority Faith.* Cambridge: Cambridge University Press, 1997.
Wilson, Andrew, and Valeriy Khmelko. "Regionalism and Ethnic and Linguistic Cleavages in Ukraine." In Taras Kuzio, ed., *Contemporary Ukraine: Dynamics of Post-Soviet Transformation*, pp. 60–80. Armonk, NY: M. E. Sharpe, 1998.
Zimmerman, William. "Is Ukraine a Political Community?" *Communist and Post-Communist Studies*, vol. 31, no. 1 (1998), pp. 43–55.

CHAPTER 4: UKRAINE'S WEAK STATE

Ash, Timothy N. "Land and Agricultural Reform in Ukraine." In Stephen Wegren, ed., *Land Reform in the Former Soviet Union and Eastern Europe*, pp. 62–86. London and New York: Routledge, 1998.
Balmaceda, Margarita M. "Gas, Oil, and the Linkages Between Domestic and Foreign Policies: The Case of Ukraine." *Europe-Asia Studies*, vol. 50, no. 2 (March 1998), pp. 257–286.
Chandler, Andrea. "State Building and Social Obligations in Post-Communist Systems: Assessing Change in Russia and Ukraine." *Canadian Slavonic Papers*, vol. 38, nos. 1–2 (March–June 1996), pp. 1–21.
Crowley, Stephen. "Between Class and Nation: Worker Politics in the New Ukraine." *Communist and Post-Communist Studies*, vol. 28, no. 1 (March 1995), pp. 43–69.
Dabrowski, Marek. "The Ukrainian Way to Hyperinflation." *Communist Economies and Economic Transformation*, vol. 6, no. 2 (June 1994), pp. 115–137.
Dabrowski, Marek, and Antczak Rafal. "Economic Transition in Russia, Ukraine and Belarus: A Comparative Perspective." In Bartlomiej Kaminski, ed.,

Economic Transition in Russia and the New States of Eurasia: The International Politics of Eurasia, vol. 8, pp. 42–80. Armonk, NY: M. E. Sharpe, 1996.

De Simone, Francisco Nadal. "Ukraine's New Currency and the Unstable Ruble Currency Area." *Communist Economies and Economic Transformation*, vol. 6, no. 1 (1994), pp. 99–112.

Hardt, John P., and Gretchen R. Rodkey. "Global Integration and the Convergence of Interests Among Key Actors in the West, Russia, Ukraine, and the Commonwealth of Independent States." In Bartolomiej Kaminski, ed., *Economic Transition in Russia and the New States of Eurasia: The International Politics of Eurasia*, vol. 8, pp. 357–385. Armonk, NY: M. E. Sharpe, 1996.

Havrylyshyn, O., Marcus Miller, and William Perrandin. "Deficits, Inflation, and the Political Economy of Ukraine." *Economic Policy*, no. 19 (December 1994), pp. 354–402.

Ishaq, Mohammed. "The Ukrainian Economy and the Process of Reform." *Communist Economies and Economic Transformation*, vol. 9, no. 4 (December 1997), pp. 501–517.

Johnson, Simon, and Oleg Ustenko. "Ukraine Slips into Hyperinflation." *RFE/RL Research Report*, vol. 2, no. 26 (25 June 1993).

Kaufmann, Daniel. "Market Liberalization in Ukraine: To Regain a Lost Pillar of Economic Reform." *Transition*, vol. 5, no. 7 (7 September 1994), pp. 1–3.

Kistersky, Leonid. "Economic Reasons for the Political Crisis in Ukraine." *Brown Journal of Foreign Affairs*, vol. 1, no. 1 (Winter 1993–1994), pp. 171–176.

Kohn, Melvin L., et al. "Social Structure and Personality Under Conditions of Radical Change: A Comparative Analysis of Poland and Ukraine." *American Sociological Review*, vol. 62, no. 4 (August 1997), pp. 614–638.

Kramer, Mark. "Blue-Collar Workers and the Post-Communist Transitions in Poland, Russia, and Ukraine." *Communist and Post-Communist Studies*, vol. 28, no. 1 (March 1995), pp. 3–11.

Krasnov, Gregory V., and Josef C. Brada. "Implicit Subsidies in Russian-Ukrainian Energy Trade." *Europe-Asia Studies*, vol. 49, no. 5 (July 1997), pp. 825–843.

Kubicek, Paul. "Post-Soviet Ukraine: In Search of a Constituency for Reform." *Journal of Communist Studies and Transition Politics*, vol. 13, no. 3 (September 1997), pp. 103–126.

Kushnirsky, Fyodr I. "Ukraine's Industrial Enterprise: Surviving Hard Times." *Comparative Economic Studies*, vol. 36, no. 4 (Winter 1994), pp. 21–39.

Kuzio, Taras. "After the Shock, the Therapy." *Transition*, vol. 1, no. 13 (28 July 1995).

_____. "Organised Crime and Corruption in Ukraine." *Jane's Intelligence Review*, vol. 9, no. 1 (January 1997).

_____. "Ukraine's Military Industrial Plan." *Jane's Intelligence Review*, vol. 5, no. 8 (August 1994).

Lapychak, Chrystyna. "Quarrels over Land Reform." *Transition*, vol. 1, no. 22 (1 December 1995).

Lazarenko, Volodymyr, and Volodymyr Zvihlianych. "Labor and Unemployment in the Ukrainian Economy." *Ukrainian Economic Review*, vol. 11, no. 3 (1996), pp. 42–52.

Miller, William L., Tatyana Koshechkina, and Ase Grodeland. "How Citizens Cope with Postcommunist Officials: Evidence from Focus Group Discussions in Ukraine and the Czech Republic." *Political Studies*, vol. 45, no. 3 (special issue, 1997), pp. 597–625.

Pleines, Heiko. "Ukraine's Organized Crime Is an Enduring Soviet Legacy." *Transition*, vol. 2, no. 5 (8 March 1996).

Rhodes, Mark. "Divisiveness and Doubt over Economic Reform." *Transition*, vol. 1, no. 6 (28 April 1995).

Rick, Simon. "Workers and Independence in Divided Ukraine." *Labour Focus on Eastern Europe*, no. 49 (Autumn 1994), pp. 18–34.

Rose, Richard. "Adaptation, Resilience, and Destitution: Alternative Responses to Transition in Ukraine." *Problems of Post-Communism*, vol. 42, no. 6 (November–December 1995), pp. 52–61.

Rosefielde, Steven. "Ukraine's Economic Recovery Potential to the Year 2000." *Journal of Ukrainian Studies*, vol. 21, nos. 1–2 (Summer–Winter 1996), pp. 165–190.

Sekarev, Alexei. "Ukraine's Crisis on the Basis of Vague Economic Policy." *Problems of Economic Transition*, vol. 37, no. 9 (1995), pp. 40–56.

Siedenberg, Axel, and Lutz Hoffmann, eds. *Ukraine at the Crossroads: Economic Reforms in International Perspective*. New York: Physica Verlag, 1999.

Smolansky, Oles M. "Ukraine's Quest for Independence: The Fuel Factor." *Europe-Asia Studies*, vol. 47, no. 1 (January–February 1995), pp. 67–90.

Tedstrom, John. "Ukraine: A Crash Course in Economic Transformation." *Comparative Economic Studies*, vol. 37, no. 4 (Winter 1996), pp. 49–67.

Varfolomeyev, Oleg. "Rival 'Clans' Mix Business, Politics, and Murder." *Transition*, vol. 3, no. 6 (4 April 1997).

Whitlock, Erik. "Ukrainian-Russian Trade: The Economics of Dependency." *RFE/RL Research Report*, vol. 2, no. 43 (29 October 1993).

Woehrel, Steven J. "Political-Economic Assessments: Ukraine." In Richard F. Kaufman and John P. Hardt, eds., *The Former Soviet Union in Transition*, pp. 961–970. Armonk, NY: M. E. Sharpe, 1993.

Zviglyanich, Volodymyr. "Public Perceptions of Economic Reform." *Transition*, vol. 1, no. 13 (28 July 1995).

CHAPTER 5:
POLITICS AND CIVIL SOCIETY

Birch, Sarah. "Electoral Systems, Campaign Strategies, and Vote Choice in the Ukrainian Parliamentary and Presidential Elections of 1994." *Political Studies*, vol. 46, no. 1 (March 1998), pp. 96–114.

———. "Nomenklatura Democratisation, Electoral Clientelism, and Party Formation in Post-Soviet Ukraine." *Democratization*, vol. 4, no. 4 (Winter 1997), pp. 40–62.

———. "The Ukrainian Parliamentary and Presidential Elections of 1994." *Electoral Studies*, vol. 14, no. 1 (March 1995), pp. 93–99.

Chudowsky, Victor. "The Ukrainian Party System." In John Micgiel, ed., *State and Nation-Building in East Central Europe: Contemporary Perspectives*, pp. 305–321. New York: Institute on East-Central Europe, 1996.
Kubicek, Paul. "Delegative Democracy in Russia and Ukraine." *Communist and Post-Communist Studies*, vol. 27, no. 4 (December 1994), pp. 423–441.
Kuzio, Taras. "Kravchuk to Kuchma: The 1994 Presidential Elections in Ukraine, 1994." *Journal of Communist Studies and Transition Politics*, vol. 12, no. 2 (June 1996), pp. 117–144.
_____. "The 1994 Parliamentary Election in Ukraine." *Journal of Communist Studies and Transition Politics*, vol. 11, no. 4 (December 1995), pp. 335–361.
_____. "Radical Nationalist Parties and Movements in Contemporary Ukraine Before and After Independence: The Right and Its Politics, 1989–1994." *Nationalities Papers*, vol. 25, no. 2 (June 1977), pp. 211–242.
_____. *Ukraine Under Kuchma: Political Reform, Economic Transformation, and Security Policy in Independent Ukraine*. London: Macmillan, 1997.
Motyl, Alexander J. *Dilemmas of Independence: Ukraine After Totalitarianism*. New York: Council on Foreign Policy, 1993.
Motyl, Alexander J., and Bohdan Krawchenko. "Ukraine: From Empire to Statehood." In Ian Bremmer and Ray Taras, eds., *New States, New Politics: Building the Post-Soviet Nations*, pp. 235–275. Cambridge: Cambridge University Press, 1997.
Prizel, Ilya. "Ukraine Between Proto-Democracy and 'Soft' Authoritarianism." In Karen Dawisha and Bruce Parrott, eds., *Democratic Changes and Authoritarian Reactions in Russia, Ukraine, Belarus, and Moldova*, pp. 330–369. Cambridge: Cambridge University Press, 1997.
Sakwa, Richard. "Democratic Change in Russia and Ukraine." *Demokratizatsiya*, vol. 1, no. 1 (Spring 1994), pp. 41–72.
Wilson, Andrew. "Parties and Presidents in Ukraine and Crimea, 1994." *Journal of Communist Studies and Transition Politics*, vol. 11, no. 4 (December 1995), pp. 362–371.
_____. "Ukraine: Two Presidents and Their Powers." In Ray Taras, ed., *Postcommunist Presidencies*, pp. 67–105. Cambridge: Cambridge University Press, 1997.
_____. "The Ukrainian Left: In Transition to Social Democracy or Still in Thrall to the USSR?" *Europe-Asia Studies*, vol. 49, no. 7 (November 1997), pp. 1293–1316.
Wilson, Andrew, and Artur Bilous. "Political Parties in Ukraine." *Europe-Asia Studies*, vol. 45, no. 4 (1993), pp. 693–703.
Wise, Charles R., and Trevor R. Brown. "The Consolidation of Democracy in Ukraine." *Democratization*, vol. 5, no. 1 (Spring 1998), pp. 116–137.
_____. "Laying the Foundation for Institutionalization of Democratic Parliaments in the Newly Independent States: The Case of Ukraine." *Journal of Legislative Studies*, vol. 2, no. 3 (Autumn 1996), pp. 216–244.

CHAPTER 6: ECONOMIC CRISIS AND REFORM

Bilokin, Serhiy. "The Kiev Patriarchate and the State." In Michael Bourdeaux, ed., *The Politics of Religion in Russia and the New States of Eurasia*. Vol. 3 of *The International Politics of Eurasia*, pp. 182–201. Armonk, NY: M. E. Sharpe, 1995.

BIBLIOGRAPHY OF SECONDARY SOURCES ■ 327

Bociurkiw, Bohdan. "Politics and Religion in Ukraine: The Orthodox and the Greek Catholics." In Michael Bourdeaux, ed., *The Politics of Religion in Russia and the New States of Eurasia*. Vol. 3 of *The International Politics of Eurasia*, pp. 131–162. Armonk, NY: M. E. Sharpe, 1995.

_____. "The Ukrainian Catholic Church in the USSR Under Gorbachev." *Problems of Communism*, vol. 36, no. 6 (November–December 1990), pp. 1–18.

_____. "The Ukrainian Greek Catholic Church in the Contemporary USSR." *Nationalities Papers*, vol. 20, no. 1 (Spring 1992), pp. 17–30.

Keleher, Serge. "Out of the Catacombs: The Greek-Catholic Church in Ukraine." *Religion in Communist Lands*, vol. 19, nos. 3–4 (Winter 1991), pp. 251–263.

Kuzio, Taras. "In Search of Unity and Autocephaly: Ukraine's Orthodox Churches." *Religion, State, and Society*, vol. 25, no. 4 (December 1997), pp. 393–415.

Lapychak, Chrystyna. "Rifts Among Ukraine's Orthodox Churches Inflame Public Passions." *Transition*, vol. 2, no. 7 (5 April 1996).

Markus, Vasyl. "Politics and Religion in Ukraine: In Search of a New Pluralistic Dimension." In Michael Bourdeaux, ed., *The Politics of Religion in Russia and the New States of Eurasia*. Vol. 3 of *The International Politics of Eurasia*, pp. 163–181. Armonk, NY: M. E. Sharpe, 1995.

Marples, David, and Ostap Skrypnyk. "Patriarch Mstyslav and the Revival of the Ukrainian Autocephalous Orthodox Church." RL 25/91, *Report on the USSR*, vol. 3, no. 2 (11 January 1991).

Martyniuk, Jaroslaw. "Religious Preferences in Five Urban Areas of Ukraine." *RFE/RL Research Report*, vol. 2, no. 15 (9 April 1993).

_____. "The State of the Orthodox Church in Ukraine." *RFE/RL Research Report*, vol. 3, no. 7 (18 February 1994).

Pospielovsky, Dmitri V. "The Russian Orthodox Church in the Post-Communist Commonwealth of Independent States (CIS)." *Modern Greek Studies Yearbook*, vol. 9 (1993), pp. 227–266.

Sutton, Jonathan. "Religious Education in Contemporary Ukraine: Some Courses of Study Analysed." *Religion, State, and Society*, vol. 22, no. 2 (June 1994), pp. 209–235, and vol. 23, no. 2 (June 1995), pp. 219–220.

CHAPTER 7: FOREIGN POLICY: FROM ISOLATION TO ENGAGEMENT

Albright, David E., and Semyen J.K. Appatov, eds. *Ukraine and European Security*. London and New York: St. Martin's Press, 1999.

Balmaceda, Margarita M. "The Role of Central Europe in Ukrainian Security." *East European Quarterly*, vol. 32, no. 3 (Fall 1998), pp. 335–351.

_____. "Ukraine, Russia, and European Security: Thinking Beyond NATO Expansion." *Problems of Post-Communism*, vol. 45, no. 1 (January–February 1998), pp. 21–29.

Bilinsky, Yaroslav. "Basic Factors in the Foreign Policy of Ukraine: The Impact of the Soviet Experience." In Frederick S. Starr, ed., *The Legacy of History in Russia and the New States of Eurasia*. Vol. 1 of *The International Politics of Eurasia*, pp. 171–192. Armonk, NY, and London: M. E. Sharpe, 1994.

328 ■ BIBLIOGRAPHY OF SECONDARY SOURCES

_____. *Endgame in NATO's Enlargement: The Baltic States and Ukraine.* Westport, CT: Praeger, 1999.

_____. "Ukraine, Russia, and the West: An Insecure Security Triangle." *Problems of Post-Communism,* vol. 44, no. 1 (January–February 1997), pp. 27–33.

Blank, Stephen. "Russia, Ukraine, and European Security." *European Security,* vol. 3, no. 1 (Spring 1994), pp. 182–207.

Brzezinski, Ian. "Polish-Ukrainian Relations: Europe's Neglected Strategic Axis." *Survival,* vol. 35, no. 3 (Autumn 1993), pp. 26–37.

Bukvoll, Tor. "Ukraine and NATO: The Politics of Soft Cooperation." *Security Dialogue,* vol. 28, no. 3 (September 1997), pp. 363–374.

Burant, Stephen R., and Voytek Zubek. "Eastern Europe's Old Memories and New Realities: Resurrecting the Polish-Lithuanian Union." *East European Politics and Societies,* vol. 7, no. 2 (Spring 1993), pp. 370–393.

Crow, Susan. "Russian Parliament Asserts Control over Sevastopol." *RFE/RL Research Report,* vol. 2, no. 31 (30 July 1993).

D'Anieri, Paul. "Dilemmas of Interdependence: Autonomy, Prosperity, and Sovereignty in Ukraine's Russia Policy." *Problems of Post-Communism,* vol. 44, no. 1 (January–February 1997), pp. 16–25.

_____. "Interdependence and Sovereignty in the Ukrainian-Russian Relationship." *European Security,* vol. 4, no. 4 (Winter 1995), pp. 603–621.

Ellis, Jason. "The 'Ukraine Dilemma' and U.S. Foreign Policy." *European Security,* vol. 3, no. 2 (Summer 1994), pp. 251–280.

Jung, Monika. "Looking Both Ways." *Transition,* vol. 1, no. 6 (28 April 1995).

Karaganov, Sergei. "Russia and the Slav Vicinity." In Vladimir Baranovsky, ed., *Russia and Europe: The Emerging Security Agenda,* pp. 289–300. Oxford: SIPRI and Oxford University Press, 1997.

Kharchenko, Ihor. "The New Ukraine-NATO Partnership." *NATO Review,* vol. 45, no. 5 (September–October 1997).

Kincade, William H., and Natalie Melnyczuk. "Eurasia Letter: Unneighborly Neighbors." *Foreign Policy,* no. 94 (Spring 1994), pp. 84–104.

Kremen, Vasily. "The East Slav Triangle." In Vladimir Baranovsky, ed., *Russia and Europe: The Emerging Security Agenda,* pp. 271–288. Oxford: SIPRI and Oxford University Press, 1997.

Kulinich, Nikolai A. "Ukraine in the New Geopolitical Environment: Issues of Regional and Subregional Security." In Adeed Dawisha and Karen Dawisha, eds., *The Making of Foreign Policy in Russia and the New States of Eurasia.* Vol. 4 of *The International Politics of Eurasia,* pp. 113–140. Armonk, NY, and London: M. E. Sharpe, 1995.

Kuzio, Taras. "The Baltics, Ukraine, and the Path to NATO." *Jane's Intelligence Review,* vol. 9, no. 7 (July 1997).

_____. "The Domestic Sources of Ukrainian Foreign Policy." In Theofil Kis, Irena Makaryk, Roman Weretelnyk, eds., *Towards a New Ukraine.* Vol. 1, *Ukraine and the New World Order, 1991–1996,* pp. 29–48. Ottawa: Chair of Ukrainian Studies, University of Ottawa, 1997.

_____. "The Domestic Sources of Ukrainian Security Policy." *Journal of Strategic Studies,* vol. 21, no. 4 (December 1998).

_____. "A Friend in Need: Kiev Woos Washington." *World Today,* vol. 52, no. 4 (April 1996), pp. 96–98.

BIBLIOGRAPHY OF SECONDARY SOURCES ■ 329

———. "NATO Enlargement: The View from the East." *European Security*, vol. 6, no. 1 (Spring 1997), pp. 48–62.
———. "Ukraine and the Expansion of NATO." *Jane's Intelligence Review*, vol. 7, no. 9 (September 1995).
———. "Ukraine and Its Future Security." *Jane's Intelligence Review*, vol. 4, no. 12 (December 1993).
———. "Ukraine and NATO: The Evolving Strategic Partnership." *Journal of Strategic Studies*, vol. 21, no. 2 (June 1998), pp. 1–30.
———. "Ukraine and the Yugoslav Conflict." *Nationalities Papers*, vol. 25, no. 3 (September 1997), pp. 587–600.
———. "Ukrainian Security Planning: Constraints and Options." In Roy Allison and Christoph Bluth, eds., *Security Dilemmas in Russia and Eurasia*, pp. 134–151. London: Royal Institute of International Affairs, 1998.
———. "A Way with Words: Keeping Kiev Secure." *World Today*, vol. 52, no. 12 (December 1996), pp. 317–319.
Larrabee, F. Stephen. "Ukraine's Balancing Act." *Survival*, vol. 38, no. 2 (Summer 1996), pp. 143–165.
Lester, Jeremy. "Russian Political Attitudes to Ukrainian Independence." *Journal of Post-Communist Studies and Transition Politics*, vol. 10, no. 2 (June 1994), pp. 193–233.
Malcolm, Neil. "The Foreign-Policy Decision Making Process in Ukraine." In *Post-Soviet Periphery: Ukraine, Transcaucasus, Central Asia, and the Russian Far East*, pp. 23–32. Tokyo: Japan Institute of International Affairs Paper no. 8, 19.
Morrison, John. "Pereyaslav and After: The Russian-Ukrainian Relationship." *International Affairs*, vol. 69, no. 4 (October 1993), pp. 677–704.
Nahaylo, Bohdan. "The Massandra Summit: Questions and Implications." *RFE/RL Research Report*, vol. 2, no. 37 (17 September 1993).
———. "Ukraine and Moldova: The View from Kiev." *RFE/RL Research Report*, vol. 1, no. 18 (1 May 1992).
Nordberg, Marc. "Domestic Factors Influencing Ukrainian Foreign Policy." *European Security*, vol. 7, no. 3 (Autumn 1998), pp. 63–91.
Pavliuk, Oleksandr. "Ukraine and Regional Cooperation in Central and Eastern Europe." *Security Dialogue*, vol. 28, no. 3 (September 1997), pp. 347–362.
———. "Ukrainian-Polish Relations: A Pillar of Regional Stability?" In Pal Dunay et al., *The Effects of Enlargement on Bilateral Relations in Central and Eastern Europe*, pp. 43–62. Paris: Institute for Security Studies, Western European Union, June 1997.
Pedchenko, Volodymyr. "Ukraine's Delicate Balancing Act." *Transitions*, vol. 4, no. 1 (June 1997).
Popadiuk, Roman. "Ukraine: The Security Fulcrum of Europe." *Strategic Forum*, no. 69 (April 1996), pp. 1–4.
Reisch, Alfred A. "Hungarian-Ukrainian Relations Continue to Develop." *RFE/RL Research Report*, vol. 3, no. 16 (16 April 1993).
Rumer, Eugene B. "Eurasia Letter: Will Ukraine Return to Russia?" *Foreign Policy*, no. 96 (Fall 1994), pp. 129–144, and no. 97 (Winter 1994–1995), pp. 178–181.
Shulman, Stephen. "Cultures in Competition: Ukrainian Foreign Policy and the 'Cultural Threat' from Abroad." *Europe-Asia Studies*, vol. 50, no. 2 (March 1998), pp. 287–303.

Snel, Gerard. "At the Border of European Security: The Case of Ukraine." In David Carlton, Paul Ingram, and Giancarlo Tenaglia, eds., *Rising Tension in Eastern Europe and the Former Soviet Union*, pp. 113–131. Aldershot: Dartmouth, 1996.

Socor, Vladimir. "Annexation of Bessarabia and Northern Bukovina Condemned by Romania." RL 256/91, *Report on the USSR*, vol. 3, no. 29 (19 July 1991).

_____. "Demirel Asserts Turkish Interests in Ukraine and Moldova." *RFE/RL Research Report*, vol. 3, no. 31 (12 August 1994).

Solchanyk, Roman. "The Crimean Imbroglio: Kiev and Moscow." *RFE/RL Research Report*, vol. 1, no. 40 (9 October 1992).

_____. "Russia, Ukraine, and the Imperial Legacy." *Post-Soviet Affairs*, vol. 9, no. 4 (October–December 1993), pp. 337–365.

_____. "Ukraine and the CIS: A Troubled Relationship." *RFE/RL Research Report*, vol. 2, no. 7 (12 February 1993).

_____. "Ukraine, the (Former) Center, Russia and 'Russia.'" *Studies in Comparative Communism*, vol. 25, no. 1 (March 1992), pp. 31–45.

_____. "Ukraine's Search for Security." *RFE/RL Research Report*, vol. 2, no. 21 (21 May 1993).

_____. "Ukrainian-Russian Summit at Dagomys." *RFE/RL Research Report*, vol. 1, no. 30 (24 July 1992).

Udovenko, Hennadiy. "European Stability and NATO Enlargement: Ukraine's Perspective." *NATO Review*, vol. 43, no. 6 (November 1995), pp. 15–18.

Umbach, Frank. "The Security of an Independent Ukraine." *Jane's Intelligence Review*, vol. 5, no. 3 (March 1994).

Vydrin, Dmitriy. "Ukraine and Russia." In Robert D. Blackwill and Sergei Karaganov, eds., *Damage Limitation or Crisis? Russia and the Outside World*, pp. 123–137. CSIA Studies in International Security no. 5. Cambridge: Center for Science and International Affairs, John F. Kennedy School of Government, and Washington and London: Brassey's, 1994.

Weydenthal, John B. "Polish-Ukrainian Rapprochement." *RFE/RL Research Report*, vol. 1, no. 9 (28 February 1992).

CHAPTER 8: UKRAINIAN DEFENSE POLICY AND THE TRANSFORMATION OF THE ARMED FORCES

Baev, Pavel, and Tor Bukvoll. "Ukraine's Army Under Civilian Rule." *Jane's Intelligence Review*, vol. 8, no. 1 (January 1996).

Clarke, Douglas L. "The Battle for the Black Sea Fleet." *RFE/RL Research Report*, vol. 1, no. 5 (31 January 1992).

Duncan, Andrew. "Ukraine's Forces Find That Change Is Good." *Jane's Intelligence Review*, vol. 9, no. 4 (April 1997).

Eberle, Sir James. "Russia and Ukraine—What to Do with the Black Sea Fleet?" *World Today*, vol. 48, nos. 8–9 (August–September 1992).

Foye, Stephen. "Civil-Military Tension in Ukraine." *RFE/RL Research Report*, vol. 3, no. 25 (18 June 1993).

Garnett, Sherman W. "The Sources and Conduct of Ukrainian Nuclear Policy." In George Quester, ed., *The Nuclear Challenge in Russia and the New States of Eurasia*. Vol. 6 of *The International Politics of Eurasia*, pp. 125–151. Armonk, NY, and London: M. E. Sharpe, 1996.
Grytsenko, Anatoliy S. *Civil-Military Relations in Ukraine: A System Emerging from Chaos*. Harmonie Paper 1. Groningen: Centre for European Security Studies, December 1997.
Izmalkov, Valerii. "Ukraine and Her Armed Forces: The Conditions and Process for Their Creation, Character, Structure, and Military Doctrine." *European Security*, vol. 2, no. 2 (Summer 1993), pp. 279–319.
Kuzio, Taras. "Border Troops of Ukraine." *Jane's Intelligence Review*, vol. 11, no. 3 (March 1999).
_____. "Civil-Military Relations in Ukraine, 1989–1991." *Armed Forces and Society*, vol. 22, no. 1 (Fall 1995), pp. 25–49.
_____. "Crisis and Reform in Ukraine—Part 1 and Part 2." *Jane's Intelligence Review*, vol. 8, nos. 10 and 11 (October and November 1996).
_____. "From Pariah to Partner: Ukraine and Nuclear Weapons." *Jane's Intelligence Review*, vol. 5, no. 5 (May 1994).
_____. "Nuclear Weapons and Military Policy in Independent Ukraine." *Harriman Institute Forum*, vol. 6, no. 9 (May 1993).
_____. "The Organization of Ukraine's Forces." *Jane's Intelligence Review*, vol. 8, no. 6 (June 1996).
_____. "The Security Service of Ukraine—A Transformed Ukrainian KGB?" *Jane's Intelligence Review*, vol. 5, no. 3 (March 1993).
_____. "Ukraine—A New Military Power?" *Jane's Intelligence Review*, vol. 4, no. 2 (February 1992).
_____. "Ukraine Revamps Its Internal Security Formations." *Jane's Intelligence Review*, vol. 10, no. 1 (January 1998).
_____. "Ukraine's 'Young Turks'—the Union of Ukrainian Officers." *Jane's Intelligence Review*, vol. 5, no. 1 (January 1993).
_____. "Ukrainian Armed Forces in Crisis." *Jane's Intelligence Review*, vol. 7, no. 7 (July 1995).
_____. "Ukrainian Civil-Military Relations and the Military Impact of the Ukrainian Economic Crisis." In Bruce Parrott, ed., *State Building and Military Power in Russia and the New States of Eurasia*. Vol. 5 of *The International Politics of Eurasia*, pp. 157–192. Armonk: M. E. Sharpe, 1995.
_____. "The Ukrainian National Guard." *Jane's Intelligence Review*, vol. 5, no. 5 (May 1993).
_____. "Ukrainian Paramilitaries." *Jane's Intelligence Review*, vol. 4, no. 12 (December 1992).
Lepingwell, John W.R. "The Black Sea Fleet Agreement: Progress or Empty Promises?" *RFE/RL Research Report*, vol. 3, no. 28 (9 July 1993).
_____. "Ukraine, Russia, and the Control of Nuclear Weapons." *RFE/RL Research Report*, vol. 3, no. 8 (19 February 1993).
_____. "Ukraine, Russia, and Nuclear Weapons: A Chronology." *RFE/RL Research Report*, vol. 3, no. 4 (28 January 1994).

332 ■ BIBLIOGRAPHY OF SECONDARY SOURCES

Mearsheimer, John J. "The Case for a Ukrainian Nuclear Deterrent." *Foreign Affairs*, vol. 72, no. 3 (Summer 1993), pp. 51–66.

Miller, Stephen E. "The Case Against a Ukrainian Nuclear Deterrent." *Foreign Affairs*, vol. 72, no. 3 (Summer 1993), pp. 67–80.

Nahaylo, Bohdan. "The Shaping of Ukrainian Attitudes Toward Nuclear Arms." *RFE/RL Research Report*, vol. 2, no. 8 (19 February 1993).

Oliynyk, Colonel Stephen D. "Emerging Post-Soviet Armies: The Case of the Ukraine." *Military Review*, vol. 74, no. 3 (March 1994), pp. 5–18.

Sauerwein, Brigitte. "Rich in Arms, Poor in Tradition: The Ukrainian Armed Forces." *International Defense Review*, vol. 26, no. 4 (1993), p. 317.

Sherr, James. "Russia-Ukraine Rapprochement? The Black Sea Fleet Accords." *Survival*, vol. 39, no. 3 (Autumn 1997), pp. 33–50.

Strekal, Oleg. "The New Secret Service." *Transition*, vol. 1, no. 10 (23 June 1995).

Tolstov, Serhij. "Ukraine's Nuclear Dilemma." *World Today*, vol. 49, no. 6 (June 1993), pp. 103–105.

Zaloga, Steven. "Armed Forces in Ukraine." *Jane's Intelligence Review*, vol. 4, no. 3 (March 1992).

Index

Administration for Bilateral Relations with CIS Countries, 225
Administration for Bilateral Relations with Russia, 225
Agrarian Party, 152, 154
Akcja Wisla (Action Vistula), 16
Alexander II, 70
Almond, Gabriel, 144
"Along the Road to Radical Economic Reform," 135, 195, 205
"Anti-Hyperinflation Program," 193–194
Anti-Monopoly Committee, 186
Antonov aircraft works, 250–251
Apathy, public political, 150–151
Arel, Dominique, 41, 56, 205
Arms sales, 249–250
Austria-Hungary, and Ukrainian identity, 53
Authoritarianism, 271
Autocephaly. *See* Ukrainian Autocephalous Orthodox Church (UAPT)
Autonomy, state, and special interests, 137–138

Baker, James, 211
Balcerowicz, Leszek, 169
Baltic republics, and civil society, 163
Bandera, Stepan, 14
Bank Ukraiina, 203
Belarus, 27, 35, 48, 270
 and Russian Orthodox Church, 74
 and Start I, 217, 218
 and suppression of Uniate Church in 1830s, 54
Belovezhskaya Pushcha meeting, 33, 34–36
Bilateralism, 225
Birch, Sarah, 129
Bizhan, Ivan, 243, 244

Black Sea Fleet and agreement, 43, 212–213, 219, 225, 226, 232, 254
Bojcun, Mark, 112
Boloto, 125, 159, 160
Brezhnev, Leonid, 21, 170
Brown, Trevor, 99–100, 116
Brubaker, Rogers, 13, 39, 40
Brzezinski, Zbigniew, 1, 222
Budgetary oversight, 122–123
 and local governance, 131–132
Budget Committee, 119
Budget deficit, 177–179
Budget System, Law on, 104, 126
Buffer, Ukraine as between Europe and Russia, 1, 63, 221–222, 231
Bunce, Valerie, 142–143
Burbulis, Gennadii, 35, 36
Bureaucracy, 90–96, 106
Burns, Nicholas, 224
Business climate, 167, 187–188
Buzduhan, Yuriy, 152–153
Byichkov, Victor, 30

Cabinet of Ministers
 functions of, 100–101
 ineffectiveness of, 109–110
 and legislative initiative, 118
Capacity, institutional, 95–97
 development of, 139
Cappelli, Ottorino, 161
Catherine the Great, 52, 70, 212
Chechnya, invasion of, 243, 244
Chernobyl disaster, 207
Chornovil, Viacheslav, 27, 59, 82, 159
 and nuclear weapons, 217, 238
Chudowsky, Victor, 155
Church of Grand Prince Volodymyr, 82
Civic national identity, 45, 47, 49, 64

Civil-military relations, 252–256
Civil Service of Ukraine, Law on the, 108
Civil service system, 106–109
Civil society
   and democratization, 144–147, 264, 265
   during Soviet regime, 141
   and guidelines for political behavior, 145
   and politics, 141–164
Clean Hands anticorruption initiative, 110
Clinton, Bill, 255
Coase, Ronald, 94
Collectivization, forced, 14
Collins, Paul, 96–97, 111–112
Commonwealth of Independent States (CIS), 10
   as a "civilized divorce," 37, 43, 209
   beginning of, 34–35, 36
   creation of, 30, 31, 33–34
   and Economic Union, 214
   and future relationship of Ukraine to, 231
   and interstate relations, 36–37, 280(n94)
   and militaries, 238, 258
   and nuclear weapons, 217, 238
   treaty written to meet Ukraine's needs, 209
Communist Party of Ukraine (KPU), 19, 23–24, 59, 148, 150
   and alliance with UPTs, 84–85
   and Declaration of Independence, 24–25
   national factions within, 21–22
   opposition to economic reform, 135–137
   and opposition to nation building, 65
   and role in Parliament, 123, 158–159
   Russian bias of, 141–142
   size and composition, 152, 161, 162
   and support for independence, 148, 213
   See also Nomenklatura
Competition policy, 186–187
"Concept of and Strategy for Economic Growth, 1999–2005," 202
Conciliatory Commission, 114
Congress of National Democratic Forces, 59, 82
Congress of Ukrainian Nationalists (KUN), 155
Congress of Ukrainian Intelligentsia, 56
Consolidation in transition to democracy, 143, 144
Constantinople Patriarch, backing of by pro-autocephaly churches, 85

Constituent Assembly, 41
Constitutional Court, 101–102
Corporate restructuring, failure of, 167
Corruption, 6–7, 140, 204, 268, 271, 294(n83)
   and arms sales, 251–252
   and fleeing of two prime ministers, 167
   in the military, 248–249, 251–252, 261
   rooting out of by Kuchma, 108, 110
Cossack uprising of 1648, 52
Council for Mutual Economic Assistance (COMECON), 173
Council of Cadres, 108, 294(n77)
Council of Defense, 238
Council of Europe, 7, 144
Council of Ministers, Law on, 110
Council of Regions, 128, 298(n137)
Council on Religious Affairs, 73, 83
Courts of Arbitrage, 101–102
Crimea
   religious practice in, 77
   Russian/Ukrainian debate over, 212–213
   separatist movement in, 57, 67, 257, 258, 268
Crimean Constitution of 1998, 65, 67
Crimean Tatar Khanate, 52
Crime rate, 140
Currency reform, 199, 200, 266

Dacko, Ivan, 86
Debt, foreign, 176, 184
Declaration of Economic Sovereignty of 1990, 24
Declaration of Independence, 24–31, 208
Declaration of Sovereignty of 1990, 24, 30, 207–208
Defense policy, 9, 233–261
   and security doctrine, 256–260
   See also Military
Deficit financing capabilities, 183–184
"Delegate democracies," 144
Demianov, Volodymyr, 134
Democratic reform, 3–4, 7
Democratization
   and civil society, 142–144, 265
   and Latin America, 142
   and South America, 4, 142
Deregulation, 187–188
Derzhavnyky (statists), 59–60, 158
Diomin, Oleh, 157
Donbas mining interests, 134, 192
Duverger, Maurice, 155, 156

INDEX ▪ 335

Eastern Ukraine, contrasted with Western Ukraine, 49–50
Ecology and Soviet policy in Ukraine, 37
Economic
  collapse after independence, 169–172
  crisis of 1998–9, 1, 203
  development and democratic reform, 3–4
  failures of Gorbachev, 20–21
  links to Ukrainian nationalism, 63, 70
  policy of Soviets to Ukraine, 37
  See also Economic reform; Economy; Institutional economics; Market economy
"Economic Growth 97," 183, 200–201
Economic reform, 1, 2, 9, 205
  and antimarket biases, 139
  and capacity of government to intervene, 95–97
  and currency, 199, 200, 266
  difficulty of establishing institutions for, 132–138
  and disaster of first four years after independence, 132
  and economic sovereignty, 189–190
  essence of, 166–167
  failures of, 3, 167, 266
  and the future, 269
  and gradualism, 168–169
  and Kravchuk's attempt to renew command economy, 194–195
  and Kravchuk's confused policies, 188–189
  and Kuchma's 1994 program, 133–137, 195–196, 204
  and Kuchma's 1995 "Correcting Reforms," 196–198
  and Kuchma's change of direction in 1998, 203
  and Kuchma's plan as Prime Minister, 190–192
  and Marchuk's program, 198–200
  political support for, 169, 204
  and "shadow economy," 172–173, 187, 200, 270, 306(n47)
  and "shock therapy," 168–169, 304(n4)
  and tax reform of 1997, 200–201
  and undermining by Rada, 204
  See also Economic; Economy; Institutional economics; Market economy

Economy
  and budget deficit, 177–179
  and business climate, 167, 187–188
  and capital flight, 175–176
  and competition policy, 186–187
  and deficit financing capabilities, 183–184
  and deregulation, 187–188
  dynamics of, 169–188
  and employment and wages, 176–177
  and expenditure control, 179
  and foreign debt, 176, 184
  and foreign investment, 175
  and funding for the military, 234, 241, 246–249, 261
  and inflation, 92, 135, 167, 177–179, 188, 190, 193–194
  performance of in 1997 and 1998, 202
  political factors in, 178
  and privatization, 167, 184–186, 196, 307–308(nn 57, 58, 59), 311–312(n117)
  and regional and local levels, 104
  "shadow," 172–173, 187, 200, 270, 306(n47)
  and tax system, 182–183
  and trade, 173–175
  Western prescriptions for, 2
  and world ranking of Ukraine, 166
  See also Economic; Economic reform; Institutional economics; Market economy
Education system and Ukrainian language, 54, 58
Election law of 1998, 156, 163
Elections
  of 1994, 123–124, 135, 144
  of 1998, 124–125, 135, 144, 201
  of 1999, 201–202, 270
Elster, Jon, 252
Employment and wages, 176–177
Energy supply, 218–219, 222, 224–225
Enterprise governance, 167, 184
Estonian Orthodox Church, 84, 85
Ethical norms of Ukrainian workers, 110
Ethnic cleansing, 14, 16
Ethnic groups
  acceptance of all in consensus of 1996 to 1998, 64
  history of, 11–12
  and national identity, 5–6, 45, 47, 49, 269
Europe, Ukrainian "return to," 63, 64, 142

European Union (EU)
  cancellation of credit, 203
  and future relationship to Ukraine,
    230–231, 267
  and the Ukraine, 222, 270
Evans, Peter, 95
Exchange rate policy, 193, 196
Executive system, 117
  development of, 113
  dual executive structure, 113–114
  Kuchma's extension of powers of,
    114–115
  and Law on Power, 114–115
  and semipresidential system, 99–100
  and signing of bills, 119
Exports, 174

Factions and parlimentarism, 154–161,
  163
Famine of 1932–3, 17, 21, 38, 68
Filaret, Metropolitan, 81, 82, 87
  and backing of Estonia, 84, 85
  and call for end of Moscow Patriarchate,
    84
Finance Ministry
  and local fiscal affairs, 104
  rebuilding of after independence, 106
Financial-Industrial Groups (FIGs), 196–197
Fiscal discipline, 92–93
Fokin, Vitold, 31, 132–133, 189, 190
Foreign borrowing, 176, 184
Foreign investment, 175
Foreign ministry, prior to independence, 40
Foreign policy, 9, 51, 60, 206–232
  and assertion of sovereignty, 206, 216,
    217–218
  balance-of-power view, 259
  before independence, 207–208
  and bilateralism, 225
  from Coup to the Commonwealth,
    208–209
  drafting of, 227–228
  future of, 229–232, 270
  and insistence on economic and political
    separation from Russia, 225
  and Kravchuk's economic plan for
    separation from USSR, 213–214
  and legal neutrality, 231
  and "neither East nor West" policy, 259
  and nonbloc status, 230, 231
  and opposition to CIS Economic Union,
    214

and place between East and West,
  229–232
and policy of Ukrainian isolation,
  213–215, 218
and recognition, 210–211, 213
and Russia, 206, 215–227
undermining of by economic problems,
  232, 266–267
and United States, 206, 215–224
See also Russia; United States
Formation of Local Government Bodies,
  Law on, 127
Formation of Local Power and Self-
  Governing Bodies, Law on, 104
"Freedom of Conscience and Religious
  Organizations, On," 73
Free speech, 146
Friendship Treaty, 226–227
Frischtak, Leila, 97, 98
"Fundamentals of National Economic
  Policy," 213
Future prospects, 262–272

Gaidar, Yegor, 35
Gargan, John, 96
Gazprom, 218–219, 316(n22)
Gellner, Ernest, 48
General Military Inspectorate, 255
Genocide, 14
Geographic boundaries and nation states,
  49, 282(n10)
Glasnost, 21, 42
Gorbachev, Michail, 20, 24, 29, 197
  and Belovezhskaya Puscha meeting,
    34–36
  economic failures of, 20–21, 42, 263
  lack of understanding of nationality
    problems, 39, 42–43
  and Referendum on Independence, 26,
    277–278(n41)
  role in demise of USSR, 10, 20–22, 31–34
  and Yeltsin, 24, 25, 32–34, 43, 209
Governmental institutions
  and economic decline, 91–93
  lack of building of during
    postindependence period, 93
  and "paradox of reforming state," 97–98
  and path dependent change, 111
Governmental system, 3, 98–113
  and administrative deficiencies, 106–109,
    138, 265
  as a unitary state, 102–105

and civil service, 106–109
and presidential system, 99–100
vestiges of Soviet regime, 98, 99, 106
and Western models of change, 111–113
Greek Catholic Church, 15
Green Party, 159
"Group of 239" KPU bloc, 25, 123
Group of Seven (G–7), and support for Kuchma's economic reform, 195
Gurfits, Eduard, 30

Haggard, Stephan, 95
Hague, Judy, 112
Hare, Paul, 186
Held, David, 95
Helsinki Movement in Ukraine, 20
Herspring, Dale, 236
Hesse, J.J., 112
Hetmanate, 11, 70
Himka, John-Paul, 54
Historical background
  decline of Soviet Union, 20–24
  prior to Gorbachev, 11–20
Historiography and nation building, 67–70
History, as a political issue, 67–70
History of Ukraine: Rus (Hrushevs'kyi), 69
Holos Ukraiiny, 29
Holovatiy, Serhiy, 109, 204, 226
Homo sovieticus policy, 38
Honadle, Beth, 96, 97
Hood, Christopher, 112
Horbulin, Volodymyr, 57, 62, 258
Hroch, Miroslav, 52–53
Hrushevs'kyi, Mykhailo, 31
  rehabilitation of, 68–69
  and Ukrainization, 55, 58
Hryvnya
  devaluation of, 176, 203
  introduction of, 199, 200
Huntington, Samuel, 143–144, 236
Hurenko, Stanislav, 24, 25, 277(n35)
Husar, Lubomyr, 80

Imports, 174
Independence, as a "civilized divorce," 37, 43, 209
Independence movement
  and Referendum of Independence, 25–31
  Ukrainian, 12, 22–23, 37, 45
Indigenization, 37–38, 53, 55
Individual initiative, de-emphasizing of, 105

Industrial-Financial Groups, Law on, 159
Industrial output, 91–2
Inflation, 92, 135, 167, 177–179, 188, 190, 193–194
Institutional economics
  and capacity to intervene, 95–97
  and contextual factors, 94–95
  theories of, 93–94
  See also Economic; Economic reform; Economy
Interests, special and group, and government capacity, 137–138
International Labor Organization (ILO), 177
International Monetary Fund (IMF), 7, 189
  cancellation of loans in 1998, 203
  and fiscal discipline under Kuchma, 92–93
  infusion of capital into Ukraine, 167
  and support for Kuchma's economic reform, 195
  and United States support of Ukraine, 222
Inter-Regional Bloc of Reforms (MRBR), 152
Interstate Economic Treaty, 174–175
Isolation and economic collapse, 218
Israel, Arturo, 90, 95, 97

Jackson, Robert, 49
Jews and removal from western Ukraine, 41, 53

Kas'ianov, H.V., 19
Kaskevych, Mykhailo, 198
Kazakhsthan and START I, 217, 218
Kebich, Vyacheslau, 33
Kharchenko, Ihor, 65
Khmelko, Valeriy, 50, 56
Kiser, Larry, 95
Kitschelt, Herbert, 162
Kliamkin, Igor, 34
Kolkowicz, Roman, 236
Korenizatsiia, 37–38
Kornai, János, 166
Korotchenya, Ivan, 43
Kozyrev, Andrei, 35
Kravchuk, Leonid, 277(n35)
  and "Anti-Hyperinflation Program," 193–194
  attempt to renew command economy, 194–195
  and "balance of power view" and NATO, 259

and Belovezhskaya Pushcha meeting, 34–36
and civil servants, 107–108
confused economic policies of, 134, 188–189, 191
and creation of "state church," 81, 82, 83, 87
and decree of military control, 238
defeat of, 127, 284(n44)
and demise of USSR, 31–34
and independence drive, 23, 25, 35–36
and interstate relations in CIS, 36–37
and local governance, 104–105
and Massandra Summit and energy agreement, 219, 228
and nation building, 59–62
and nuclear weapons ownership, 217
and "Party of Power," 137–138, 152
and political problems at time of independence, 40
and possible intervention by Soviet or Russian forces, 237
and Presidential Representatives, 126, 127, 292(n52), 297(n129)
and promotion of Ukrainian language, 60
and Referendum on Independence, 26–28, 29, 30–31, 277–278(n41)
and relationship to Gorbachev, 33–34
role in KPU, 24
and State Commission on Administrative Reform, 108–109, 136
and struggle with Kuchma, 191–192
and Yeltsin, 33–34, 37
Krawchenko, Bohdan, 108
Kremen', Vasyl, 61
Kubicek, Paul, 59–60, 144
Kuchma, Leonid, and 1995 "Correction Reforms," 196–198
Kuchma, Leonid
and arms sales, 250
and CIS as "civilized divorce," 43, 209
and civil servants, 108–109
and "Correcting Reforms" of 1995, 196–198
and deregulation, 187–188
economic change of direction in 1998, 203
economic plan as Prime Minister, 190–192
economic reform package of 1994, 133–137, 195–196, 204

and establishment of presidential dominance, 128
and fiscal discipline, 92–93
and Law on Power, 128–129
and local governance, 104–105
and nation building, 62–64
and "neither East nor West" view, 259–260
and presidential election of 1999, 200–201
and presidential power issues, 99–100
and rebuilding of relationship with Russia, 206
religious policies of, 83, 87
and restructuring of the military, 242, 245
and Russian policy, 224–227
and struggle with Kravchuk, 191–192
and view of Hrushevs'kyi, 69
Kuzio, Taras, 5, 50
Kuzmuk, Oleksandr, 246, 247
Kyivan Rus', 51, 69, 87
Kyiv as right home of Metropolinate, 71, 82
Kyiv Currency Exchange, 134
Kyiv International Institute of Sociology, 75

Language, 19, 54, 60, 64
books published in Ukrainian, 56, 57–58
continuation of Russian, 58, 61
nation destroying Soviet policy towards Ukrainian, 39
and Soviet promotion of Russian, 55, 264
transition towards Ukrainian, 62–63, 264
and trend toward bilingualism, 280(n102)
Ukrainian and the military, 58, 241
"Languages, On" Law, 24
Latin America, 2, 4, 142
Law. *See individual laws by name*
Lazarenko, Pavlo, 110, 200, 313(n147)
and Economic Growth '97, 200–201
Lebed, Mykola, 14
"Left" in Ukrainian politics, 152–153
Legislative function
budgetary oversight, 122–123
committee structure and staff, 119–121
development of, 116, 118–125
See also Verkhovna Rada
Legitimation, crisis of, 140
Liber, George, 38, 50
Liberalization in transition to democracy, 143

INDEX ■ 339

Linz, Juan J., 4, 49, 164, 282(n9)
Lisbon Protocol, 217–218
"Little Russian," 16–17, 52
  ideology, and Orthodox Church-Moscow Patriarch, 71–72
  and the New Soviet Man, 18
  policy in Ukraine, 38–39, 55
  and Shcherbyts'kyi era, 19–20
Local Councils, Law on, 105
Local governance, 104–105, 125–132, 297(n119)
Local Self-Government, Law on, 102–103, 125–126, 131
Lopata, Anatoliy, 244–245, 255
Lopatin, Vladimir, 237, 258
Lubachivsky, Myroslav, 78
Lukashenka, Aleksandr, 27
Lukianenko, Ivan, 30
Lukianenko, Levko, 27, 151
Luzhkov, Yuri, 227
L'viv University, 54

Makhno, Nestor, 12
Marchuk, Yevhen, 196, 198–200, 313(n140)
Market economy
  biases against, 139
  institutional basis of transition to, 90–96, 170
  See also Economic reform
Masol, Vitaliy, 132, 133, 196
Massandra Summit, 219, 228, 254
Media, mass, 144, 302(n32)
Migration, 55, 56
Military, 208, 233–261, 267
  and civilian control, 235, 236
  and corruption, 248–249, 251–252, 261
  and creation of CIS, 36
  and creation of independent forces, 234, 317(n6)
  decree asserting Ukrainian ownership and control of, 237–238
  and economic limits, 234, 241, 246–249
  establishment of and sovereignty, 237
  lack of interference in politics, 235, 236, 252–256, 260
  and NATO, 258–260
  and oath of allegiance, 238, 239, 240–241
  physical and moral crises in, 246–249
  professionalization of, 244, 245–246, 261
  and relations in Soviet Union, 236, 237
  and relations with civil sector, 252–256

  restructuring and reorienting, 234, 242–245
  role in state-building in Western Europe, 235
  and security doctrine, 256–260
  and Shmarov plan, 242–245, 255
  size and downsizing of, 233, 241–242
  and state building, 235, 239
  theoretical issues relative to, 235–236
  and threat, lack of, 237, 256–258
  Ukrainianization of, 240–241
  and Ukrainian language, 58, 241
  See also Defense policy; Nuclear weapons
Military-industrial complex, 234, 267
  and arms production, 249
  cooperation with Russia, 251
  restructuring of, 249–252
Ministry of Finance. *See* Finance Ministry
Ministry of International Economic Relations and Trade, 225
Molotov-Ribbentrop Pact, 12
Monopolies, 186–187, 197, 308(n63)
"Monopolization and Preventing Unfair Competition, On Containing," 186
Moroz, Oleksandr, 115, 135, 153, 156, 157–158
Morozov, Konstantin, 238, 254
Moscow as home of Metropolinate, 71, 82
Motyl, Alexander J., 5, 22
  and inheritance from Soviets in Ukraine, 40–41
  and "shock therapy," 168, 304(n4)
  and Ukrainian nation, 28
Mstyslav, Patriarch, 81, 82, 87
Musiaka, Viktor, 157
Myths, national, 67–70

Nation
  definition of, 48–49
  versus state, 11, 45, 47, 49–50
National Bank of Ukraine (NBU), 99–100, 189
  and currency reform, 199, 200, 266
  and exchange rate, 193
  and legislative initiative, 118
  reestablishment of government control over, 203
National Communist wing of the Communist Party, 59
National Democratic Party, 27, 71
National identity
  definition of, 48–49

development of, 4, 5–6, 264
and the future, 269
historical development of, 11–20, 37–38
lack of, 7, 45, 263–264
and nation building, 45–70
in pre-Russian times, 12
and religious belief, 74, 75
Soviet relationship to Ukrainian, 37–38
tsarist Russian suppression of, 52–53, 54–55
and Ukraine as a quasi-state, 41–42, 49
and Ukrainian SSR, 17, 18–19
and unity and democratization, 161
and western Ukraine, 29
National Institute of Strategic Studies, 29
Nationalism and Gorbachev, 20–22
National Security and Defense Council, 57, 62, 227, 258
National Security Concept of 1997, 64
Nation building. *See* National identity
Nation building
during Kravchuk era, 59–62
during Kuchma era, 62–64
historical legacy, 59
and the military, 235, 239
and national identity, 45–70
in post-Soviet Ukraine, 57–64
stages of, 50–51
and teaching of Ukrainian history, 68–70
NATO. *See* North Atlantic Treaty Organization
Nazarbayev, Nursultan, 33
Nazi regime, 14, 41
Nelson, Joan, 95
Nepotistic relations, 6–7
New Economic Policy, 37
Newland, Chester, 90, 112
New Soviet Man, 18, 43
New Ukraine bloc, 152
Nomenklatura
and cabinet ministries, 118
continued control by, 106, 107, 109, 110, 148, 189
distribution of property to, 186
Kravchuk's working with, 114
and streamlining of government of 1996, 200
support for initial separation from Russia, 213
North, Douglass C., 93
North Atlantic Treaty Organization (NATO), 221, 222, 226
and future relationship to Ukraine, 230–232
and Kuchma's "neither East nor West" view, 259–260
and military, 258–260
and the Ukraine, 222, 270
and Ukraine bilateral agreement, 229, 231
See also Partnership for Peace program
Norton, Peter, 116
Nuclear Nonproliferation Treaty, 221
Nuclear weapons
and demise of USSR, 42, 208, 237, 279(n88)
and Lisbon protocol, 217–218, 232
and Massandra Summit, 219, 228, 254
and "strategic forces," 238
and Trilateral Agreement of January 1994, 216–217
Ukraine as lawful owner of share, 216–217
Ukraine's assertion as nonnuclear state, 211, 216, 257
U.S./Russian reduction relative to, 216
Western fears relative to, 210–211, 215

Oath of allegiance, 238, 239, 240–241
Oblasts, central government supervision of, 102
Offe, Claus, 4, 5, 252
Oliynyk, Borys, 24, 277(n36)
Olson, David, 116
"On Measures to Accelerate Administrative Reform," 136
Organization for Economic Cooperation and Development (OECD), 107
Organization for Security and Cooperation in Europe (OSCE), 144
Organization of Ukrainian Nationalists (OUN), 13, 14, 16
Orthodox Church
competition between factions of, 72
and resistance to Communism, 74
three branches of, 71–72
See also Ukrainian Autocephalous Orthodox Church; Ukrainian Orthodox Church-Kyiv Patriarchate; Ukrainian Orthodox Church-Moscow Patriarch
Ostrom, Elinor, 95

"Paradox of reforming state," 97–98

Parliament. *See* Verkhovna Rada
Parliamentary politics, 147–165
Parlimentarism, Ukrainian, 154–161
Partnership for Peace program (NATO) and the military, 235
   Ukrainian participation in, 1, 222, 230
   See also North Atlantic Treaty Organization (NATO)
Party of Democratic Revival (PDVU), 152
Party of Economic Revival of the Crimea, 66–67
"Party of Power," 137–138, 152, 155
Party system, development of, 148–154
Paskhomenko, Sergei, 33
Pavlychko, Dmytro, 23–24
Peasant Party of Ukraine, 135, 154, 158–159
People's Democratic Party (NDPU), 64, 66–67, 152, 154
Perestroika, 42
Period zastoiy (period of stagnation), 170
Peter the Great, 52
Pivden'mash, 250, 251
Pliushch, Ivan, 24–25, 40
Pluralism, extreme, 143–144
Poland, 2–3, 12–13, 15–16, 41, 52, 53
Polish-Lithuanian Commonwealth, 52
Political culture, 145
Political institutions, development of, 5
Political parties, 123, 148–154, 265, 269–270
Political problems at time of Independence, 39–40
Politics. *See* Executive system; Legislative function; Nation building; State
Politics and the military, 235, 236, 252–256, 260
Pope, Roman Catholic, 16, 81
Power, Law on, 114–115, 118, 128–129
Presidential elections of 1999, 2
Presidential office. *See* Executive system
Presidential Representatives, 126, 127, 292(n52), 297(n129)
Presidium, 118, 123
Preuss, Ulrich, 252
Prime minister, 116, 132
Privatization, 167, 184–186, 196, 307(nn 57, 58, 59), 311–312(n117)
Privatization, Law on, 191
Progressive Socialist Party, 65, 159
Property rights, 94
Prosvita Society, 54
Pustovoitenko, Valeriy, 132, 201, 269
Putsch of 1991, 10, 23, 25, 35

Pye, Lucian, 145
Pynzenyk, Victor, 173

Quadruple transition, 3–6, 143

Raions, 102
Rationing coupons, 189, 190
Recognition, international, 210–211, 213
"Red Directors" group, 192, 194
Referendum on a "renewed (Soviet) federation" of 1991, 24, 27
Referendum on Independence of 1991, 25–31, 277(n40)
Regional governance, 104–105
Regionalism, 66–67, 126–127, 161–163
Religion, 14, 15, 73
   and destruction of indigenous Churches, 18
   high level of adherence to, 74–75
   and pluralism, 86–87, 264–265
   regional distribution of believers, 76–77
   revival of from late 1980s, 72, 74
   and state and society, 71–89
Representatives of the President of Ukraine, Law on, 126
   See also Presidential Representatives
Republican Party of Ukraine, 27
"Right" in Ukrainian politics, 152–153
Roeder, Philip, 113
Roman Catholic communities, 76
Romania, state treaty with, 225–226
Romaniuk, Volodymyr, 83
Rose, Aidan, 112
Ruble zone, Ukrainian departure from, 190, 214
Rudenko, Vasyl, 127–128
Rudnytsky, Lysiak, 41
Rueschemeyer, Dietrich, 95
Rukh. *See* Ukrainian Popular Movement
Russia
   as a military threat, 256–258, 260
   and CIS, 34, 36–37, 211, 279(n77), 280(n94)
   and control of nuclear weapons, 239
   and energy supply to Ukraine, 218–219, 222, 224–225, 306(n33)
   and failures compared with Ukraine, 3
   and formation of its military, 238–239
   and future foreign affairs with Ukraine, 229–232
   and historical control of Ukraine, 40, 52

and influence on Ukrainian culture, 58–59
language and culture of, 58–59, 61
as minority in Ukraine, 56
and nationhood, 11, 34
negative view of by nationalists, 60
and non-support of USSR, 43
and political ties with Ukraine, 33
and recognition of Ukraine, 211
and regional and ethnic differences, 3
and relationship to United States, 215–224
relations with Ukraine from 1994 on, 224–227
and Serbia, 221
as SFSR, 34
strategic partnership with Ukraine, 258, 260
tsarist, and Ukraine, 11–12
Ukrainian separation from, 213
and Western scholarly study, 2
Russian Federation, 18–19, 36, 74, 281(n112)
Russian Federation Defense Committee, 237
Russian Liberal Democratic Party, 154
Russian Orthodox Church
  as agent of Russian influence, 71
  and autonomous UPTs, 83–84
  forced union with Uniate Church, 14
  its claim to entire CIS territory, 80
  number of Ukrainian members, 75
  and Ukraine, 18
Russian-Ukrainian interstate agreement of May 1997, 40, 43
Rustow, Dankwart, 161

Sartori, Giovanni, 155
Saunders, David, 52, 54–55
Schedler, Andreas, 143
Secession, 161–162
Semenov, Viktor, 43
Semipresidential system, 99–100
Separatism, 66–67, 257, 258, 268
Sequencing, 6
Sevastopol, 212, 226, 227
"Shadow Economy," 172–173, 187, 200, 270, 306(n47)
Shakhrai, Sergei, 35
Shaposhnikov, Evgenii, 36, 237
Shcherbysts'kyi, Volodymyr, 12, 19–20
Shelest, Petro, 19
Shevchenko Scientific Society, 54

Shmarov, Valeriy, 242–245, 248, 253, 254, 255
Shukhevych, Yury, 154
Shushkevich, Stanislav, 31–32, 33, 34–35
Slavic union, idea and support for, 57, 211
Slipyj, Isoyf, 78
Smith, Anthony, 48
Smoliy, Valeriy, 68
Social Democrats, 152–153
Socialist opposition to economic reform, 135–137
Socialist Party of Ukraine (SPU), 25–26, 153, 158–159
Social scientific paradigms, Western, 7–8
Social welfare benefit programs, slashing of during Kuchma's regime, 93
Solidarity, 16
Sovereignty, 206, 216, 217–218, 226
Soviet legacy in Ukraine, 6–7, 10–11, 37–44
Speaker of Verkhovna Rada, 118
Stalin, Joseph
  and halt of indigenization campaign, 53
  and national homelands policy, 38
  and Ukrainian famine of 1932–3, 21, 53
  and United Nations seat for Ukraine, 207
Starovoitova, Galina, 33
Start II, 216, 217
START I treaty, 216, 217
State, 90–140, 271
State autonomy and special interests, 137–138
State Center of Employment, 176
State church, 60, 72, 81–83, 85
State Commission on Administrative Reform, 108–109, 136
State Committee on Problems of Development of Business Enterprise, 187
State Committee on Religious Affairs, 83
State-owned enterprises, subsidies to, 92
State Power and Local Government, Law on, 99, 100
State Property Fund, 191, 192
State versus nation, 11, 45, 47, 49–50
Stepan, Alfred, 4, 164
Stetsko, Yaroslav, 14
Strategic location, 1
Suny, Ronald, 39
Supreme Court, 100–101
Symonenko, Valentyn, 30
Synder, Jack, 217
Szporluk, Roman, 279(n77)

INDEX ■ 343

Talanchuk, Petro, 60
Tax system, 182–183, 200–201, 268–269, 271
Television, and Russian culture, 58–59
Tilly, Charles, 235
Tkachenko, Oleksandr, 135, 156–157
Tolochko, Petro, 67
Trade with CIS and Russia, 174–175
Transformation, 3
Transitional incompatibilities, 6
Transitions
  quadruple, 3–6
  Western social scientific theories of, 7–8
Treaty of Periaslav of 1654, 11, 31, 53, 82
Treaty of Riga of 1921, 12
Trilateral Agreement on Nuclear Weapons of January 1994, 216–217, 221
Tsarist Russia
  and suppression of Ukrainian identity, 52–53, 54–55
  and Ukraine, 11–12
Tuleyev, Aman, 70
Turshynsky, Hennadiy, 30
"Two-turnover test" of democratization, 144

Ukraine as Soviet Socialist Republic, 16–17
Ukrainian Academy of Public Administration (APA), 108
Ukrainian Autocephalous Orthodox Church (UAPT), 71, 77, 80
  and conversion of Metropolitan Filaret, 81
  and national identity, 86
  and rift with UPTs-KP, 85–86
Ukrainian Catholic. *See* Ukrainian-Greek Catholic (Uniate) Church (UHKTs)
Ukrainian Catholic Church. *See* Ukrainian-Greek Catholic (Uniate) Church (UHKTs)
Ukrainian Constitution of 1977, 42
Ukrainian Constitution of 1996, 42, 64, 65, 142, 144, 285(n59), 298–299(n145)
  and Crimea, 66
  and elimination of Presidium, 118
  and governmental reform, 98
  and Law on Power, 114–116
  and local governance, 125, 129–132
  and presidential power, 100, 114–116
  and religious equality, 85
  and unitary state, 102–105

Ukrainian-Greek Catholic (Uniate) Church (UHKTs), 15, 54, 71, 73, 78–81
  forced union with Russian Orthodox, 14
Ukrainian Insurgent Army (UPA), 14, 16
Ukrainian Interbank Currency Exchange (UICE), 193, 196
Ukrainian Nationalist Assembly (UNA), 153, 154, 155
Ukrainianophile movement, 54
Ukrainian Orthodox Church, 18, 81–82
  and call for unification and autocephaly, 87–88
Ukrainian Orthodox Church-Kyiv Patriarchate (UPTs-KP), 71, 76, 82–86
  and conversion of Metropolitan Filaret, 81
  number of members of, 75
  and rift with UAPTs, 85–86
Ukrainian Orthodox Church-Moscow Patriarchate (UPTs-MP), 59, 87
  number of members of, 75
  and Russian Orthodox Church, 71–72
Ukrainian Popular Movement (Rukh), 20, 150, 162, 213
Ukrainian Republican Party (URP), 151
Ukrainian-Russian treaty, 65, 67, 87–88
Ukrainian Socialist Party, 135
Ukrspetsexport, 174
Unemployment, 176–177
Uniate Church. *See* Ukrainian-Greek Catholic (Uniate) Church
Union of Brest of 1596, 78–79
Union of Ukrainian Officers, 239
Union Party, 67
Union Treaty of 1922, 12, 31, 207
  annulment of, 33, 35, 42, 209
Unitary state, 63–64, 129
United Nations
  mission to, 40, 207
  peacekeeping operations and Ukraine, 235, 248
United Social Democratic Party of Ukraine, 25, 61
  and support of Kuchma, 63, 64
United Soviet Socialist Republic (USSR)
  disintegration of, 10, 20–24, 31–37
  ending of and military, 236–237
  failure of its Soviet nation building programs, 39
  and lack of civil society, 141
  legacy in Ukraine, 6–7, 10–11, 37–44
  and national identity of Ukraine, 37–39

Ukraine as inheritor of shares of assets
of, 216–217
United States, 215–224
aid, 1, 224
backing of Gorbachev over Yeltsin, 210
and fear of collapse of Soviet Union,
210–211
relationship to Ukraine until mid-1994
based on Russia, 215, 220
and souring of relationship with Russia,
220–221, 232
and Ukrainian nuclear weapons, 210,
215, 216–219
and warming up to Ukraine, 221–222,
224
Unity faction, 155, 159, 161

van Gennep, Arnold, and stages of nation
building, 50–51
Varrenikov, General, 237
Vatican, 79–80
Verkhovna Rada, 23, 272
and Declaration of Independence, 24–25
and foreign policy decisions, 228
functions of, 100–101
1994 majoritarian election of, 154,
155–156
and opposition to Kuchma, 195–196,
201–202
and political parties, 123–125, 150
and relationship to President (Law on
Power), 99–100, 114–116
See also Legislative function
Volodymr, Patriarch, 83
Vydryn, Dmytro, 142

Wages, 177
Wanner, Catherine, 50, 62, 67–68
Watson, Hugh Seton, 48
West
and future affairs with Ukraine, 229–232
heritage of, 5
and recognition of Ukraine, 210–211
and scholarship, 2
Western Ukraine
and civil society and political parties, 143
contrasted with Eastern Ukraine, 49–50
and nationalism, 14–15, 40, 41
and nation building, 53
and number of religious believers, 76
Wilson, Andrew, 50, 59
Wise, Charles, 99–100, 116
World Bank, 7, 97, 106, 166, 189–190
cancellation of loans in 1998, 203
and institutional development, 111
and transition economies, 90
and United States prodding to help
Ukraine, 224
Writers Union of Ukraine, 56

Yeltsin, Boris, 18
and Belovezhskaya Pushcha meeting,
34–36, 209
and demise of USSR, 31–34
and dissolution of Russian Parliament,
220
and domination of Russia in CIS, 36–37
and Gorbachev, 24, 25, 32–34, 43, 209
and Kravchuk, 33–34, 37
and nuclear weapons policy, 216, 217,
238
and relationship to United States, 210,
216, 220
and signing of Black Sea Fleet agreement
and Friendship Treaty, 226–227
Yushchenko, Victor, 200

Zaslavsky, Victor, 39
Zhirinovsky, Valdimir, 153–154, 244
Zimmerman, William, 50
Zinko, Ihor, 129
Zviahilskiy, Yukhim, 110, 134, 192,
193
Zviglyanich, Volodymyr, 189